Fostering Child & Adolescent Mental Health in the Classroom

Fostering Child & Adolescent Mental Health in the Classroom

Raymond J. Waller Editor

Piedmont College
University of Georgia

SAGE Publications
Thousand Oaks ▪ London ▪ New Delhi

For information:

Sage Publications, Inc.
2455 Teller Road
Thousand Oaks, California 91320
E-mail: order@sagepub.com

Sage Publications Ltd.
1 Oliver's Yard
55 City Road
London EC1Y 1SP
United Kingdom

Sage Publications India Pvt. Ltd.
B-42, Panchsheel Enclave
Post Box 4109
New Delhi 110 017 India

Printed in the United States of America

Library of Congress Cataloging-in-Publication Data

Fostering child and adolescent mental health in the classroom / [edited by] Raymond J. Waller.
p. cm.
Includes bibliographical references and index.
ISBN 1-4129-0906-6 (cloth) — ISBN 1-4129-0907-4 (pbk.)
1. Mentally ill children—Education. 2. Child mental health. 3. Child psychopathology—Diagnosis. I. Waller, Raymond J.
LC4165.F67 2006
371.92—dc22 2005029813

This book is printed on acid-free paper.

06 07 08 09 10 8 7 6 5 4 3 2 1

Acquisitions Editor: Diane McDaniel
Editorial Assistant: Erica Carroll
Production Editor: Diane S. Foster
Copy Editor: Linda Gray
Typesetter: C&M Digitals (P) Ltd.
Proofreader: Scott Oney
Indexer: Molly Hall

CONTENTS

Acknowledgments

My sincere thanks are offered for the grace of the eminent researchers and educators who contributed their scholarship, time, expertise, and faith in the importance of this book. Dr. Donna Andrews, my boss, provided an unparalleled level of support. I am not sure that this book could have been completed without the diligent and tireless help of my coworker and voice of reason, Diane Bresson. I am sure that it wouldn't have been completed without the professionalism of the people at Sage, including Diane McDaniel, Marta Peimer, Erica Carroll, and others I don't even know about. I offer my gratitude to the academic reviewers of this text, who provided continuous, salient feedback throughout the process: C. Ann Wentz, Park University; Pam L. Warrick, University of Arkansas at Little Rock; Donna H. Schumacher-Douglas, University of Northern Iowa; Sarah Templin, Purdue University; Dan Schwartz, Saint Louis University; Sue A. Rieg, Indiana University of Pennsylvania; Judith Ableser, University of Michigan–Flint; Laura A. Barwegen, Wheaton College; and Diana Rogers-Adkinson, University of Wisconsin–Whitewater.

My final and most heartfelt thanks are to my eternal helpers—Katie, Sarah, and Emily.

INTRODUCTION

Raymond J. Waller
Jeffrey P. Douglass

Nine-year-old white male brought to the emergency room by mother, aunt, and female friend of the mother. Patient loudly cursing all three adults. Each adult observed making (different) threats to child. Patient reportedly on several medications. Patient reportedly "messed up" home computer. When scolded by mother, patient ran outside yelling that "ghosts were touching" him.

Thirteen-year-old black male brought to emergency room by parents for taking an overdose of Celexa. Patient was sent home from school for fighting with another student. Patient has a history of suicide attempts. Patient tested positive for benzodiazepines and cannabis. Patient has been prescribed Risperdal, but patient reports that he is grinding it up and snorting it up his nose rather than swallowing it.

Fourteen-year-old white female brought to emergency room by mother. Patient reportedly has previous diagnoses of attention deficit hyperactivity disorder and bipolar disorder. Patient not currently taking medication. Mother states that patient is "out of control" and has been trying to hurt herself. Scratch is visible on arm.

Fifteen-year-old white male brought to emergency room by guardians. Patient reportedly was "breaking up the house and threatening to hurt himself." Parents report being highly career oriented. Patient reports wanting parents more involved in his life.

Fifteen-year-old white female brought to emergency room by police. Patient had run away from home to have sex with boyfriend. Patient apprehended in bed having sex with 19-year-old boyfriend. Boyfriend was arrested. Patient has a history of running away and suicidal ideations. Patient was alert, verbal, and oriented. Patient reports being "very interested in sex" and "getting experience."

These brief case studies may initially appear quite different, but they have similarities. First, each of these children was seen in a rural hospital emergency room. Furthermore, each child has a history of emotional and behavioral problems that could be threatening. And finally, each of these children was in school the day after their emergency room visit.

> Nine-year-old multiracial male brought to emergency room by police. Patient has diagnostic history of migraines, Tourette's syndrome, and bipolar disorder. Patient had been apprehended going door-to-door in his neighborhood with a knife, a roll of magnets, a compass, and a level. Patient reported that he was trying to find a time machine. Patient had been sent home from school for being disruptive. Patient was disoriented in emergency room. Patient attempted to bite emergency room staff. Patient placed in restraints. Blood and urine screens negative for alcohol and drugs.

> Fourteen-year-old white female brought to emergency room by law enforcement. Patient had been fighting with sister and pulled a knife. Patient was disarmed by police.

> Twelve-year-old white male brought to the emergency room by police. Patient made suicide threat because he did not want to go back to mental health after-school program (patient had been one time). Patient reports plan to kill himself with a knife. Patient reports uncontrollable anger. Patient taking Prozac and Neurontin. Family reports previous inpatient psychiatric hospitalization.

These children were also seen in a hospital emergency room, but each of these children was involuntarily committed to treatment in an inpatient psychiatric facility. They were back in school within 2 weeks.

The demands placed on school personnel have never been greater, and some indications suggest that the needs of children have never been greater. On top of addressing the educational responsibilities that compose the primary expectation placed on them, educators are likely to be the first professionals to confront mental health needs in children and respond appropriately, despite a lack of training or focus for most educators in the area of child and adolescent mental health.

The purpose of this book is to help address the void created by the lack of training in recognizing and addressing mental health problems in the classroom. It is intended for preservice and currently practicing teachers and confronts some of the most common mental health issues experienced by children. The primary goal is to provide readers with some suggestions regarding how they might be able to help students with mental health issues. In addition, case vignettes are provided to help teachers conceptualize how students with specific problems may present in class and to identify support strategies for these students. The case studies are not necessarily intended to offer advice about how problems should be addressed. Rather, they are intended (a) to demonstrate that teachers actually confront mental health problems in the classroom and are often blindsided by them and (b) to show that teachers have done the best they could do to help students in need. We hope that teachers can learn from their experiences and that this material may help them to be more proactive in their classrooms and schools, implementing strategies that serve the various needs and the best interests of all their students. To maximize its use, the book offers a number of features:

EXPERTISE

A variety of nationally known educators and scholars have contributed their knowledge to ensure a high degree of fidelity for the information provided.

CASE VIGNETTES

As previously mentioned, case vignettes are provided to discuss clinical situations in the school setting. Readers are encouraged to consider the actions taken, the outcome observed, and brainstorm alternative strategies that they might use in a similar situation.

GLOSSARY DEFINITIONS

Key terms appear in boldface type in each chapter. These terms are defined in the Glossary at the end of the book.

THINKING AHEAD

Prereading questions are provided at the beginning of each chapter to facilitate synergy, promote the integration of previous and current learning, and stimulate thinking about readers' work, internship, practicum, or prospective field activity.

DISCUSSION QUESTIONS

Discussion questions at the end of each chapter prompt preemptive contingency planning and integrate both shared experiences and freshly assimilated information.

TEACHER FOCUS

Although many books on child and adolescent mental health have been written for mental health professionals, few have focused specifically on the needs of educators. This book fills a void by being written for teachers and by providing classroom explicit strategies to support students with a variety of mental health needs.

FOR ADDITIONAL HELP

Finally, each chapter includes Internet resources to assist with further information. While we encourage readers to access mental health professionals in the school system for support, consultation, and collaboration, we know that there will be times that they need immediate information or when they want to learn more about a particular topic. The Web sites provided—many of them award winners—were included to provide ancillary help when teachers need it.

Part I

Introduction to Child and Adolescent Mental Health

Chapter 1

The Educator's Role in Child and Adolescent Mental Health

Raymond J. Waller

Diane J. Bresson

Katherine S. Waller

PREREADING QUESTIONS

As you read this chapter, reflect on the following questions and issues:

1. We frequently hear about the shortage of classroom teachers. What are some of the reasons that you think a shortage exists?
2. What would you guess are some of the most common job-related difficulties reported by veteran teachers?
3. Do you think that students today face the same challenges as children from previous decades, or do children today experience more significant challenges? What are those challenges?
4. Should teachers play a role in fostering mental health in their students? If so, what responsibilities do they have? If not, who is responsible for meeting the mental health needs of students?

Teaching is more demanding today than it has ever been. Few researchers would disagree with this statement, and even fewer professional educators would disagree. Myriad factors intermesh to contribute to the challenge. Poor pay has been a longtime complaint. Newer factors related to the difficulties that teachers report include (a) increased bureaucratic demands; (b) the contradictory demands of federal No Child Left Behind (NCLB) legislation, which many teachers feel places them in the position of being "accountable" based on measures that do not measure the effectiveness of their teaching; (c) the cumbersome requirements of the Individuals with Disabilities Education Act (IDEA), which many teachers have not been educated about; (d) concerns about institutional safety in a time of several high-profile episodes of horrific school violence; (e) heightened concerns about personal liability in an era of resolution through civil mediation; and (f) what seems to be an all-time low in the credibility afforded to teachers by the body politic. It is not surprising, therefore, that a drastic shortage in teachers is forecast to worsen in coming years. Perhaps many prospective education graduates find themselves asking the same question as Ogden (2002), who pondered rhetorically,

> Why would a bright student . . . go into a low-paying, low-respect job where the primary responsibility is to expose . . . a small group of people, a sizable proportion of whom could care less about anything of an intellectual nature, in a place where they do not wish to be, to something that all but a few will find totally irrelevant. (p. 367)

What does surprise many is that this shortage is not due primarily to the number of people who enter the field but is instead the result of teacher attrition (Harrell, Leavell, van Tassel, & McKee, 2004; National Commission on Teaching and America's Future [NCTAF], 2003). Teacher training, like most areas of professional training, involves intense commitment, sacrifice, and expense. Unlike most other college training curricula, although there are a few other exceptions (e.g., nursing), teacher training prepares students to leave the college classroom and immediately obtain employment doing a *specific job.* Although the following example is extreme, it seems as unlikely for teachers to successfully undertake obtaining a degree in education and then to leave education as it would be to see a physician go through medical school and then leave the field of medicine. Many people obtain college degrees in a given field of study (although they are not trained to obtain a specific job in that field) and, after graduation, obtain employment in a field unrelated to their course of study. Intuitively, one would not expect this to be the case in education. Therefore, the issue of attrition of professional educators warrants consideration.

One third of beginning teachers leave the field within 5 years (Darling-Hammond, 2001), and the attrition rate is even higher in schools in communities with high poverty rates (Ingersoll, 2001) and in urban locales (McCreight, 2000); attrition is the most severe for teachers in the field of special education (Brownell, Sindelar, Bishop, Langley, & Seo, 2002). Issues such as those listed earlier in the chapter are among some that are the targets of familiar investigation, but two that occur with great frequency have yet to be mentioned: job dissatisfaction and the behavior of students. Job dissatisfaction is inferred to be a given, since teachers leave the profession of education in greater numbers than people leave most other professions. In fact, dissatisfaction with the field often goes hand in hand with the behavior of students, which many new teachers find to be appreciably more challenging than they had anticipated.

We have heard—rarely, we are glad to say—that the students of today are "getting worse," and popular media and impression often reinforces this belief.

Although we disagree with statements such as this on both philosophical and evidentiary grounds, there is a point here that is worthy of exploration. Furthermore, the unanticipated level of challenge presented by student behavior to new teachers is exacerbated by a common criticism debated both within the professional literature and too often heard by professional educators, which is that "most professors do not expand on the realities but concentrate on the theories [of teacher education]" (Walters, 2004, p. 58). We agree that teacher training should focus primarily on practical applications to classroom problems, including effective instruction strategies and behavior management approaches. Moreover, teachers routinely take courses in behavior management in fulfillment of degree requirements. However, we also acknowledge that the needs of children in many areas are more momentous and complex than teacher education programs have systematically addressed. Children with atypical behavior problems, particularly children experiencing **mental health problems**, are in need of specialized behavior management strategies and, more important, behavioral supports that most teachers are not trained to provide. Thus, this book has two primary foci: (a) to respond to the need for practical strategies to support students with mental health issues and (b) to redress the need to provide educators with specific training in the mental health issues commonly seen in school-age children and adolescents.

Gratefully, the data show that, at least in some domains, things are improving for students in this country. For example, the Child Welfare League (2005) reports the following:

- The high school dropout rate has decreased.
- The number of children in juvenile justice facilities has decreased.
- The number of arrests for children under the age of 18 has decreased.

From the standpoint of **mental health**, however, America's students are in crisis. In addition, both the **incidence** and **prevalence** of many of the mental health issues that affect school-age children show clear signs of increasing. At any given time, 1 of every 10 school-age children suffers from a mental health problem significant enough to disrupt that child's functioning in a major area of life, but fewer than 20% of these children receive any form of mental health treatment (U.S. Department of Health and Human Services, 2000). One of the best national studies available reported that the highest prevalence rate of mental health issues occurs in people aged 15 to 24 (Kessler et al., 1994), and this study did not evaluate children younger than 15. In fact, some studies indicate that *most* children will experience a diagnosable mental health problem during the child and adolescent years.

IDEA and NCLB have both encouraged the **inclusion** of students with identified disabilities into the general education setting, and teacher training programs have responded to the need by providing inclusive teaching strategies in the curricula of many college programs. The special education label that predominately serves students who have been identified for special education services is **emotional disorders** (EDs), also referred to as emotional/behavioral disorders (EBDs). Students who are identified as having an ED are likely to be placed into the regular education setting. Unfortunately, research findings consistently reveal that teachers in regular education feel unprepared to meet the needs of students with disabilities (Pivik, McComas, & LaFlamme, 2002), even though, in the 1998 school year, 47% of students with identified disabilities were educated in general education classrooms 79% of the time (U.S. Department of Education, 2001). From this standpoint, it is in one's best professional interest to be familiar with the strategies outlined in the following chapters, as the following veteran teacher discovered:

My 25th year of teaching elementary school has been the most challenging. In all my years of teaching, I have never had a more needy class. Most of my 28 fifth-grade students struggle academically, and 10 of them have standardized test scores that qualify them for intervention services. Three of my students speak no English, and 1 of those students is also legally blind, which obviously makes communication even more difficult. Six of my students are labeled with disabilities and are served part-time in a special education resource classroom. These special education students present some of my biggest challenges.

Jeremy is labeled as emotionally disordered. He was already being served in special education when his mother passed away last year. She died suddenly with no warning that she was ill. The grandmother is now raising Jeremy and his sister. Jeremy does very little class work. It's not that he doesn't try, but he moves and writes so slowly that he has barely gotten his name on a sheet of paper before the rest of the class has completed the assignment. Jeremy rarely speaks or interacts at all with any of his teachers or classmates.

Tamara's mother also died a couple of years ago. Her mother was murdered. Like Jeremy, Tamara is also labeled as emotionally disordered. Tamara's response to her mother's death has been the opposite of Jeremy. Tamara is very loud, disruptive, and often disrespectful. She has yelled and made insulting comments to some of the other teachers. Most of her disrespectfulness toward me has been with defiant comments that she mumbles very quietly. Tamara does not get along well with girls, and she has been in two fights this year. With the boys, Tamara is quite flirtatious. In her fourth-grade year, Tamara was sexually abused and possibly raped by a male relative. Since then, Tamara has had several incidents at school involving sexual comments and notes to male classmates.

Jackson is in special education part of the day because of his ADHD. His mother is in jail for drug possession. Jackson has an explosive temper, and he often lashes out at classmates. Carlos also fights with classmates, although he is not labeled with any sort of disability. He was considered for the gifted program, but his disruptive behavior disqualified him for that program. Carlos was recently suspended for beating a younger, smaller student in the face and head as the younger child sat defenseless on the bus.

I have to keep Bill far away from Jackson and Carlos. Although he is very bright, Bill is served in special education for ADHD, but recently he has been diagnosed with other mental health problems. His counselor says that he is hearing voices, and he has attempted to stab a family member with a knife. At school, Bill is targeted for teasing and bullying by the other children. Bill is always very sweet and respectful toward me, though. He rarely does any written work, but he generally gets all the answers right on the weekly tests and quizzes.

Many of my students are struggling with issues like divorce and family violence. I know that their behavior at school is related to all the things going on at home. Each morning, as the students arrive I go to their desks and say, "Good morning. How are you? I'm glad you're here." I ask them about things that I know are going on in their lives, and I give them a hug or a pat on the back to let them know I care. I have tried to build a bond with my class. Even with all the challenges going on in these children's lives, we go on with learning. No one considers the personal lives of children when standardized test scores are analyzed. These children will be expected to do as well as children from more privileged homes and neighborhoods.

Many students with mental health problems do not qualify for special education services. Therefore, children with a variety of mental health needs will be in your classroom, and you will be the primary source of school-based support for these students. To be eligible for services under the label ED, the problem must, according to the federal definition, negatively affect student academic performance. This is problematic for a variety of reasons. A student may suffer quietly with depression without necessarily having any noticeable drop in academic performance. Yet another student may be extremely fastidious about her schoolwork but be experiencing suicidal thoughts. Obviously, the academic performance of all students who are suffering will not be negatively affected. There are several other criticisms of the definition of ED, but they can be summed up by a major researcher in the area of ED, who has referred to the definition as being close to "nonsense" (Kauffman, 2005, p. 18). Thus, even if a student appears to be experiencing a clear mental health problem, the subjective nature of defining ED and the procedural difficulties that some educators face can prevent or drastically slow the access to services.

THE TEACHER'S ROLE IN FOSTERING THE MENTAL HEALTH OF CHILDREN

This chapter began with an acknowledgment of the difficulty of contemporary teaching. It seems only prudent to offer to current and prospective teachers the following encouragement: Rather than adding to your workload by giving you the additional stress of feeling responsible for students with mental health problems, you should know that you are already helping children who have mental health problems by fostering one of the most valuable tools available—**psychological resilience**. Gootman (1996) summarized the research findings about the potential contribution of educators to fostering psychological resilience in children by clearly stating that it is the empathy, trust, and patience from teachers, *not* the assignment of additional duties to the professional responsibilities of teachers, that are paramount in supporting the development of protective factors in students.

Psychological Resilience

Although the exact definition of psychological resilience varies, it can be elucidated as follows: If you were to evaluate a group of children who had been exposed to really bad events, some examples of which are discussed in later chapters of this book, a lot of those children would suffer as a result of that exposure, and many would develop mental health problems. However, a detail that has interested numerous mental health professionals is that there will be a subgroup of children who do not seem to suffer significantly and seem to be *protected* against exposure to bad events. This prompted some researchers to investigate these protected children, to see what it was that kept them from suffering to the extent that other children do. This investigation led to the discovery of several things that protected children seem to have in common that the adversely affected children did *not* seem to have. These factors, often referred to as protective factors, seem to foster the phenomenon of psychological resilience in children.

An alternative method of investigating mental health problems is to look at **risk factors**. A variety of risk factors have been found to increase the odds that an individual will experience a negative mental health impact. A long list of **psychosocial** risk factors have been found to be associated with the development of mental health problems, including low levels of family cohesion, not living with both biological parents (Cuffe, Mckeown, Addy, & Garrison, 2005), low socioeconomic status, and a history of child maltreatment (Harvey & Delfabbro, 2004). Additional risk factors relating to specific mental health problems are discussed in subsequent chapters.

Although this book stipulates a variety of risk factors associated with the development of mental health problems, we hope to offer several strategies for you to implement to cultivate psychological resilience in your students. We think it is important for educators to focus primarily on protective factors for two primary reasons. First, teachers, like most other professionals, have little influence over risk factors. It is simply not within their purview to control whether poverty exists or whether families separate. However, they can have a dramatic influence on the factors associated with resilience. Second, the strategies outlined below are conducive to the training teachers are receiving or have received during their professional training.

SPECIFIC STRATEGIES TO PROMOTE PSYCHOLOGICAL RESILIENCE

Be There

Despite difficulties that may exist in the life of a child, one factor repeatedly found to be protective is having positive interactions with an adult (Anthony & Kohler, 1987; Garmezy, 1993; Werner & Smith, 1992). In fact, the availability of an adult with whom a child shares a positive relationship is probably the most extensively reported predictor of psychological resilience (Masten & Coatsworth, 1998). It is unfortunate that our society seems to be in a period of valuing teachers less, and it is appalling that educators sometimes seem to accept this dilution. Teachers are in a position unique to the lives of children. Teachers spend more time with children than any other professionals. Even when a child's home environment is less than optimal, a teacher can provide a positive, stabilizing presence. When teachers are suspicious that a child is experiencing a mental health problem, their first thought is to refer the child to someone "who can help them," such as a counselor, social worker, or psychologist. In fact, these professionals can provide specialized care to students experiencing mental health problems, but it is difficult to say the care provided by mental health personnel is more valuable than—or even competes with—the protective impact of a positive, supportive teacher.

Model Support of All Students

Classrooms today are inundated with diversity. Culture, ethnicity, and sexual orientation are examples of diversity that may be encountered. How the teacher addresses issues of diversity can set the tone for how everyone in the classroom manages student differences. Younger students may be especially attuned to any biases subtly manifested by the teacher. Evidence suggests that some people in our society still discriminate based on race (e.g., Waller, DeWeaver, Myers, & Thyer, in press). Adolescents who identify themselves as being homosexual commit suicide at an extremely high rate, which could speak to the level of social isolation and disapproval they experience (Harrison, 2003). Furthermore, society at large tends to frequently relate to individuals with mental health problems in a negative way. Indeed, in one study of animated Walt Disney movies, it was discovered that 85% of the 34 movies evaluated made references to mental illness, and that most references to mental illness (frequently referred to as "crazy" or "nutty") were made in such a way as to insult or socially isolate the person being referred to (Lawson & Founts, 2004). Since Walt Disney is the foremost producer of animated movies viewed by children worldwide (Giroux, 1999), many children are exposed at a very young age to the idea that there is something fundamentally amiss with those who experience a mental health problem. Teachers are in an unparalleled position to model acceptance of those who are different and to facilitate positive peer interactions and social competence (Garmezy, Masten, & Tellegen, 1984).

Be Positive

Many classroom and schoolwide behavior management plans are based on punishment of inappropriate behavior rather than support of positive behavior. Likewise, it is easy to get into a pattern of content instruction that is somewhat negative or intimidating to students. Competitive classroom practices can emphasize areas of failure rather than focus on success. A positive self-perception and an optimistic outlook have been found to be protective factors (Masten, 2001), which can be actively influenced by the educational setting. Varieties of instructional practices de-emphasize competition and have been shown to be effective in facilitating learning. Examples of teaching techniques likely to foster optimism and learning include **cooperative learning** and **mastery learning**, although these are by no means the only two possibilities. Furthermore, many people may be inclined to think that optimism is an intrinsic characteristic and that one is either born with it or without it. To the contrary, optimism has been found to be learned, and the corollary is that optimism can be taught. An eminent psychologist and researcher, Martin Seligman (1991), has written a book titled *Learned Optimism: How to Change Your Mind and Your Life* that provides explicit strategies on increasing optimism.

Teach Problem Solving

Children who are psychologically resilient are effective, active problem solvers (Garmezy, 1993). Adapt your teaching to facilitate investigation and successful problem resolution rather than relying on rote data memorization. Although there are certainly "facts" that must be learned and on which subsequent information is built, true learning is demonstrated by an ability to assimilate a variety of information, develop perspective, and understand the flow of cause and effect and the variables that interact to influence outcomes. Problem-solving skills are not taught through instructional strategies that are observed too frequently—for example, extensive use of worksheets and passive seatwork activities. Students who have learned to think and solve problems are much more likely to be able to generalize these skills from the academic setting to difficulties in their own lives.

Encourage Self-Management

Self-management has been used extensively as a method to improve behavioral and academic performance (Shimabukuro, Prater, Jenkins, & Edelen-Smith, 1999). Self-management focuses attention on teaching the student to evaluate his or her own performance (Huff & DuPaul, 1998), which has been reported to be another skill that facilitates psychological resilience (Masten, 2001). Self-management includes a variety of procedures that give students responsibility for their own behavior, including techniques such as self-monitoring, self-assessment, self-delivered rewards, and self-selected rewards (e.g., Hughes, Harner, Killian, & Niharos, 1995; Hughes, Hugo, & Blatt, 1996). Furthermore, once self-management plans have been developed and implemented, these techniques have received favorable feedback from teachers (Fuchs, Fuchs, & Bahr, 1990).

Contrive Positive Peer Interactions

Some students in your classroom will not interact well with other students. This creates a substantial problem for two reasons. First, having effective social skills and positive social interactions is a protective factor and appears to facilitate psychological resilience. Second, the opposite is clearly true—having poor social skills and being socially isolated are significant risk factors associated with a variety of undesirable outcomes. Therefore, it is in the best interest of your students for you to contrive a variety of opportunities for positive social interaction. Fortunately, a variety of effective strategies have been found that provide opportunities for positive social interaction, enhance academic achievement, and improve behavior. These strategies are frequently subsumed under the heading of **peer-mediated interventions**. Examples include peer monitoring, peer tutoring, peer counseling, and peer assessment (Topping & Ehly, 1998; Utley & Mortweet, 1997), but one quality that adds to the attraction of all these techniques is that they "rel[y] heavily on a relatively abundant resource (i.e., students) and place comparatively modest demands on scarcer resources (i.e. educators)" (Dufrene, Noell, Gilbertson, & Duhon, 2005, p. 75).

SUMMARY

Teachers face more challenges today than during any other time. Students present with more challenges than ever before, particularly in the area of mental health needs. Clear evidence suggests that a variety of mental problems are increasing in frequency, and access to and availability of services for students with mental health needs have not improved for decades. In the face of such need, it is easy for educators to accept the responsibility of this burden borne by so many of today's students. But teachers should resist the propensity to shoulder a burden that is outside the purview of their professional training and focus.

Educators should acknowledge, however, that they can have a positive impact on children's mental health. Teachers can play an incalculable role in fostering psychological resilience in children, which can serve to protect them from exposure to a variety of risk factors. The strategies suggested in this chapter are classroom techniques that can assist in the development of these protective factors. They are techniques that have been found to be effective, while actually tending to decrease, rather than increase, one's workload. In addition, the impact of protective factors seems to be cumulative so that the more of these strategies a teacher implements, the more protection a student may cultivate.

Teachers are among the most involved adults in the lives of children. In our society, physicians maintain a high level of professional prestige, whereas teaching has lost credibility. Ironically, a child may go through life and rarely, if ever, see a physician. The same cannot be said of educators. If a child begins to show symptoms of a mental health problem, teachers are likely to be the first professionals to see them. Thus, teachers can also play an indispensable role in recognition of problems, referral, participation in interdisciplinary planning, advocacy, and monitoring of their students and can do so without making a difficult job impossible. To assist in this, and to fill a void in most teacher training programs, the majority of the remainder of this book is devoted to helping teachers recognize the most common mental health issues seen in children and adolescents and to offer strategies on how they can help encourage and support all their students.

DISCUSSION QUESTIONS

1. Evidence suggests that a variety of mental health problems in children are increasing. What are some strategies that you can use in your classroom to effectively support these students?
2. What are the rights of students with mental health needs in the school setting? What resources are available for such students?
3. The case study in this chapter highlights the difficulties faced by a teacher who was trying to meet the needs of several students in her classroom who had special needs. What other ideas do you have for ways that she could have handled these cases? Are there other sources of help that she might have sought? If so, what are they?
4. What schoolwide policies, procedures, or programs are available where you work to support the needs of students with mental health problems?

FOR ADDITIONAL HELP

	Organization	*Web Address*	*Description*
The Educator's Role in Child and Adolescent Mental Health	American Academy of Child and Adolescent Psychiatry (AACAP) Facts for Families	www.aacap.org/publications/factsfam/index.htm	The goal of AACAP is to provide concise and up-to-date information on mental health-related issues that affect children, teenagers, and their families.
	Our-Kids	www.our-kids.org	Our-Kids is a network of parents, caregivers, and others who are working with children with physical and/or mental disabilities and delays.

REFERENCES

Anthony, E., & Kohler, B. (Eds.). (1987). *The invulnerable child.* New York: Guilford Press.

Brownell, M. T., Sindelar, P. T., Bishop, A. G., Langley, L. K., & Seo, S. (2002). Special education teacher supply and teacher quality: The problems and what states, districts, and schools can do about them. *Focus on Exceptional Children, 35*(2), 1–16.

Child Welfare League of America. (2005). *State child welfare agency survey.* Washington, DC: Author.

Cuffe, S. P., Mckeown, R. E., Addy, C. L., & Garrison, C. Z. (2005). Family and psychosocial risk factors in a longitudinal epidemiological study of adolescents. *Journal of the American Academy of Child and Adolescent Psychiatry, 44,* 121–129.

Darling-Hammond, L. (2001). The challenge of staffing our schools. *Educational Leadership, 58*(8), 12–17.

Dufrene, B. A., Noell, G. H., Gilbertson, D. N., & Duhon, G. J. (2005). Monitoring and implementation of reciprocal peer tutoring: Identifying and intervening with students who do not maintain accurate implementation. *School Psychology Review, 34,* 74–86.

Fuchs, D., Fuchs, L., & Bahr, M. (1990). Mainstream assistance teams: A scientific basis for the art of consultation. *Exceptional Children, 57,* 128–139.

Garmezy, N. (1993). Vulnerability and resilience. In D. C. Funder & R. D. Parke (Eds.), *Studying lives through time: Personality and development* (pp. 377–398). Washington, DC: American Psychological Association.

Garmezy, N., Masten, A. S., & Tellegen, A. (1984). The study of stress and competence in children: A building block for developmental psychopathology. *Child Development, 55,* 97–111.

Giroux, H. A. (1999). *The mouse that roared: Disney and the end of innocence.* New York: Rowman & Littlefield.

Gootman, M. E. (1996). Child abuse and its implications for early childhood educators. *Preventing School Failure, 40,* 149–153.

Harrell, P., Leavell, A., van Tassel, F., & McKee, K. (2004). No teacher left behind: Results of a five-year study of teacher attrition. *Action in Teacher Education, 26*(2), 47–59.

Harrison, T. W. (2003). Adolescent homosexuality and concerns regarding disclosure. *Journal of School Health, 73,* 107–112.

Harvey, J., & Delfabbro, P. H. (2004). Psychological resilience in disadvantaged youth: A critical review. *Australian Psychologist, 39,* 3–13.

Huff, K. E., & DuPaul, G. J. (1998). Reducing disruptive behavior in general education classrooms: The use of self-management strategies. *School Psychology Review, 27*(2), 290–303.

Hughes, C., Harner, M. L., Killian, D. J., & Niharos, F. (1995). The effects of multiple-exemplar self-instruction training on high school students' generalized conversational interactions. *Journal of Applied Behavior Analysis, 28,* 201–218.

Hughes, C., Hugo, K., & Blatt, J. (1996). Self-instructional intervention for teaching generalized problem-solving within a functional task sequence. *American Journal on Mental Retardation, 100,* 565–579.

Ingersoll, R. M. (2001). Teacher turnover and teacher shortages: An organizational analysis. *American Educational Research Journal, 38*(3), 499–534.

Kauffman, J. M. (2005). *Characteristics of emotional and behavioral disorders of children and youth* (8th ed.). Upper Saddle River, NJ: Pearson.

Kessler, R. C., McConagle, K. A., Zhao, S., Nelson, C. B., Hughes, M., Eshleman, S., Wittchen, H. U., & Kendler, K. S. (1994). Lifetime and 12-month prevalence of *DSM-III-R* psychiatric disorders in the United States: Results from the National Comorbidity Study. *Archives in General Psychiatry, 51,* 8–19.

Lawson, A., & Founts, G. (2004). Mental illness in Disney animated films. *Canadian Journal of Psychiatry, 49,* 310–314.

Masten, A. S. (2001). Ordinary magic: Resilience processes in development. *American Psychologist, 56,* 227–238.

Masten, A. S., & Coatsworth, J. D. (1998). The development of competence in favorable and unfavorable environments: Lessons from research on successful children. *American Psychologist, 53,* 185–204.

McCreight, C. (2000). *Teacher attribution, shortage, and strategies for teacher retention.* Texas A&M University. (ERIC Document Reproduction Service No. ED444986)

National Commission on Teaching and America's Future. (2003). *No dream denied: A pledge to America's children* (Document No. 4269). Washington, DC: Author.

Ogden, W. R. (2002). The real crisis in the classroom: Where have all the teachers gone? *Education, 123,* 365–375.

Pivik, J., McComas, J., & LaFlamme, M. (2002). Barriers and facilitators to inclusive education. *Exceptional Children, 69,* 97–107.

Seligman, M. E. P. (1991). *Learned optimism: How to change your mind and your life.* New York: Simon & Schuster.

Shimabukuro, S. M., Prater, M. A., Jenkins, A., & Edelen-Smith, P. (1999). The effects of self-monitoring of academic performance on students with learning disabilities and ADD/ADHD. *Education and Treatment of Children, 22*(4), 397–415.

Topping, K., & Ehly, S. (1998). Introduction to peer-assisted learning. In K. Topping & S. Ehly (Eds.), *Peer-assisted learning* (pp. 1–23). Mahwah, NJ: Erlbaum.

U.S. Department of Education. (2001). *Twenty-third annual report to Congress on the implementation of the Individuals with Disabilities Act.* Washington, DC: U. S. Government Printing Office.

U.S. Department of Health and Human Services, Health Resources and Services Administration, Maternal and Child Health Bureau. (2004). *The national survey of children with special health care needs chartbook, 2001*. Rockville, MD: Author.

Utley, C. A., & Mortweet, S. L. (1997). Peer-mediated instruction and interventions. *Focus on Exceptional Children, 29*(5), 1–23.

Waller, R. J., DeWeaver, K. L., Myers, L., & Thyer, B. A. (in press). A correlational study of the impact of discrimination on disposition during hospital emergency services contacts. *Social Work in Mental Health.*

Walters, H. (2004). Why teachers leave the profession. *Delta Kappa Gamma Bulletin, 71*(3), 58–60.

Werner, E. E., & Smith, R. S. (1992). *Overcoming the odds: High risk children from birth to adulthood.* Ithaca, NY: Cornell University Press.

Chapter 2

A Teacher's Guide to Understanding the *Diagnostic and Statistical Manual of Mental Disorders (DSM-IV-TR)*

Denise M. Green

PREREADING QUESTIONS

As you read this chapter, reflect on the following questions and issues:

1. What are your own ideas about mental illness? How do these ideas shape your teaching style?
2. How do you feel about being informed that you have a child in your classroom who has a mental illness?
3. Are you familiar with some of the most common childhood mental health diagnoses? Are you willing to find out the side effects of medication that a child in your classroom may be taking? What are some of the classroom effects that might result from having students who take medication?
4. What are the resources available within your school system to refer and assist a child who is having difficulties in your classroom?

The classroom is not a stagnant or self-contained environment. Each morning, the outside world begins, with all its complexities and needs, and affects the students collecting in rooms for the lessons of the day. Each child comes from a unique social environment and has his or her own psychological makeup and genetic inheritance to deal with amid the work of reading, writing, and arithmetic. It would be overly optimistic to believe that all children are cared for appropriately at home, have no emotional problems, and arrive at school free from mental illness. Prevalence indicators in the *Diagnostic and Statistical Manual of Mental Disorders* (*DSM-IV-TR*; American Psychiatric Association, 2000) show that school-age children with Mental Retardation make up 1% of the population, Learning Disorders affect from 2% to 10%, Communication Disorders affect from 3% to 7%, Attention Deficit/Hyperactivity Disorder affects from 3% to 7%, Conduct Disorder affects from 1% to 10% (higher among males), and Oppositional Defiant Disorder affects from 2% to 16% (*DSM-IV-TR,* 2000). Although there is a lot of variability in these estimates of the number of students affected by mental health issues, what immediately becomes clear is that these problems very much affect the lives of children. Given this information, the likelihood that at least one child with emotional problems will be in any teacher's classroom is a strong one. This chapter is designed to help you understand how mental illnesses are broadly defined, how the current system of mental health providers reports these illnesses, and how to find out additional information about an illness a child in your classroom may have. The chapter includes a vignette demonstrating how an educator can work collaboratively with an interdisciplinary team to help develop effective intervention planning through a difficult situation affecting a child and the classroom.

The complexities of mental illness are not simple. Mental illness is—arguably, by necessity—a multifaceted concept. The term *mental illness* is professionally used to summarize the current diagnosable mental disorders as listed in the *DSM-IV-TR* (2000) and the *International Classification of Diseases* (*ICD-9-CM*; 1997). There are many definitions, ranging from the technical to laymen's terms, for the conditions and symptoms of a mental disorder. A simple and very applicable definition of mental disorders is provided by the surgeon general's report on mental health (U.S. Department of Health and Human Services [DHHS], 1999). This report defines mental disorders as "health conditions that are characterized by alterations in thinking, mood, and behavior (or some combination thereof) associated with distress and/or impaired functioning" (p. 5).

Several components are considered when determining the diagnosis of a mental disorder. The first component is a pattern of *significant clinical behaviors;* the second component is a *significant level of distress or disability;* and the third component is a *significant increase in risk factors.* It is the critical combination of these three **constructs** evaluated within the social and cultural environment of the individual that makes up a mental disorder as defined by the *DSM-IV-TR*.

APPROACHES TO USE OF THE *DSM-IV-TR*

Applicability of the Categorical Approach

The *DSM-IV-TR* follows a long-term medical tradition of grouping, defining, and separating mental disorders based on inclusive and exclusive criteria. The benefits of this form of classification are numerous. First, it allows for a uniform and universal way of relaying information about a disorder. Second, it lends itself to **empirical** evaluation and research toward progression of treatment. Third, it allows a professional to rule out a condition based on criteria. Finally, it allows for the resolution of a condition based on criteria. However, no matter how beneficial the categorical approach is, there are several limitations that the professional should be aware of to optimize understanding of the *DSM-TV-TR*.

The first limitation (and possibly the greatest criticism of the *DSM-IV-TR* method of diagnosis) is in the lack of definitive clarity of the categorical approach. There is no absolute limit or dividing line between mental disorders. In truth, two individuals may have the same diagnosis and not share similar symptoms of the disorder. A teacher may have one child with Attention Deficit Disorder who is noticeably overactive and another child with the same diagnosis who does not complete any seatwork and is easily distracted. These characteristics of the categorical approach make a diagnosis of the borderline cases difficult and leave the mental health professional to rely on research, experience, and clinical judgment. Another issue affected by this lack of definitive clarity is if and when a child has a mental disorder that is typically considered an adult disorder. Some examples of these disorders are found in children diagnosed with Bipolar Disorder, Schizophrenia, eating disorders, and major depression with psychotic features. Most children with a diagnosis that is typically considered an adult disorder are often placed on potent medications to help control the symptoms. These medications have their own effects on a child in addition to the problems associated with the mental illness and, frequently, have not been approved by the Food and Drug Administration for use with children. Furthermore, many of these potent medications affecting brain chemistry have not been evaluated for long-term safety with children. In summary, the categorical approach does allow for greater flexibility—this, in turn, necessitates the individual or advocate to insist on a skilled evaluation with the use of multiple sources of information. It is important that educators understand what the particular diagnosis means and the implications it holds for that child in the context of the classroom and that they realize that there is room for error in the diagnostic process.

Clinical Judgment

The *DSM-IV-TR* is a primary tool for reference concerning mental disorders in multiple settings. This manual is designed to be used by professionals across a variety of disciplines, including clinical, educational, and research areas. However, this flexibility across disciplines does not negate the absolute necessity of specific training. Clinical judgment is a developmental aspect of diagnosis. Factors such as education, licensure, training, exposure, and philosophy are variants that all have an impact on clinical judgment. It is essential for the proper use of the manual and for the accuracy of a diagnosis that the professional using the *DSM-IV-TR* has expertise and trained clinical skills concerning mental illness and mental disorders regardless of the discipline background. It cannot be stressed enough that multiple sources of information and experience in mental health are paramount in making an accurate diagnosis. For a child to be accurately diagnosed, it is most important that information concerning how the child is functioning is collected from as many people as might be useful, including the primary caretaker and other involved adults, a specialist in evaluating childhood disorders, and teachers involved with the child.

Social and Cultural Issues

The environmental contexts within which behaviors are formed and take place are important to consider when evaluating an individual. The *DSM-IV-TR* specifically provides three types of information for consideration when dealing with social and cultural diversity. First, information concerning cultural variants is provided within the text of specific clinical disorders. These cultural variations can include reactions to trauma, interactions with individuals outside a child's culture, responses to failure, and overall demeanor in a public place. Second, Appendix I (*DSM-IV-TR,* 2000) summarizes cultural syndromes not included in the text. An example of a cultural syndrome that resembles anxiety, depression, or somatoform disorders (*DSM-IV-TR,* 2000) is as follows:

> *brain fag:* A term initially used in West Africa to refer to a condition experienced by high school or university students in response to the challenges of schooling. Symptoms include difficulties in concentrating, remembering, and thinking. Students often state that their brains are "fatigued." (p. 900)

The third piece of information is an outline (also found in Appendix I) designed to assist the clinician in assessing the impact of cultural influences on the individual's behavior and symptoms. It is important to recognize that although a culture may identify or sanction a particular behavior or group of behaviors, this does not remove the behaviors or symptoms from being a mental disorder. An example of this is the acceptance of fasting behavior within certain cultures. Even when fasting is an accepted cultural behavior, severe food restriction may be diagnosed as Anorexia. The significance of the behaviors, the distress and/or disability to the individual, and the increased risk factors as a result of these behaviors must still be evaluated.

UNDERSTANDING A *DSM-IV-TR* DIAGNOSIS

The Multi-Axis Assessment

The *DSM-IV-TR* uses a five-tiered system to provide a broad and comprehensive assessment of the individual's mental, medical, and psychosocial well-being as well as evaluation of environmental variables and level of functioning. These specific areas of focus allow for the development of a picture or story about the individual, the issues he or she faces, and the environmental influences. These five areas of assessment are addressed by five axes in the *DSM-IV-TR* (2000, p. 27), which are as follows:

Axis I Clinical Disorders

Other Conditions That May Be a Focus of Clinical Attention

Axis I diagnosis is the condition that is the focus of treatment for that child. A common example of an Axis I diagnosis is Attention Deficit Disorder. Another frequent Axis I diagnosis is Major Depressive Disorder or Bipolar Disorder. It is very common that these diagnoses are accompanied with medication.

Axis II Personality Disorders

Mental Retardation

Axis II diagnoses commonly seen in children are Conduct Disorder and Oppositional Defiant Disorder. In addition, recorded here are Mental Retardation disorders.

Axis III General Medical Conditions

Axis III is used to record any medical condition. Common problems listed here for children may be hearing problems, injuries, surgeries, nutritional problems, and any congenital disorders.

Axis IV Psychosocial and Environmental Problems

Axis IV allows the evaluator the opportunity to document the living conditions, both past and present, that may have helped shape and influence the child's diagnosis.

Axis V Global Assessment of Functioning

Axis V is a numeric value taken from a scale that summarizes the functioning level of the child at the time of the assessment.

Although the exact causes (etiology) of the majority of mental disorders remain unknown, the factors that shape mental disorders are within our grasp to understand. The combination of biological, psychological, and social/cultural factors that interact to produce or exacerbate a mental disorder is the cumulative focus of assessment for diagnosis in the multi-axial system used in the *DSM-IV-TR*. It cannot be stressed enough that the diagnosis of a mental illness needs to be made with input from a variety of adults involved in the child's life, then compiled and evaluated by an expert. Additional aspects of formulating an accurate diagnosis include consideration of severity of symptoms, areas of impaired functioning, and increased risk factors the child may be experiencing.

THE FIVE AXES AND WHAT THEY MEAN

Axis I: Clinical Disorders and Other Conditions That May Be a Focus of Clinical Attention

Axis I is considered the principal diagnosis or reason for seeking professional help. In some instances, more than one disorder may be listed on Axis I. In this case, the first disorder listed should indicate the reason for treatment. There are also instances where there is no disorder on Axis I. This situation is represented by the Code V71.09 (No Diagnosis or Condition). If the diagnosis has not yet been made or the professional feels further information is needed before a diagnosis is given, the Code 799.9 (Diagnosis or Condition Deferred) is used. The following is a list of clinical disorders or other conditions currently considered on Axis I (*DSM-IV-TR*, 2000):

Disorders Usually First Diagnosed in Infancy, Childhood, or Adolescence (This section contains most of the disorders of children and adolescence: Learning Disorders, Motor Skills Disorder, Communication Disorders, Pervasive Developmental Disorders, Attention-Deficit and Disruptive Behavior Disorders, Feeding and Eating Disorders of Infancy and Early Childhood, Tic Disorders, and Elimination Disorders)

Delirium, Dementia, and Amnestic and Other Cognitive Disorders

Mental Disorders Due to a General Medical Condition

Substance-Related Disorders

Schizophrenia and Other Psychotic Disorders

Mood Disorders

Anxiety Disorders

Somatoform Disorders

Factitious Disorders

Dissociative Disorders

Sexual and Gender Identity Disorders

Eating Disorders

Sleep Disorders

Impulse-Control Disorders Not Elsewhere Classified

Adjustment Disorders

Other Conditions That May Be a Focus of Clinical Attention (Psychological factors affecting medical conditions, Medication-Induced Movement Disorders, Relationship Problems, Problems related to Abuse or Neglect, Noncompliance with Treatment, Malingering) (p. 28)

Axis II: Personality Disorders and Mental Retardation

This axis is reserved for the disorders of personality and mental retardation. The diagnosis of a personality disorder is generally not given to a child or adolescent. Personality disorders are generally reserved for adults. Commonly, a child or adolescent will have a Disruptive Behavior Disorder such as Conduct Disorder or Oppositional Defiant Disorder rather than a personality disorder. Usually, if the problem is of unusual severity, a diagnosis of personality disorder will be given to a child or adolescent. If Axis II is the primary diagnosis, this should be qualified by "Principle Diagnosis" or "Reason for Visit." The following is a list of disorders currently noted on Axis II (*DSM-IV-TR,* 2000):

Paranoid Personality Disorder

Narcissistic Personality Disorder

Schizoid Personality Disorder

Avoidant Personality Disorder

Schizotypal Personality Disorder

Dependant Personality Disorder

Obsessive-Compulsive Personality Disorder

Borderline Personality Disorder

Personality Disorder Not Otherwise Specified

Histrionic Personality Disorder

Mental Retardation

Antisocial Personality Disorder (p. 28)

Axis III: General Medical Conditions

This axis is reserved for listing pertinent medical problems that influence the overall management of the individual's condition. The inclusion of this axis is in keeping with the philosophy "that the causes of health and disease are generally viewed as a product of the interplay or interaction between biological, psychological, and sociocultural factors" (U.S. DHHS, 1999, p. 49). Listing general medical conditions accentuates and gives respect to the powerful mind and body relationship. The biopsychosocial model—as put forward by George L. Engel (1977)—stresses the multiple factors involved in the development and the outcome of well-being and illness. This model embraces the inseparable relationship that humans share as biological organisms, psychological beings, and sociocultural creatures.

Axis IV: Psychosocial and Environmental Problems

The inclusion of psychosocial and environmental problems within the domain of mental disorders embraces the belief that the person is not separate from the influences or impact of a child's environment. This environment includes not only the physical surroundings (poverty or homelessness) but also the impact of family (birth, death, sexual or physical abuse) and sociocultural influences (education, occupation, difficulty with acculturation). Most psychosocial and environmental problems should be indicated on Axis IV except when these problems are also the primary focus of clinical attention. In this case, these problems should be listed on Axis I. The following is a list of psychosocial and environmental problems coded on Axis IV (for a more detailed explanation of each problem area, see pages 31 and 32 of the *DSM-IV-TR*):

Problems with primary support group

Problems related to the social environment

Educational problems

Occupational problems

Housing problems

Economic problems

Problems with access to health care services

Problems related to interaction with the legal system/crime

Other psychosocial and environmental problems (*DSM-IV-TR,* 2000, p. 31)

Axis V: Global Assessment of Functioning of the Individual (GAF)

This axis requires the clinical judgment of the professional to provide an overall assessment of the individual's functioning capabilities. The GAF Scale (*DSM-IV-TR,* 2000, p. 34) is divided into 10 areas, ranging from "superior functioning in a wide range of activities" to "persistent danger of severely hurting self or others." The GAF Scale can be used to provide the individual's highest-functioning level compared with his or her current level (to demonstrate decline) or improving functioning level compared with start of treatment (to demonstrate treatment efficacy). Criticism of the GAF Scale centers on the perceived subjectivity of assigning a score. In rebuttal to this criticism, use of the scale by an experienced clinician reduces subjectivity, providing an accurate numeric assignment to the individual's functioning level and a description that gives meaning to the score. The following is a partial list of the GAF Scale (for a complete list, see *DSM-IV-TR,* 2000):

(100–91) Superior functioning in a wide range of activities . . .

(80–71) If symptoms are present, they are transient and expectable . . .

(60–51) Moderate symptoms . . .

(40–31) Some impairment in reality testing or communication . . .

(20–11) Some danger of hurting self or others . . .

(10–1) Persistent danger of hurting self or others . . . (p. 34)

The *DSM-IV-TR* and the Individuals with Disabilities Education Act

The Individuals with Disabilities Education Act (IDEA), also known as Public Law 94-142, sets guidelines (amid significant criticisms from many professional groups (e.g., the National Mental Health Association, 1986) for determining when children can be labeled as having federally acknowledged disabilities such as "seriously emotionally disturbed," "mentally retarded," or "learning disabled." These labels are used for the purposes of ensuring that appropriate educational services are available for all students, regardless of disability. It is important to keep in mind that to be served under an IDEA category, the student must be experiencing academic problems. Thus, a student could suffer from a mental health problem and not be eligible for services under the IDEA.

However, the *DSM-IV-TR* plays the pivotal role in a child's ability to access special services within a school system. It is imperative that a specialist in children's disorders work in concert with the school, teachers, and parents to develop an accurate picture of what is going on in that child's world and to help develop strategies to meet that child's needs. The reality of a teacher's world is that you will have in your classroom children who are mentally and emotionally disabled. You must work with school psychologists, special education teachers, and parents as a team to develop an Individual Education Plan (IEP) that meets the educational needs of the student with a disability. It is helpful for you to gain information and understanding of the disorder with which the student is diagnosed and to be familiar with possible effects of any medication that has been prescribed to treat the disorder.

Teachers play an important role in the process of gathering information about a student who is experiencing difficulty. As the following case study illustrates, the information teachers gather can be used in the diagnosis and treatment intervention planning for students with mental health disorders. This vignette is somewhat different from the others in this book in that this case is written by a teacher who is working with the school psychologist and interdisciplinary team to help compile information that could be used to formulate a diagnosis and educational plan.

Eight weeks into the school year, Christopher was placed in my class. At 10 years old, Christopher was small for his age. His teeth were crooked, and some looked broken. Records from his other school had not arrived, so all I knew about Christopher was that he and his single mother had recently moved here from another state, back to his mother's original home.

After the first week I consulted with the school social worker about my concerns, and I documented the following observations:

- *Christopher has not returned any homework or signed papers from his mother. When he is asked, he replies "I don't know" and runs off. I noticed that his book bag is full of papers.*
- *Christopher is failing in reading.*
- *Christopher has difficulty staying in his seat. Frequently he will get up, even in the middle of a lesson, to get something off of a shelf or engage in some other distraction.*
- *The playground monitors report that Christopher does not wait his turn. He does not play well with the other children. There have been several instances when he has been put in time-out for fighting. He does not seem to have any friends.*
- *I have noticed that Christopher is not clean. He sometimes has on dirty clothes in the morning. His teeth are not brushed and his nails and hands are dirty.*
- *Christopher does not eat well. He complains about being hungry, but is unable to finish the food he is given at school. He has not brought in money to pay for his meals, but the lunchroom still provides meals at my request. I am not certain how long they will continue to provide Christopher a regular meal, because school policy requires the lunchroom to provide a peanut butter sandwich for students who do not pay.*

I realized that moving to a new home and new school was a big adjustment, so I decided to try a few things in the classroom to get a better feel for what was going on with Christopher. I implemented the following plan for two weeks:

- *Christopher was moved to the front of the classroom, and seated with a quiet group of well-behaved children.*

- *I counted the number of times that Christopher got out of his chair during five-minute intervals at set times of the day.*
- *I asked the lunchroom monitors to make note of disruptive behavior in the lunchroom and report this to me.*
- *I asked the playground monitors to count the times Christopher got in arguments, initiated play with other children, broke into a line, or disrupted others playing.*
- *I tried to contact Christopher's mother to get more information about this situation.*

After two weeks, I was not able to help Christopher improve on his behavior, complete school work, decrease fights with other children, or eat well. I was not successful in scheduling a meeting with his mother. I did obtain information from Christopher's last school. Records from the previous school indicated similar problems had existed there. There had been a referral to the school psychologist; however, the family moved before an assessment could be completed. I organized my information and began the process for referral for a psychological evaluation.

It took approximately two months to engage the family, complete the evaluation, and develop an IEP. During this time, I discovered that Christopher's mother had brought him here to escape an abusive relationship with Christopher's father. There was also a formal report that the father also abused Christopher, and a case with Family and Children's Services (from the old home) concerning this abuse was still open. Further complicating the issue was the fact that the mother did not have a high school education. She worked nights and was asleep when Christopher got up in the morning. The grandmother with whom they lived was in poor health and could provide only minimal assistance to Christopher. The school social worker was able to initiate referrals for assistance from several agencies to help Christopher and his mother. The following Axis I–V assessment was made concerning Christopher after school testing and a formal evaluation by a child specialist:

Axis I: 314.00 Attention-Deficit/Hyperactivity Disorder, Predominantly Inattentive Type
315.00 Reading Disorder
V61.20 Parent-Child Relational Problem

Axis II: V62.89 Borderline Intellectual Functioning

Axis III: Anemia

Axis IV: Problems related to the social environment; Educational problems; Economic problems; Problems with primary support group

Axis V: GAF of 40, Major impairments in school and with family relationships.

As a result of the evaluation, Christopher began to receive services in special education in a resource reading class. Through Family and Children's services, his mother was referred to the Department of Labor for employment training. She also was able to take parenting classes on the weekend to learn how to deal with Christopher's problems. Christopher was placed in an after-school program that assists with homework and daily living skills for children. The state child support recovery agency pursued obtaining child support from the father for Christopher. The school psychologist referred Christopher and his mother to a local child psychiatrist for additional evaluation and treatment. The school social worker, the school psychologist, the special education teacher, and I continue to monitor Christopher's progress, and I provide emotional and educational supports as needed.

SUMMARY

Mental illness is a complex phenomenon. In modern times, mental illness is defined within a matrix that combines biological influences, psychological influences, and social/cultural influences. The *DSM-IV-TR* embraces this model of mental illness conceptualization and treatment by providing a multi-axis diagnostic grid for assessment and evaluation. The *DSM-IV-TR* also provides categorical conditions and severity-of-illness criteria for diagnostic purposes. The *DSM-IV-TR* provides a universal, common, and accepted language that allows professionals to communicate across services. As a closing comment, it is important to remember that mental illness is not what a person is, it is a condition that he or she has.

DISCUSSION QUESTIONS

1. As you reflect on the material in this chapter, can you think of ways that your training and contact can help students with mental health problems?
2. Is it reasonable to expect teachers to contribute to the promotion of mental health in America's students? Why or why not?
3. What strategies do you use or do you plan to use to optimize socialization opportunities for students with mental health problems, since these students often become ostracized from peers?

FOR ADDITIONAL HELP

	Organization	*Web Address*	*Description*
A Teacher's Guide to Understanding the *Diagnostic and Statistical Manual of Mental Disorders (DSM-IV-TR)*	WebMD Health	http://my.webmd.com/webmd_today/home/default.htm	WebMD provides valuable health information, tools for managing your health, and support to those who seek information, including information on mental health and medication issues.

REFERENCES

American Psychiatric Association. (2000). *Diagnostic and statistical manual of mental disorders* (4th ed., text revision). Washington, DC: Author.

Engel, G. (1977). The need for a new medical model: A challenge for biomedicine. *Science, 196*, 129–136.

ICD-9-CM: International Classification of Diseases (9th rev., clinical modification). (1997). Chicago: American Medical Association.

National Mental Health Association. (1989). *Severely emotionally disturbed children: Improving services under Education of the Handicapped Act* (P.L. 94-142). Washington, DC: Author.

U.S. Department of Health and Human Services. (1999). *Mental health: A report of the surgeon general.* Rockville, MD: Government Printing Office.

Chapter 3

Dealing With Problem Behavior in the Classroom

A Behaviorological Perspective

Jerome D. Ulman

PREREADING QUESTIONS

As you read this chapter, reflect on the following questions and issues:

1. Why do children engage in behaviors that get them into trouble?
2. What advantages are there to seeking out and using research-based strategies for behavior management?
3. What is a functional behavioral assessment (FBA), and how is it related to a behavior intervention plan (BIP)? What are the procedures at your school for how to conduct an FBA?

The primary goals of educators should be to provide young people with academic knowledge and social skills that will enable them to become caring individuals, critical thinkers, and adults who contribute to the betterment of society. Educators are key players in improving society. In addition to promoting academic achievement, educators also have the important task of engendering prosocial behavior in their students—a task that is even more important today because, too often, parents are defaulting on this social responsibility in the home. Increasingly, educators are dealing with disruptive behavior—actions that impede instruction and induce a social atmosphere of generalized disrespect for others—in their classrooms (e.g., Burley & Waller, 2005). Knowing what countermeasures a teacher should take continues to be a controversial issue. Yet daily, from one moment to the next, teachers must make decisions about the actions to take in response to the behavior of their students, not only about academic performance but also about deportment.

When you are faced with problem behavior in your classroom, your interpretation of what is causing that behavior and what to do about it becomes central to your responsibility as a teacher, which is providing your students with essential academic and social skills. This chapter focuses on how to deal with problem behavior in the classroom from a *behaviorological perspective.* The radical departure this perspective takes from the *psychological perspective* can best be appreciated by contrasting them.

FOLK PSYCHOLOGY PERSPECTIVE

Educators attempt to deal with unacceptable classroom behavior on the basis of some kind of theory about behavior, even if, by default, their "theory" is merely an implicit set of assumptions about why children act the way they do. Many teachers operate on the basis of **folk psychology** (sometimes called pop psychology), a "commonsense" approach expressed in ordinary talk about putative psychological phenomena. But as Albert Einstein (1879–1955) reminded us, "Common sense is the collection of prejudices acquired by age 18." Routinely, folk psychology is nothing more than an outgrowth of whatever notions student teachers may have learned about behavior from their supervising teachers at the beginning of their professional careers. Based on the folk psychology approach to understanding and dealing with behavior problems, a common reaction of teachers is to show some form of disapproval. Although, initially, disapproval may to some extent suppress the undesired behavior, such improvements are often short-lived. More often than not, measures such as reprimanding, using "time-out," sending recalcitrant students to the principal's office, or sentencing them to in-school suspension or detention do not appear to reduce disruptive behaviors and may even make the problem behavior worse. When every trick in the book of disciplinary folklore has been attempted and yet the problem behavior persists, what are we to do? One useful answer might be, Question your theory of behavior.

BEHAVIOROLOGICAL PERSPECTIVE

How does the behaviorological perspective differ from other perspectives that purport to explain behavior? There are two diametrically opposed ways to understand the causes of behavior: (a) as the result of some hypothetical inner causes (inner agencies) or (b) as actions that are largely a function of other events. The former account characterizes not only folk psychology but also a large portion of mainstream psychology. The latter characterizes the behaviorological perspective—arguably, one that should be as basic to education as germ theory is to medicine. The goal, then, is to provide you with general guidelines for developing behaviorologically informed teaching practices that have been shown to be highly effective in dealing with behavior problems.

The natural science of **behaviorology** is the study of contingent relations between behavior and other events; it systematically excludes accounts of behavior based on notions of an inner causal agency such as ego, self, or similar trait-type psychological concepts. This science began with the pioneering research of B. F. Skinner in the 1930s. We will be concerned primarily with **applied behavior analysis**, the engineering aspect of behaviorology. The literature on the technology of behavior change includes the procedural details for implementing various behavioral interventions (see *Journal of Applied Behavior Analysis,* http://seab.envmed.rochester.edu/jaba/jabaindx.asp). The aim here is not to review this technical literature but, rather, to offer a way to think about behavior problems in an effective manner—that is, as a practical guide to understanding and dealing with behavior problems in the classroom.

WHAT ARE CONTINGENCIES?

We cannot see contingencies directly, but we can observe their effects over time. This causal mechanism controls behavior that we call **operant** (actions that *operate* on the environment, in contrast to reflex-like responses), discovered by B. F. Skinner's pioneering research on pigeon behavior in the highly controlled experimental environment of the operant conditioning chamber. Skinner demonstrated that by careful manipulation of contingency relations, behavior could be predicted and controlled with great precision. Subsequent operant research demonstrated the operation of several kinds of contingency arrangements: positive reinforcement, the contingent presentation of reinforcing events; negative reinforcement, the contingent removal of aversive events (i.e., escape and avoidance behavior); positive punishment, the contingent presentation of aversive events; and negative punishment, the contingent removal of reinforcing events.

The accumulation of a huge body of experimental research over a 70-year period, in both laboratory and applied settings, has confirmed that operant contingencies are as real as any other causal mechanism in the natural sciences. The scope of this chapter does not allow elaboration of these causal mechanisms, but the important point is that the only way we can identify the mechanisms of reinforcement and punishment is by observing their effects on behavior. Although their effects (changes in behavior) cannot be captured in a photograph, they can be observed and recorded over time. These are real causal mechanisms, not invented hypothetical constructs.

Contingencies are always operating in the classrooms, and they influence the behavior of everyone in the room—students, teachers, instructional assistants, everyone (even the hamster in the cage). Learning to see how contingencies operate in the classroom is not a simple task, however. It will require that you learn the precise meaning of some technical terms. It will also require that you learn some basic behavioral assessment procedures. The pivotal behaviorological term is **contingencies**: the functional relations between actions and other events. Contingencies consist of relations between behavior, events that follow the behavior (postcedent events), and the situation within which the behavior occurs (antecedent events). The concept of behavior is straightforward: simply, what someone does or says (i.e., talking, too, is operant behavior).

Postcedent Events

Some of these events constituting a contingency relation are **postcedents**—events that immediately follow certain actions. When the actions produce those postcedent events, they are called **consequences**—our primary concern when analyzing contingencies. Here are some examples of consequences: The effect of typing a word in a word processing document (i.e., a word appearing on the computer screen) is a consequence of the fingers pressing keys on a keyboard in a particular sequence. The consequence of a student getting out of his or her seat without permission during a seatwork period may be that this action evokes a reprimand from the teacher. Some consequences increase the actions they follow and are therefore defined as **reinforcing consequences**. If the out-of-seat behavior increases following the teacher's reprimanding, then the reprimands are reinforcing consequences. Other consequences decrease the actions they follow and are therefore defined as **punishing consequences**. If the out-of-seat behavior decreases following the teacher's reprimanding, then the reprimands are punishing consequences (at least for the time being). Whether a consequence is reinforcing or punishing is determined solely by its effect on behavior. If you praised the particular actions of a student—say, always completing his or her homework assignment before class—and as a result you subsequently observed that his or her assignment was not completed before class, you should strongly suspect that your praise is not functioning as a reinforcing consequence and may even be punishing.

Some postcedent events are not consequences; they simply occur adventitiously following a particular action but may nonetheless affect that behavior. The bowler who talks to the ball after releasing it down the alley illustrates such superstitious conditioning (i.e., the event of getting a strike is not a consequence of talking to the ball). The essential point to remember is that *actions are selected by their consequences.* This is a behavioral law that is as valid as any other law in the natural sciences and your most powerful tool in learning to manage behavior in your classroom. We can choose to ignore this behavioral law, of course, just as we might choose to ignore the law of gravity, but we do so at our own peril. Whether we like it or not, just as gravity will cause us to fall on our face when we trip over a curb, consequences can produce problem behavior in the classroom, and changes in consequences can replace them with desired behavior. Hence, it is to your advantage to see contingencies in operation in your classroom so that you can do something effective about them and their behavioral effects. But how do we go about "seeing contingencies"?

ANTECEDENT EVENTS

By virtue of the fact that a particular set of stimuli are always present when a behavior is reinforced or punished, **antecedent events** may come to control behavior. These antecedent events, along with postcedent events, constitute a contingency relation (i.e., a three-term contingency relation: antecedent-behavior-postcedent). Antecedent stimuli consistently correlated with the delivery of reinforcing or punishing consequences acquire control of the behavior. Presenting a stimulus previously correlated with reinforcement will evoke a behavior (these are called **discriminative stimuli**); presenting a stimulus previously correlated with punishment will suppress a behavior (these are called conditioned **aversive stimuli**). For example, when a teacher who has consistently reinforced on-task behavior in a classroom enters that classroom, there will be a dramatic increase in on-task behavior among the students. When a principal who has consistently employed punishment enters a classroom of unruly students, their misbehavior will immediately be suppressed.

FUNCTIONAL BEHAVIORAL ASSESSMENT

How does knowing about behavioral contingencies translate into steps that will allow you to deal effectively with problem behavior in your classroom? This question leads us to a brief consideration of **functional behavioral assessment** (**FBA**). The purpose of FBA is to identify the actual variables responsible for the behavior of concern, thereby leading to an intervention that will do away with the problem. As a teacher, you need to be aware of FBA because it is a requirement of federal law. Since the 1997 reauthorization of the Individuals with Disabilities Education Act (IDEA), schools are required to conduct an FBA if there is to be a change in school placement due to the behavior of a student who has qualified for special education services (i.e., a student with an Individual Educational Program, or IEP). IDEA also stresses the need for an FBA for positive behavior support programming—that is, the use of nonaversive strategies that teach students new skill repertoires that replace the old problem behaviors. But IDEA does not spell out what an FBA should be. What one school district calls an FBA may differ markedly from that of another school district. In one school, the FBA may be a one-page checklist or brief questionnaire, whereas another school may require extensive time-consuming documentation. When performing an FBA, it is one thing to meet the requirements of the law but quite another to identify real causal mechanisms responsible for producing and maintaining problem behaviors in the classroom. Whether or not an FBA leads to the development of an effective behavior intervention plan is not a matter of extensive documentation but of the accuracy of the assessments made in conducting the FBA. This chapter does not aim to provide you with the skills required to conduct an FBA but, rather, aims to highlight this assessment approach.

Psychological FBAs

A psychological FBA assumes that behavior is the result of some hypothetical inner cause (inner agency). The putative causal variables from psychology such as attitudes, expectations, cognitions, and the like are easy to hypothesize but less than helpful for the purpose of planning effective behavioral interventions. With psychology as the guide, one simply observes some action, labels it using some psychological term, and then concludes that the action has now been explained by that term—so the label now becomes the cause of the problem. For example, Mary has difficulty reading, so we thus surmise that she has a **learning disability**. As we continue to observe Mary's reading problem, we now know why—she is learning disabled. Jack repeatedly hits other children, thus we conclude that he has a **conduct disorder**. Jack continues to hit other children because of this disorder. And so on *ad infinitum.* In these cases, the actions observed are empirical (or if the actions are merely reported to you, they may be actual), but the causal mechanisms purported to account for the actions are not real. Skinner fittingly called such terms

explanatory fictions—they appear to explain behavior, but in reality they explain nothing. They are simply illogical circular arguments. Moreover, psychological theories (including folk psychology) look at the form but not the function of the behavior. It is the form of the behavior, not its function, that is usually judged and labeled as inappropriate. Following are some examples:

- Sam is aggressive.
- Jane is disruptive.
- Fred is impulsive.

What do we do about the aggressive, disruptive, or impulsive actions? Labels will not provide the answer. We must focus not on what the student *is* but on what the student *does*—the function of that behavior. The following case vignette approaches classroom behavior problems from the behaviorological perspective and shuns explanatory fictions:

Bobby is a 9-year-old, third-grade male identified as learning disabled with difficulty attending to academic work throughout the school day. His general education teacher, Mrs. Roberts, reports that he frequently talks out and plays with items that are in and on his desk, behavior that sometimes disturbs other students in the classroom. His off-task behavior usually continues for a couple of minutes or until he is redirected back to what he is supposed to be doing. This problem behavior usually occurs during lecture or small-group time in his regular classroom. Mrs. Roberts has observed that this problem behavior is most likely to be "set off" during reading or note taking and begins when he is no longer giving her eye contact—often "getting a glazed look in his eyes." Although Mrs. Roberts reminds Bobby to get back on task, this regularly does not work unless she stops what she is doing, walks over to his desk, and talks to him. When asked about the likely function (consequence) of the off-task behavior, she states, "I feel he is doing this to get attention from the students or his teachers, and very possibly to get out of doing assignments." When asked what behavior might serve the same function for the student that is appropriate within the same classroom context, Mrs. Roberts relates, "Bobby could get attention by doing his work and receiving praise." When asked for other information that might contribute to an effective intervention—for example, conditions under which the problem behavior was observed not to occur—she replies, "Bobby does not play with items at his desk when given simple tasks to complete or when he is given tasks that he actually likes, such as doing art projects."

When Bobby was observed during a half-hour reading group, the following sequence of events was recorded: Mrs. Roberts gives the reading group assignment >> Bobby plays with his pencil >> Mrs. Roberts tells Bobby to stop playing with his pencil >> Bobby responds while laughing, "Yes, Mrs. Roberts" >> Mrs. Roberts ignores Bobby's remark >> Mrs. Roberts begins small-group instruction >> Bobby begins whistling >> Mrs. Roberts reminds Bobby that he has an assignment to complete and to raise his hand if he has a question >> Bobby raises his hand >> Mrs. Roberts helps Bobby begin his assignment >> Bobby finishes his assignment. From the observation of this sequence of events (antecedent-behavior-postcedent pattern), it is apparent that Bobby plays with items on his desk and makes noises when Mrs. Roberts gives instructions for individual work. Bobby receives attention from the teacher and his peers for his problem behavior and does not complete seatwork until he gets assistance from the teacher.

Overall, the function of Bobby's problem behavior (based on this informal functional behavioral assessment, or FBA) is attention from the teacher and classmates and escape from doing his assigned tasks. Because he completes assignments only with teacher assistance, Bobby may be having difficulty with the tasks he is given. From this informal assessment, the behavior intervention plan is as follows: The desired behavior is that Bobby will monitor his appropriate work behavior (working quietly and not playing with items at his desk). Mrs. Roberts will respond nonverbally (nodding, etc.) for appropriate behavior. For an entire class period of appropriate behavior, Bobby will also receive tangible rewards or extra time to engage in a preferred activity such as an art project. Thus, the potential reinforcing consequences for appropriate behavior are nonverbal teacher attention, positive feedback from self-monitoring, and rewards for longer periods of on-task behavior. Now, instead of receiving teacher attention for playing at his desk or making noise or both, Bobby will receive attention for doing his seatwork quietly. Significantly, Mrs. Roberts will also determine if the tasks she assigns Bobby are too difficult for him—and if so, make appropriate adjustments in his assignments.

Postscript. The behavior intervention was actually implemented, and Bobby's problem behavior was subsequently replaced with appropriate classroom behavior. The reward system was gradually removed, and Mrs. Roberts easily maintained the desired behavior with occasional contingent attention to improvements in Bobby's (adjusted) academic work. Thus, *treatment validity* (also referred to as treatment fidelity) was established. The remainder of the chapter is intended to help you develop behavior intervention strategies that will be effective in reducing disruptive classroom behaviors, as did the plan outlined above.

Behaviorological FBAs

The function of a behavior requires a more thorough analysis:

- Sam hits other children when they do not comply with his demands.
- Jane makes animal noises when the teacher is attending to other children.
- Fred, without being called on, frequently blurts out answers.

We would like to observe what happens after Sam hits other children, after Jane makes animal noises, after Fred blurts out an answer. The assessment of such relationships is the focus of behaviorological FBA.

A behaviorologically guided FBA can allow us to determine what is responsible for a given behavior in the classroom, the real identifiable variables that account for the behavior in question. We can then plan our intervention accordingly. When viewed from the behaviorological rather than a bureaucratic perspective, the amount of documentation is irrelevant.

What is important are the kinds of variables assessed and how accurately they are assessed. This chapter is not intended as a guide for you to develop competence in conducting FBA (a topic that alone would require, minimally, an entire chapter—see Chandler & Dahlquist, 2002; also see the Web site http://cecp.air.org/fba/default.asp). Rather, FBA will be discussed as an assessment approach, an overview of which will allow you to grasp the understanding that the operation of contingencies determines behavior.

Setting Events

In addition to the events that immediately precede and follow behavior, contextual variables must also be taken into account for performing an FBA or understanding classroom behavior in general. Hence, when working with students, we also need to consider **setting events**, situational or contextual factors that affect how a student will respond to antecedent and consequent events. "Setting events may be divided into three categories: physiological/biological, physical/environmental, and social/situational" (Chandler & Dahlquist, 2002, p. 55). For example, setting events may include things happening in the student's life outside the classroom that are affecting the behavior of concern. For example, Jane recently started to be mainstreamed more often into the regular classroom. She has begun to take math (an area of strength and interest) in the general education classroom. In this example, receiving recognition for her accomplishments may be having a positive "ripple effect" in the resource room as evidenced by a decrease in her problematic attention-seeking behavior. Tom has recently moved to his father's home where he is not properly supervised. He stays up half the night playing video games and consequently takes naps at school. Bob did not receive his medication this morning, and his hyperactivity subsequently increased. Jimmy has been diagnosed as having Attention Deficit Hyperactivity Disorder and is now on stimulant medication (a biological variable).

Thus, FBAs evaluate behavior functionally, not structurally—that is, they focus (a) on what the student *does,* not what the student *is,* and (b) on the events functionally related to what the student does (or does not do). The aim of an FBA is **treatment validity**: the extent to which it contributes to the development of an effective behavioral intervention program. The old saying that "the test of the pudding is in the eating" holds true with FBA. Did the use of the assessment information result in a plan for behavior intervention that actually produced the desired change in the target behavior?

Assessing Antecedent-Behavior-Postcedent Relations in the Classroom

Short of conducting a formal FBA, then, how do you go about making an educated guess about the variables that control operant behavior? For your guess to be behaviorologically informed, you need to be somewhat familiar with the questions that a properly conducted FBA would address. Basically, such an FBA would carefully consider the conditions just prior to and during occurrence of the behavior of concern, the behavior itself, and the events that immediately follow the behavior. This procedure is often referred to as an *A-B-C analysis* (antecedents-behaviors-consequences), but it would be more correct to call it an *A-B-P analysis* (antecedents-behaviors-postcedents). Briefly, the following are areas that the FBA must carefully assess.

Defining Behavior and Identifying Important Antecedent and Postcedent Events

Behavior. State the specific behavior about which you are concerned. Unwanted behavior (behavioral excesses) is relatively easy to specify because its occurrence is so obvious. Desired behavior that rarely occurs is somewhat more difficult to track. Avoid targeting the absence of behavior such as being quiet (i.e., if a dead person can do it, it is not behavior). Also avoid using ambiguous behavioral descriptions such as noncompliance. There are many forms of noncompliance.

Antecedents. Describe where the behavior occurs and the particular conditions present just before and during the time that the behavior is observed. At what time of the day does the behavior usually occur? What activities are going on while the behavior occurs? What people (teacher, peers, etc.) are around when the behavior tends to occur? In short, what appears to set off or consistently precede the behavior of concern? Also, don't forget to consider possible setting events, either immediate (e.g., temperature in the classroom) or remote (level of sleep deprivation, medication, etc.).

Postcedents. The FBA literature typically states something such as, "Define the intent or the function that the behavior appeared to serve. Was it power, control, attention, etc.?" There is a problem with such terms. "Intention" can lead us astray, prompting us to speculate about what may be going on in the student's mind. What does *control* mean? As for *attention,* the important considerations are the particular events that are called to attention and exactly when such events occur with respect to the specified behavior. In particular, do these events tend to immediately follow the behavior? Overall, postcedent events can be classified within a two-by-two table as follows:

		Behavior Effect	
		Behavior Increased	*Behavior Decreased*
Condition Changes	*Something Presented*	Positive reinforcement	Positive punishment
	Something Removed	Negative reinforcement	Negative punishment

What we are trying to determine here is not the *purpose* of the behavior (a term that can too easily steer us toward folk psychology formulations) but the nature of the events that typically follow the behavior—their function as a causal mechanism. These events are two-dimensional; that is, (a) they are either presented or removed following the behavior and (b) they either increase or decrease the behavior they follow. When we say that something is "presented" or "removed" we do not necessarily mean that these are deliberate actions. For example, a teacher who gives attention to out-of-seat behavior by saying, "Johnny, sit down" may not be aware that her attention is functioning as a causal mechanism (positive reinforcement) responsible for the very behavior she is trying to reduce. She certainly would not be "presenting" attention in order to increase that behavior. Nonetheless, attention *occurs* immediately following the out-of-seat behavior.

The FBA Interview

In summary, FBA is not a set of assessment techniques; it is an *assessment approach* to identifying possible causes of problem behavior. FBAs are conducted for two purposes: (a) to meet the legal requirements of IDEA and (b) to develop an effective positive behavioral intervention plan. This chapter does not address the legal aspects, nor will it provide details about various assessment procedures routinely employed in FBA. Of the assessment methods used in FBA, the indirect method of formal behavioral interviewing is most appropriate for our purpose. The following is a list of questions an interviewer might ask to collect information about antecedents and postcedents (adapted from Milterberger, 2004, p. 264).

Antecedents

- When does the problem behavior usually occur?
- Where does the problem behavior usually occur?
- Who is present when the problem behavior occurs?
- What activities or events precede the occurrence of the problem behavior?
- What do other people say or do immediately before the problem behavior occurs?
- Does the student engage in any other behavior before the problem behavior?
- When, where, with whom, and in what circumstances is the problem behavior least likely to occur?

Postcedents

- What happens after the problem behavior occurs?
- What do you do when the problem behavior occurs?
- What do other people do when the problem behavior occurs?
- What changes after the problem behavior occurs?
- What does the student get after the problem behavior?
- What does the student get out of or avoid after the problem behavior?

You will note that each question asks about the events that immediately precede and follow the student's problem behavior. Instead of interviewing someone else, however, you would be answering these questions yourself. If you are team teaching or have an instructional assistant in your classroom, you would, of course, want to interview that person as well. In circumstances where you feel it would be appropriate, it may also be useful to interview the student who is displaying the problem behavior. Your goal at this point is to formulate a hypothesis (educated guess) about what contingency arrangement is most likely causing the problem behavior. The behavioral interview will be useful to the extent that it approximates that of a well-conducted behaviorological FBA—one that focuses on contingent relations between behavior and other events. To become adept with FBA, you need to learn how to see these contingent relations going on about you, the functional relations among particular actions of your students and other events—both antecedent and postcedent—including, especially, your own actions. From such observations you will be able to identify the variables (causal mechanism) controlling the problem behaviors and then design effective interventions.

PLANNING BEHAVIOR INTERVENTIONS

The purpose of a behaviorological FBA is to develop a positive and proactive set of strategies to remediate the behavior problem. The effectiveness of a particular problem-solving approach depends on its accuracy in identifying the variables responsible for the behavior problem. So how do you determine if your assessment is accurate? The ultimate test is whether or not it leads directly to an effective intervention in your classroom—that is, whether it has treatment validity. But that test is after the fact. How can you decide on a particular plan at the onset of the problem-solving process? The answer lies in classroom-based research. Based on a colossal body of empirical research in school settings, there is no question that applied behavior analysis has achieved this distinction—to wit, well over 200 classroom behavior management studies reported in the *Journal of Applied Behavior Analysis* (http://seab.envmed.rochester.edu/jaba/jabaindx.asp) as well as dozens of books on the subject (some are much better than others).

What Kind of Behavior Problem?

First, you need to determine what kind of problem you are encountering, along with the nature of the consequences responsible for it. Reducing behavior problems to their simplest terms, you are dealing with either a "cannot do" *skill problem* or a "will not do" *performance problem,* and the maintaining consequences are either that the student gets something or avoids something. Thus, we have four broad possibilities: For skill problems, the student may get attention from peers for immature behavior (lacks appropriate social skills) or for failing to comprehend your assignment (lacks prerequisite academic skills). For performance problems, the student may get more attention for inappropriate behavior than for appropriate behavior (although equally capable of either behavior) or may avoid asking you for assistance with a difficult task (capable but hesitant).

Developing the Behavior Intervention Plan

Next, you need to develop a **behavior intervention plan** (**BIP**). Determine if an informal intervention will suffice. For example, suppose Jerry is bothering Jean in class. As an informal solution, try moving Jerry to a desk on the other side of the room. That may end the problem. If the problem persists and Jerry begins to annoy his new neighbor, then a more systematic intervention plan is needed. A systematic plan begins with a definition of the problem behavior that is observable and measurable. Again, the scope of this chapter precludes an adequate guideline on the measurement of behavior (see Van Houton & Hall, 2001). For our purpose, perhaps it will do to state that in many cases, behavior measurement can be fairly simple. One of the easiest ways to measure behavior is to count how many times it occurs in a specified period of time. The behavior needs to be defined so that you can tell when it begins and ends. We can count talking out, being out of one's seat (although a duration measure using a stopwatch may be better for students who tend to wander around the room once they are out of their seat), the number or percentage of arithmetic problems answered correctly, and so on. Then you need to draw a simple behavioral graph consisting of a vertical scale for the behavior and a horizontal scale for the time dimension (see Figure 3.1). Label the behavioral scale up the

Figure 3.1 Sample Behavior Chart

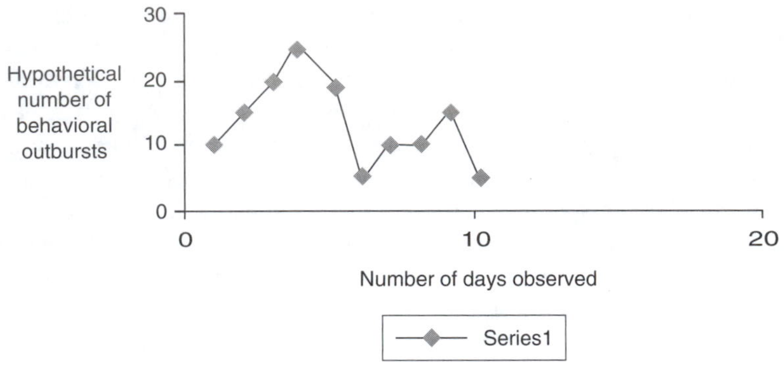

side (e.g., "Number of Minutes of In-Seat Behavior") and the time scale across the bottom of your graph (e.g., "Days"). Each day during the same time and activity and for a fixed period of time (e.g., 15 minutes), count the number of times the behavior occurs. Then graph your data by placing a data point at the intersection of the day and the point on your behavior scale corresponding to your count. As you plot data points from day to day, connect them with a line (forming a data path). Next, measure the behavior several days before you begin your intervention. This part of your graph is called the baseline. Then draw a vertical line as long as your behavioral scale between day lines to separate the baseline phase from the intervention phase—which we will now discuss.

A BIP is a written plan that describes the behavioral intervention you designed to address a problem behavior. The purpose of a BIP is to alter the social or physical environment or both so that it will prevent the problem behavior from occurring by making it less effective, efficient, and relevant while—and this is the heart of the matter—developing an alternative acceptable behavior that will be more effective, efficient, and relevant. That is, teach a viable replacement behavior. As examples, if the problem is out-of-seat behavior, reinforce in-seat behavior. If it is running in the hall, reinforce walking in the hall. If it is talking out, reinforce raising a hand before speaking. If it is off-task behavior, reinforce on-task behavior. If the writing assignment is only half-done, reinforce the satisfactorily completed product. See if you can replace the problem behavior with an educationally meaningful behavior. For more serious behavior such as fighting, more intrusive interventions may be needed. Although the reference list includes texts that address the reduction of dangerous behavior, it might be helpful to seek the assistance of a competent behavioral consultant.

If your intervention plan attempts to teach an acceptable alternative behavior, but the new behavior is not more effective, efficient, and relevant than the problem behavior for the student, the plan is not likely to be successful. Effective *BIPs are directly linked to FBAs.*

Basic Intervention Strategies

In general, a BIP specifies intervention features in four main areas: (a) teaching acceptable replacement behaviors—strategies for teaching replacement behaviors (e.g., modeling,

Figure 3.2

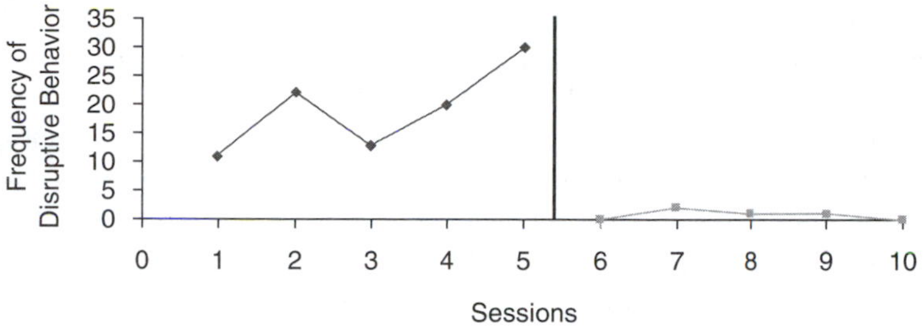

corrective feedback, positive reinforcement); (b) antecedent manipulations—strategies that involve removal or modification of triggering antecedents or programming antecedent stimuli that trigger the replacement behavior; (c) consequence manipulations—strategies that involve the removal or modification of maintaining consequence stimuli, or the addition of other consequence stimuli that positively reinforce and maintain the replacement behavior; and (d) setting event manipulations—strategies that involve the removal or modification of factors that perpetuate the problem behavior, or the addition of strategies that nullify such factors. The intervention strategy that you develop should be implemented in a way that is effective, yet least intrusive to the student, and consistent with established professional standards. And it must be implemented in the way you designed it, an important consideration if you are team teaching or if you have an instructional assistant in your classroom. The plan should include clear, written directions outlining *who, what, when, where,* and *how.*

Finally, you need to continue to measure the target behavior each day in exactly the way you did during the baseline phase and plot the date on your behavioral graph (see Figure 3.2). At the top of your graph, you should write "Baseline" to the left of your phase-change line, and to the right, provide a descriptive label for the intervention (e.g., "Contingent Praise"). As you plot data during the intervention phase, you can compare the data paths during the baseline and intervention phase to see if the measured behavior is improving. If after several days the intervention is not sufficient to effect a noticeable change in the behavior, you should reexamine your intervention. Is it being carried out consistently? If it involves consequence manipulations, do these manipulations immediately follow the target behavior? Are antecedents or setting events being changed appropriately? And so on. If you troubleshoot and the BIP is still not successful, it may be necessary for you to conduct further assessment and adjust the BIP accordingly.

One hallmark of the behaviorological approach to solving behavior problems in the classroom is, "If at once you don't succeed, try, try again." You will have the enormous advantage of determining in a timely way whether or not you are succeeding. And if you are not succeeding, a behavior-change technology of demonstrated effectiveness is available for your use. Again, seeing the *Journal of Applied Behavior Analysis* is a strong recommendation.

SUMMARY

One of the biggest obstacles standing in the way of effective behavior management in the classroom is reliance on folk psychology to solve problems. Folk psychology is based on the assumption that behavior (desired or undesired) is caused by some hypothesized inner agency, such as "Billy is a good-natured boy" or "Mary has a mean streak in her." The behaviorological perspective takes another position; while not ruling out the effects of genetic inheritance (there are inborn individual differences in behavior) and physiological variables, the behavior change technology derived from behaviorology focuses on the manipulation of environmental variables in the context within which the behavior of concern is manifested. Thus, the behaviorological approach posits that problem behaviors that occur in the classroom are the result of causal variables that are potentially identifiable. By recognizing the fact that student behavior is caused by a particular set of variables operating in the classroom environment, with a properly conducted functional behavioral assessment these causal variables can be identified and systematically altered, thereby eliminating the problem behavior—usually, by replacing it with a desired behavior. Although the scope of this chapter precludes providing an adequate guide for conducting a thorough FBA, it does offer a scientifically based frame of reference for understanding and eliminating problem behavior. To the extent that you understand how contingencies control classroom behavior, you will be better prepared to deal with problem behaviors when they do arise and—even more important—prevent them from occurring in the future as they are replaced with desired and educationally meaningful behavior.

DISCUSSION QUESTIONS

1. What are the differences between behaviorological and folk psychology approaches to understanding and dealing with behavior problems?
2. Provide an original example of an *explanatory fiction*. What makes it a fiction?
3. What is applied behavior analysis, and how is it related to behaviorology?
4. The subject matter of behaviorology necessarily includes important technical terms. Can you answer the following technical questions?
   a. What are the two types of punishment?
   b. What is the difference between positive and negative reinforcement?
   c. What is the difference between consequences and postcedents?
   d. What are contingencies?
5. Suppose you were interviewing another teacher about antecedent and postcedent events in relation to a student's problem behavior. Give some examples of questions you should ask. (Note: When you encounter behavior problems in your classroom, these are questions you should ask yourself, becoming at once both interviewer and interviewee.)

FOR ADDITIONAL HELP

	Organization	*Web Address*	*Description*
Dealing With Problem Behavior in the Classroom	New York University Child Study Center	www.aboutourkids.org	Dedicated to advancing the field of child mental health through evidence-based practice, science, and education
	Center for Effective Collaboration and Practice	http://cecp.air.org/preventionstrategies/Default.htm	Research-based and practical information for parents and professionals about behavior problems in children

REFERENCES

Burley, R., & Waller, R. J. (2005). Effects of a collaborative behavior management plan on reducing disruptive behaviors of a student with ADHD. *Teaching Exceptional Children Plus, 1*(4). Retrieved October 22, 2005, from http://escholarship.bc.edu/education/tecplus/vol1/iss4/art2

Chandler, L. K., & Dahlquist, C. M. (2002). *Functional assessment: Strategies to prevent and remediate challenging behavior in school settings.* Upper Saddle River, NJ: Merrill/Prentice Hall.

Milterberger, R. G. (2004). *Behavior modification: Principles and procedures* (3rd ed.). Belmont, CA: Wadsworth/Thomson.

Van Houton, R., & Hall, R. V. (2001). *The measurement of behavior: Behavior modification* (3rd ed.). Austin, TX: Pro-Ed.

Part II

Mental Health Issues Frequently Confronted in the Classroom

Chapter 4

Elimination Disorders

Susan Mortweet VanScoyoc

PREREADING QUESTIONS

As you read this chapter, reflect on the following questions and issues:

1. What is an elimination disorder?
2. How likely will it be that a teacher will have a student with an elimination disorder in the classroom in any given year?
3. How can a teacher respectfully and discretely address the needs of a student with an elimination disorder?
4. Should teachers be required to play a role in managing the elimination disorder of a student?

Elimination disorders in the academic setting can present a unique challenge to school personnel. Some specialized knowledge of these disorders is important to handle a student's symptoms appropriately and with sensitivity. The two elimination disorders that present most frequently in the school setting are fecal soiling (encopresis) and daytime wetting (diurnal enuresis). The purpose of this chapter is to describe symptoms, etiology, and prevalence of encopresis and enuresis, and to offer specific suggestions that can be used by school personnel to discretely assist a student with these disorders in the school setting.

ENCOPRESIS

Definition and Etiology

Encopresis is defined as the involuntary passing of stool in places other than the toilet in children who are at least 4 years old. Students diagnosed with encopresis have a history of soiling their underwear. The most common causes of encopresis are biological—specifically, constipation and stool withholding. Stool that is not passed regularly through the colon becomes dry and hard and stretches out the muscles of the colon. The nerves in the colon also get stretched out, impairing their ability to alert the student's brain that it is time to pass stool. Over time, the student may simply pass stool into his or her underwear without feeling it. This unawareness of feces in the underwear and its resulting odor is common for students with encopresis, although sometimes it is difficult for parents, teachers, and peers to comprehend.

Since the 1950s, the classification of encopresis as a psychiatric disorder has been challenged (e.g., Davidson, 1958). A small percentage of students with encopresis may have severe psychopathology and may have bowel movements outside the toilet as an intentional act. Overall, however, many studies have shown that children with encopresis do not differ significantly with respect to behavioral or emotional problems when compared with their peers without encopresis (Cox et al., 2003; Friman, Mathews, Finney, Christophersen, & Leibowitz, 1988; Ling, Cox, Sutphen, & Borowitz, 1996). A study that included adolescents with encopresis found that these participants did exhibit more behavioral problems than normative peers (Benninga, Voskuijl, Akkerhuis, Taminiau, & Buller, 2004). The authors reported that the participants with encopresis also experienced more social problems than a comparative group of peers with recurrent abdominal pain. Unfortunately, the results were not reported by age to offer some guidance as to what age-group experienced the most difficulties in these areas.

Prevalence

An estimated 1% to 2% of children aged 6 to 11 years are reported to suffer from encopresis, more commonly boys than girls (Loening-Baucke, 2002). The incidence of encopresis is highest in children aged 5 to 10 years, with a decrease in adolescence (North American Society for Pediatric Gastroenterology, Hepatology and Nutrition, n.d.). Some children with **developmental disabilities** experience more constipation and related bowel problems, including fecal incontinence, than do their peers (Bosch et al., 2002). Thus, school personnel working with students served in special education or inclusive classrooms may see a higher rate of problems with elimination than do those working in the general education setting.

Table 4.1 Summary of Facts About Encopresis

- Encopresis is the involuntary passing of stool in places other than the toilet.
- The most common causes of encopresis are constipation and stool holding.
- Students with encopresis often have to take medication to help them go to the bathroom regularly.
- Students with encopresis may need to engage in daily toilet sits at specific times to facilitate successful toileting.
- Encopresis may resolve for some students within a year, but for others problems with intermittent constipation and soiling will remain.
- Students with encopresis often do not know when they have soiled in their underwear and cannot smell the odor.
- Students with encopresis typically do not have more behavior problems than displayed by their peers.
- Students with encopresis may have to modify their diet to include high fiber choices and reduced dairy intake.
- Students with encopresis often require positive reinforcement to encourage cooperation with their treatment plan.

Treatment

The treatment for encopresis often involves a complex medical and behavioral plan. Students are often prescribed medications to facilitate the regular passing of stools. They are also encouraged to modify their diet to include an increase in daily fiber intake and a decrease in dairy products, which can aggravate constipation. Behavioral components such as scheduling toilet sits and rewarding the student for cooperating with the treatment regimen are also important. Parent education is also a key component, given the misconceptions about soiling and the tendency for parents to try to use punishment to improve the problem (Stark et al., 1997). The success of treatment for encopresis can vary from student to student. Research studies on children treated with the medical-behavioral model suggest that about half the participants are in remission at 1 to 4 years posttreatment, with the remaining demonstrating ongoing mild or intermittent constipation (Levine, 1976; Rockney, McQuade, Days, Linn, & Alario, 1996). Table 4.1 summarizes the important facts about encopresis discussed above.

ENURESIS

Definition and Etiology

Enuresis is described as the repeated voiding of urine outside the toilet, either intentionally or involuntarily, by children over the age of 5 years. Daytime (diurnal) enuresis, as opposed to bedwetting at night, is obviously more disruptive in the school environment and thus is the focus of this chapter. A student with enuresis may experience increased urgency, urination frequency, and the complete or partial loss of bladder control. Diurnal enuresis may be caused by a urinary tract infection, a structural or anatomical abnormality, or a neurological problem such as those experienced by a student with spina bifida. Poor daytime toileting habits may also contribute to diurnal enuresis (American Urological Association, n.d.). Students may ignore the early warning signs that their bladder is full and in need of emptying, only to respond too late

Table 4.2 Summary of Facts About Enuresis

• Enuresis is the repeated voiding of urine outside the toilet.	• Students with enuresis may experience increased urgency, urination frequency, and loss of bladder control.
• School-age children may develop an unhealthy habit of trying to suppress their urge to urinate.	• Students may try to avoid using restrooms that are unclean, that are unsafe, or that do not allow for privacy.
• Diurnal enuresis is a common problem for students of elementary school age.	• Students with special needs may experience more problems with enuresis.
• Medications and behavioral strategies are used to treat enuresis.	• Students with enuresis may need to have unrestricted access to a clean, safe bathroom.

as the urgency increases and they cannot get to the toilet in time. School-age children may make an unhealthy habit of suppressing the urge to urinate in order to comply with inflexible toileting schedules at school or to avoid having to use an unsafe, unsanitary, or public bathroom setting (Cooper, Abousally, Austin, Boyt, & Hawtrey, 2003). Other less common explanations include developmental immaturity, insufficient toilet training, or psychological stress (American Academy of Child and Adolescent Psychiatry [AACAP], 2004). Finally, some students report having episodes of enuresis related to laughing, appropriately called "giggle incontinence" (Chandra, Saharia, Shi, & Hill, 2002).

Prevalence

Diurnal enuresis can be a common problem for children. One study of more than 3,000 students who were 7 years old found that 6% of them experienced some kind of dysfunctional voiding (Hjalmas, 1992). Approximately 3% of the girls and 2% of the boys experienced day wetting at least once a week. A more recent study of school-age children found that 5% to 15% of the participants experienced daytime incontinence (Farhat et al., 2000). Students with Attention Deficit Hyperactivity Disorder (ADHD) have also been found to have significantly higher rates of enuresis than their peers without ADHD (Duel, Steinberg-Epstein, Hill, & Lerner, 2003).

Treatment

If a specific etiology can be found for enuresis, such as a urinary tract infection, a specific medical treatment is prescribed. If, however, a medical examination does not reveal a known etiology, supportive behavioral strategies and medication may be used (AACAP, 2004). The treatment of diurnal enuresis may include behavioral strategies such as increased monitoring, scheduled voiding, overlearning, and reinforcement. Overlearning can be described as a procedure that results in the child's being trained to a higher rate of performance than would normally be expected (Christophersen & Mortweet, 2001). For example, a child may be asked to drink extra fluids to make it more difficult for him or her to avoid urinating, thereby offering more training opportunities to urinate appropriately (e.g., Houts, 1996). Medications may also be considered by a child's health care provider, including imipramine and DDAVP (desmopressin acetate). Behavioral and pharmacological treatments are both successful in managing enuresis. Children receiving nonpharmacological

Table 4.3 Ways to Assist the Student With an Elimination Disorder at School

Allow unrestricted access to a clean bathroom

- ✓ Allow the student to use the restroom as needed and not just during scheduled restroom breaks.
- ✓ Allow access to a restroom with privacy.
- ✓ Develop a private signal system with the student to encourage the use of the restroom without disrupting the class.
- ✓ Do not wait for the student to notice an odor. Discreetly excuse from class when YOU notice a problem.

Provide a way for the student to clean up

- ✓ Allow student access to a change of clothing, especially underwear and pants.
- ✓ Allow student access to wet cleansing wipes and plastic bags to assist with cleanup and clothing disposal.
- ✓ Suggest to parents that the student with encopresis be provided with toilet paper that can be flushed to assist with cleanup.
- ✓ Seek out these supplies from donation resources if needed.

Be sensitive to emotional needs

- ✓ Be discreet when interacting with a student about elimination issues.
- ✓ Do not berate or humiliate the student regarding elimination problems.
- ✓ Do not tolerate teasing or bullying.
- ✓ Provide adequate supervision of bathroom breaks.

Allow adequate restroom time and accommodations for missed work

- ✓ Do not ask students to rush their toileting.
- ✓ Do not penalize students for missed work resulting from time in the bathroom.
- ✓ Do not keep a student in from recess for toileting problems or regimen requirements.
- ✓ Treat needed accommodations as seriously as those needed for any student with a medical condition.

Cooperate with the health care plan

- ✓ Meet with parents to discuss treatment needs at school.
- ✓ Ask for consent to talk with health care providers if needed.
- ✓ Provide scheduled toilet sits, unrestricted access, dietary accommodations, and daily reporting of symptoms as requested.
- ✓ Recognize the additional needs of students with special learning or behavioral issues.

Be an informed advocate

- ✓ Seek out information about the student's particular elimination disorder and treatment.
- ✓ Share information with necessary staff.
- ✓ Report noncompliance with treatment needs by other staff.
- ✓ Report unsanitary or unsafe bathroom conditions.

treatments may have a more lasting positive outcome (Houts, Berman, & Abramson, 1994). Table 4.2 provides a summary of facts about enuresis.

HOW TO ASSIST THE STUDENT WITH AN ELIMINATION DISORDER

There are many ways to help a student manage an elimination disorder at school. Although the nuances of each student's care will be individual, some suggestions should apply to most students suffering from encopresis or enuresis. These recommendations can encourage students to respond to their "call to stool or urinate," increasing the likelihood of treatment success and symptom resolution. Students with elimination disorders will also feel supported by their school personnel, knowing that their condition is taken seriously and that no teasing by other students will be tolerated. A summary of these recommendations is found in Table 4.3. A brief case vignette is presented below to illustrate the issues often experienced by a student with an elimination disorder, as well as the strategies found to be useful in the school setting.

Adam is an 8-year-old male attending third grade in an urban elementary school. He is described by his teacher and parents as a typically developing child who is shy, unwilling to ask for help, and isolated from his peers. Adam does not display any significant behavior problems at home or school and, once engaged, typically enjoys interacting with children and adults.

Adam has a long history of problems with constipation. Even as a toddler, he required suppositories and a strict diet to maintain adequate stooling. A few months into his third-grade year, Adam's parents took him to see his primary care physician because they had noticed Adam had stool in his underwear and often smelled of feces. After a medical examination, he was diagnosed with encopresis, prescribed a stool-softening medication, and then referred to a pediatric psychologist for behavior management strategies.

At school, Adam had many days when he would soil before or after school, resulting in a foul odor. Many students asked to be moved away from Adam, and his teacher also reported difficulties assisting him due to the smell. She often recommended he take unfinished work home with him instead of spending the time needed to address his questions in class. The teacher found it difficult to discuss Adam's odor with him and had a hard time understanding how he could not smell it. She chose not to say anything or to ask Adam to go to the restroom to clean up, because she did not want to embarrass him. She also had not discussed her concerns with his parents, once again, not sure how to bring up the subject for a student clearly old enough to be toilet trained.

Adam's parents discussed his toileting habits and the increased amount of uncompleted work that Adam was experiencing at school. Consent was obtained for the psychologist to talk with the teacher. After discussing the teacher's concerns about Adam's toileting problems and odor, an intervention plan was discussed with the teacher. It was recommended that she share this plan with the school nurse, counselor, and any other personnel who interacted with Adam on a regular basis. This intervention included the following: (a) Adam's parents would be asked to bring a change of clothes, some flushable toilet paper, and a plastic bag to transport any dirty clothes. (b) School personnel would send Adam to the nurse's office any time they smelled a fecal odor on Adam. They were not to wait for Adam to smell the odor or question him about whether or not he could smell the odor. (c) Adam and his teacher were to work out a private signal system so that if Adam needed to use the restroom, he could do so without interrupting the teacher. (d) Adam was to be allowed to use the restroom in the nurse's office if he requested to have the privacy he needed to have a complete bowel movement. (e) Lunch personnel were instructed to offer Adam juice instead of milk as a way of limiting his dairy intake. This intervention assisted school personnel in understanding Adam's needs and contributed to his overall treatment plan. Initially, Adam was resistant to the private signal system, but as he saw that most children ignored the fact that he left the room and that he did not get in trouble for leaving, he became more compliant with the plan. His increased attempts to use the toilet at school assisted in the management of his symptoms, which resulted in consistent stooling after school and reducing his soiling and odor at school.

Allow Unrestricted Access to a Clean Bathroom

In general, students with elimination disorders should have unrestricted access to a clean bathroom and should not be asked to wait for scheduled breaks if they feel the need to eliminate. For students with encopresis, access to a restroom with more privacy than the group restroom can be helpful. By allowing the student to use the restroom in the nurse's office, for example, the student does not have to worry about other children noticing that he or she is taking a long time or that the odor from the stall is strong. When the student needs to use the restroom, a private signal can be given to the teacher so that the student may use the restroom without having to interrupt the teacher. For example, the student can put a laminated card on the corner of his or her desk to indicate that a restroom break is needed. Of course, some teachers may fear that a student may take advantage of this unrestricted usage and abuse the system to get out of doing class work. As mentioned previously, most students with elimination disorders do not differ from their peers with respect to behavior problems. Furthermore, most students with elimination disorders are uncomfortable with their problems and do not want to appear different from their peers. Thus, a student who might "abuse" unrestricted bathroom privileges may be in the minority. A more frequent problem might indeed be encouraging a student to use the system set in place to assist with toileting needs. For example, 67% of the teachers surveyed by Cooper et al. (2003) encountered reluctance on the part of a student to let them know of a urine or fecal incontinence, especially for students in kindergarten through second grade.

The private signal system can also be used if the teacher smells an odor from the student when the student does not seem to be aware of the smell. The teacher can then initiate the private signal so that the student may use the restroom. As mentioned previously, it is not uncommon for a student with an elimination disorder to not smell his or her own urine or bowel movement. (The experience for them may be similar to the adult who wears too much aftershave or cologne yet seems oblivious to the looks of disdain and the breath holding that occur when he or she enters an elevator.) Thus, teachers should always request that the student go to the restroom or nurse's office to clean up without waiting for the student or peers to notice and should not berate the student for not noticing the smell.

Allow Adequate Time in the Restroom and Accommodations for Missing Class Work

When students are in the restroom, they should not be asked to rush. The student must be given time to listen to internal cues in order for elimination to be complete and successful. Any work that is missed by the student should not be counted against him or her, nor should the student have to stay in from recess to make it up. Other arrangements should be made to help the student complete missing work. The needs of a student with an elimination disorder are as important and worthy of accommodations as the needs of a student with any other kind of medical condition, such as diabetes. Students with diabetes would not be penalized for the work missed while going to the nurse's office to manage their low blood sugar. Similarly, students with encopresis or enuresis should not be penalized or belittled for their treatment needs.

Provide a Way for the Student to Clean Up

Students should also have a change of clothes available to them, specifically underwear and pants, in the nurse's office or with their teacher. If parents are not reliable in bringing such clothing, donations from local charities can be an option for having age-appropriate clothing available for any child who may need a change of clothes. A supply of wet cleansing wipes and plastic bags to assist in cleanup and discrete disposal of soiled clothing are also recommended. The bag can then be given to the student at the end of the day to take home. If a student rides the bus home, increasing the likelihood of being teased for carrying smelly clothes, extra effort should be made to clean out the clothes as much as possible at school first. For the student with encopresis, a supply of toilet paper that can be flushed may be kept in the private restroom that he or she has access to in order to facilitate adequate wiping after a bowel movement. Once again, parents should be asked to provide this supply, or a donation from local merchants or manufacturers could be sought.

Cooperate With the Health Care Plan

One of the best ways to help a student with an elimination disorder in the school setting is to assist the student's parents with the treatment regimen that has been prescribed to address the problem. If direct communication is necessary, the student's parents should be asked to sign a consent form for school personnel to talk with the health care providers who are working with the student outside the school setting. For students with encopresis and enuresis, assisting with the treatment plan may include allowing scheduled toilet sits in addition to allowing the student to use the toilet as needed. For students with encopresis, additional requirements from school personnel may include providing the parent with weekly lunch menus, allowing the student to supplement food intake at school with high-fiber snacks, and offering the student nondairy beverage options at mealtimes. School personnel can also assist parents by informing them of any known accidents or voiding abnormalities during the school day. Some students in the classroom, such as those with ADHD or a borderline IQ, may have difficulties adhering to a treatment plan and therefore may be less successful in resolving their voiding problems (Crimmins, Rathbun, & Husmann, 2003). Thus, even more assistance from school personnel may be required for these types of students to facilitate treatment success.

Be Sensitive to Emotional Needs

Children with elimination disorders may be at risk for experiencing increased social and interpersonal problems compared with their peers without these disorders. Students with elimination disorders are often the victims of misunderstanding by parents and teachers, who blame the student for the problem. They may be belittled by adults indignant that they are not "acting their age" or humiliated by not being allowed access to clean up their underwear. Socially, students with encopresis may be subject to teasing and social isolation due to the odor associated with soiling. Students with enuresis may be at risk for emotional or physical abuse from family members, anxiety about detection of their problems by peers, and low self-esteem (Warzak, 1993).

It is not difficult to understand why school personnel need to be discreet and sensitive when assisting a student with an elimination disorder. Accommodations for the student should be made willingly and without the message that the student is a source of frustration or does not truly have a medical condition. As mentioned previously, teachers should develop a private way for the student to indicate that he or she needs to use the bathroom, as well as to indicate to the student that the teacher has detected a reason for the student to excuse himself or herself. Teachers should also enforce a zero-tolerance policy for teasing students with elimination disorders. Adequate supervision during bathroom breaks should be provided to decrease incidents of ridicule or bullying. If such supervision is not possible, the student should be allowed to use a private or safer bathroom than that used for a group restroom break.

Be an Informed Advocate

Most school personnel do not receive information about normal and abnormal elimination habits for students. Thus, when a student is in need of assistance, all personnel who will be interacting with that student should educate themselves about the particular condition and treatment needed for success in symptom management or resolution. Staff members can then advocate for that student's rights in all academic settings. For example, lunchroom personnel can be informed that the student needs a nondairy beverage option, unsanitary bathroom conditions can be reported to the appropriate administrators, and successful strategies to accommodate a flexible toileting schedule can be passed along to next year's teachers. In addition to communicating with the student's parents and health care providers, a Web site with useful information is offered by the North American Society for Pediatric Gastroenterology, Hepatology and Nutrition (NASPGHAN) at www.naspgn.org. In short, many school personnel will have misconceptions that a student's elimination disorder is nothing more than a behavioral and emotional problem, easily resolved with the right consequences. School personnel with more accurate information about elimination disorders must advocate for students with such problems to decrease the negative physiological and psychological consequences these students may experience.

SUMMARY

Elimination disorders, contrary to common assumptions, are not volitional behaviors that manipulative children use to control adults or situations they do not like. Elimination disorders usually involve behaviors over which children have no control. In fact, a medical cause is common. Elimination disorders can cause significant emotional duress in children and can result in ostracism by peers. Teachers can play a tremendous role in supporting students with this type of problem. In fact, for children who are in school, teachers are often an indispensable part of the intervention team. Furthermore, teachers can help prevent additional issues from arising in children with elimination disorders resulting from the anxiety, teasing, and exclusion that can occur. Elimination disorders are a perfect example of a student problem that can be helped dramatically by your sensitive and patient response.

DISCUSSION QUESTIONS

1. More students with serious and chronic medical conditions are surviving and attending school, often in need of accommodations and care by school personnel. Many schools do not have school nurses to assist with such care. How can teachers be more prepared to assist such students? What role should parents play in providing care to medically complex students or for those with chronic health care needs in the school setting? Should school personnel be allowed to refuse the provision of accommodations?
2. Section 504 of the Rehabilitation Act of 1973 provides a legal basis for plans (called (504 plans) to be developed to assist students in the regular classroom who have an impairment in one or more major life areas. The purpose of these plans is to provide support for students so that they can function effectively in the general education setting. What are the rights of students with medical care needs in the school setting? Do they qualify for special 504 plans to accommodate their needs? What resources are available for teachers to learn more about the rights of such students?
3. The case discussed in this chapter highlights the teacher's hesitancy to get involved in this student's problems with soiling and odor. How else might she have handled the situation? What are some of the challenges of addressing personal hygiene types of issues in the school setting?

FOR ADDITIONAL HELP

	Organization	*Web Address*	*Description*
Elimination Disorders (Enuresis and Encopresis)	NASPGHAN	www.naspgn.org	North American Society for Pediatric Gastroenterology, Hepatology and Nutrition
	KidsHealth	http://kidshealth.org	The largest and most visited site available, providing doctor-approved health information about children from before birth through adolescence

REFERENCES

American Academy of Child and Adolescent Psychiatry. (2004). Summary of the practice parameter for the assessment and treatment of children and adolescents with enuresis. *Journal of the American Academy of Child and Adolescent Psychiatry, 43,* 123–125.

American Urological Association. (n.d.). *Pediatric conditions: Bladder.* Retrieved April 3, 2004, from www.urologyhealth.org/pediatric/index.cfm?cat=03&topic=91

Benninga, M. A., Voskuijl, W. P., Akkerhuis, G. W., Taminiau, J. A., & Buller, H. A. (2004). Colonic transit times and behaviour profiles in children with defecation disorders. *Archives of Disease in Childhood, 89,* 13–16.

Bosch, J., Mraz, R., Msbruch, J., Tabor, A., Van Dyke, D., & McBrien, D. (2002). Constipation in young children with developmental disabilities. *Infants and Young Children, 15,* 66–77.

Chandra, M., Saharia, R., Shi, Q., & Hill, V. (2002). Giggle incontinence in children: A manifestation of detrusor instability. *Journal of Urology, 168,* 2184–2187.

Christophersen, E. R., & Mortweet, S. L. (2001). *Treatments that work: Empirically supported strategies for managing childhood problems.* Washington, DC: American Psychological Association.

Cooper, C. S., Abousally, C. T., Austin, J. C., Boyt, M. A., & Hawtrey, C. E. (2003). Do public schools teach voiding dysfunction? Results of an elementary school teacher survey. *Journal of Urology, 170,* 956–958.

Cox, D. J., Ritterband, L. M., Quillian, W., Kovatchev, B., Morris, J., Sutphen, J., & Borowitz, S. (2003). Assessment of behavioral mechanisms maintaining encopresis: Virginia encopresis-constipation apperception test. *Journal of Pediatric Psychology, 28,* 375–382.

Crimmins, C. R., Rathbun, S. R., & Husmann, D. A. (2003). Management of urinary incontinence and nocturnal enuresis in Attention-Deficit Hyperactivity Disorder. *Journal of Urology, 170,* 1340–1350.

Davidson, M. (1958). Constipation and fecal incontinence. *Pediatric Clinics of North America, 62,* 261–275.

Duel, B. P., Steinberg-Epstein, R., Hill, M., & Lerner, M. (2003). A survey of voiding dysfunction in children with attention deficit-hyperactivity disorder. *Journal of Urology, 170,* 1521–1524.

Farhat, W., Bagli, D., Darius, J., Capolicchio, G., O'Reilly, S., Merguerian, P. A., Khoury, A., et al. (2000). The dysfunctional voiding scoring system: Quantitative standardization of dysfunctional voiding symptoms in children. *Journal of Urology, 164,* 1011–1015.

Friman, P. C., Mathews, J. R., Finney, J. W., Christophersen, E. R., & Leibowitz, M. (1988). Do encopretic children have clinically significant behavior problems? *Pediatrics, 82,* 407–409.

Hjalmas, K. (1992). Functional daytime incontinence: Definitions and epidemiology. *Scandinavian Journal of Urology and Nephrology, 141*(Suppl.), 39–44.

Houts, A. C. (1996). Behavioral treatment of enuresis. *Clinical Psychologist, 49,* 5–6.

Houts, A. C., Berman, J. S., & Abramson, H. (1994). Effectiveness of psychological and pharmacological treatments for nocturnal enuresis. *Journal of Consulting and Clinical Psychology, 62,* 737–745.

Levine, M. D. (1976). Children with encopresis: A study of treatment outcome. *Pediatrics, 56,* 845–852.

Ling, W., Cox, D. J., Sutphen, J., & Borowitz, S. (1996). Psychological factors in encopresis: Comparison of patients to nonsymptomatic siblings. *Clinical Pediatrics, 35,* 427.

Loening-Baucke, V. (2002). Encopresis. *Current Opinion in Pediatrics, 14,* 570–575.

North American Society for Pediatric Gastroenterology, Hepatology and Nutrition. (n.d.). *Fecal soiling (encopresis).* Retrieved March 1, 2004, from www.naspgn.org/sub/Encopresis.htm

Rockney, R. M., McQuade, W. H., Days, A. L., Linn, H. E., & Alario, A. J. (1996). Encopresis treatment outcome: Long-term follow-up of 45 cases. *Journal of Developmental and Behavioral Pediatrics, 17,* 380–385.

Stark, L. J., Opipari, L. C., Donaldson, D. L., Danovsky, M. B., Rasile, D. A., & Del Santo, A. F. (1997). Evaluation of a standard protocol for retentive encopresis: A replication. *Journal of Pediatric Psychology, 22,* 619–633.

Warzak, W. J. (1993). Psychosocial implications of nocturnal enuresis. *Clinical Pediatrics* (Special Suppl.), 38–40.

Chapter 5

Mood Disorders

Major Depressive Disorder, Dysthymic Disorder, and Bipolar Disorder

Amy C. Traylor

M. Elizabeth Vonk

PREREADING QUESTIONS

As you read this chapter, reflect on the following questions and issues:

1. What is the difference between a student who is experiencing "normal" mood swings and one who is suffering from a mood disorder? What warning signs, if any, should you look for and when might immediate action be warranted?
2. What do you feel are personal strengths and weaknesses that might affect your ability to assist a student with a mood disorder?
3. There are many state and district policies and procedures aimed at teacher and school responsibilities regarding the report and treatment of students displaying symptoms of illnesses such as mood disorders. Are you aware of these policies and procedures as they apply to you? Where could you seek further information on these policies and procedures?

Major Depressive Disorder, **Dysthymic Disorder**, and **Bipolar Disorder** all belong to a category of disorders known as **mood disorders**. For many years, the diagnosis of these disorders occurred solely among the adult population because it was widely believed that children did not suffer from these illnesses. The reasons for this idea were the beliefs that younger children did not possess the developmental maturity necessary to feel depressed or have feelings of hopelessness and that adolescents were "supposed" to be "moody" as they adapted to changes related to puberty, establishment of a personal identity, and changes in relationships with family and peers (Miezitis, 1992). Over the past few decades, however, increased attention has been paid to the idea that children and adolescents are susceptible to these disorders and deserve to be taken seriously and provided treatment. Likewise, there is a growing appreciation of the need for research pertaining to depression in children and adolescents, and professionals from a variety of fields are working to understand the mysteries of these illnesses in relation to children and adolescents.

This chapter focuses on three mood disorders that most commonly affect students: Major Depressive Disorder, Dysthymic Disorder, and Bipolar Disorder. First, we explore the underlying causes of mood disorders. Next, we examine each mood disorder in more detail. Each of these sections begins with a brief vignette to introduce the disorder and then examine the scope, signs and symptoms, relationships to other illnesses, clinical treatment, and outcomes of each disorder. Classroom interventions are discussed in the third section. Finally, an in-depth case study is provided to demonstrate how a mood disorder could manifest itself in an adolescent and how treatment strategies might be effective. It is important to remember when reading this chapter that, just as each child in a classroom is different, each child with a mood disorder will present with somewhat different symptoms and will respond differently to the techniques employed. The information provided here is meant to provide a general idea of how to identify and support children suffering from these mood disorders. However, flexibility and creativity are keys in helping these children succeed in the classroom.

UNDERLYING CAUSES OF MOOD DISORDERS

Although it is generally accepted that both biological and **psychosocial** factors play a role in adult mood disorders, there is little consensus as to the causes of such problems in children and adolescents. However, it is suggested that four factors may put children and adolescents at risk of mood disorders: family and genetic factors, gender factors, biological factors, and cognitive factors.

Family and Genetic Factors

Family factors, be they guided by issues of nature or nurture, undoubtedly play a major role in the establishment of child and adolescent mood disorders. Some studies appear to provide substantial evidence linking major mood disorders to genetics (Duffy, 2000). However, others argue that it is impossible to determine if genetics play an actual role in childhood disorders or if similarly distressed parents simply create an environment that increases the likelihood of disorders developing in their children. In their literature review of studies exploring the link between genetics and mood disorders, Rice, Harold, and Thapar (2002) note that both environmental and genetic influences are included in most family studies and that twin and adoption studies vary widely in their estimations of a link between genetics and mood disorders. Thus, they conclude, such studies provide few firm conclusions regarding the role of genetics in childhood mood disorders. However, the role of the family should not be discounted as a factor in the development of child and adolescent mood disorders. Studies of children seen at clinics for mood disorders indicate that 20% to 50% of that population has a family history of similar illnesses (Kovacs, Devlin, Pollack, Richards, & Mukerji, 1997). Other studies have shown that children of affected parents are three times more likely than children of nonaffected parents to experience a mood disorder (Birmaher, Ryan, Williamson, Brent, & Kaufman, 1996a; Birmaher, Ryan, et al., 1996b), indicating that family factors, whether genetic or environmental, are, indeed, a major factor in understanding the cause of mood disorders.

Gender Factors

Gender does not appear to play a major factor in early childhood mood disorders, but differences do occur once children reach adolescence. By this time, afflicted girls outnumber boys 2 to 1 (Schlozman, 2001). One reason for this difference may be that adolescent girls are more social, depend more on positive social relationships, and are, therefore, more vulnerable to social losses than most boys, thus increasing their vulnerability to interpersonal stress (Allgood-Merten, Lewinsohn, & Hops, 1990). There is also some evidence that, unlike boys, girls use coping methods that entail more focused, repetitive thinking about stressful events (Nolen-Hoeksema & Girgus, 1994). Finally, mood disorders may be evident in girls who are unhappy with the changes in their bodies as a result of puberty. These physical changes, combined with greater social vulnerability and specific coping methods, may result in a higher prevalence of mood disorders among adolescent girls.

Biological Factors

Although poorly understood, biological factors are thought to play a role in child and adolescent mood disorders. Some features of such illnesses, including changes in sleep and appetite, are related to a part of the brain called the hypothalamus, which is, in turn, closely related to the pituitary gland. Although gland abnormality is a recognized feature of adult mood disorders, very little research has been conducted in this area with children and adolescents (Birmaher, Ryan, et al., 1996a, 1996b). As more research is conducted, the role of biological functions will become clearer, potentially making treatment more efficacious.

Cognitive Factors

The relationship between cognitive factors and mood disorders has received considerable attention from researchers. A child or adolescent with cognitive traits that predispose him or her to such illnesses generally exhibits a pessimistic attitude. Such a child may assume personal blame for negative events, expect consistently negative outcomes, and believe a singular negative event will last indefinitely. This child may take a negative view of positive events, stating that luck or someone else's efforts caused them to occur. The child may react in a more passive, helpless, or ineffective manner to negative events than do those who view events positively (Seligman, 1975). It is unknown if this cognitive pattern precedes a mood disorder, is evident only during episodes of illness, or is the consequence of previous episodes of illness (Lewinsohn, Steinmetz, Larson, & Franklin, 1981). It is known, however, that these negative patterns may contribute to feelings of hopelessness that have been associated with mood disorders and suicide (Overholser, Adams, Lehnert, & Brinkman, 1995).

Other risk factors may be linked to the development of mood disorders in children and adolescents. Social factors such as divorce or other family disruption, death, serious illness, abuse or neglect, or any other event that negatively affects a young person may contribute to the evolution of a mood disorder and should not be taken lightly, particularly in children and adolescents who exhibit other risk factors.

MAJOR DEPRESSIVE DISORDER

Megan is a 15-year-old female who has always excelled in school and enjoyed spending time with her friends and family. However, her parents have recently expressed concern to the school about possible drug involvement. Over the course of the past 2 months, her grades have fallen dramatically. She frequently falls asleep during her morning classes and expresses little interest in subjects that were once her favorites. She has stopped attending club meetings and functions and is withdrawn and irritable around her peers. When confronted with the change in her behavior, she becomes defensive and teary and denies that any problem exists.

Scope of the Illness

Major Depressive Disorder (depression) may be the most recognized of the mood disorders—and for good reason. Studies have consistently suggested that between 1% and 3% of children in the United States suffer from depression (Birmaher & Brent, 1998; Costello, Mustillo, Erkanli, Keeler, & Angold, 2003). Among adolescents, the prevalence rates rise dramatically (Angold & Costello, 2001), with estimates of 20% to 50% of adolescents exhibiting symptoms of major depression at any given time (Kessler, Avenevoli, & Merikangas, 2001; Petersen, Compas, Brooks-Gunn, Stemmler, & Grant, 1993). Although major depression obviously occurs in younger children, symptoms increase from childhood to adolescence with a marked increase appearing between 13 and 15 years and peaking at 17 to 18 years (Angold, 1988; Radloff, 1991).

Signs and Symptoms

An episode of major depression lasts an average of 7 to 9 months in children and adolescents; it is characterized by many of the features seen in adult major depression (Birmaher, Ryan, et al., 1996a, 1996b). It should be noted that children and adolescents often experience periods of moodiness or sad, withdrawn behavior. This does not mean that every child who appears sad or "out of sorts" is suffering from Major Depressive Disorder. The major differences between a child who is exhibiting "normal" mood shifts and one who has major depression are the number of symptoms present and the length of time the symptoms are present. According to the

Diagnostic and Statistical Manual of Mental Disorders (*DSM-IV-TR*, American Psychiatric Association, 2000), a child or adolescent must demonstrate *five or more* of the following symptoms *for 2 or more weeks* before a diagnosis of major depression can be made:

1. Persistent sad or irritable mood
2. Loss of interest in activities once found to be pleasurable
3. Change in appetite and/or sleeping habits
4. **Psychomotor retardation** or **agitation**
5. Lack of energy
6. Feelings of worthlessness or inappropriate guilt
7. Difficulty concentrating
8. Recurrent thoughts of death or suicide

Young children tend to voice more **somatic** concerns than do adolescents or adults, frequently complaining of headaches or stomachaches. In addition, they are likely to demonstrate regressive behaviors such as increased separation anxiety or reluctance to engage with other people. Adolescents, on the other hand, are more likely to complain of symptoms such as poor sleep, low energy, appetite changes, and decreased interest in activities (Schlozman, 2001). Furthermore, they are more likely to demonstrate interpersonal difficulties and voice suicidal ideation and feelings of hopelessness than young children (Harrington, 1989; Simeon, 1989).

Comorbidity

Approximately two thirds of children and adolescents diagnosed with major depression suffer from another mental disorder (Angold & Costello, 1993) such as anxiety disorders, Posttraumatic Stress Disorder, Conduct Disorder, Oppositional Defiant Disorder, learning disorders, Attention Deficit Disorder/Attention Deficit Hyperactivity Disorder (ADD/ADHD), or substance abuse or dependence. Separation anxiety is commonly seen in younger children, while adolescents may exhibit signs of personality disorders. Mood disorders do not always occur exclusively of one another; children and adolescents can be diagnosed with concurrent major depression and dysthymia—a condition known as "**double depression**." Studies vary on the rate at which children with major depression also present with dysthymia, with percentages varying from 17% to 70% (Ferro & Carlson, 1994; Flament, Cohen, Choquet, Jeammet, & Ledoux, 2001; Goodman, Schwab-Stone, Lahey, Shaffer, & Jensen, 2000). Similarly, Bipolar Disorder develops in 20% to 40% of depressed children (Strober, Lampert, Schmidt, & Morrell, 1993).

It should also be noted that major depression is common among children with medical disorders, with approximately 7% of general medical patients also exhibiting symptoms of depression (Guetzloe, 1991) and with patients with some medical needs having rates of depression much higher. With acute conditions, the depression may be temporary; for children with ongoing medical concerns, major depression may be considered a primary disability coinciding with their physical ailments.

Clinical Treatment

Treatment for major depression can be approached with psychotherapy, pharmacology, or more frequently, a combination of the two in tandem with targeted interventions at home and school. The choice of initial intervention should be based on factors such as age of the child, contextual issues such as interpersonal or school problems, and chronicity of depressive illness. Generally, a multimodal approach is used because pharmacology alone cannot address all the issues potentially affecting a child or adolescent suffering from major depression.

Two types of psychotherapeutic intervention have been found effective in relieving depression for children and adolescents. Cognitive behavioral therapy focuses on changing negative cognitions such as "I'm no good" or "Nothing goes right for me," which are frequently voiced by depressed children and adolescents. The other intervention, interpersonal therapy, helps the child or adolescent work on disturbed personal relationships that may have contributed to the onset of depression. These therapies have demonstrated efficacy among children and adolescents, especially when continued *after* remission of symptoms has occurred; this allows the child and family to further assimilate new skills, alleviate environmental stressors, and explore how thoughts and behaviors might contribute to a relapse.

Research demonstrates that pharmacology, particularly when used in conjunction with psychotherapy, is effective for adults, yet few studies exist to speak to the efficacy of medication for children and adolescents. Trials conducted with the antidepressant fluoxetine (Prozac) showed that this medication is safe and effective for short-term treatment of severe, persistent major depression (Emslie et al., 1997), and Prozac remains the only medication of its type approved by the U.S. Food and Drug Administration for use in the treatment of depression with children and adolescents (National Institute of Mental Health, 2005). Children receiving medication should initially be placed on a relatively low dosage and monitored for side effects. If the child is responding to the medication and feeling relatively few side effects, but depressive symptoms have not substantially abated, the doctor may choose to increase the dosage. Common side effects of medication include impulsive or silly behavior, gastrointestinal symptoms, restlessness, headaches, and changes in sleep or appetite. Typically, a child responding well to medication will continue taking it for at least 6 months after remission of symptoms.

Outcomes

It is important to identify children and adolescents suffering from major depression. Although many children and adolescents diagnosed with major depression go on to have depressive episodes in adulthood, with proper treatment, children can develop social and coping skills necessary to interact with others and weaken the cycle of depression. Left untreated, major depression can worsen and lead to poorer psychosocial functioning, greater **comorbidity**, and possibly, suicide.

DYSTHYMIC DISORDER

Emily is a 13-year-old female who draws little attention to herself. She performs moderately well in school, participates in some school activities, and has a few friends. Although she was an outgoing child, she has withdrawn gradually over the past 2 years and rarely appears to be happy or excited about much of anything. She lacks concentration during class and frequently appears sleepy. When asked how she feels about herself and her future, she generally replies in negative or uncertain terms.

Scope of the Illness

Dysthymic Disorder (dysthymia) is a chronic depressive disorder seen in approximately 0.6% to 4.6% of children and 1.6% to 8.0% of adolescents (Lewinsohn, Hops, Roberts, Seeley, & Andrews, 1993). The average age of onset is somewhat lower than for that of major depression, with studies demonstrating a range between 5 and 16 years of age (Klein, Schwartz, Rose, & Leader, 2000; Lewinsohn, Rohde, Seeley, & Hops, 1991). As with major depression, dysthymia occurs at the same rate in children, but girls are twice as likely as boys to develop the illness during adolescence (Fleming & Offord, 1990).

Signs and Symptoms

Dysthymia is often considered a chronic state of depression. Although the symptoms are not as intense as with Major Depressive Disorder, the duration of a single episode may last as long as 2.5 to 3.4 years (Kovacs, Obrosky, Gatsonis, & Richards, 1997; Lewinsohn et al., 1991). With this in mind, it is important to remember that many children and adolescents will experience times during which they demonstrate many symptoms identical to those of dysthymia. The major indicators that dysthymia may be present are the number of symptoms present and the length of time they are present. According to the *DSM-IV-TR* (2000), symptoms in a child or adolescent must be present for *at least 1 year* and must include *two of the following seven symptoms:*

1. Poor appetite or overeating
2. Insomnia or **hypersomnia**
3. Low energy or fatigue
4. Low self-esteem
5. Poor concentration or difficulty making decisions
6. Feelings of hopelessness
7. Irritability or excessive anger

Compared with children who have Major Depressive Disorder, children suffering from dysthymia demonstrate fewer melancholic symptoms, fewer feelings of guilt, less impaired concentration, and less preoccupation with death. Disobedience and irritability, while not typical symptoms of dysthymia in adults, are perhaps the most recognized symptoms of dysthymia in children (Kovacs, Akiskal, Gatsonis, & Parrone, 1994). Because dysthymia can last for such a long period of time, a suffering child may not recognize that there is a problem and may not complain of symptoms. Therefore, it is important that those around the child be vigilant about symptomology.

Comorbidity

Dysthymia is often associated with many other conditions, including anxiety disorders, behavioral problems, and substance abuse. Studies show that approximately 50% of adolescents with dysthymia have additional disorders, including anxiety, Conduct Disorder, and ADHD (Kovacs et al., 1994). In one particular study, 59% of subjects with dysthymia also had Generalized Anxiety Disorder, 28% had simple phobias, 18% had separation anxiety, 14% had Obsessive-Compulsive Disorder, 13% had Social Phobia, and 10% had Panic Disorder, thus demonstrating a strong association between dysthymia and anxiety disorders (Masi et al., 2003). The same study also explored the comorbidity between dysthymia and disorders such as ADHD, Oppositional Defiant Disorder, and Conduct Disorder and found that 35% of subjects suffered from both dysthymia and one of these disorders (Masi et al., 2003).

Children and adolescents with dysthymia are also at risk for developing Major Depressive Disorder, resulting in double depression. Children with double depression generally have longer and more intense episodes, higher likelihood of having additional mental illnesses, more suicidality, and higher rates of functional impairment than do children suffering solely from major depression or dysthymia (Kovacs et al., 1994). There are two lines of reasoning hypothesizing the coexistence of major depression and dysthymia. First, the two disorders and their overlap may actually be different manifestations of the same disorder or two steps within a continuum of depression. Second, the two disorders are, indeed, two separate disorders, and the co-occurrence may be the result of environmental or genetic factors (Nobile, Cataldo, Marino, & Molteni, 2003). In whatever way the disorders are linked, children and adolescents with double depression recover but often relapse quickly, with an estimated 84.4% rate of relapse (Klein et al., 2000).

Clinical Treatment

Very few studies have been conducted on the treatment of children and adolescents with dysthymia. Treatment for dysthymia is similar to that for major depression, including the use of the same medications and psychotherapeutic interventions. But because of the chronic nature of the illness, treatment may require longer periods of time (Keller et al., 2000), and special consideration is given to functional impairment, which may not improve as depressive symptoms abate (Klein et al., 2000). Following careful assessment, individualized treatment should be initiated at multiple levels, including individual psychotherapy, pharmacology, and family therapy. Education about the disorder and psychosocial support are crucial elements of any treatment plan (Emslie & Mayes, 1999). As with Major Depressive Disorder, medications may be continued for 6 to 9 months following remission of symptoms. It may also be beneficial to continue supportive therapy sessions to maintain social, emotional, and academic functioning and to monitor for relapse.

Outcomes

As with Major Depressive Disorder, early identification and treatment of children and adolescents with dysthymia is critical. Children and adolescents with dysthymia run a high risk of both relapsing and developing other mood disorders. Data suggest that almost every individual suffering from dysthymia will develop Major Depressive Disorder at some point in his or her life (Klein et al., 2000). However, this cycle may be weakened if treatment is sought at the onset of illness. In addition, psychosocial impairment is common in children and adolescents with dysthymia because the long duration of the illness inhibits their ability to develop skills needed for appropriate social interaction. Again, early intervention is crucial in assisting these children to develop social skills necessary for creating and maintaining meaningful relationships.

BIPOLAR DISORDER

Christopher is an 8-year-old male who can be wildly unpredictable. He may be darkly morose, talking of suicide, but become silly and immature to the point of alienating his peers a few days, or even hours, later. At other times, he is obstinate and defiant, suggesting that he knows better than others and sees no reason to comply with the teacher's instructions. Without provocation, he can fly into an explosive rage, lashing out verbally and physically at those around him. He has been diagnosed as having ADHD, but the medications are not alleviating his symptoms.

Scope of the Illness

Bipolar Disorder in children and adolescents is typically misdiagnosed as ADHD, Major Depressive Disorder, or as one of several other illnesses. Therefore, it is difficult to determine prevalence rates for Bipolar Disorder in youths. It has been suggested, however, that 1% of adolescents meet the criteria for Bipolar Disorder, with 6% of adolescents meeting some, but not all, of the criteria necessary for a diagnosis (Wilens & Wozniak, 2003). Similarly, it is difficult to determine age of onset for Bipolar Disorder. Some researchers feel that it may have an **insidious onset**, reporting that parents have stated that their child had "always" demonstrated an abnormal mood (Wilens & Wozniak, 2003).

Signs and Symptoms

Bipolar Disorder involves unusual shifts in mood, energy level, and functioning as the child alternates between states of depression, as described above, and **mania**. These shifts can occur over time or can manifest themselves in a **mixed state** in which the child may alternate states over the course of a day. The *DSM-IV-TR* criteria for Major Depressive Disorder listed earlier in the chapter apply to Bipolar Disorder. The *DSM-IV-TR* (2000) symptoms for mania include the following:

1. Severe change in mood, either overly irritable or silly
2. Overly inflated self-esteem, thoughts of grandiosity
3. Increased energy and decreased need for sleep
4. Increased talking, talking too much, too fast
5. Distractibility

6. Increased goal-directed activity, physical agitation, or hypersexuality
7. Excessive involvement in risky behaviors

Children and adolescents in the depressive stage of Bipolar Disorder exhibit many of the symptoms seen in children with Major Depressive Disorder. In the manic stage, children and adolescents are more likely to be irritable or prone to destructive rages than silly or euphoric. Indeed, a child who exhibits severe ADHD-like behavior with excessive, rageful outbursts and mood changes may have Bipolar Disorder.

Comorbidity

Children and adolescents suffering from Bipolar Disorder may suffer from a number of other mental illnesses. Most commonly associated with Bipolar Disorder are ADHD, Oppositional Defiant Disorder, Conduct Disorder, and anxiety disorders. In addition, substance abuse may be present in children and adolescents with Bipolar Disorder (Wilens & Wozniak, 2003). Sometimes, however, it is difficult to differentiate between childhood disorders, and thus, a child technically may be diagnosed with only one disorder while suffering from two or more at the same time. Indeed, some studies demonstrate a very high linkage between both ADHD (West, McElroy, Strakowski, Keck, & McConville, 1995) and Conduct Disorder (Kovacs & Pollock, 1995) and Bipolar Disorder. Masi and her colleagues (2001) found that anxiety disorders were prevalent in their sample of children and adolescents with Bipolar Disorder, with almost 42% manifesting symptoms of more than one anxiety disorder. Among their sample, 44% also had Obsessive-Compulsive Disorder, 39.5% had Social Phobia, and 25.6% had Panic Disorder. They also noted that ADHD and Conduct Disorder were present in 27.9% of the children and adolescents they studied.

Clinical Treatment

Very little research has been conducted on treatment efficacy for children and adolescents with Bipolar Disorder. As with the other mood disorders, a combination of psychotherapy and pharmacology are recommended. Lithium (Eskalith, Lithobid) is typically prescribed to children and adolescents to stabilize mood. Generally, antidepressants are not recommended because they may invoke a manic state. Anticonvulsants, which are usually used to treat epileptic seizures, have demonstrated some effectiveness in mood stabilization for Bipolar Disorder. The three anticonvulsants most commonly used are carbamazepine (Tegretol), valproic acid (Depakene), and phenytoin (Dilantin). Each of these drugs has the potential for severe long-term side effects, so the use of these medications for Bipolar Disorder treatment should be limited. Furthermore, the efficacy of using these drugs for the purpose of treating Bipolar Disorder is still under investigation; thus, use of these medications should be monitored closely by the child's doctor (Sweeney & Forness, 1997).

Outcomes

Bipolar Disorder generally is considered a chronic condition with a high possibility of relapse. Often, children and adolescents with Bipolar Disorder are at risk for poorer academic perfomance, disturbed interpersonal relationships, increased rates of substance abuse, legal difficulties, multiple hospitalizations, and increased rates of both suicide attempts and completions (Lewinsohn, Klein, & Seeley, 1995; Strober et al., 1995). Although frequent misdiagnosis often prevents it, early intervention may play a role in limiting these outcomes.

CLASSROOM INTERVENTIONS

It is obvious that many of the symptoms manifested in mood disorders are not conducive to high classroom functioning; however, we know that without early intervention, children and adolescents suffering from these disorders are likely to suffer setbacks in a number of arenas. Therefore, if a child appears to be suffering from a mood disorder, it is critical to alert the parents to the possibility of the need for professional evaluation. Before making contact with a child's parents, however, it is important to consult with school administrators about the school district's policies regarding recommendation of professional services. One concern for the school in this case is the issue of financial responsibility. If a teacher makes a recommendation for professional services to a parent, is the district responsible for paying for that service? Policies may vary between districts and on a case-by-case basis. Therefore, it is important to be aware of specific district policies and to consult with administrators who may be able to provide more precise guidance in this area.

When talking with parents about the need for evaluation, being prepared with a specific list of symptoms, as well as the ways in which these behaviors are affecting their child's academic performance, may be helpful because parents may not be aware of the problem or may want to attribute the child's behavior to "normal" mood swings. The parents may be more likely to seek treatment if a school psychologist, school social worker, or counselor is able to corroborate the signs seen in the classroom and provide possible venues for treatment. Parents sometimes become defensive or angry when confronted by school personnel about behavioral issues, and it is important to reassure them that their child is not "crazy" but may be in need of some additional help to maintain optimal performance in the classroom. Again, either consulting with a school psychologist or counselor or, even better, having one present when talking with the parent may be helpful in addressing parents' specific concerns about their child's mental health. If a parent is reluctant to pursue treatment, it may be due to denial or lack of information about treatment options, but it may also be that the parent is dealing with a mental illness of his or her own. Persistence on the part of school personnel may be necessary to ensure proper treatment for students in need.

Students who voice feelings of wanting to harm themselves should not be taken lightly. They are in need of immediate intervention, and it is best to speak with school administrators about the protocol for handling such a crisis. It is important to remember that in all states, all teachers are considered to be mandated reporters. This means that teachers are required by law to report incidents in which a student or other individual discloses information about wanting to do harm to self or others. Being familiar with state laws, as well as with district policy and procedure, and addressing such situations is imperative. For more information about suicidal children and adolescents, refer to the chapter on suicide (Chapter 14) in this book.

Once a child is diagnosed with a mood disorder, the decision may be made, based on the severity of illness and the child's additional needs, to develop an Individual Education Plan (IEP). Many children with mood disorders may not exhibit the educational needs necessary to qualify for special education services, or the parents may not want their child to be considered for such services. In such situations, if simple accommodations might help the child, instituting a 504 plan (see Discussion Question 2 in Chapter 4) may be an effective intervention strategy. Regardless of what action is taken, several things can be done within a classroom setting to make it more inviting to a child suffering from a mood disorder:

Work as a Team and Maintain Communication. It is important that everyone involved in the child's treatment—for example, parents, educators, and mental health clinicians—be aware of one another and work together toward the child's improvement. Discussing the child's symptoms with both the child and parents allows everyone involved to target potential problem behaviors and prepare strategies. Also, it is helpful to keep abreast of new developments in treatment. If a child has started or stopped taking a medication, be aware of possible side effects or other complications and make arrangements accordingly. Give and receive suggestions from others on the treatment team regarding behavior management techniques. Sometimes parents or clinicians have helpful methods that have worked for them that they are willing to share to facilitate the learning process. Likewise, the teacher may need to show a parent effective classroom methods for teaching a child to prepare for schedule changes or to organize belongings. Treatment meetings with the mental health practitioner and family can be particularly helpful in facilitating communication and cooperation among those involved with the child. These meetings allow all parties to hear how the child is progressing in other arenas and to become aware of any changes being considered in the child's treatment regimen, as well as to provide the teacher an opportunity to voice praise or concerns for the child's classroom performance. Of course, it may not always be practical or possible to attend every treatment meeting for every child; indeed, teachers are not required to attend these meetings if it requires extra time on their parts. However, attending these meetings is in the best interest of the child, and likewise, school support of teacher participation in these meetings is in the child's best interest. In cases where treatment team meeting attendance is not an option, it may still be helpful to be aware of when these meetings occur in order to provide input about the child's classroom issues and receive information about changes in treatment through the child's parents. It may also be helpful to maintain a journal of daily behavior for the child or to send progress reports to parents and mental health practitioners so that there is an ongoing record of the child's classroom behavior and performance. Maintaining open lines of communication will help everyone work more efficiently toward treatment goals and may curtail potential crises before they occur.

Create a Safe, Noncritical Classroom Environment. It is important that the child knows that school personnel are allies, so it is essential to be persistent with communication, even if the child responds irritably or with resentment. Try to communicate warmth and caring and be attentive if approached by the child. Facilitate and acknowledge success in the classroom by assigning tasks that the child is likely to master, and provide praise and reassurance on a regular basis. Because withdrawal from others is often seen in children and adolescents with mood disorders, it is important to involve the child in classroom activities or special tasks and to encourage appropriate social skills. Discuss diversity with the entire class and develop a classroom culture based on respect for others. Do not allow bullying, name-calling, or other hurtful behavior to have a place in the classroom; these actions can contribute to the negative self-perceptions inherent in mood disorders.

Provide Accommodations for Periods of More Troubled Functioning. When a child is experiencing problems, maintaining focus in class may prove difficult. Discuss with the child and parents possible accommodations for these times. Some of the following suggestions may require the development of an IEP, and the educational and treatment teams should be brought together to determine if such a step is merited or if other measures can be taken. In any case, seating assignments can be considered. The child may need to be placed near the front of the class for frequent on-task cues or near the door if medication side effects necessitate frequent trips to the bathroom. Further considerations regarding side effects may include having a water bottle to combat dry mouth or using a laptop computer if tremors make writing difficult. Designating a "safe place" either within or outside of the classroom provides the student a place to which he or she may go if feeling overwhelmed or out of control. Adjusting a student's schedule may alleviate problems due to the sleep issues often seen in mood disorders. Testing accommodations may be necessary to reduce stress and anxiety. Simple, inexpensive changes such as the ones suggested here are just a starting point. Depending on the strengths and needs of any given child, the treatment team should be able to develop a plan of accommodation that will allow the child to be successful in the classroom.

Remain Calm and Flexible. This is perhaps the most important to remember. Children suffering from mood disorders are in pain, not physically but emotionally. Often, they demonstrate that by lashing out at or retreating from those who are trying to help them. The ability to be calm and consistent instills trust by showing that you are not likely to react unpredictably. Like everyone else, these children have "good" days and "bad" days. They may need additional support on the bad days. Having a flexible "game plan" for both types of days may curtail problems before they occur. Furthermore, interventions may not work continuously over time. It is important to remain flexible, explore new options, and ask for help when it is needed to maintain a classroom conducive to learning for all students.

Now that general information and classroom strategies regarding mood disorders have been presented, the following brief case study will demonstrate how this information and these strategies could be used.

Melissa is a 14-year-old, Caucasian female in the ninth grade who lives in a suburban community. She is considered by her teachers to be a "typical" student who makes average to above-average grades and participates in a few extracurricular activities. She is not considered overly popular but has a few close friends with whom she spends time after school and on weekends. Over a period of 2 months, Melissa's science teacher noticed a change in her. Melissa had always appeared to enjoy science, and she excelled in it. However, she had begun neglecting homework assignments, and her usual good grades were slipping. She was participating only minimally in classroom discussions and activities, sometimes falling asleep, and no longer appeared interested in the class content. When her teacher approached her with concerns about her performance, Melissa irritably snapped that she was having trouble concentrating and did not want to talk about it. She appeared to be holding back tears. The teacher agreed to drop the subject for the present but made it clear to Melissa that she was concerned and would be available to talk with Melissa whenever she was ready. The teacher spoke with some of Melissa's other teachers, who noted that they, too, were noticing changes in Melissa's behavior and performance, but most had written off these changes as normal mood swings.

The teacher made a list of Melissa's behaviors and how these were affecting her performance in science class and spoke with the school social worker, who agreed that, given the duration and number of problems that Melissa was having, there could be a problem and felt that it might be a good idea if Melissa's parents were contacted. It was also decided that the school social worker would meet one-on-one with Melissa. It was not certain that Melissa was clinically depressed, but he wanted to determine if there were more serious concerns related to suicidal ideation, or thoughts about suicide, that needed to be addressed immediately, regardless of her potential for diagnosis.

Having met with Melissa and been satisfied that there was no cause for immediate concern, the school social worker contacted Melissa's mother to see if she had noticed any changes in Melissa. At first, her mother was guarded about providing any information, but after several reassurances that Melissa's best interest was everyone's main concern, she admitted that she had noticed some changes, but was hoping they would disappear on their own. In the course of this interview, Melissa's mother also stated that there was a family history of depression and that Melissa's older brother had received therapy for issues of depression several years ago. She further stated that she had been concerned about Melissa for some time because she was "the type of child who never saw the bright side of anything." Melissa's mother agreed to meet with the school social worker, teacher, and Melissa to determine a course of action.

At the meeting, Melissa's mother, teacher, and the mental health practitioner spoke with Melissa about their concerns and stressed that they wanted to help her in any way possible. Melissa tearfully responded that she did not need help and did not want to be a part of the meeting. She sat silently next to her mother for the rest of the meeting, apparently lost in her own thoughts. The remainder of the treatment team decided that the school social worker would conduct a full assessment of Melissa's functioning, using information gathered from teacher and parent interviews; parent, teacher, and child rating scales; and behavioral observation. Because Melissa's family had sufficient insurance, her mother volunteered to take Melissa to the doctor for a physical to rule out any physical causes for the changes they had seen. The school social worker's assessment indicated that Melissa met the criteria for Major Depressive Disorder, and Melissa's family doctor concurred with this diagnosis. She suggested that Melissa try a trial of fluoxetine while the school social worker and Melissa's teacher and parents developed additional strategies to aid Melissa's recovery.

The treatment team consisting of Melissa's parents, her science teacher, and the school social worker again met with Melissa to discuss the findings and develop some ways in which they could assist her. She protested her involvement in the process, but responded to questions posed to her by the team about strategies that might be helpful to her. The team decided to meet biweekly in the beginning of Melissa's treatment to stay abreast of medication and behavioral issues that arose and agreed that they would later switch to monthly meetings as Melissa's situation stabilized. They agreed that an IEP probably was not appropriate for Melissa but that some minor changes at home and school might be effective.

The school social worker stated his intention to "check in" on Melissa and serve as an advocate for her with her other teachers. He and Melissa agreed to a weekly meeting during which she could discuss any problems she might be experiencing or concerns she might have. He also reminded her of his open-door policy and affirmed his support of her and concern for her needs. Her parents, too, agreed to advocate for Melissa with school officials and teachers and to make a greater effort toward increasing communication with her. When the subject of family therapy was brought up, they were informed that the school did not provide that service or reimbursement to families who received that service away from school but that it might be beneficial if they could afford it. The school social worker provided them with the names of some providers, with the reminder that the school could not be financially responsible for such services.

Melissa's teacher felt she could demonstrate support by providing additional praise for the efforts Melissa made in class and by encouraging her to participate in activities. Melissa agreed that small-group activities where she would have to participate, but would not be "singled out," might be most effective for her. The teacher also noted that this would increase her interaction with other students in the class from whom she had recently withdrawn. She emphasized to Melissa that she would expect her to take part in the class and complete assignments. However, she also acknowledged that this was a difficult time for her and expressed her desire to help and support her through it. She asked Melissa to let her know if she was experiencing medication side effects or if there were other issues with which she might be able to assist her.

Melissa's team worked together to support her through the initial stages of her treatment. All team members made the commitment to engage in open and active communication so that everyone involved was aware of important issues, such as medication side effects and changes, and treatment progress and setbacks. They shared strategies and techniques they found effective for increasing interaction, encouraging participation in activities, and maintaining schedules. Melissa's other teachers, encouraged by her science teacher and the school social worker began providing periodic input, increasing the scope of team communication. In the classroom, Melissa's teacher initially had difficulty encouraging Melissa to participate but did not give up, even when Melissa resisted help. She also noticed a gradual change not only in Melissa but in the rest of her class as she instituted a "no grumbling" policy. She encouraged her students to maintain a positive outlook and focus on their strengths and the strengths of others. With the institution of this new class policy, many students, including Melissa, appeared to be enjoying class more and exhibiting greater self-esteem.

By the end of the school year, Melissa was exhibiting renewed interest in the activities and classes she once enjoyed and was no longer falling asleep in the middle of class. Her grades were better, and she was spending more time with friends and less time alone. She continued to have periodic mood swings, but they were more consistent with the "normal" mood swings seen in so many adolescents. With the support of her teachers and parents, who knew what signs to observe, she quickly rebounded from periods of sadness or moodiness. Her treatment team decided that there was no need to meet on a monthly basis but agreed to come together should the situation change and Melissa's depression return.

SUMMARY

Mood disorders (Major Depressive Disorder, Dysthymic Disorder, and Bipolar Disorder) are serious illnesses that, left untreated, can have dynamic effects on the psychosocial development and later mental health of children and adolescents. Identification and early intervention are crucial to curtailing the effects of these illnesses, which respond to both psychotherapeutic and pharmacological treatment.

Teachers are well placed to notice warning signs of these illnesses and alert parents and other school personnel about potential problems and the need for clinical assistance. Within the classroom, they have a responsibility to work with the child and other members of the treatment team to assist the child in regaining full functioning. Initiating and maintaining good communication, creating a safe classroom environment, providing necessary accommodations, and remaining calm and flexible can assist a child with a mood disorder to get on the road to remission and ensure that the classroom will be a place of enrichment and learning for all students.

DISCUSSION QUESTIONS

1. The authors state that communication is crucial to providing effective treatment for a student with a mood disorder. How might one best communicate with parents who are reluctant to accept that their child may need help or who are openly resistant to school involvement in the situation? How might one best express concerns about classroom issues or potential treatment options to a treatment team? What might be the most effective way to communicate with parents and treatment providers when face-to-face contact is not an option?

2. It can be difficult to provide accommodations for one student in a sensitive manner while ensuring that the needs of all other students are being met as well. How might a teacher go about developing a class environment in which students respect individual differences and where accommodations can be provided so as not to draw attention to them while meeting the needs of the other students in the class?

3. Many children display some symptoms of mood disorders but do not meet full criteria for those disorders. This condition is known as "subthreshold." How might one provide support to a student displaying subthreshold symptoms of a mood disorder, and are there any difficulties that might present themselves when trying to provide that support?

4. In the prereading section, you were asked to consider your personal strengths and weaknesses as they pertained to working with students who have mood disorders. What strategies for working with these students are most aligned with your personal strengths? What strategies might prove more difficult for you to carry out given your

weaknesses? How might you work to address those personal needs to provide the best possible care for such students?

5. Several risk factors were mentioned as potential elements in the development of mood disorders. Think about ways in which these factors may link together to produce mood disorders. Are there other factors that you feel may contribute to the development of such disorders?

FOR ADDITIONAL HELP

	Organization	*Web Address*	*Description*
Mood Disorders: Major Depressive Disorder, Dysthymic Disorder, and Bipolar Disorder	Depression and Related Affective Disorders Association (DRADA)	www.drada.org/Facts/childandadolescent.html	DRADA's mission is to alleviate the suffering arising from depression and bipolar illness by assisting self-help groups, providing education and information, and lending support to research programs
	Council for Exceptional Children	http://ericec.org/faq/bipolar.html	The Council for Exceptional Children is an association for special educators. CEC works to improve the educational success of individuals with disabilities and/or gifts and talents.

REFERENCES

Allgood-Merten, B., Lewinsohn, P. A., & Hops, H. (1990). Sex differences and adolescent depression. *Journal of Abnormal Psychology, 99*(1), 55–63.

American Psychiatric Association. (2000). *Diagnostic and statistical manual of mental disorders* (4th ed., text revision). Washington, DC: Author.

Angold, A. (1988). Childhood and adolescent depression: Epidemiological and aetiological aspects. *British Journal of Psychiatry, 152*(5), 601–617.

Angold, A., & Costello, E. J. (1993). Depressive comorbidity in children and adolescents: Empirical, theoretical, and methodological issues. *American Journal of Psychiatry, 150*(12), 1779–1791.

Angold, A., & Costello, E. J. (2001). The epidemiology of depression in children and adolescents. In I. M. Goodyer (Ed.), *The depressed child and adolescent* (2nd ed., pp. 143–178). New York: Cambridge University Press.

Birmaher, B., & Brent, D. (1998). Practice parameters for the assessment and treatment of children and adolescents with depressive disorders. *Journal of the American Academy of Child and Adolescent Psychiatry, 37*(10 Suppl.), 63–83.

Birmaher, B., Ryan, N. D., Williamson, D. E., Brent, D. A., & Kaufman, J. (1996a). Childhood and adolescent depression: A review of the past 10 years, Part II. *Journal of the American Academy of Child and Adolescent Psychiatry, 35*(12), 1575–1583.

Birmaher, B., Ryan, N. D., Williamson, D. E., Brent, D. A., Kaufman, J., Dahl, R. E., Perel, J., & Nelson, B. (1996b). Childhood and adolescent depression: A review of the past 10 years, Part I. *Journal of the American Academy of Child and Adolescent Psychiatry, 35*(11), 1427–1439.

Costello, E. J., Mustillo, S., Erkanli, A., Keeler, G., & Angold, A. (2003). Prevalence and development of psychiatric disorders in childhood and adolescence. *Archives of General Psychiatry, 60,* 837–844.

Duffy, A. (2000). Toward effective early intervention and prevention strategies for major affective disorders: A review of antecedents and risk factors. *Canadian Journal of Psychiatry, 45*(4), 340–349.

Emslie, G. J., & Mayes, T. L. (1999). Depression in children and adolescents: A guide to diagnosis and treatment. *CNS Drugs, 11*(3), 181–189.

Emslie, G. J., Rush, A. J., Weinberg, W. A., Kowatch, R. A., Hughes, C. W., Carmody, T., & Rintelmann, J. (1997). A double-blind, randomized, placebo-controlled trial of fluoxetine in children and adolescents with depression. *Archives of General Psychiatry, 54*(11), 1031–1037.

Ferro, T., & Carlson, G. A. (1994). Depressive disorders: Distinctions in children. *Journal of the American Academy of Child and Adolescent Psychiatry, 33*(5), 664–670.

Flament, M. F., Cohen, D., Choquet, M., Jeammet, P., & Ledoux, S. (2001). Phenomenology, psychosocial correlates and treatment seeking in major depression and dysthymia of adolescence. *Journal of the American Academy of Child and Adolescent Psychiatry, 40*(9), 1070–1078.

Fleming, J. E., & Offord, D. R. (1990). Epidemiology of childhood depressive disorders: A critical review. *Journal of the American Academy of Child and Adolescent Psychiatry, 29,* 571–580.

Goodman, S. H., Schwab-Stone, M., Lahey, B. B., Shaffer, D., & Jensen, P. S. (2000). Major depression and dysthymia in children and adolescents: Discriminant validity and differential consequences in a community sample. *Journal of the American Academy of Child and Adolescent Psychiatry, 39*(6), 761–770.

Guetzloe, E. C. (1991). *Depression and suicide: Special education students at risk.* Reston, VA: Council for Exceptional Children.

Harrington, R. C. (1989). Child and adult depression: Concepts and continuities. *Israeli Journal of Psychiatric Related Disorders, 26*(1–2), 12–29.

Keller, M. B., McCullough, J. P., Klein, D. N., Arnow, B., Dunner, D. L., Gelenberg, A. J., et al. (2000). A comparison of nefazodone, the cognitive behavioral-analysis system of psychotherapy, and their combination for the treatment of chronic depression. *New England Journal of Medicine, 342*(20), 1462–1470.

Kessler, R. C., Avenevoli, S., & Merikangas, K. R. (2001). Mood disorders in children and adolescents: An epidemiological perspective. *Biological Psychiatry, 49,* 1002–1014.

Klein, D. N., Schwartz, J. E., Rose, S., & Leader, J. B. (2000). Five-year course and outcome of dysthymic disorder: A prospective, naturalistic follow-up study. *American Journal of Psychiatry, 157*(6), 931–939.

Kovacs, M., Akiskal, H. S., Gatsonis, C., & Parrone, P. L. (1994). Childhood-onset dysthymic disorder: Clinical features and prospective naturalistic outcome. *Archives of General Psychiatry, 51*(5), 365–374.

Kovacs, M., Devlin, B., Pollack, M., Richards, C., & Mukerji, P. (1997). A controlled family history study of childhood-onset depressive disorder. *Archives of General Psychiatry, 54*(7), 613–623.

Kovacs, M., & Pollack, M. (1995). Bipolar disorder and comorbid conduct disorder in childhood and adolescence. *Journal of the American Academy of Child and Adolescent Psychiatry, 34*(6), 715–723.

Kovacs, M., Obrosky, D. S., Gatsonis, C., & Richards, C. (1997). First-episode major depressive and dysthymic disorder in childhood: Clinical and sociodemographic factors in recovery. *Journal of the American Academy of Child and Adolescent Psychiatry, 36*(6), 777–784.

Lewinsohn, P. M., Hops, H., Roberts, R. E., Seeley, J. R., & Andrews, J. A. (1993). Adolescent psychopathology: Prevalence and incidence of depression and other DSM-III-R disorders in high school students. *Journal of Abnormal Psychology, 102*(1), 133–144.

Lewinsohn, P. M., Klein, D. N., & Seeley, J. R. (1995). Bipolar disorders in a community sample of older adolescents: Prevalence, phenomenology, comorbidity, and course. *Journal of the American Academy of Child and Adolescent Psychiatry, 34*(4), 454–463.

Lewinsohn, P. M., Rohde, P., Seeley, J. R., & Hops, H. (1991). Comorbidity of unipolar depression: I. Major depression with dysthymia. *Journal of Abnormal Psychiatry, 100*(2), 205–213.

Lewinsohn, P. M., Steinmetz, J. L., Larson, D. W., & Franklin, J. (1981). Depression-related cognitions: Antecedent or consequence? *Journal of Abnormal Psychology, 90,* 213–219.

Masi, G., Millepiedi, S., Mucci, M., Pascale, R. R., Perugi, G., & Akiskal, H. S. (2003). Phenomenology and comorbidity of dysthymic disorder in 100 consecutively referred children and adolescents: Beyond DSM-IV. *Canadian Journal of Psychiatry, 48*(2), 99–105.

Masi, G., Toni, C., Perugi, G., Mucci, M., Millepiedi, S., & Akiskal, H. S. (2001). Anxiety disorders in children and adolescents with bipolar disorder: A neglected comorbidity. *Canadian Journal of Psychiatry, 46*(9), 797–802.

Miezitis, S. (1992). *Creating alternatives to depression in our schools.* Seattle, WA: Hogrefe & Huber.

National Institute of Mental Health. (2005). *Antidepressant medications for children and adolescents: Information for parents and caregivers.* Retrieved November 1, 2005, from www.nimh.nih.gov/healthinformation/antidepressant_child.cfm

Nobile, M., Cataldo, G. M., Marino, C., & Molteni, M. (2003). Diagnosis and treatment of dysthymia in children and adolescents. *CNS Drugs, 17*(13), 927–946.

Nolen-Hoeksema, S., & Girgus, J. S. (1994). The emergence of gender differences in depression during adolescence. *Psychological Bulletin, 115*(3), 424–443.

Overholser, J. C., Adams, D. M., Lehnert, K. L., & Brinkman, D. C. (1995). Self-esteem deficits and suicidal tendencies among adolescents. *Journal of the American Academy of Child and Adolescent Psychiatry, 34*(7), 919–928.

Petersen, A. C., Compas, B. E., Brooks-Gunn, J., Stemmler, M., Ey, S., & Grant, K. E. (1993). Depression in adolescents. *American Psychologist, 48,* 155–168.

Radloff, L. S. (1991). The use of the Center for Epidemiological Studies Depression Scale in adolescents and young adults. *Journal of Youth and Adolescence, 20,* 149–166.

Rice, F., Harold, G., & Thapar, A. (2002). The genetic aetiology of childhood depression: A review. *Journal of Child Psychology and Psychiatry, 43*(1), 65–79.

Schlozman, S. C. (2001). The shrink in the classroom: Too sad to learn? *Educational Leadership, 60*(7), 80–81.

Seligman, M. E. P. (1975). *Helplessness: On depression, development, and death.* San Francisco: Freeman.

Simeon, J. G. (1989). Depressive disorders in children find adolescents. *Psychiatric Journal of the University of Ottawa, 14*(2), 356–363.

Smucker, M. R., Craighead, W. E., Craighead, L. W., & Green, B. J. (1986). Normative and reliability data for the children's depression inventory. *Journal of Abnormal Child Psychology, 14*(1), 25–39.

Strober, M., Lampert, C., Schmidt, S., & Morrell, W. (1993). The course of major depressive disorder in adolescents: Recovery and risk of manic switching in a follow-up of psychotic and nonpsychotic subtypes. *Journal of the American Academy of Child and Adolescent Psychiatry, 34*(6), 724–731.

Strober, M., Schmidt-Lackner, S., Freeman, R., Bower, S., Lampert, C., & DeAntonio, M. (1995). Recovery and relapse in adolescents with bipolar affective illness: A five-year naturalistic, prospective follow-up. *Journal of the American Academy of Child and Adolescent Psychiatry, 34*(6), 724–731.

Sweeney, D. P., & Forness, S. R. (1997). An update on psychopharmacologic medication: What teachers, clinicians, and parents need to know. *Intervention in School and Clinic, 33*(1), 4–22.

West, S. A., McElroy, S. L., Strakowski, S. M., Keck, P. E., Jr., & McConville, B. J. (1995). Attention deficit hyperactivity disorder in adolescent mania. *American Journal of Psychiatry, 152*(2), 271–273.

Wilens, T. E., & Wozniak, J. (2003). Bipolar disorder in children and adolescents: Diagnostic and therapeutic issues. *Psychiatric Times, 20*(8), 55–61.

Chapter 6

CHILDHOOD ANXIETY DISORDERS

Joseph A. Himle

Daniel J. Fischer

Michelle Van Etten Lee

Jordana R. Muroff

PREREADING QUESTIONS

As you read this chapter, reflect on the following questions and issues:

1. Have you ever known anybody who seemed to be excessively anxious in one or more areas of life?
2. How likely will it be that a teacher will have a student with an anxiety disorder in the classroom in any given year?
3. How can a teacher be supportive of a student with an anxiety disorder?
4. Can teachers make anxiety problems in children worse? If so, how?

Although the experience of fear and anxiety is a part of normal development for school-age children and adolescents, there is a subgroup of children for whom fear and anxiety are so distressing and disabling that psychiatric diagnosis and intervention are warranted. This chapter begins by addressing the difference between normal fears, adaptive fears, and clinical anxiety disorders followed by discussion regarding the prevalence and impact of childhood anxiety disorders. Finally, several important childhood anxiety disorders are described separately, along with disorder-specific information on prevalence, onset, functional impairment, and clinical presentation, particularly in school settings. This chapter ends with discussion of state-of-the-art psychosocial treatments for childhood anxiety disorders, with special attention to intervention in the school setting.

NORMATIVE FEAR VERSUS CLINICAL ANXIETY DISORDERS

Childhood anxiety can be considered normative, adaptive, or indicative of a psychological disorder, depending on the developmental level of the child, the nature of the fear, and the impact on the child's life. Anxiety that is adaptive, such as a learned fear of touching a hot stove, usually endures over time. Experience teaches children how to distinguish between dangerous and nondangerous situations, when to be afraid, when to avoid, and how to cope with anxiety-provoking circumstances that are unavoidable (Nesse & Williams, 1996; Spence, 1994). These skills are vital to normal functioning. Other fears are normative for certain developmental levels and usually remit on their own. However, fear, anxiety, and avoidance are no longer adaptive when they cause significant distress, when they are out of proportion to the real threat involved, and when fear and avoidance interfere with normal activities (e.g., fear of the dark that persists into adolescence; fear of becoming ill by touching a public surface). These persistent and impairing anxiety problems would likely be classified as clinical anxiety disorders. Although these conditions can remit over time, many youths with anxiety disorders require formal intervention.

CHILDHOOD ANXIETY DISORDERS: PREVALENCE, FUNCTIONAL IMPAIRMENT, COURSE, CO-OCCURRING CONDITIONS

Anxiety disorders are by far the most common emotional disorders experienced by children and adolescents (Schniering, Hudson, & Rapee, 2000). Between 10% and 21% of children and adolescents experience clinical signs and symptoms of some anxiety disorder over the course of a year (Anderson, Williams, McGee, & Silva, 1987; Kashani & Orvaschel, 1988, 1990). Social, physical, and academic functioning are often impaired when an anxiety disorder is present. Socially, children and adolescents with anxiety disorders may suffer severe self-consciousness, irritability, peer rejection or neglect, unpopularity, social withdrawal and avoidance, parental dependency, and difficulty with problem solving, assertiveness, maturity, and personal autonomy (Dadds & Barrett, 2001; Kashani & Orvaschel, 1990; Messer & Beidel, 1994; Panella & Henggeler, 1986; Rubin & Clark, 1983; Strauss, Frame, & Forehand, 1987). Physically, they may complain of fatigue, stomachaches, headaches, flushing, trembling, nausea, restlessness, excessive sweating, heart palpitations, dizziness, or shortness of breath. Academic performance may also be hampered by inconsistent school attendance, failure to participate in class, and concentration difficulties (Dadds & Barrett, 2001; Dulcan, Martini, & Lake, 2003).

THE COST OF ANXIETY

It is not uncommon for children and adolescents with anxiety disorders to have anxiety problems into adulthood. Those childhood anxiety disorders that persist into adulthood may also be associated with notable financial and occupational burden in addition to the social, physical, and academic toll incurred in the early years (Kendall, 1992a). Data from the Burden of Disease Project (Murray & Lopez, 1996) ranked anxiety disorders as one of the most significant health problems, surpassing most physical health problems as well as most other mental health difficulties (Dadds & Barrett, 2001). In 1990, the annual cost attributed to adult anxiety disorders was estimated at $42.3 billion, or $1,542 per sufferer (Greenberg et al., 1999).

Not surprisingly, an added cost to childhood anxiety disorders is the elevated risk for developing other psychiatric conditions. Given the emotional distress and avoidance behavior inherent in anxiety disorders, it follows that those children and adolescents with anxiety disorders would be vulnerable to conditions such as depression and substance abuse. A child or adolescent with an anxiety disorder is much more likely to develop substance use disorders, depression, and other anxiety problems than youths without an anxiety disorder (Dadds & Barrett, 2001). Comorbidity with depression is particularly high (45%), with anxiety preceding the depression in two thirds of cases (Kovacs, Gatsonis, Paulauskas, & Richards, 1989). In fact, childhood anxiety disorders have been described as a common first step in a path toward adolescent depression, although childhood depression does not reliably predispose a youth to develop future anxiety problems (Cole, Peeke, Martin, Truglio, & Seroczynski, 1998; Dadds & Barrett, 2001). Others suggest that childhood anxiety and depression are so intertwined that they are best viewed as existing along a developmental continuum where anxiety predates depression (Dobson, 1985; Schniering et al., 2000). In terms of substance abuse, adolescents may use alcohol and other substances as a form of self-medication to relieve tension, anxiety, and distress (Bukstein, Brent, & Kaminer, 1989; Clark & Neighbors, 1996; Greenbaum, Foster-Johnson, & Petrila, 1996; Wittchen, Stein, & Kessler, 1999). Anxiety symptoms may also occur as a result of alcohol and substance use or during withdrawal (Schuckit & Hesselbrock, 1996). Early intervention for youths with anxiety disorders may reduce the likelihood of developing substance abuse, depression, and other comorbid psychiatric conditions (Bukstein et al., 1989).

Although childhood anxiety disorders are prevalent, distressing, and commonly linked with other psychiatric problems, they often go unrecognized and untreated. Given the relatively recent recognition of childhood anxiety disorders as specific clinical entities, professionals and parents often do not identify such disorders as problematic until the child's functional level is greatly impaired. Anxiety experienced during childhood is often viewed as mere shyness or conscientiousness or as a "phase" that the child will outgrow. This chapter discusses various childhood anxiety disorders with specific attention to how they may present in school. It is our hope that this information will assist educators in differentiating between normal and excessive fears and will facilitate appropriate referrals and interventions for children with suspected anxiety disorders.

THE ANXIETY DISORDERS

Separation Anxiety Disorder

Separation Anxiety Disorder (SAD) is a common childhood anxiety disorder and is the only anxiety condition confined to the childhood disorders section of the *Diagnostic and Statistical Manual of Mental Disorders* (*DSM-IV-TR*; American Psychiatric Association, 2000). The essential feature of SAD is excessive fear and anxiety concerning anticipated or actual separation from home, parents, or other attachment figures. Separation anxiety is a normal developmental phenomenon from approximately the ages of 7 months to 6 years (Bernstein & Borchardt, 1991). In SAD, the anxiety and reactions to separation are extreme and must be beyond what would be expected given the child's age and developmental level. SAD is expressed by recurrent, intense distress when separation is anticipated or actually takes place. The fear associated with leaving the safety of home and the comfort of parents may escalate into crying, temper tantrums, or panic attacks and may cause significant interference with academic, social, and emotional development. Children may display a range of functional impairment resulting from SAD. Mild impairment may include hesitancy to leave home or play outside, or to attend birthday parties, social gatherings, or other outings unless the parents are attending or are readily accessible. Moderate levels of functional impact may include refusal to stay with a babysitter, avoidance of sleepovers away from home, and increasing frequency and severity of **somatic** complaints, such as nausea and headaches. Children who develop excessive attachments to a teacher or other school personnel or who make attempts to call home during the school day may also evidence moderate impairment. These children may become distraught and difficult to soothe during morning drop-offs at school, create disruption in the classroom, and necessitate school-based intervention plans. In its most severe form, children with SAD become frantic in their efforts to stay with or reconnect with their parents. Severe impairments include constant clinging and shadowing of parents, vomiting, refusal to attend school or regular attempts to leave school grounds prematurely to reunite with parents, and refusal to sleep apart from parents.

According to *DSM-IV-TR* (2000) criteria, the excessive anxiety associated with SAD is evidenced by three or more of the following symptoms: (a) recurrent excessive distress when separation from home or major attachment figures occurs or is anticipated; (b) persistent and excessive worry about losing or possible harm befalling a major attachment figure; (c) persistent and excessive worry that an untoward event will lead to separation from a major attachment figure (e.g., getting lost or being kidnapped); (d) persistent reluctance or refusal to go to school or elsewhere because of fear of separation; (e) persistent and excessive fear or reluctance to be alone or without major attachment figures at home or without significant adults in other settings; (f) persistent reluctance or refusal to go to sleep without being near a major attachment figure or to sleep away from home; (g) repeated nightmares involving the theme of separation; (h) repeated complaints of physical symptoms (such as headaches, stomachaches, nausea, or vomiting) when separation from major attachment figures occurs or is anticipated. SAD symptoms are enduring rather than limited to a single episode and must cause clinically significant distress or impairment in social, academic, occupational, or other important areas of functioning. Diagnostic criteria for SAD also require that symptoms are present for 4 or more weeks and occur in children aged 18 or under.

The clinical presentation of SAD has considerable developmental variation. As mentioned earlier, separation anxiety is a part of normal child development in toddlers and preschoolers, and as a result, the clinical diagnosis of the disorder during this phase of life should be made with caution. Children who are 8 years old and younger tend to present with unrealistic worry about harm coming to their parent(s), have nightmares about separation, and refuse to attend school. Children 9 to 12 years of age are more likely to present with excessive distress at times of separation, such as when confronted with sleepovers, camps, or school trips. Adolescents aged 13 to 16 most often present with school refusal coupled with a variety of physical and somatic complaints, such as stomach upset, vomiting, and headaches (Bernstein & Borchardt, 1991).

Prevalence estimates for SAD range from 3.2% to 4.1% (Kashani & Orvaschel, 1990). SAD can begin at any age from preschool up to age 18 but is most frequent before puberty (Bernstein & Borchardt, 1991; Bowen, Offord, & Boyle, 1990). The mean age of onset of SAD is 7.5 years (Last, Perrin, Hersen, & Kazdin, 1992). Studies examining sex ratio of SAD are inconsistent, with some studies reporting that SAD is more common in females (Compton, Nelson, & March, 2000; Costello, 1989), whereas other reports show no sex differences (Last et al., 1992). Although traditionally characterized and assessed as a disorder unique to childhood, the core symptoms of separation anxiety, involving excessive and often disabling distress when faced with actual or perceived separation from major attachment figures, may persist into adulthood.

Behavioral inhibition and temperamental variables appear to be predictive of the development of childhood anxiety disorders and exhibit moderate heritability (Bierderman et al., 1993). Separation anxiety has been linked as a risk factor for the development of other anxiety disorders, particularly Panic Disorder (Battaglia et al., 1995). Caregiver's social supports and life stresses have also been implicated as risk factors in contributing to the development of SAD (Silverman & Dick-Niederhauser, 2004). Observational studies have also provided evidence of a relationship between an overinvolved parenting style and childhood anxiety disorders (Hudson & Rapee, 2001). This could indicate that children with anxiety disorders can have inadequate opportunity or may fail to master early fears through the process of habituation as a result of parent-child interactional patterns. However, it is unclear whether such patterns are the cause of or in response to excessive child anxiety states.

Social Anxiety Disorder

Social Anxiety Disorder (SocAD) is a relatively newly recognized psychiatric disorder. SocAD was first identified as a clinical problem in 1980 with the third edition of the *Diagnostic and Statistical Manual of Mental Disorders* (*DSM-III*; American Psychiatric Association, 1980). SocAD has been identified as one of the most prevalent child and adolescent psychiatric disorders (Beidel, Ferrell, Alfano, & Yeganeh, 2001). SocAD is likely to manifest itself in the school setting, and as such, it is a particularly important childhood anxiety disorder for school personnel to familiarize themselves with.

SocAD, also known as Social Phobia, is defined by the *DSM-IV-TR* (2000) as "a marked and persistent fear of one or more social situations in which the person is exposed to unfamiliar people or to possible scrutiny by others" (p. 456). In the face of a feared social situation, a person with SocAD will experience anxiety or intense distress such as a "situationally bound or situationally disposed panic attack" or engage in avoidance. Such avoidance of the feared social situation negatively impacts "normal routine, social activities, or occupational/academic functioning" (p. 456). SocAD is classified as generalized if the individual fears most social situations.

Although most of the diagnostic criteria for adults and children overlap, the *DSM-IV-TR* includes four separate criteria that specifically relate to youths with SocAD. First, the child must have the ability to form and maintain appropriate social relationships and the anxiety must manifest itself in peer settings, not just in situations primarily involving adults. Second, because their cognitive capacity and perceptual skills are not yet developed, children, unlike adults, are not expected to recognize that their social fears are excessive or unreasonable. Because brief, discrete periods characterized by social anxiousness are often seen as a normal part of development, persons younger than 18 years of age must exhibit social fears for at least 6 months. Furthermore, children's behavioral responses to social anxiety may be characterized by crying, tantrums, and the like, which often differ from social anxiety symptoms experienced by adults.

SocAD is prevalent among children and adolescents. Studies examining the prevalence of SocAD among children and adolescents indicate lifetime prevalence rates of 5% to 15% in the United States (Heimberg, Stein, Hiripi, & Kessler, 2000; Lewinsohn, Hops, Roberts, Seeley, & Andrews, 1993). The mean age of onset is relatively young, occurring around early to middle adolescence (Liebowitz, Gorman, Fyer, & Klein, 1985), with an average age of onset being cited as 15.5 years (Schneier, Johnson, Hornig, Liebowitz, & Weissman, 1992). However, children have been diagnosed with SocAD as early as 8 years of age (Beidel & Turner, 1998; Kashdan & Herbert, 2001). Finally, social anxiety among children tends to be equally prevalent in boys and girls (Beidel & Turner, 1998). The etiological pathway for SocAD is unknown, but genetic predisposition, maladaptive familial environment, or other negative social experiences have been cited as possible causes of SocAD (Beidel & Turner, 1998; Kashdan & Herbert, 2001; Whaley, Pinto, & Sigman, 1999).

Social anxiety appears to negatively affect youths functioning across numerous domains. Because of the social nature of the school environment, it is not surprising that the expression of social anxiety is often most notable in school. The school environment typically requires class participation, in-class public speaking, group activities, student initiative to request assistance from teachers, and ongoing interaction with peers. Younger children with SocAD often resist interacting with teachers, peers, or both; resist using the school restroom; and experience excessive anxiety when reading, writing, or eating in front of peers (Beidel & Turner, 1998). Physical manifestations of social anxiety in this age-group often include stomachaches, headaches, flushing, choking, rapid heartbeat, and trembling (Beidel, Christ, & Long, 1991). As students enter adolescence, greater freedom and independence can further accentuate school-based impairment resulting from social anxiety (Kashdan & Herbert, 2001). An adolescent with social anxiety may view making a mistake while giving a speech, being picked on by peers, or being rejected by a romantically interesting peer as a "social trauma," and that trauma may serve as a critical event that moves a socially apprehensive adolescent toward a clinical diagnosis of SocAD. Functional impairments for adolescents with SocAD often include few or no friends, academic problems, inability to establish romantic relationships, substance use and abuse, and poor social skills (Albano, DiBartolo, Heimberg, & Barlow, 1995; Beidel, Turner, & Morris, 1999; DeWit, MacDonald, & Offord, 1999; La Greca & Lopez, 1998; Wittchen et al., 1999). In addition, children and adolescents with social anxiety tend to perceive less social support (La Greca & Lopez, 1998), exhibit more negative emotions (Beidel, 1991; Inderbitzen-Nolan & Walters, 2000), and have more "social pessimism" (Albano, 1995; Spence, Donovan, & Brechman-Toussaint, 1999). Compared with younger children, adolescents with SocAD may engage in more fighting, have problems with truancy, and exhibit more oppositional, depressed, and antisocial behaviors (Davidson, Hughes, George, & Blazer, 1993; Kashdan & Herbert, 2001).

Often, children and adolescents with SocAD are not recognized as having such difficulties until it worsens to the point of school refusal and other more significant behavioral avoidance (Beidel & Morris, 1995). Because of the disorder's newness and the ambiguity of its symptoms at times being perceived as mere shyness or typical adolescent behavior, SocAD commonly goes unrecognized and untreated by both professionals (i.e., mental health practitioners, physicians, teachers, school counselors) and nonprofessionals (i.e., parents, care providers) (Kashdan & Herbert, 2001).

Selective Mutism

Selective Mutism is another childhood psychiatric disorder that is seen as a subtype, a developmental manifestation of, or closely related to, SocAD (Black & Uhde, 1995; Dummit et al., 1997). Studies illustrate that nearly all children diagnosed with Selective Mutism (97%) also met criteria for SocAD. Selective Mutism is described by the *DSM-IV-TR* (2000) as "the persistent failure to speak in specific social situations (in which there is an expectation for speaking) despite speaking in other situations" (p. 127). Furthermore, the "disturbance must interfere with educational achievement or with social communication and last at least one month (or not be limited to the first month of school)" (p. 127). However, a substantial proportion of children and adolescents with Selective Mutism are never referred for treatment (Black & Uhde, 1995).

Despite growing interest in this disorder, little is known about the prevalence and characteristics of Selective Mutism (Bergman, Piacentini, & McCracken, 2002). It is thought to be a rare psychiatric disorder, affecting fewer than 1% of school-age children (Dow, Sonies, Scheib, & Moss, 1995). Selective Mutism typically manifests before the age of 5 years old (*DSM-IV-TR*, 2000; Steinhausen & Juzi, 1996), although it is typically not diagnosed until the child enters kindergarten or first grade, when verbal skills become more important (Dow et al., 1995). Selective Mutism appears to be more common among girls (Bergman et al., 2002). The school setting is often a very challenging environment for children with Selective Mutism (Bergman et al., 2002; Black & Uhde, 1995; Dummit et al., 1997), given the expectation that children offer comments in class, work on group projects, read aloud or give speeches, and interact with teachers and peers. It is important that such expectations and requests for participation not be withdrawn. Nonverbal forms of communication should not be reinforced by such withdrawals, nor should others (peers and/or other adults) be permitted to speak for the child with Selective Mutism (Kehle, Madaus, Baratta, & Bray, 1998; Krysanski, 2003). It is critical to determine that the lack of speech is not due to neurological reasons, cognitive difficulties, or auditory problems (Krysanski, 2003). Although Selective Mutism is considered difficult to treat, adaptations of behavioral treatments that will be discussed later in this chapter have been shown effective. Adaptations to behavioral approaches include the use of audiotape, videotape, and electronic equipment for voice production (Kee, Fung, & Ang, 2001). Other approaches include gradually bringing teachers and schoolmates into settings where the child is more likely to speak and having the child reward himself or herself when he or she accomplishes identified behaviors (Kehle et al., 1998). Collaboration between school personnel, parents, and mental health professionals to address Selective Mutism is also recommended. Selective Mutism can be complicated, because it can be comorbid with other problems. Apparent comorbidity and obtaining cooperation with school personnel were two of the problems seen by the teacher in following case.

In January, Megan R., a kindergartner, was placed in my classroom. Megan had actually been on my roll at the beginning of the school year, but her family had moved to another county over the summer. The family moved back to our county during winter holidays. During our January teacher planning day, a brief Individual Education Plan (IEP) meeting was held to discuss placement and goals for Megan. It appeared that Megan had been quite disruptive during fall semester in her previous school. The teachers there had recommended a full reevaluation. Megan was subsequently labeled with an Emotional Behavior Disorder (EBD), and a behavior intervention plan was developed that addressed tantrum behaviors. The IEP team decided that Megan should be placed in my classroom so that she could receive services that would provide accommodations for her disability.

On Megan's first day in my class, there were no disruptive outbursts. Megan actually never spoke a word. After her babysitter dropped her off, she stood for a long time staring at the floor. I tried to speak to her in a comforting, encouraging way, but she would not speak or make eye contact. I decided to let her have some time to warm up. At lunchtime, Megan had still not spoken. She did sit at her desk and use a pencil to shade out letters on a worksheet. When it was time for lunch, Megan refused to leave the classroom. I guided her out the door, but Megan began crying, spitting, biting herself, and pulling out her hair.

It took weeks to get Megan to leave my classroom without a major tantrum. Each day I wrote a note to Megan's mother describing her day. Megan's mother was surprised that Megan was reluctant to travel around school since this had never been a problem before. Her mother insisted that once Megan got to know us, she would talk like any other child. Each day, however, Megan continued to speak no more than a few sentences—if that. Sometimes she would say "hi" and smile for the first 15 minutes of school, but after that, she would sit quietly at her desk for the rest of the day. At the end of her first month, Megan spoke few sentences each day and pulled her hair each time she had to leave the classroom. I realized Megan may be selectively mute, so I spoke to the counselor, principal, and school psychologist about her.

Although she rarely spoke, Megan would seek affection by attempting to lean on me or sit in my lap when I worked at my desk. As I built rapport with Megan, one of the ways that I got Megan to speak (in monosyllables or short phrases) was to require that she ask for items that she wanted—toys, snacks, her favorite book, and so on. My teacher's aide, Ms. Johnson, would give Megan these things in anticipation of what Megan wanted without requiring her to ask. She would say, "I bet you want a cracker," rather than asking her what she wanted for snack. I spoke to Ms. Johnson about this several times. I explained the importance of encouraging Megan to verbalize her wants. Unfortunately, Ms. Johnson continued to speak for Megan.

Six weeks after Megan came to my class, she began having wetting accidents several times a week. When it became apparent that these weren't isolated accidents, I spoke to Megan's mother about the wetting. She agreed to take Megan to the doctor. Megan's mother never took her to the doctor and the wetting got worse. Megan refused to use the restroom at school, and she wet her pants throughout the day. I became very concerned when Megan wet her pants three times on the class field trip to a local park. Megan had already used up her dry clothes, and no one would bring her any more. She had to stay in wet clothes throughout the day. Megan's mother said she felt like the wetting was intentional and asked that I put Megan in time-out each time she wet.

Rather than punish Megan for wetting her pants, I made a referral to the school counselor. I explained to the counselor that Megan was rarely speaking at school, she wet her pants throughout the day, and she injured herself when she had to leave her desk. The counselor made a referral to the school social worker. In addition, I spoke to the school psychologist about Megan.

Generalized Anxiety Disorder

The core diagnostic feature of Generalized Anxiety Disorder (GAD) is recurrent, excessive anxiety and worry that occurs most of the time, nearly every day (see *DSM-IV-TR*, 2000). A child with GAD typically experiences multiple worries about several topics throughout the day. Common worries for children with GAD include concern about peer relationships, academic performance, health, personal attacks, and natural disasters (Weems, Silverman, & La Greca, 2000). Children with GAD find it very difficult to control and manage their worries and often feel accompanying restlessness, irritability, fatigue, muscle tension, concentration problems, and difficulty falling or staying asleep. Occasional worries are common for children and adults. However, to meet diagnostic criteria for GAD, youths must experience multiple daily worries that are difficult to control coupled with at least one of the accompanying symptoms listed earlier, more days than not, for at least 6 months. Although worry is a normal part of development for children and adolescents, the main difference among clinic-referred children with GAD is the intensity of their worries (Perrin & Last, 1997).

GAD is common in youths, with prevalence estimates of 3% among children and over 10% among adolescents (Costello, Stouthamer-Loeber, & DeRosier, 1993). Children with GAD often continue to meet diagnostic criteria for the disorder for many years after the onset of the condition (Keller et al., 1992). GAD in childhood can lead to significant functional impairments (e.g., school problems, trouble with peers), especially when family disruption or low levels of parental education and income are present (Manassis & Hood, 1998). Functional hardships are especially notable when GAD occurs with other psychiatric disorders. Common comorbidities include Major Depressive Disorder (6.4%), Separation Anxiety Disorder (24.8%), Social Phobia (31.2%), Specific Phobia (48.6%), Attention Deficit Hyperactivity Disorder (18.3%), and Oppositional Defiant Disorder (10.1%) (Verduin & Kendall, 2003). Comorbid GAD and depression is a particularly troublesome combination in that this comorbidity carries increased risk of unemployment, financial disability, and increased need for mental health services in adulthood (Last, Hanson, & Franco, 1997).

In the classroom environment, GAD can present in several ways. Children with GAD can be observed wringing their hands, shifting in their seats, and complaining of headaches, stomachaches, and fatigue. Clearly, many children with GAD can also be quite irritable with classmates and teachers, which can lead peers and teachers to withdraw or become quite punitive with these children. Even more common than irritability, worry often affects children with GAD to such an extent that it is apparent to teachers and classmates. Worry is often made apparent by complaints that children with GAD make about fearful anticipation regarding upcoming assignments, new experiences, or changes in routines. Children with GAD commonly seek reassurance (Strauss et al., 1987), and teachers can often be faced with multiple concerns from students with GAD regarding their school performance, including requesting more detailed assignment descriptions and asking for more help on assignments than their peers without GAD. Peers who begin to observe a child with GAD complaining and worrying may begin to tease, branding him or her as weak, a "worry wart," a "baby," or nervous. Being teased by peers or annoying their teachers can further add to the list of worries that most children with GAD are troubled with.

Beyond the formal treatment strategies outlined in the treatment sections below, teachers who interact with children who have GAD can help in several ways. One helpful method is to encourage children with GAD to take a more balanced view of their academic performance. Aiming for straight A's may not be in the best interest of a child with GAD. Teachers can also help students by reminding them to use what they know about probability to judge the chances of the worrisome events actually taking place. Teachers can also assist children with GAD by encouraging them to view the consequences of their worries, if they were to come true, as not so terrible. Clearly, a final consideration for classroom teachers is to stay away from the temptation to shelter children with GAD by allowing them to avoid responsibilities in the classroom or with their schoolwork. Supporting avoidance can only contribute to a worsening of GAD over the long haul.

Obsessive-Compulsive Disorder

Obsessive-Compulsive Disorder (OCD) is a prevalent, chronic, and disabling anxiety disorder, often with onset in childhood and commonly persisting throughout adulthood. The defining features of OCD are recurrent obsessions or compulsions that cause marked distress, occur for at least 1 hour per day, or cause a significant impact in functioning (*DSM-IV-TR*, 2000). Persons suffering from OCD are aware, at least at some point during the course of their illness, that their thoughts or behaviors are excessive or unreasonable. *Obsessions* are persistent, intrusive thoughts, images, or ideas that are inappropriate, excessive, and anxiety provoking. Most commonly, obsessions involve concerns about contamination, doubts about whether something was done correctly, concerns about symmetry or order, fears about harm coming to oneself or a loved one, or fears of committing aggressive or sexual acts. Because obsessions are associated with such distress, the person usually tries to suppress them or to "neutralize" them by performing particular behaviors or routines. For example, contamination obsessions are usually accompanied by severe avoidance of perceived germs coupled with excessive hand-washing rituals. These repetitive behaviors, rituals, or mental acts designed to reduce the anxiety associated with the obsessions are called *compulsions*. The most common compulsions involve cleaning, checking, ordering and arranging, counting, and repeating behaviors. OCD sufferers feel driven to perform their compulsions, despite awareness (usually) that the compulsions are either excessive or not connected in any realistic way to their obsessive fear (e.g., repetitive counting to a "lucky" number to keep a loved one safe from harm). Often, the compulsions must be performed in a ritualistic fashion and can involve very elaborate routines. Although most OCD sufferers experience both obsessions and compulsions, some patients may have one feature without the other. A diagnosis is given when symptoms are severe enough to cause marked distress, take significant time, or cause notable functional impairment.

Recent community studies estimate that the lifetime prevalence of OCD is approximately 2.5% (Karno, Golging, Sorenson, & Burnam, 1988). Age of onset is often in early adulthood, but varies by gender, with onset usually occurring between ages 6 and 15 years for males and between 20 and 29 years for females (Burke, Burke, Regier, & Rae 1990; *American Psychiatric Association,* 1994; Noshirvani, Kasvikis, Marks, Tsakiris, & Monteiro, 1991; Rasmussen & Eisen, 1992). The average age at onset in referred children and adolescents is about 10 years (Geller, Biederman, Griffin, & Jones, 1996; Hanna, 1995), but onset has been reported as early as 2 years of age (Rapoport, 1989).

Although there are more females in virtually all studies of OCD in adults (up to a 2:1 ratio of females to males), most studies of referred children and adolescents have found that OCD is more common in boys than girls (Bland, Newman, & Orn, 1988; Geller et al., 1996; Hanna, 1995; Last & Strauss, 1989). However, the sex ratio in clinical studies may be influenced by clinical severity in addition to earlier onset among males (Hanna, 1995).

OCD is often associated with severe disruption in academic, family, and social functioning (Adams, Waas, March, & Smith, 1994; Leonard et al., 1993). The course of OCD is typically chronic, with symptoms waxing and waning in severity over time, often increasing with life stress, and only very rarely remitting fully. Even with beneficial treatment, a large percentage of children with OCD continue to be bothered by symptoms as adults (Berg, Rapoport, & Wolff, 1989; Flament et al., 1989; Hollingsworth, Tanguay, & Grossman, 1980; Leonard et al., 1993; Warren, 1960; Zeitlin, 1986). Comorbidity is common, with an estimated 74% to 84% of children and adolescents suffering another lifetime psychiatric diagnosis (Flament et al., 1988; Flament et al., 1989; Hanna, 1995; Leonard et al., 1993; Riddle et al., 1990; Swedo, Rapoport, Leonard, Lenane, & Cheslow, 1989). Comorbid depression (20%–73%) (Flament et al., 1990; Geller et al., 1996) and anxiety disorders (33%–50%) (Geller et al., 1996; Swedo et al., 1989) are most common, but Attention Deficit Hyperactivity Disorder (10%–33%) (Geller et al., 1996; Swedo et al., 1989), Oppositional Defiant Disorder (11%–43%) (Geller et al., 1996; Hanna, 1995), and tic disorders (57%) (Leonard et al., 1992) are also prevalent. In about 50% of these cases, the comorbid anxiety or depressive disorders are thought to be a secondary reaction to the OCD (Swedo et al., 1989).

OCD may present in a variety of ways in the classroom. This includes extreme distractibility and inattentiveness (due to internal focus on obsessions); excessive concern about neatness, symmetry, order, and routines; perfectionism with writing, reading, or homework, indicated by excessive erasure marks or rewriting to the point of indecipherable ink marks on paper or holes in assignments; excessive slowness or incompletion of work, possibly due to checking and repeating rituals; avoidance of touching "germy" surfaces or other children, possibly by use of tissues or shirtsleeve to touch door handles, and so on; frequent bathroom trips, for compulsive voiding of the bowels and bladder or compulsive hand washing; frequent checking or repeating behaviors (with locker, book bag, desk); unusual habits such as patterned walking through hallways or doorways, touching or tapping self or objects in repetitive, routine fashion; counting floor squares or ceiling tiles or words and numbers on blackboard; and tardiness or absenteeism, possibly indicating a difficulty to leave home on time due to compulsive checking or cleaning routines.

Teachers observing one or more of these behavioral tendencies reliably over time are advised to discuss these observations with the student's family with the prospect of referring the child for a formal psychiatric evaluation.

TREATMENT OF ANXIETY DISORDERS IN CHILDHOOD

Cognitive-behavioral therapy (CBT) is generally viewed as the psychotherapeutic method of choice when treating pediatric anxiety disorders. Several studies have documented the effectiveness of (a) individual child-focused CBT, (b) CBT with an emphasis on increased parental involvement, and (c) group CBT that uses peer participation in the treatment process (Barrett, Dadds, & Rapee, 1996; Fischer, Himle, & Hanna, 1998; Flannery-Schroeder & Kendall, 2000; Kendall, 1994). All three forms of CBT are time limited and incorporate several different CBT methods, including affective education, cognitive techniques, exposure-based interventions, relaxation training, self-monitoring, and positive reinforcement.

Affective Education

Affective education is the process of helping anxious children to identify and better understand the physiological, behavioral, and cognitive signs of fear and anxiety (Kendall, 1992b). This tripartite model of emotion serves as the framework for intervention; techniques for coping include strategies in managing troubling physical sensations, alternative and productive behavioral responses, and cognitive coping statements (Wagner, 2002).

A child can be introduced to the concept of feelings by identifying facial expressions in magazines, pictures, drawings, or video clips. The child learns to identify the expressions, muscle responses, and body postures associated with a variety of emotions. This model is then used to help children understand anxiety. For example, a child with separation anxiety may be asked to imagine a scenario in which his or her mother is late for school pickup. The child is asked what his or her thoughts and behaviors would be in response to this situation. Through exercises like this, children learn to identify the physiological and somatic responses of anxiety, including muscle tension, gastrointestinal distress, heart palpitations, wobbly legs, lightheadedness, and racing thoughts. Patterns of anxious thinking are also identified. These may include predictions of something bad happening or other negative interpretations of events. Children can also learn to identify actions associated with anxiety, including avoidance behaviors.

Care should be taken to normalize the experience of anxiety and the usefulness of the fight-or-flight response triggered when a person is in real danger. Affective education focuses on helping children understand that excessive anxiety is not fatal and that it can be managed with coping skills. The dangers of anxiety-driven avoidance are also discussed during this phase of treatment. Avoidance serves to increase and maintain excessive anxiety responses through negative reinforcement or escape and avoidance learning (Marks, 1987). Affective education relies on the clinicians' ability to use stories, illustrations, and metaphors to help the child with extreme anxiety to better understand anxious feelings, problematic patterns of avoidance, and maladaptive strategies for managing anxious feelings.

Cognitive Intervention

Affective education, which is a type of cognitive intervention, develops support for the central notion that thinking affects the way we feel and behave. Children with anxiety disorders often predict that something catastrophic is about to occur and are unable to tolerate the uncertainty of life. Cognitive interventions are geared toward helping children with anxiety disorders identify and challenge patterns of anxious thinking, more accurately assess uncertainty, and develop realistic responses and coping self-statements, which often reduce excessive anxiety. The goal of cognitive interventions is not to try to get the child to think more positively but rather to test out distorted thoughts and use the power of nonnegative thinking (Kendall, Aschenbrand, & Hudson, 2003) to reduce anxiety.

The child must learn to identify common distorted thoughts that are present during times of extreme anxiety. This can be accomplished with younger children through the use of play activities and drawings, whereas self-monitoring, role plays, imagery, and direct practice is commonly used with older children and adolescents. These techniques often yield several distorted anxiety-producing thoughts. The clinician and child then work together to examine the accuracy and helpfulness of these distorted cognitions and develop nonnegative alternative coping self-statements. The child is taught to use several sources of information to respond to distorted, frightening thoughts. These sources include the youth's past experiences, modeling and experiences of others (such as peers, siblings, and parents), and current and prospective self-experiences. Because avoidance is a common strategy for anxious children, behavioral experiments (see exposure techniques below) can be used to collect this prospective data and as evidence to dispute anxiety-producing thoughts. To facilitate skill development in using cognitive strategies, the youth is asked to complete a daily journal in which fear-producing thoughts are identified and replaced by truthful, nonnegative alternatives. Children who have difficulty with journaling may be asked as daily homework to carry and review index cards created during therapy sessions that have self-statements already identified and written out for the child to use as a coping tool. With regular and consistent practice, children can develop the cognitive coping skills needed to counter anxiety and to fight back against the temptation to avoid challenging situations.

Cognitive interventions are used for all the disorders outlined earlier in this chapter. For youths with GAD, much of the cognitive intervention would focus on distorted perceptions about the likelihood of the occurrence of terrible events (e.g., natural disasters, health problems, etc.). The clinician would typically question the child about how often he or she has predicted that these events may occur, how many times they have actually occurred, and whether the child may be able to cope if something bad actually happened. Because children suffering from SocAD or Selective Mutism often predict that social encounters will turn out badly, the cognitive therapy would likely focus on whether it is really so terrible to have someone act in a rejecting way and whether the child is really sure that it is not worth the time to try to interact with others. For children with SAD, cognitive interventions would typically focus on the likelihood that the child will really "fall apart" if separated from his or her parent in addition to focusing on the likelihood that something horrible will happen to either the child or the parent when he or she is away. For youths with OCD, cognitive interventions usually center on coping self-statements (e.g, "It is just my OCD, I can fight it!" "The OCD is trying to bully me, do not back down"), which are used to facilitate compliance with exposure exercises.

Exposure Techniques

An essential component of most intervention plans for children with anxiety disorders is graded exposure therapy (Kendall, 1994). This strategy calls for the anxious youth to confront feared situations in a way that allows for his or her anxiety to first increase and then decrease over time. The idea of confronting fearful situations to become less afraid in the future is often seen as a logical and straightforward approach for most children, parents, and school personnel.

The essential component of exposure therapy is to arrange confrontations with fearful situations such that a child can feel a sense of mastery over the feared situation. This sense of mastery is achieved by arranging gradual confrontations, moving from easier to more difficult encounters, in what is usually referred to as an *exposure hierarchy.* To maximize the effectiveness of exposure therapy, several "golden rules" should be followed: Exposure to feared situations should be performed frequently (usually daily) and repetitively for at least 1.5 hours at a time if possible; exposure typically involves the use of a 0 (*calm*) to 10 (*terror*) rating scale that the child uses to report the level of anxiety experienced during each exposure exercise; the ratings are then used to pace the progressive difficulty of the exposure tasks, with pacing determined by the child; children are also taught to focus their attention on the exposure exercises rather than attempting to distract themselves to reduce their anxiety; and finally, each exposure trial should be arranged so that the child can experience mastery over the final exposure exercise of the session.

The general principles of exposure therapy are modified to fit the various anxiety disorders experienced by youths. Children with social anxiety are typically asked to encounter social situations such as making comments in class, talking to other children in the lunchroom, and asking for information in stores and other public situations. Children with separation anxiety are often asked to practice spending prolonged periods away from their parents. Finally, children with obsessions and compulsions may be asked to confront challenging stimuli such as dirt, germs, using the stove, or making mistakes on homework while attempting to prevent engagement in rituals to reduce their anxiety.

Relaxation

Progressive muscle relaxation is a commonly used method for managing anxious sensations (see Ost, 1987, for a complete description). Progressive muscle relaxation involves systematically tensing and relaxing muscle groups. Moderate tension is normally applied to one muscle group at a time for 5 seconds followed by approximately 15 to 20 seconds of rest before the next muscle group is sequentially tensed and relaxed. The tension and rest exercises can be described using the analogy of a stiff robot and a limp rag doll (Kendall, 1992b). Although the sequence of muscle groups involved in progressive muscle relaxation varies to some extent, the typical progression begins with clenching the right fist, progressing through the right arm, followed by the left fist and arm to the face, neck, shoulders, trunk and back, and finally down through the legs and feet. Throughout the relaxation exercises, the youth is encouraged to attend to the feelings experienced during the tension phase and to compare them to the sensations during the relaxation phase of the muscle tension sequence. The goal is to assist the youth in learning the difference between muscle tension and relaxation. As this distinction is noted repeatedly during the progressive muscle relaxation exercises, children usually become able to identify signs of muscle tension throughout the course of their daily lives.

Progressive muscle relaxation involves three phases. The first phase typically includes daily muscle relaxation exercises performed as homework and should be expected to last around 20 minutes. These exercises are typically continued for 1 to 2 weeks. The second phase of progressive muscle relaxation is known as the release-only phase. The goal of this stage is to reduce the amount of time it takes to achieve a state of relaxation, by eliminating the muscle tension aspect of the exercise. The youth is allowed to apply tension to a given muscle group only if problems achieving relaxation are encountered. Homework typically involves having the person practice release-only relaxation at least one time daily for 1 to 2 weeks. The final phase involves cue-controlled relaxation, which further reduces the time it takes for the youth to achieve a state of relaxation. This stage focuses on breathing techniques and establishing a relationship between the self-instruction "relax" and a state of increased relaxation. Once cue-controlled relaxation is mastered, youths can use this technique to control anxiety in stressful situations.

Relaxation exercises are particularly relevant for youths with GAD, SAD, and SocAD. Relaxation exercises are best used for ongoing, enduring anxiety, but they play a somewhat more limited role as a method to manage specific fearful encounters. Specific encounters such as talking to peers for a child with SocAD or frightening separations from parents for children with SAD are best addressed using the exposure therapy paradigm.

Self-Monitoring and Positive Reinforcement

Self-monitoring is used throughout the treatment process. The primary goal of self-monitoring is to help the child or adolescent learn to identify the physical sensations of anxiousness and anxiety-producing triggers (situational, cognitive) and to rate anxiety levels and evaluate intervention results. Positive reinforcement is used to reward effort and compliance with the other CBT techniques. Reinforcement approaches typically involve parental praise and tangible rewards, encouragement from teacher/school personnel, and self-reinforcement.

SUMMARY

Anxiety is a common, developmentally normative and necessary aspect of childhood. However, anxiety is not considered adaptive when it becomes developmentally inappropriate, prolonged, and very distressing and has a negative impact on social, familial, and academic functioning. Parents and school personnel often face the challenge of determining if a child's anxiety is normal and something he or she will outgrow or whether it is a problem that warrants assessment and intervention. The discussion about the normative occurrences of anxiety and the nature of the disorders described in this chapter should be helpful in making what can often be a difficult distinction. Wagner (2002) uses four criteria to help make the distinction between normal anxiety and an anxiety disorder; to be considered a disorder, anxiety should (a) be disproportionate, (b) cause disruption by interfering with functioning, (c) be significantly distressing, and (d) be present for a sustained period of time. The treatment techniques described in this chapter are performance based and geared toward helping the child develop the coping skills needed to manage anxious arousal. Children learn necessary skills to detect undesirable and unhelpful anxious feelings and to use these physical sensations as signals to enact the coping strategies learned in treatment. School personnel can play a significant role in identifying and assessing developmentally inappropriate and excessive anxiety, as well as assisting the child and parents in carrying out coping-based intervention strategies.

DISCUSSION QUESTIONS

1. In any of your college classes, have you ever observed a classmate who did poorly on a test or assignment due to anxiety? How did he or she respond? Did the instructor make accommodations for the person? If so, what sorts of accommodations were made?
2. What are some of the routine activities of the school day that could exacerbate anxiety problems?
3. Have you ever known a student who seemed to be "turned off of school"? Did it appear that anxiety could have been a factor? If so, how?
4. One of the components of effective treatment for anxiety disorders is exposure to the feared stimulus. Consider the example of test anxiety. What are some supports that you could use that would provide support to a student with this problem without allowing him or her to engage in complete avoidance of tests?

FOR ADDITIONAL HELP

	Organization	*Web Address*	*Description*
Childhood Anxiety Disorders	Anxiety Disorders Association of America (ADAA)	www.adaa.org	The ADAA promotes the early diagnosis, treatment, and cure of anxiety disorders and is committed to improving the lives of the people who suffer from them.
	National Institute of Mental Health (NIMH)	www.nimh.nih.gov/healthinformation/anxietymenu.cfm	NIMH is the lead federal agency for research on mental and behavioral disorders.

REFERENCES

Adams, G. B., Waas, G. A., March, J. S., & Smith, M. C. (1994). Obsessive compulsive disorder in children and adolescents: The role of the school psychologist in identification, assessment, and treatment. *School Psychologist Quarterly, 9,* 274–294.

Albano, A. M. (1995). Treatment of social anxiety in adolescents. *Cognitive and Behavioral Practice, 2,* 271–298.

Albano, A. M., DiBartolo, P. M., Heimberg, R. G., & Barlow, D. H. (1995). Children and adolescents: Assessment and treatment. In R. G. Heimberg, M. R. Liebowitz, D. A. Hope, & F. R. Schneier (Eds.), *Social phobia: Diagnosis, assessment, and treatment* (pp. 387–427). New York: Guilford Press.

American Psychiatric Association. (1980). *Diagnostic and statistical manual of mental disorders* (3rd ed.). Washington, DC: Author.

American Psychiatric Association. (1994). *Diagnostic and statistical manual of mental disorders* (4th ed.). Washington, DC: Author.

American Psychiatric Association. (2000). *Diagnostic and statistical manual of mental disorders* (4th ed., text revision). Washington, DC: Author.

Anderson, J. C., Williams, S., McGee, R., & Silva, P. A. (1987). *DSM-III* disorders in preadolescent children: Prevalence in a large sample from a general population. *Archives of General Psychiatry, 44,* 69–76.

Barrett, P. M., Dadds, M. R., & Rapee, R. M. (1996). Family treatment of childhood anxiety: A controlled trial. *Journal of Consulting and Clinical Psychology, 64,* 333–342.

Battaglia, M., Bertella, S., Politi, E., Bernardeschi, L., Perna, G., Gabriele, A., & Bellodi, L. (1995). Age at onset of panic disorder: Influence of familial liability to the disease and of childhood separation anxiety disorder. *American Journal of Psychiatry, 152,* 1362–1364.

Beidel, D. C. (1991). Social phobia and overanxious disorder in school-age children. *Journal of the American Academy of Child and Adolescent Psychiatry, 30,* 545–552.

Beidel, D. C., Christ, M. G., & Long, P. J. (1991). Somatic complaints in anxious children. *Journal of Abnormal Child Psychology, 19,* 659–670.

Beidel, D. C., Ferrell, C., Alfano, C. A., & Yeganeh, R. (2001). The treatment of childhood social anxiety disorder. *Psychiatric Clinics of North America, 24,* 831–846.

Beidel, D. C., & Morris, T. L. (1995). Social phobia. In J. S. March (Ed.), *Anxiety disorders in children and adolescents* (pp. 181–211). New York: Guilford Press.

Beidel, D. C., & Turner, S. M. (1998). *Shy children, phobic adults: Nature and treatment of social phobia.* Washington, DC: American Psychological Association.

Beidel, D. C., Turner, S. M., & Morris, T. L. (1999). Psychopathology of childhood social phobia. *Journal of the American Academy of Child and Adolescent Psychiatry, 38,* 643–650.

Berg, C., Rapoport, J., & Wolff, R. (1989). Behavioral treatment for obsessive-compulsive disorder in childhood. In J. Rapoport (Ed.), *Obsessive-compulsive disorder in children and adolescents.* Washington, DC: American Psychiatric Press.

Bergman, R. L., Piacentini, J., & McCracken, J. T. (2002). Prevalence and description of selective mutism in a school-based sample. *Journal of the American Academy of Child and Adolescent Psychiatry, 41,* 938–946.

Bernstein, G. A., & Borchardt, C. M. (1991). Anxiety disorders of childhood and adolescence: A critical review. *Journal of the American Academy of Child & Adolescent Psychiatry, 30,* 519–532.

Bierderman, J., Rosenbaum, J. F., Bolduc-Murphey, E. A., Faraone, S. V., Charloff, J., Hirshfeld, D. R., & Kagan, J. (1993). A 3-year follow-up of children with and without behavioral inhibition. *Journal of the American Academy of Child & Adolescent Psychiatry, 32,* 814–821.

Black, B., & Uhde, T. W. (1995). Psychiatric characteristics of children with mutism: A pilot study. *Journal of the American Academy of Child and Adolescent Psychiatry, 34,* 847–856.

Bland, R. C., Newman, S. C., & Orn, H. (1988). Lifetime prevalence of psychiatric disorders in Edmonton. *Acta Psychiatrica Scandinavica, 77,* 24–32.

Bowen, R. C., Offord, D. R., & Boyle, M. H. (1990). The prevalence of overanxious disorder and separation anxiety disorder: Results from the Ontario Child Health Study. *Journal of the American Academy of Child & Adolescent Psychiatry, 29,* 753–758.

Bukstein, O. G., Brent, D. A., & Kaminer, Y. (1989). Comorbidity of substance abuse and other psychiatric disorders in adolescents. *American Journal of Psychiatry, 146,* 1131–1141.

Burke, K. C., Burke, J. D., Regier, D. A., & Rae, D. S. (1990). Age of onset of selected mental disorders in five community populations. *Archives of General Psychiatry, 47,* 511–518.

Clark, D. B., & Neighbors, B. (1996). Adolescent substance abuse and internalizing disorders. *Child and Adolescent Psychiatric Clinic of North America, 5,* 45–57.

Cole, D. A., Peeke, L. G., Martin, J. M., Truglio, R., & Seroczynski, A. D. (1998). A longitudinal look at the relation between depression and anxiety in children and adolescents. *Journal of Consulting and Clinical Psychology, 66,* 451–460.

Compton, S. N., Nelson, A. H., & March, J. S. (2000). Social phobia and separation anxiety symptoms in community and clinical samples of children and adolescents. *Journal of the American Academy of Child & Adolescent Psychiatry, 39,* 1040–1046.

Costello, E. J. (1989). Child psychiatric disorders and their correlates: A primary care pediatric sample. *Journal of the American Academy of Child & Adolescent Psychiatry, 28,* 851–855.

Costello, E. J., Stouthamer-Loeber, M., & DeRosier, M. (1993). *Continuity and change in psychopathology from childhood to adolescence.* Paper presented at the annual meeting of the Society for Research in Child and Adolescent Psychopathology, Santa Fe, NM.

Dadds, M. R., & Barrett, P. M. (2001). Practitioner review: Psychological management of anxiety disorders in childhood. *Journal of Childhood Psychology and Psychiatry, 42,* 999–1011.

Davidson, J. R. T., Hughes, D. L., George, L. K., & Blazer, D. G. (1993). The epidemiology of social phobia: Findings from the Duke Epidemiological Catchment Area Study. *Psychological Medicine, 23,* 709–718.

DeWit, D. J., MacDonald, K., & Offord, D. R. (1999). Childhood stress and symptoms of drug dependence in adolescence and early adulthood: Social phobia as a mediator. *American Journal of Orthopsychiatry, 69,* 61–72.

Dobson, K. S. (1985). The relationship between anxiety and depression. *Clinical Psychology Review, 5,* 307–324.

Dow, S. P., Sonies, B. C., Scheib, D., & Moss, S. E. (1995). Practical guidelines for the assessment and treatment of selective mutism. *Journal of the American Academy of Child and Adolescent Psychiatry, 34,* 836–846.

Dulcan, M. K., Martini, D. R., & Lake, M. B. (2003). *Concise guide to child and adolescent psychiatry* (3rd ed.). Washington, DC: American Psychiatric Press.

Dummit, I. E. S., Klein, R. G., Tancer, N. K., Asche, B., Martin, J., & Fairbanks, J. A. (1997). Systematic assessment of 50 children with selective mutism. *Journal of the American Academy of Child and Adolescent Psychiatry, 36,* 653–660.

Fischer, D. J., Himle, J. A., & Hanna, G. L. (1998). Group behavioral therapy for adolescents with obsessive-compulsive disorder: Preliminary outcomes. *Research on Social Work Practice, 8,* 629–636.

Flament, M. F., Koby, M. F., Rapoport, J. L., Berg, C. J., Zahn, T., Cox, C., et al. (1990). Childhood obsessive-compulsive disorder: A prospective follow-up study. *Journal of Child Psychology & Psychiatry & Allied Disciplines, 31,* 363–380.

Flament, M. F., Rapoport, J. L., Berg, C. Z., Walter, S., et al. (1989). Obsessive-compulsive disorder in adolescence: An epidemiological study. *Annual Progress in Child Psychiatry and Child Development,* 499–515.

Flament, M. F., Whitaker A., Rapoport, J. L., Davies, M., Berg, C. Z., Kalikow, K., et al. (1988). Obsessive-compulsive disorder in adolescence: An epidemiological study. *Journal of the American Academy of Child and Adolescent Psychiatry, 27,* 764–771.

Flannery-Schroeder, E. C., & Kendall, P. C. (2000). Group and individual cognitive-behavioral treatments for youth with anxiety disorders: A randomized clinical trial. *Cognitive Therapy and Research, 24,* 251–278.

Geller, D. A., Biederman, J., Griffin, S., & Jones, J. (1996). Comorbidity of juvenile obsessive-compulsive disorder with disruptive behavior disorders. *Journal of the American Academy of Child and Adolescent Psychiatry, 35,* 1637–1646.

Greenbaum, P. E., Foster-Johnson, L., & Petrila, A. (1996). Co-occurring addictive and mental disorders among adolescents: Prevalence research and future directions. *American Journal of Orthopsychiatry, 66,* 52–60.

Greenberg, P. E., Sisitsky, T., Kessler, R. C., Finkelstein, S. N., Berndt, E. R., Davidson, J. R. T., Ballenger, J. C., & Fyer, A. J. (1999). The economic burden of anxiety disorders in the 1990s. *Journal of Clinical Psychiatry, 60,* 427–435.

Hanna, G. L. (1995). Demographic and clinical features of obsessive-compulsive disorder in children and adolescents. *Journal of the American Academy of Child and Adolescent Psychiatry, 34,* 19–27.

Heimberg, R. G., Stein, M. B., Hiripi, E., & Kessler, R. C. (2000). Trends in the prevalence of social phobia in the United States: A synthetic cohort analysis of changes over four decades. *European Psychiatry, 15,* 29–37.

Hollingsworth, C., Tanguay, P., & Grossman, I. (1980). Long-term outcome of obsessive-compulsive disorder in childhood. *Journal of the American Academy of Child and Adolescent Psychiatry, 19,* 134–144.

Hudson, J. L., & Rapee, R. M. (2001). Parent-child interaction and the anxiety disorders: An observational analysis. *Behaviour Research & Therapy, 39,* 1411–1427.

Inderbitzen-Nolan, H. M., & Walters, K. S. (2000). Social anxiety scale for adolescents: Normative data and further evidence of construct validity. *Journal of Clinical Child Psychology, 29,* 360–371.

Karno, M., Golging, J. M., Sorenson, S. B., & Burnam, M. A. (1988). The epidemiology of obsessive-compulsive disorder in five U.S. communities. *Archives of General Psychiatry, 45,* 1094–1099.

Kashani, J. H., & Orvaschel, H. (1988). Anxiety disorders in mid-adolescence: A community sample. *American Journal of Psychiatry, 145,* 960–964.

Kashani, J. H., & Orvaschel, H. (1990). A community study of anxiety in children and adolescents. *American Journal of Psychiatry, 147*(3), 313–318.

Kashdan, T. B., & Herbert, J. D. (2001). Social anxiety disorder in childhood and adolescence: Current status and future directions. *Clinical Child and Family Psychology Review, 4*(1), 37–61.

Kee, C., Fung, D., & Ang, L. (2001). The electronic communication device for selective mutism. *Journal of the American Academy of Child and Adolescent Psychiatry, 40,* 389.

Kehle, T. J., Madaus, M. R., Baratta, V. S., & Bray, M. A. (1998). Augmented self-modeling as a treatment for children with selective mutism. *Journal of School Psychology, 36,* 247–260.

Keller, M. B., Lavori, P. W., Wunder, J., Beardslee, W. R., Schwartz, C. E., & Roth, J. (1992). Chronic course of anxiety disorders in children and adolescents. *Journal of the American Academy of Child and Adolescent Psychiatry, 31,* 595–599.

Kendall, P. C. (1992a). Childhood coping: Avoiding a lifetime of anxiety. *Behavioural Change, 9,* 1–8.

Kendall, P. C. (1992b). *Coping cat workbook.* Ardmore, PA: Workbook.

Kendall, P. C. (1994). Treating anxiety disorders in children: Results of a randomized clinical trial. *Journal of Consulting and Clinical Psychology, 62,* 100–110.

Kendall, P. C., Aschenbrand, S. G., & Hudson, J. L. (2003). Child focused treatment of anxiety. In A. E. Kazdin & J. R. Weisz (Eds.), *Evidenced-based psychotherapies for children and adolescents* (pp. 81–100). New York: Guilford.

Kovacs, M., Gatsonis, C., Paulauskas, S. L., & Richards, C. (1989). Depressive disorders in childhood: IV. A longitudinal study of comorbidity with and risk for anxiety disorders. *Archives of General Psychiatry, 46,* 776–783.

Krysanski, V. L. (2003). A brief review of selective mutism literature. *Journal of Psychology, 137,* 29–40.

La Greca, A. M., & Lopez, N. (1998). Social anxiety among adolescents: Linkages with peer relationships and friendships. *Journal of Abnormal Child Psychology, 26,* 83–94.

Last, C. G., Hanson, C., & Franco, N. (1997). Anxious children in adulthood: A prospective study of adjustment. *Journal of the American Academy of Child and Adolescent Psychiatry, 36,* 645–652.

Last, C. G., Perrin, S., Hersen, M., & Kazdin, A. E. (1992). *DSM-III-R* anxiety disorders in children: Sociodemographic and clinical characteristics. *Journal of the American Academy of Child & Adolescent Psychiatry, 31,* 1070–1076.

Last, C. G., & Strauss, C. C. (1989). Obsessive-compulsive disorder in childhood. *Journal of Anxiety Disorders, 3,* 295–302.

Leonard, H. L., Lenane, M. C., Swedo, S. E., Rettew, D. C., Gershon, E. S., & Rapoport, J. L. (1992). Tics and Tourette's disorder: A 2- to 7-year follow-up of 54 obsessive-compulsive children. *American Journal of Psychiatry, 149,* 1244–1251.

Leonard, H. L., Swedo, S. E., Lenane, M. C., Rettew, D. C., Hamburger, S. D., Bartko, J. J., et al. (1993). A 2–7 year follow-up study of 54 obsessive-compulsive children and adolescents. *Archives of General Psychiatry, 50,* 429–439.

Lewinsohn, P. M., Hops, H., Roberts, R. E., Seeley, J. R., & Andrews, J. A. (1993). Adolescent psychopathology: I. Prevalence and incidence of depression and other *DSM-III-R* disorders in high school students. *Journal of Abnormal Psychology, 102,* 133–144.

Liebowitz, M., Gorman, J. M., Fyer, A. J., & Klein, D. F. (1985). Social phobia: Review of a neglected anxiety disorder. *Archives of General Psychiatry, 42*(7), 729–736.

Manassis, K., & Hood, J. (1998). Individual and familial predictors of impairment in childhood anxiety disorders. *Journal of the American Academy of Child & Adolescent Psychiatry, 37,* 428–434.

Marks, I. M. (1987). *Fears, phobias, & rituals.* New York: Oxford University Press.

Messer, S. C., & Beidel, D. C. (1994). Psychosocial correlates of childhood anxiety disorders. *Journal of the American Academy of Child & Adolescent Psychiatry, 33,* 975–983.

Murray, C. J. L., & Lopez, A. D. (1996). *The global burden of disease.* Boston: Harvard University Press.

Nesse, R., & Williams, G. C. (1996). *Why we get sick: The new science of Darwinian medicine.* New York: Vintage Books.

Noshirvani, H. A., Kasvikis, Y., Marks, I. A., Tsakiris, F., & Monteiro, W. O. (1991). Gender-divergent etiological factors in obsessive-compulsive disorder. *British Journal of Psychiatry, 148,* 260–263.

Ost, L. G. (1987). Applied relaxation: Description of a coping technique and review of controlled studies. *Behaviour Research and Therapy, 25,* 397–410.

Panella, D., & Henggeler, S. W. (1986). Peer interactions of conduct-disordered, anxious-withdrawn, and well-adjusted Black adolescents. *Journal of Abnormal Child Psychology, 14,* 1–11.

Perrin, S., & Last, C. G. (1997). Worrisome thoughts in children referred for anxiety disorder. *Journal of Clinical Child Psychology, 26,* 181–189.

Rapoport, J. L. (1989). *The boy who couldn't stop washing.* New York: Dutton.

Rasmussen, S. A., & Eisen, J. L. (1992). The epidemiology and clinical features of obsessive compulsive disorder. *Journal of Clinical Psychiatry, 53,* 743–758.

Riddle, M. A., Scahill, L., King, R., Hardin, M. T., Towbin, K. E., Ort, S. I., et al. (1990). Obsessive-compulsive disorder in children and adolescents: Phenomenology and family history. *Journal of the American Academy of Child and Adolescent Psychiatry, 29,* 766–772.

Rubin, K. H., & Clark, M. L. (1983). Preschool teachers' ratings of behavioural problems: Observational, sociometric and social-cognitive correlates. *Journal of Abnormal Child Psychology, 11,* 273–286.

Schneier, F. R., Johnson, J., Hornig, C. D., Liebowitz, M. R., & Weissman, M. M. (1992). Social phobia: Comorbidity and morbidity in an epidemiologic sample. *Archives of General Psychiatry, 49,* 282–288.

Schniering, C. A., Hudson, J. L., & Rapee, R. M. (2000). Issues in the diagnosis and assessment of anxiety disorders in children and adolescents. *Clinical Psychology Review, 20,* 453–478.

Schuckit, M., & Hesselbrock, V. (1996). Alcohol dependence and anxiety disorders: What is the relationship? *American Journal of Psychiatry, 153,* 139–140.

Silverman, W. K., & Dick-Niederhauser, A. (2004). Separation anxiety disorder. In T. L. Morris & J. S. March (Eds.), *Anxiety disorders in children and adolescents* (2nd ed., pp. 164–188). New York: Guilford Press.

Spence, S. H. (1994). Preventative strategies. In T. H. Ollendick (Ed.), *International handbook of phobia and anxiety disorders in children and adolescents* (pp. 453–474). New York: Plenum Press.

Spence, S. H., Donovan, C., & Brechman-Toussaint, M. (1999). Social skills, social outcomes, and cognitive features of childhood social phobia. *Journal of Abnormal Psychology, 108,* 211–221.

Steinhausen, H. C., & Juzi, C. (1996). Elective mutism: An analysis of 100 cases. *Journal of the American Academy of Child and Adolescent Psychiatry, 35,* 606–614.

Strauss, C. C., Frame, C., & Forehand, R. (1987). Psychosocial impairment associated with anxiety in children. *Journal of Clinical Child Psychology, 16,* 235–239.

Swedo, S. E., Rapoport, J. L., Leonard, H., Lenane, M., & Cheslow, D. (1989). Obsessive-compulsive disorder in children and adolescents: Clinical phenomenology of 70 consecutive cases. *Archives of General Psychiatry, 46,* 335–341.

Verduin, T. L., & Kendall, P. C. (2003). Differential occurrence of comorbidity within childhood anxiety disorders. *Journal of Consulting and Clinical Psychology, 32,* 290–295.

Wagner, A. P. (2002). *Worried no more: Help and hope for anxious children.* Rochester, NY: Lighthouse Press.

Warren, W. (1960). A study of adolescent inpatients and the outcome six or more years later. *Journal of Child Psychology and Psychiatry, 6,* 141–160.

Weems, C. F., Silverman, W. K., & La Greca, A. M. (2000). What do youth referred for anxiety problems worry about? Worry and its relation to anxiety and anxiety disorders in children and adolescents. *Journal of Abnormal Child Psychology, 28,* 63–72.

Whaley, S. E., Pinto, A., & Sigman, M. (1999). Characterizing interactions between anxious mothers and their children. *Journal of Consulting & Clinical Psychology, 67,* 826–836.

Wittchen, H. U., Stein, M. B., & Kessler, R. C. (1999). Social fears and social phobia in a community sample of adolescents and young adults: Prevalence, risk factors, and comorbidity. *Psychological Medicine, 29,* 309–323.

Zeitlin, H. (1986). *The natural history of psychiatric disorder in children.* Oxford, UK: Oxford University Press.

Chapter 7

Attention Deficit Hyperactivity Disorder

Nina Yssel

PREREADING QUESTIONS

As you read this chapter, reflect on the following questions and issues:

1. How can we serve students with ADHD in public schools?
2. Does ADHD present the same way in all students? If not, what are some differences that can be seen?
3. What are some of the strengths and weaknesses associated with ADHD?
4. How do characteristics of ADHD change with age?
5. What are possible causes of ADHD?

Attention Deficit Hyperactivity Disorder (ADHD) is one of the most common and impairing of childhood psychological disorders (Wells, 2004) and one of the most common reasons children are referred to mental health practitioners in the United States (Barkley, 1998). It is also probably fair to say that few childhood conditions or disorders elicit the controversy that surrounds ADHD. Most of us know at least one child with this label, and many people have strong opinions about ADHD interventions, specifically stimulant medication. The overdiagnosis and overmedication of students with ADHD is a topic widely explored in the popular media, and it becomes increasingly difficult for the layperson to distinguish between myths and facts where ADHD is concerned.

Although ADHD is viewed as a disorder of current times, in reality it is not a new phenomenon. In the 1950s, the concept of the "brain-injured child" was researched by Strauss, who claimed that the psychological disturbances or behavioral deficits were, de facto, evidence of brain injury (cited in Barkley, 1998). Reported use of medication actually predates the work of Strauss. Stimulants have been prescribed since the 1930s when researchers such as Bradley reported on the efficacy of amphetamines in reducing disruptive behavior and improving the academic performance of students with behavior disorders (cited in Barkley, 1998). The use of medication, particularly in the United States, is the focus of the current controversy that has characterized the treatment of ADHD.

You may have come across some of the following misconceptions regarding ADHD:

- All children with ADHD will outgrow it.
- ADHD is a disability area addressed by the Individuals with Disabilities Education Act (IDEA).
- ADHD is caused by poor parenting.
- ADHD is caused by certain foods, specifically sugar.
- Medication can actually "diagnose" ADHD: Children with ADHD will improve when taking medication; children without ADHD will show no effect when taking medication.
- ADHD is only found in the United States.
- All children with ADHD are eligible for special education.
- All children with ADHD are hyperactive. (Hallahan & Kauffman, 2003; Weyandt, 2001)

This chapter attempts to clear up the confusion and presents you with the information you will need to make appropriate referrals and recommendations.

DEFINITION AND TERMINOLOGY

The criteria of the American Psychiatric Association's (APA) *Diagnostic and Statistical Manual of Mental Disorders* (*DSM-IV-TR*; APA, 2000) are used to diagnose ADHD (see Table 7.1). For many years, the APA used the general term Attention Deficit Disorder (ADD) to refer to all individuals with the condition, but it currently uses ADHD as the general term with three subtypes:

ADHD-IA: Predominantly Inattentive

ADHD-HI: Predominantly Hyperactive-Impulsive

ADHD-C: Combined (Forness & Kavale, 2002)

Table 7.1 Diagnostic Criteria for Attention Deficit Hyperactivity Disorder (ADHD)

ADHD-IA Subtype: Symptoms of Inattention

- Fails to give close attention to details, makes careless mistakes
- Has difficulty sustaining attention
- Does not seem to listen
- Does not follow through or finish tasks
- Has difficulties organizing tasks and activities
- Avoids or dislikes tasks requiring sustained effort
- Loses things needed for tasks or activities
- Is easily distracted by extraneous stimuli
- Is often forgetful in daily activities

ADHD-HI Subtype: Symptoms of Hyperactivity and Impulsivity

- Fidgets with hands or feet or squirms in seat
- Leaves seat in classroom or in other situations
- Runs about or climbs excessively
- Has difficulty playing or engaging in leisure activities quietly
- Talks excessively
- Acts as if "driven by motor" and cannot sit still
- Impulsivity
- Blurts our answers before questions are completed
- Has difficulty waiting in line or awaiting turn in games or activities
- Interrupts or intrudes on others

ADHD-C: Combined Subtype

- Symptoms of both IA and HI

SOURCE: American Psychiatric Association (2000). Reprinted with permission from the Diagnostic and Statistical Manual of Mental Disorders, Copyright 2000. American Psychiatric Association.

Please note that the symptoms, which are listed in Table 7.1, should "have persisted for at least 6 months to a degree that is maladaptive and inconsistent with developmental level" (*DSM-IV-TR,* 2000, p. 92). That is, the behaviors should occur considerably more frequently and severely than those observed in peers at the same developmental level. The *DSM-IV-TR* criteria also require that problem behaviors be observed in multiple contexts (school, home, and social interactions). These criteria lack clear operational procedures for determining if a criterion is met, and the *DSM-IV-TR* acknowledges that there are no standardized tests at this point to establish a definitive diagnosis of this condition (Raymond, 2000).

It is important to remember that not all children will be affected to the same degree and that ADHD effects are on a continuum ranging from mild to severe. The guidelines from *DSM-IV-TR* (2000) are the following:

- Mild: few if any symptoms in excess of those required to make the diagnosis; minimal or no impairment in school or social functioning
- Moderate: symptoms or functional impairment intermediate between "mild" and "severe"

- Severe: many symptoms in excess of those required to make the diagnosis; significant and pervasive impairment in functioning at home and in school with peers

SERVICES

How and where do we serve students with ADHD in our schools? ADHD is not a separate category under the IDEA, but students may qualify for services under the category of Other Health Impaired. A student with other health impairments has "limited strength, vitality, or alertness, including a heightened sense of alertness with respect to the educational environment." The latter criterion, along with "adversely affects a child's educational performance," allows students with ADHD to qualify for services under this category (U.S. Department of Education, 1999). As a result, the number of children identified as Other Health Impaired has increased substantially—from 53,165 in 1991 to 220,931 in 2000 (Lerner, 2003).

A large number of students with ADHD who qualify for services under the IDEA may already receive services under other existing disability categories, most likely under the categories of learning disabilities and emotional disorders (Dowdy, Patton, Smith, & Polloway, 1998). On the other hand, those students with ADHD whose educational performance is not seriously affected, and therefore do not qualify for special services under the IDEA, may be eligible for services under Section 504 of the Rehabilitation Act (see Box below).

SECTION 504 OF THE REHABILITATION ACT

Section 504 is a provision of the Rehabilitation Act of 1973 that extends to individuals with disabilities the same kind of protection extended to individuals discriminated against on the basis of race and gender. Originally aimed at employment discrimination, Section 504 addresses protection in areas such as public schools, higher education, social services, health care, and transportation—that is, any program or activity receiving federal financial assistance (Henley, Ramsey, & Algozzine, 2002).

PREVALENCE AND COMORBIDITY

Determining the true prevalence of ADHD is difficult because it cannot be strictly defined and precisely measured (Barkley, 1998; Loechler, 1999). Barkley (1998) points out that this problem pertains not only to ADHD but to all psychiatric disorders. Therefore, percentages will vary because of different diagnostic criteria and methods used to define and assess ADHD (Weyandt, 2001). Estimates of the existence of ADHD in the school-age population range from figures as liberal as 30% (Dowdy et al., 1998), to 3% to 5% of children or adolescents (Forness & Kavale, 2002). Most experts seem to agree on 3% to 5%, which means that in a typical class of 25, at least 1 student may have ADHD (Loechler, 1999).

The *DSM-IV-TR* definition is not used worldwide; in Europe and Britain, the World Health Organization definition is more commonly accepted, resulting in fewer students being identified with ADHD. This definition requires *both* significant inattention and hyperactivity in an individual. British psychologists believe that this stringent definition could reduce the risk of identifying children from cultures or backgrounds where expected school behaviors might not be instilled from early childhood (Smith, 2004). On the other hand, Hallahan and Kauffman (2003) cite several researchers who had found prevalence rates as high as that of the United States (e.g., 6%–9% in China, 12%–19% in Columbia, but only 1%–2% in the Netherlands).

As in the case of learning disabilities, boys outnumber girls, with ratios ranging from 3:1 (Lerner, 2003) to even 10:1 (Wells, 2004). Gender research shows that boys seem to be more hyperactive and have more acting-out problems than do girls, whereas girls have greater problems with attention (Hallahan & Kauffman, 2003; Weyandt, 2001). The question is whether boys may be overidentified and girls underidentified and whether gender bias may exist in referrals. Although these questions may be valid, they cannot account for the disparity in prevalence rates (Hallahan & Kauffman, 2003). Barkley (1998) argues that "there may be some gender-linked mechanism involved in the expression of the disorder" (p. 85).

ADHD is often associated with one or more comorbid conditions: In the case of Oppositional Defiant Disorder, we find an overlap of 35% to 60%, Conduct Disorder 30% to 50%, Anxiety Disorder 25% to 40%, and then an overlap of 10% to 26% between ADHD and Specific Learning Disabilities (Forness & Kavale, 2002). **Comorbidity** between emotional disorders and ADHD has also been reported: Raymond (2000) considers antisocial, aggressive behavior or conduct disorders the most frequent problem behavior associated with ADHD.

IDENTIFICATION/ASSESSMENT

There is no single test to diagnose ADHD; it is, in fact, a multifaceted process (Children and Adults With Attention-Deficit/Hyperactivity Disorder [CHADD], 2003; Weyandt, 2001). Salend and Rohena (2003) explained the multifaceted identification process as seeking to

> collect data to identify the student's academic, behavioral, and social behaviors and medical, family, experiential, and developmental history. These data are then analyzed to identify learning and behavioral patterns and to determine if students have an ADD that meets the diagnostic criteria specified by the American Psychiatric Association. (p. 262)

If the presence of ADHD is suspected, it is important to note that (a) other conditions and problems (e.g., anxiety, depression) may cause symptoms similar to those exhibited by children with ADHD (CHADD, 2003) and that (b) many children (who do not have ADHD) may present difficulties with attention, impulsivity, and hyperactivity (Weyandt, 2001). When considering an escalating cycle of referrals, Snider, Busch, and Arrowood (2003) point out that teachers should be aware that a lack of attention and inappropriate behaviors may not necessarily be a result of ADHD; this kind of behavior may often be attributed to the need for attention or to avoid school tasks. It is, of course, extremely important to rule out these factors before considering ADHD.

According to Barkley (1998), there should be three components to assessment:

1. A medical examination to rule out conditions such as brain tumors or thyroid problems as possible causes of hyperactivity or inattention
2. A clinical interview of parents and child to learn about the child's physical and psychological characteristics, as well as family dynamics and social interactions
3. Teacher and parent rating scales (examples of such rating scales are the Connors scales and the ADHD–Rating Scale IV)

Finally, when conducting ecological assessment, which includes rating scales and interviews as mentioned above, one should always be sensitive to cultural or linguistic factors (Raymond, 2000) that may have an impact on children's behavior.

CHARACTERISTICS

When asked to describe a child with ADHD, most people will probably first mention the excessive movement and distractibility—in other words, the child who is on the go all the time. Before examining the validity of such descriptions, we need to focus on the strengths of the individual with ADHD. We often forget about strengths and too easily accentuate the difficulties. Turnbull, Turnbull, Shank, and Smith (2004) emphasize the importance of focusing on the strengths that people have and point out that students with ADHD have the ability to **hyperfocus**. They may also exhibit strengths such as creativity, high energy, and intuitiveness (Flint, 2001). Flint describes the minds of many people with ADHD as follows: "The ideas come and go, changing from one topic to another with an awesome rapidity and proliferation. With this many ideas, new ones pop up with regularity" (p. 65).

When it comes to areas of difficulty, Barkley (1998) groups these into three common areas:

Reduced Impulse Control and a Need for Instant Gratification. These behaviors have academic and social consequences; in the classroom, they may result in an inability to focus on long-term goals (Smith, Polloway, Patton, & Dowdy, 2004) and difficulty in completing assignments. In the social realm, the impulsive student might interrupt conversations and make inappropriate remarks; he or she is often ostracized by peers because of an inability to control behaviors and emotions. Social alienation is, unfortunately, not limited to just a small number—the majority of all persons with ADHD experience problems in peer relations and social skills (DuPaul & Stoner, 2003; Hallahan & Kauffman, 2003). The effects of social rejection should be a major concern for educators: As Richard Lavoie (1994) so convincingly argues in the video *Last One Picked, First One Picked On*, the effects of social skills deficits can be far more devastating than academic problems.

Limited Sustained Attention. Distractibility and off-task behavior are characteristics that certainly have negative implications in the classroom. Because of lower rates of on-task behavior compared with classmates, students with ADHD complete less independent work (DuPaul & Stoner, 2003), which is one explanation for why they underachieve academically. Students with ADHD also often demonstrate difficulties with organizational and study skills (Flint,

2001), working memory (i.e., difficulty remembering to do things), using time effectively, using internal language or self-talk to monitor behavior and make decisions, emotional immaturity, and often, high levels of performance but low levels of accuracy (Smith et al., 2004).

Excessive Task-Irrelevant Activity. The student with ADHD is often very fidgety and restless, resulting in behaviors such as pencil tapping and other forms of excessive movement (Smith et al., 2004). Other characteristics may include a preference for less structured activities such as climbing rather than fine-motor tasks, a preference that often leads to much frustration given the strong emphasis on fine-motor skills in schools (Carbone, 2001).

Students with ADHD are indeed at risk for a number of significant difficulties. In addition to academic underachievement and social skills problems, we may also observe high rates of noncompliance and aggression (DuPaul & Stoner, 2003). Raymond (2000) listed the following characteristics as being often associated with ADHD (also see the box below):

- Low frustration tolerance
- Mood instability
- Poor self-esteem
- Temper outbursts
- Rejection by peers
- Excessive, insistent demands that requests be met
- Oppositional behavior
- Antagonism and aggression

Children who have comorbid ADHD and aggression (i.e., Oppositional Defiant Disorder or Conduct Disorder) may more often exhibit (compared with children with ADHD and no aggression) antisocial behaviors such as lying, stealing, and fighting (Barkley, 1998) and possibly substance abuse (DuPaul & Stoner, 2003; Hallahan & Kauffman, 2003). It is clear that effective early intervention is of utmost importance for these students.

Contrary to earlier beliefs that children outgrow ADHD, we now know that this is not invariably the case: "The effect of ADHD over time leads to increasing problems with learning, conduct, emotional development, and health" (Raymond, 2000, p. 129). Only about 20% to 35% of children with ADHD will not experience the problems and limitations of ADHD as adults (Smith et al., 2004). The adult with ADHD may exhibit problems with relationships, organization, or keeping a job (Raymond, 2000).

Characteristics of Preschoolers, Elementary School Age Children, and Adolescents With ADHD

It might be helpful to classroom teachers and parents to consider the effects of ADHD that have been determined to vary with age:

Preschoolers diagnosed with ADHD demonstrate excessive gross motor activity, often accompanied by aggressive acts, noncompliance, and destructive behavior. The latter can be ascribed to impulsiveness (Weyandt, 2001). *Elementary school age* students might possibly demonstrate less motor activity and more fidgeting and restlessness. Now students typically have difficulty with task completion and tolerance with frustration. We still notice the impulsive behaviors, disruptiveness in class, and noncompliant behaviors. Social difficulties are apparent during this age (Lerner, 2003). During *adolescence,* the excessive motor behavior is no longer a problem. The adolescent with ADHD has continued problems with academic work, self-control, low self-esteem, and peer relations. Aggression becomes a concern; in addition, there is a risk of developing depression, problems with substance abuse, and antisocial behaviors (Lerner, 2003). During adolescence, school performance often becomes more inconsistent.

POSSIBLE CAUSES OF ADHD

Brain Damage

Although several theories are offered, the exact cause of ADHD is not known. At the beginning of the 20th century, the cause of inattention and hyperactivity was attributed to brain damage. As in the case of learning disabilities, however, research has determined that ADHD may result from neurological dysfunction rather than from actual brain damage. With neuroimaging techniques such as MRIs (magnetic resonance imaging) and PET (positron emission tomography) scans in the latter part of the century, researchers were able to document the neurological basis of ADHD (Hallahan & Kauffman, 2003; Smith et al., 2004). Hallahan and Kauffman (2003) cite several studies that identified abnormalities in three areas of the brain in persons with ADHD—the frontal lobes, basal ganglia, and cerebellum.

Pre- and Postnatal Events

Barkley (1998) notes low birth weight, complications during pregnancy, and strep infection being associated with ADHD. Turnbull and others (2004) refer to teratogens (agents such as chemicals capable of causing developmental abnormalities) that could increase the likelihood that a child would develop ADHD. Some of these include (prenatal) maternal smoking and alcohol or drug abuse and poor maternal nutrition.

Hereditary Factors

Research does not support the belief that ADHD is caused by specific genetic mutations or chromosomal abnormalities; research does, however, support a hereditary basis for this disorder (Weyandt, 2001) evidenced by a higher prevalence rate in certain families (Smith et al., 2004). There is reportedly evidence that families with children with ADHD might have a higher incidence of psychological and psychiatric problems such as depression, anxiety, substance abuse, antisocial disorders, and ADHD—in short, certain families may be biologically more vulnerable and at greater risk for disorders such as ADHD (Weyandt, 2001).

Ecological Causes

Again, the exact cause of ADHD is not known. However, as in the case of learning disabilities and mild mental retardation, researchers have identified environmental factors that may contribute to the development of ADHD. For example, Salend and Rohena (2003) cite lead poisoning, allergy-producing substances, infection, and birth trauma as factors that may contribute to the manifestation of ADHD.

One study suggests that hyperactivity might be a response to an environment with insufficient stimulation (Raymond, 2000), and another study suggests that attention problems may be associated with early exposure to television (Christakis, Zimmerman, DiGiuseppe, & McCarty, 2004).

A lack of clear-cut causes and explanations has possibly fostered the myths and unfounded theories that attempt to explain the etiology of ADHD, such as sugar, fluorescent lighting, disinfectants, yeast, food coloring, preservatives, aspartame, sugar, and poor parenting (Barkley, 1998; Weyandt, 2001). Poor parenting and teaching have also been particularly singled out as factors that may result in ADHD. Research, however, has found that, whereas poor teaching and parenting styles may exacerbate disruptive classroom behaviors, they do not cause ADHD (Weyandt, 2001).

Interventions

The increase in prescriptions for ADHD medication—reportedly a 35% increase in a 5-year period (Smith, 2004)—is a source of concern for many. During the last decade, we have been exposed to widespread media coverage of the uses and abuses of medication—a phenomenon that has created much confusion, especially with parents who are unsure of the treatment they should pursue for their child. Experts in the field, however, are in agreement that the most effective treatment for ADHD is a combination of behavioral and pharmacological interventions (Barkley, 1998; Forness, Walker, & Kavale, 2003).

Medication

First-Tier Medication: Psychostimulants

Most experts on ADHD are in favor of the use of psychostimulants. Stimulant medications (e.g., Ritalin, Adderall, Dexedrine, Cylert, and Concerta) are usually the first medications considered (Forness et al., 2003). Whereas it may seem paradoxical to prescribe stimulants to a hyperactive child, stimulant medications actually stimulate the brain to allow the child to be more focused. It seems that psychostimulants are effective for more than 75% of individuals with ADHD (Lerner, 2003).

Second-Tier Medications: Nonstimulants

Some children do not respond to stimulant medications and may be treated with nonstimulants. In 2002, the Food and Drug Administration approved atomoxetine (Strattera), a new medication that is neither a stimulant nor an antidepressant. Atomoxetine is a prescription medication but is not a controlled substance like psychostimulants. The effects of this medication

Table 7.2 Medications

Drug Name	*Potential Side Effects*	*Duration of Action*
1. Psychostimulants		
Methylphenidate: Ritalin, Metadate, Focalin, Concerta	Loss of appetite, difficulty sleeping, irritability, rebound effect, motor tics when dosage is too high	Short acting: 34 hrs Long acting: 6–8 hrs 10–12 hrs
Mixed salts of a single-entity amphetamine product: Adderall, Adderall XR	Same as above	3.5–8 hrs
Dextroamphetamine: Dexedrine	Same	6–8 hrs
2. Nonstimulants		
Strattera (neither stimulant nor antidepressant)	Nervousness, sleep problems, fatigue, stomach upset, dizziness, and dry mouth	24-hr coverage from dosing 1 to 2 times a day
Antidepressants: imipramine (Tofranil)	As above; also, accelerated heart rate.	Often 24-hr effect

SOURCE: CHADD (2003) and Lerner (2003).

are reportedly not seen until the person has been taking it regularly for 3 to 4 weeks (CHADD, 2003). Other medications that may be prescribed if psychostimulants are not effective are antidepressants, such as Tofranil, Norpramin, or Wellbutrin (Forness et al., 2003; Lerner, 2003).

Side Effects

The most common side effects of medications for ADHD include loss of appetite, difficulty sleeping, motor tics (usually managed by lowering the dose), and headaches (CHADD, 2003). Snider et al. (2003) stress the need for teacher awareness of the risks of stimulant medication. Results of their study showed that most teachers were unaware of the possible side effects of stimulant medication and the potential for abuse. They also point out that there is a common misconception that ADHD can be confirmed if a child's behavior improves when taking stimulant medication and suggest that "this sense of validation may bolster their confidence and contribute to an escalating cycle of referrals of stimulant medication" (p. 52). Snider and colleagues further argue that the behavior and concentration of children *without* ADHD will improve if placed on stimulant medication as well. See Table 7.2 for information about some of the medications most often prescribed.

Behavioral Interventions

Behavioral interventions include providing structure—for example, establishing predictable routines and expectations at home and in school. When children meet these expectations, they are rewarded. It is also important to note that we should not expect perfect behavior or immediate improvement but rather for the child to accomplish small steps gradually

(Forness et al., 2003). Consistency is extremely important and should be stressed in parent and teacher education. Two short vignettes illustrate the importance of consistency and home-school collaboration.

Vignette 1: Ms. Harper, third-grade teacher

Sean came to our school as a third grader. I was unaware of his problems, but after 10 minutes in my classroom on the first day, I realized it was going to be an uphill battle to get Sean to sit still and learn. He was not taking any medication in spite of the severity of what I found out was ADHD. In addition to financial difficulties that made it difficult for this family to afford medication, Sean's mother also wanted him to have a fresh start at "the new school" without medication. Those were extremely difficult days for me. He could not sit still or follow classroom procedures. Even walking to the lunchroom proved to be a challenge. Sean could not stay in line; he actually couldn't walk! Running, skipping, walking backward—those were some behaviors I saw during the simple activity of going to lunch. In the classroom, he was so disruptive that I had to focus on him entirely. Sean was mean to the other kids and consequently alienated them. I hate to admit it, but I was in tears nearly every day. All my years of teaching experience did not prepare me for this student!

His mother finally decided to have Sean take medication, after 7 extremely difficult weeks for everyone—including Sean, of course. We decided to communicate with daily notes home and that his mother would reward Sean at home for a good daily report. I noticed a marked improvement almost immediately. Sean completed assignments and stayed on task; unfortunately, he was far behind academically by this time. He was also diagnosed with a learning disability during his third-grade year. Social skills were still a problem; Sean was no longer bothering the other kids, but he kept to himself. I wish I could say that the improvements continued; unfortunately, Mom was not consistent with medication or with rewards for good behavior.

This year he is in fourth grade, and his current teacher remarked yesterday that Sean's behavior is very immature. I have noticed that Sean is in the office often, and it seems as if everybody has given up on him. I cannot help but wonder what will happen to Sean in junior high and high school.

Vignette 2: Mr. Huston, sixth-grade teacher

Andy has come a long way. The first few days of the school year were rough, to say the least. This kid was all over the place and in trouble all the time. He was impulsive and said the most inappropriate things; he rarely completed assignments and did not take responsibility for anything. Andy was also extremely disorganized—I can go on and on about the problems but have to add that he was a likeable kid in spite of all the difficulties. His parents were involved in his education but simply did not know how to deal with his academic and social problems. They were not in favor of medication and said that they had read too many unfavorable things about medication.

The parents, the school counselor, and I met and agreed on a structured behavior management plan, and the parents suggested that it might be time for a trial period of medication; I think they realized that something drastic had to be done if this kid was to graduate successfully from high school one day. We all knew Andy had a lot of potential. The combination of medication and behavior management was successful. Andy became far more responsible and also interested in his work once he realized that study and organizational skills could help him be successful. He started playing basketball and is a member of the student council.

Andy still has some problems, but the improvement has been remarkable. He feels good about himself and has good friends. They are excited to go to junior high next year.

WHAT CAN TEACHERS DO?

Barkley (1998) points out that teachers' knowledge of and attitude about ADHD is critical for the success of children with ADHD in school. Barkley cited the work of Abramowitz and O'Leary (1991) in reminding teachers that ADHD is treatable but not curable and that although interventions can have a positive impact, children may continue to experience some difficulty in academic and social functioning. Moreover, it is important for teachers to remember that students with ADHD might be significantly behind in social skills and organization and may need more structure, more salient positive consequences, and more consistent negative consequences (Barkley, 1998) than nondiagnosed peers.

As mentioned at the beginning of this section, a highly structured learning environment, using effective teaching strategies such as direct instruction, is imperative for the student with ADHD (Smith, 2004). Carbone (2001) suggests arranging the classroom in a traditional row-seating pattern because it is more structured and predictable; when children are seated at tables with other classmates, they are too easily distracted.

Zentall, Moon, Hall, and Grskovic (2001) advise teachers to break down tasks into smaller segments, allow students to work in different settings (e.g., high table or on the carpet), and plan assignments with a varied response format. They emphasize the importance of ongoing feedback and reinforcement. Barkley (1994) underscores the necessity for and effectiveness of frequent and salient rewards. In Barkley's video, *ADHD in the Classroom,* we have an excellent demonstration of a behavior management plan in a classroom; the students receive feedback and rewards every 30 minutes.

Most parents and teachers who work with children with ADHD are fully aware of their difficulties with organization: They forget to do their assignments or leave them at home; they forget their locker combinations and lose their assignments; their desks and bedrooms might be extremely messy. In addition to difficulties with organization and untidiness of school materials, there are often the problems of time management and illegible handwriting (Austin, 2003; Carbone, 2001). For students with ADHD to be successful, organizational and learning strategies have to be taught, starting as early as possible.

Garrick Duhaney (2003) summarizes the most important considerations when working with students with ADHD as follows:

- Phrase rules concisely and in the students' language and post them in a prominent place for frequent review
- State rules in positive terms
- Follow the rules of firmness, fairness, and consistency
- Discuss consequences for breaking rules, rewards for appropriate behavior, and the reasons why classroom rules exist
- Administer, as promptly as possible, previously agreed upon punishments rewards; respond to misbehaving in a quiet, slow voice, refrain from becoming visibly irritated to avoid compromising the effect of the punishment
- Face students when talking to them, as facial expressions will teach students to use and understand proper body language
- Avoid being trapped into arguments as this is a no win situation (p. 273)

SUMMARY

ADHD is a controversial but certainly not a "trendy" problem. It is, however, a complex condition and possibly very challenging for teachers and parents. Students with ADHD often demonstrate social skills problems that exacerbate the academic difficulties they might encounter. You may find that they are among some of the brightest and most creative students that you will teach. Although the behaviors of students with ADHD can present problems in the traditional classroom setting, there are effective ways to facilitate the learning of these students. With appropriate intervention that includes several options including medical, educational, and psychological counseling (Hallahan & Kauffman, 2003), the student with ADHD can experience a high level of academic achievement and successfully transition into adulthood and education beyond the secondary level. The benefits of early intervention must be emphasized; however, most children will need effective long-term planning to be successful and find fulfillment as adults. The things that you do as the classroom teacher can make all the difference in facilitating the accomplishments of these—and all—your students.

DISCUSSION QUESTIONS

1. Discuss the importance of collaboration between home and school when planning successful interventions for the student with ADHD. How does this pertain to Sean and Andy in the vignettes? What should have been done differently in Sean's case?

2. Identify at least five strategies that teachers can implement to help their young students with ADHD be successful in the classroom. Would these strategies be effective for adolescents with ADHD?

3. Discuss the controversy surrounding medication use in the treatment of ADHD.

4. What role does the environment play in ADHD? Consider diversity and cultures, media, societal expectations, and technology in your discussion.

FOR ADDITIONAL HELP

	Organization	*Web Address*	*Description*
Attention Deficit Hyperactivity Disorder	Children and Adults With Attention Deficit/Hyperactivity Disorder (CHADD)	www.chadd.org	CHADD is the nation's biggest nonprofit agency for people with ADHD.
	Big's Place	www.bigsplace.com	Big's Place is an award-winning Web site containing information on ADD and other mental health issues.

REFERENCES

American Psychiatric Association. (2000). *Diagnostic and statistical manual of mental disorders* (4th ed., text revision). Washington, DC: Author.

Austin, V. L. (2003). Pharmacological interventions for students with ADD. *Intervention in School and Clinic, 38*(5), 289–296.

Barkley, R. A. (1994). *ADHD in the classroom* [Video]. New York: Guilford.

Barkley, R. A. (1998). *Attention deficit hyperactivity disorder: A handbook for diagnosis and treatment.* New York: Guilford Press.

Carbone, E. (2001). Arranging the classroom with an eye (and ear) to students with ADHD. *Teaching Exceptional Children, 34*(2), 72–81.

Children and Adults With Attention-Deficit/Hyperactivity Disorder. (2003). *CHADD Fact Sheet #3: Evidence-based medication management for children and adults with AD/HD.* Retrieved October 31, 2005, from www.chadd.org/fs/fs3.pdf

Christakis, D. A., Zimmerman, F. J., DiGiuseppe, D. L., & McCarty, C. (2004). Early television exposure and subsequent attentional problems in children. *Pediatrics, 113*(4), 708–713. Retrieved November 4, 2005, from http://pediatrics.aappublications.org/cgi/content/full/113/4/708?ijkey=52d829973ad856722f5eabdacffa55b6b97e8fbe

Dowdy, C. A., Patton, J. R., Smith, T. E. C., & Polloway, E. A. (1998). *Attention-deficit/hyperactivity disorder in the classroom.* Austin, TX: PRO-ED.

DuPaul, G. J., & Stoner, G. (2003). *ADHD in the schools: Assessment and intervention strategies.* New York: Guilford Press.

Flint, L. J. (2001). Challenges of identifying and serving gifted children with ADHD. *Teaching Exceptional Children, 33*(4), 62–69.

Forness, S. R., & Kavale, K. A. (2002). Impact of ADHD on school systems. In P. S. Jensen & J. R. Cooper (Eds.), *Attention deficit-hyperactivity disorder: State of the science best practices* (pp. 1–20, 24). Kingston, NJ: Civic Research Institute.

Forness, S. R., Walker, H. M., & Kavale, K. A. (2003). Psychiatric disorders and treatments: A primer for teachers. *Teaching Exceptional Children, 36*(2), 42–49.

Garrick Duhaney, L. M. (2003). A practical approach to managing the behaviors of students with ADD. *Intervention in School and Clinic, 38*(5), 267–279.

Hallahan, D. P., & Kauffman, J. M. (2003). *Exceptional learners.* Boston: Allyn & Bacon.

Henley, M., Ramsey, R. S., & Algozzine, R. F. (2002). *Characteristics of and strategies for teaching students with mild disabilities.* Boston: Allyn & Bacon.

Lavoie, R. D. (1994). *Learning disabilities and social skills: A teacher's guide* Last One Picked . . . First One Picked On. Alexandria, VA: PBS Video.

Lerner, J. W. (2003). *Learning disabilities: Theories, diagnosis, and teaching strategies.* Boston: Houghton Mifflin.

Loechler, K. (1999). Frequently asked questions about ADHD and the answers from the Internet. *Teaching Exceptional Children, 31*(6), 28–31.

Raymond, E. B. (2000). *Learners with mild disabilities: A characteristics approach.* Needham Heights, MA: Allyn & Bacon.

Salend, S. J., & Rohena, E. (2003). Students with attention deficit disorders: An overview. *Intervention in School and Clinic, 38*(5), 259–266.

Smith, D. D. (2004). *Introduction to special education: Teaching in an age of opportunity.* Boston: Pearson Education.

Smith, T. E. C., Polloway, E. A., Patton, J. R., & Dowdy, C. A. (2004). *Teaching students with special needs in inclusive settings.* Boston: Pearson Education.

Snider, V. E., Busch, T., & Arrowood, L. (2003). Teacher knowledge of stimulant medication and ADHD. *Remedial and Special Education, 24*(1), 46–56.

Turnbull, R., Turnbull, A., Shank, M., & Smith, S. J. (2004). *Exceptional lives: Special education in today's schools.* Upper Saddle River, NJ: Pearson Education.

U.S. Department of Education. (1999, March 12). Final regulations for the 1997 Individuals with Disabilities Education Act. *Federal Register.*

Wells, K. C. (2004). Treatment of ADHD in children and adolescents. In P. M. Barrett & T. H. Ollendick (Eds.), *Handbook of interventions that work with children and adolescents: Prevention and treatment* (pp. 343–368). Chichester, UK: John Wiley.

Weyandt, L. L. (2001). *An ADHD primer.* Needham Heights, MA: Allyn & Bacon.

Zentall, S. S., Moon, S. M., Hall, A. M., & Grskovic, J. A. (2001). Learning and motivational characteristics of boys with ADHD and/or giftedness. *Exceptional Children, 67*(4), 499–519.

Chapter 8

Oppositional Defiant Disorder

Julie Sarno Owens

Lauren Richerson

PREREADING QUESTIONS

As you read this chapter, reflect on the following questions and issues:

1. What factors should you consider when attempting to work collaboratively with the parents of a child with oppositional behavior?
2. What can educators do to avoid power struggles with children with oppositional behavior?
3. Have you ever watched a parent or teacher get into a power struggle with a strong-willed child? Describe what happened.
4. Self-assessment: Imagine a student who demonstrates oppositional behavior in the classroom. How might you engage in positive interactions with this child? What behavior strategies could you use to enhance the student-teacher relationship?

Nearly two thirds of children with an emotional and behavioral disorder spend approximately 60% of their school day in a regular education classroom (Ohio Department of Mental Health & Ohio Department of Education, 2003). Teachers must be prepared to address the academic and behavioral needs of these children. Many children with emotional and behavioral disorders exhibit noncompliant, defiant, and oppositional behaviors that are frequent and deviant enough from the norm to warrant special attention and intervention from educators and mental health professionals. In many cases, implementing effective, evidence-based intervention strategies prior to a referral for an evaluation for special education services can adequately meet the educational needs of these children and will reduce their disruptive classroom behaviors.

The goal of this chapter is to provide information that will allow educators to identify, understand, and address the behaviors of children with **Oppositional Defiant Disorder** (ODD). With the knowledge and strategies provided in this chapter, we hope that you will have the tools necessary to address the needs of children with ODD, such that the education of *all* other children in your classroom is ensured and such that unnecessary referrals for special education evaluations are minimized. In the pages that follow, we describe the characteristic behaviors of ODD, how ODD is distinct from other childhood mental health problems, and the cycle of coercive adult-child interactions that contribute to the maintenance of oppositional and defiant behavior. Then, we provide 10 evidence-based intervention strategies to prevent or ameliorate this type of interaction. We also offer a case vignette to illustrate the use of these strategies.

WHAT IS OPPOSITIONAL DEFIANT DISORDER (ODD)?

ODD has been defined as a "recurrent pattern of negativistic, defiant, disobedient, and hostile behavior toward authority figures" (American Psychiatric Association, 2000, p. 100). The most recent edition of the *Diagnostic and Statistical Manual of Mental Disorders* (*DSM-IV-TR*; American Psychiatric Association, 2000) states that to meet the criteria for a diagnosis of ODD, this pattern of behavior must have been present for at least 6 months, during which four (or more) of the following symptoms must be present:

1. Often loses temper
2. Often argues with adults
3. Often actively defies or refuses to comply with adults' requests or rules
4. Often deliberately annoys people
5. Often blames others for his or her mistakes or misbehavior
6. Is often touchy or easily annoyed by others
7. Is often angry or resentful
8. Is often spiteful or vindictive

For any of the above-described symptoms to be considered "present," the symptom must be exhibited at a frequency and severity level that is developmentally inappropriate for the child's mental and chronological age. Furthermore, a diagnosis of ODD requires that the symptoms cause significant impairment in at least one of three domains (i.e., social interactions, academic functioning, or occupational functioning) and that the symptoms cannot be better explained by another disorder (e.g., Bipolar Disorder, Conduct Disorder). Impairment in functioning refers to how the child's symptoms interfere with academic performance, daily functioning (e.g., routines), self-esteem, and healthy relationships with educators, peers, siblings, and parents. Thus, although the above-described behaviors may be observed in many children from time to time, a diagnosis of ODD should be made only if the oppositional and defiant behaviors are persistent and severe enough to interfere with academic, social, or emotional development or some combination of these.

Estimates of the prevalence of ODD suggest that as many as 16% of children may meet criteria for the disorder (*DSM-IV-TR*, 2000; Loeber, Burke, Lahey, Winters, & Zera, 2000). Thus, in a given classroom of 25 children, it is likely that you will have 1 to 4 children who demonstrate this type of behavior. During elementary school, boys are more likely than girls to meet criteria for ODD (Loeber et al., 2000). However, during adolescence, the rates of ODD in boys and girls appear to be equal (*DSM-IV-TR,* 2000; Loeber et al., 2000).

WHAT DOES ODD LOOK LIKE IN THE CLASSROOM?

In the classroom, the oppositional and defiant child is likely to argue frequently with teachers, peers, and aides. For example, in response to an instruction, the oppositional child may remark, "I don't have to," "No," or "You can't make me." The child may assert an elaborate rationale to explain why he or she should not be required to follow the instruction. When an educator exercises authority over a child with ODD, the child may respond by muttering under his or her breath, yelling, threatening, or calling the educator names to provoke a response. If, in response to the verbal attacks of a child with ODD, an educator engages the child in an argument or lecture, the educator is likely to learn that the child strongly desires to speak the last word in any verbal confrontation. Furthermore, it may seem as if the child is enjoying the experience of intentionally frustrating the educator and causing emotional arousal. It is quite normal for educators to feel angered and disrespected by this behavior.

Children with ODD are typically identified as such because of their strained relationships with authority figures; however, these children tend to have difficulties in their interactions with peers as well. For instance, the child with ODD is likely to engage in behaviors that provoke other students such as teasing, mocking, excluding others, or offering condescending glances. Furthermore, the child with ODD often misperceives the behavior of other children as provoking and, consequently, is highly reactive to these perceived offenses. Finally, when educators observe or are informed of the child's misbehavior, the child typically is quick to place the blame on others. Clearly, these behaviors detract attention from both the education of the student with ODD and other students in the classroom.

UNDERSTANDING THE FAMILIES OF CHILDREN WITH ODD

Studies indicate that the parents of children with ODD are more likely to report a history of mental health problems, family violence (i.e., hitting or throwing things at their spouses), and a previous conviction for a criminal offense than are parents of children with no diagnosis (Frick et al., 1992; Rowe, Maughan, Pickles, Costello, & Angold, 2002; Schachar & Wachsmuth, 1990). With regard to family functioning, children with ODD are nearly 3 times more likely than other children to experience at least one of the following conditions: (a) be a teenage parent, (b) have four or more siblings in the home, (c) live in a single-parent household or a blended family, and (d) experience frequent moves and exposure to foster care (Rowe et al., 2002). Furthermore, there is some evidence that parents of children with ODD are more likely than parents of nondiagnosed children to use overly harsh discipline strategies, provide inadequate supervision, and blame their child for family problems (Rowe et al., 2002).

It is noteworthy that the research does not clearly indicate whether the presence of these factors leads to ODD, if the presence of ODD leads to these factors, if the cause is bidirectional, or if additional factors lead to both ODD and the associated factors. However, it is widely acknowledged that there is no single factor to which the development of ODD can be attributed (Burke, Loeber, & Birmaher, 2002). Instead, there appear to be multiple causal factors that vary across individuals.

Given the above-described family characteristics, it is clear that children with ODD experience significant stress in the home environment that they subsequently bring into your classroom and into their interactions with you. That is not to say that the child's parents are to blame for his or her misbehavior. Indeed, Gerald Patterson (1976; cited in Carlson, Tamm, & Hogan, 1999), a leader in the field of children's mental health, has suggested that the child with disruptive behavior problems is typically both "the victim and architect" of negative adult-child interactions.

Educators are encouraged to consider two factors when collaborating with the parents of children with ODD. First, educators are encouraged to solicit input from the child's parents before making recommendations or offering suggestions. In some cases, parents will have found successful solutions or responses to the child's challenging behavior. Educators may be able to apply such strategies in the classroom. In addition, when parents feel that their child's teacher is willing to listen to their ideas, they may be more willing to work collaboratively. For example, it is not uncommon for a parent to feel defensive or offended when educators offer suggestions for managing his or her child's behavior. That is not to say that the educator's recommendations are not appropriate, but educators are encouraged to consider the timing of the recommendations offered to parents.

Second, educators should keep in mind that working with the parents of children with ODD may present its own challenges because the parents may be struggling with their own mental health issues, as well as the stress created by their child's behavior problems. As an adult who has interacted with a child with ODD, you can understand how frustrating and stressful this experience can be. Imagine how much more stressful it might be to live with a child with ODD. If educators can recognize and empathize with the parents' distress, parents may be more willing to work collaboratively with educators toward the improvement of the child's behavior. In addition, if parents and educators can refrain from directly or indirectly blaming each other for the child's behavior, together they can become an influential and effective intervention team with a common goal of breaking the cycle of negative adult-child interactions.

In summary, the child with ODD presents many challenges for educators. However, it is important not to lose hope for the possibility of change in this child or in your relationship with this child. Indeed, if the child with ODD does not receive early intervention, he or she is at risk for additional mental health problems in adolescence and adulthood (Burke, Loeber,

& Lahey, 2003). For example, research has shown that ODD is often a precursor to Conduct Disorder (Burke et al., 2002; Cohen & Flory, 1998; Rowe et al., 2002), which, as described below, is characterized by severely delinquent behaviors such as aggression, truancy, deceit, and theft. Thus, it is very important for educators to use evidence-based classroom interventions and to work collaboratively with parents and mental health professionals to address the needs of the child with ODD and the environment in which he or she lives.

HOW IS ODD DIFFERENT FROM OTHER CHILDHOOD MENTAL HEALTH PROBLEMS?

ODD and Attention Deficit Hyperactivity Disorder (ADHD)

It is fairly common for children with ODD to also meet criteria for Attention Deficit Hyperactivity Disorder (ADHD). For example, studies suggest that 9% to 37% of children with ODD also meet criteria for ADHD (Angold & Costello, 1996; Carlson, Tamm, & Gaub, 1997; Simonoff et al., 1997). However, despite the overlap between ODD and ADHD, educators are encouraged not to assume that children with ODD will always have ADHD.

Many studies indicate that educators tend to be fairly accurate raters of the presence and severity of symptoms of inattention, hyperactivity/impulsivity, and oppositionality and defiance. For example, in one study (Stevens, Quittner, & Abikoff, 1998), 100 teachers watched two videotapes and rated behaviors of the child depicted in the videotape. One video depicted a child demonstrating appropriate behavior. The second video depicted either a child demonstrating inattentive and hyperactive/impulsive behaviors (ADHD symptoms) or a child demonstrating oppositional and defiant behaviors (ODD symptoms). In general, the teachers rated the ADHD child as demonstrating high levels of inattention and hyperactivity/impulsivity and rated the child with ODD as demonstrating high levels of oppositional behaviors.

However, a closer look at the data (Stevens et al., 1998) indicated that when ODD behaviors were present, teachers also made higher ratings of inattention and hyperactivity/impulsivity (despite the fact that the child did not demonstrate these behaviors). This suggests that teachers may mistakenly perceive that ADHD symptoms are present when a child is demonstrating only ODD symptoms. Because it is very common and helpful for teachers to complete rating scales used in determining whether or not a child meets the criteria for a diagnosis (e.g., Carlson et al., 1997), it is important to be aware of the subtle differences associated with these two disorders.

The reason it is critical for educators to understand and recognize the difference between ODD and ADHD is that the mental health treatments for ODD and ADHD are very different. Although there is substantial support for the effectiveness of medication (e.g., Ritalin, Adderall, Concerta) in the treatment of ADHD, there is virtually no evidence to suggest that medication is an effective treatment for children with ODD (Society of Clinical Child and Adolescent Psychology, 2003). Indeed, the only treatment that has received sufficient empirical support to meet the criteria for a "well-established," evidence-based treatment for children with ODD is behavioral intervention that includes strategies such as praise, giving effective instructions, time-out procedures, active ignoring skills, and contingency management strategies (Brestan & Eyberg, 1998; Society of Clinical Child and Adolescent Psychology, 2003; Webster-Stratton, 1996). Thus, educators should not be surprised to learn that a child with oppositional and defiant behaviors is not taking medications. Although behavioral interventions implemented in the home and school settings are considered well-established evidence-based treatments for ADHD and ODD, medication is considered to have this status only in the treatment of ADHD.

ODD and Conduct Disorder

To meet criteria for Conduct Disorder (CD) under the definitions provided in the *DSM-IV-TR* (2000), a child must demonstrate a persistent pattern of behavior in which the basic rights of others or societal norms or rules are violated. Behaviors that fall within this domain include aggression toward people and animals, intentional destruction of others' property, setting fires, stealing, lying, and truancy. Both ODD and CD fall within the category of disruptive behavior disorders; however, the disruptive behaviors of children with ODD are typically thought of as less severe than those of CD children. That is, children with ODD typically do not demonstrate aggression toward peers, adults, or animals and typically do not engage in stealing or intentional destruction of property. ODD is characterized by verbal defiance, whereas CD is characterized by physical assault on a person or on one's property. However, in many cases, children demonstrate behaviors that are characteristic of both ODD and CD. For example, approximately 25% to 57% of children who meet the criteria for ODD also meet the criteria for CD (Biederman et al., 1996; Rowe et al., 2002). Although the idea is controversial (Schachar & Wachsmuth, 1990), many believe that ODD represents a less severe form of CD (Rey et al., 1988), suggesting that many children with ODD progress down a developmental pathway that starts with ODD and transitions to CD. It is, therefore, important to provide evidence-based behavioral treatment as early as possible to shift children with ODD onto a more developmentally and behaviorally appropriate trajectory.

COERCION THEORY

Gerald Patterson and his colleagues have spent decades researching the mechanisms by which children develop antisocial and delinquent behaviors. Patterson's model (Patterson, Reid, & Dishion, 1992) is termed the *coercion model* because it is based on the finding that **coercive exchanges** (i.e., those that attempt to dominate others by force such as through threatening, yelling, aggression, etc.) between children and their parents maintain and even exacerbate children's development of disruptive and antisocial behaviors. This pattern of interaction might be commonly referred to in some settings as power struggles. For example, a child may have a particularly difficult temperament or personality that may not match well with that of his or her parents. This mismatch might result in hostile, aggressive, and/or coercive parent-child interactions. As coercive exchanges continue, this style of interaction becomes a habit for both the parent and the child and may occur so often that the parent and child know no other way of interacting. Furthermore, as the child develops a coercive style of interaction with his or her parents, this style of interaction can also generalize to relationships in other settings, such as the student-teacher relationship in the classroom. Therefore, it is not uncommon for educators to unintentionally engage in coercive interactions as a result of the negative emotions that their students with ODD elicit from them. Unfortunately, these exchanges maintain the coercive interaction pattern and lead to continued conflict between the child and educator.

Although parents and educators may play a role in coercive exchanges, neither parents nor educators are fully responsible for them. In the next few paragraphs, we discuss how to

Table 8.1 Principles of Behavioral Theory

	Positive	*Negative*
Provide	Positive reinforcement (increases behavior)	Punishment (decreases behavior)
Remove	Punishment (response-cost) (decreases behavior)	Negative reinforcement (increases behavior)

recognize the coercive pattern and how to avoid coercive traps. This knowledge often empowers educators to more effectively monitor their responses to oppositional and defiant behaviors, recognize the signs of coercive exchanges, and break the negative cycle of coercive traps as they arise.

First, let us briefly review some basic principles of behavioral theory. In general, when a behavior is *reinforced* (through either positive or negative reinforcement), the behavior is likely to increase in the future. When a behavior is *punished* (either by providing something negative or by removing something positive), the behavior is likely to decrease in the future. As shown in Table 8.1, positive reinforcement occurs when you provide something positive following a given behavior (upper left). Providing rewards that are contingent on a specific behavior *increases* the likelihood that the behavior will occur again. For example, providing children with 15 minutes of computer time in response to their completion of their class work increases the likelihood that they will complete class work in the future. Punishment occurs when you provide something negative following a given behavior (upper right). Providing punishment that is contingent on a specific behavior *decreases* the likelihood that the behavior will occur again. For example, requiring that the child write 50 sentences following an aggressive act, in theory, decreases the likelihood that aggression will occur in the future.

Another form of punishment is known as response-cost (lower left). Response-cost occurs when you remove something positive following a given behavior. Removing something positive *decreases* the likelihood that the behavior will occur again. For example, removing the child's recess privilege following his or her use of disrespectful language decreases the likelihood that the child will be disrespectful again. Time-out is an additional example of response-cost. The child is removed from an activity following inappropriate behavior, which decreases the likelihood of inappropriate behavior in the future.

A more challenging concept to understand is negative reinforcement. Negative reinforcement (lower right) increases the likelihood of a behavior's occurrence, but it does so through the removal of something negative following a given behavior. Removing something negative contingent on a specific behavior actually *increases* the likelihood of that behavior occurring in the future. Negative reinforcement can be used effectively in the classroom to increase children's desirable behaviors. For example, a teacher may remove children's homework over the weekend in response to their completion of homework throughout the week. In this case, removing a negative event (weekend homework) following the completion of weekday homework increases the likelihood that students will complete their weekday homework in the future.

However, negative reinforcement also may occur in such a way that undesired behaviors displayed by the child or adult are accidentally reinforced. This type of negative reinforcement occurs frequently in the context of coercive exchanges. For example, sending a student to the office because he or she is making obnoxious noises instead of doing his or her work can increase the likelihood that the student will make obnoxious noises to avoid work in the future. In this situation, class work is a negative experience for the student, and this negative experience is removed (by sending the student to the office) when he or she makes loud, obnoxious noises. Thus, if going to the office is not a negative consequence for this student, removal from the classroom actually increases the likelihood that the student will make loud noises again.

To illustrate a coercive exchange as described in Patterson and colleagues' (1992) coercive model, let us consider an example of a typical interaction between a parent and a young child with disruptive behavior problems. Imagine that while at the grocery store, the child asks the parent to buy him or her candy. The parent refuses, but the explanation does not appease the child. The child, thus, restates his or her request in a louder, high-pitched voice. The parent refuses again, and the child begins to cry and whine excessively. The parent, wanting to avoid embarrassment and further escalation of the child's annoying behavior, gives in and buys the child the candy. When the parent gives the child the candy, the whining and crying (negative event) stops (is removed). Thus, the parent's behavior (giving in to the child) is negatively reinforced, increasing the likelihood that the parent will engage in this behavior in the future to remove the negative event (i.e., whining and crying). In the immediate situation, this may be effective for the parent because it quiets the child and reduces embarrassment. However, without intending to, the parent also positively reinforces the child's negative and coercive behavior (i.e., whining and crying) by providing candy. Thus, in the long term, the coercive child behavior (whining and crying) will actually increase because the parent has provided something positive following the behavior.

Now imagine that the same parent and child are at home, and the parent asks the child to stop playing and pick up his or her toys. The child, engaged in play activity, does not respond. The parent repeats the request, and the child responds, "In a minute!" The parent gets frustrated and threatens to punish the child (e.g., with a spanking), who then complies with the instruction. Thus, the parent's coercive behavior (i.e., harsh and angry threats) is positively reinforced (the child complied). Harsh parenting is likely to increase in the future. Furthermore, the child's noncompliant behavior may have been positively reinforced, in that he or she may have experienced a sense of control as a result of witnessing the parent's emotional reaction to his or her behavior. If this is the case, then the likelihood that the child will "test the limits" with the parent (i.e., comply with instructions just before the threat is carried out) in the future is increased.

In both cases, the child engaged the parent in a battle for control of the situation. In the first example, the parent acquiesced (i.e., was coerced by the child), whereas in the second example, the parent harshly asserted authority (i.e., used coercion to get what he or she wanted from the child). Although there were short-term benefits for the parent in both situations, the long-term costs are great (i.e., unintentional reinforcement of negative child behavior, continued harsh or lax parenting) because these types of interactions perpetuate coercive parent and child behavior and are likely to lead to deterioration of the child's behavior and the parent-child relationship.

In the case of the child who has ODD, the coercive behaviors used to obtain reinforcement are reflected in the diagnostic criteria for the disorder: arguing, blaming others, annoying others, becoming angry, and engaging in temper tantrums. The fact that these behaviors are typically directed toward adults indicates that these children have a history of battling with adults for control. Thus, it is extremely important for educators to refrain from engaging in coercive exchanges, because this would serve only to perpetuate the child's negative interactions with adults. Instead, educators are encouraged to recognize the child's use of coercion and respond in ways in which their authority is preserved without inadvertently reinforcing inappropriate behavior or giving the child the opportunity to escalate his or her coercive behavior. Although this is easier said than done, below we provide several evidence-based interventions for achieving this goal.

When interacting with children with ODD, the goal is to increase appropriate behaviors and decrease the inappropriate or disruptive behaviors. Thus, educators should primarily focus on the left-hand column in Table 1: positive reinforcement and effective discipline that employs response-cost principles. Typically, behavior problems such as those demonstrated by children with ODD are maintained over time because children are inadvertently reinforced for their display of disruptive behavior. The reinforcement may be positive (e.g., through the acquisition of attention, stimulation, assistance, a sense of control) or negative (e.g., through the avoidance of tasks, punishment, anxiety, embarrassment, undesired activities).

ADDRESSING ODD IN THE SCHOOL SETTING

Rationale

Although it is typically assumed that mental health problems are addressed in the offices and clinics of psychologists, social workers, and psychiatrists, public schools represent a setting in which therapeutic educators, often in collaboration with mental health professionals, can implement effective behavioral interventions. There are numerous reasons why schools are advantageous as an environment for addressing the emotional and behavioral problems of children with disruptive behaviors. First, research indicates that there is a critical link between children's mental health and their success in school such that children whose mental health problems are not addressed often fail in school (Ohio Department of Mental Health & Ohio Department of Education, 2003).

Second, schools provide educators and mental health professionals with a unique opportunity to identify and respond to behavioral problems early in their development. When problems are identified early, they can be addressed before they become severe. Furthermore, when educators collaborate with mental health professionals to implement school-based interventions to prevent and address behavioral problems, they are reaching children who may not otherwise receive mental health services (Flaherty, Weist, & Warner, 1996; Weist, Lowie, Flaherty, & Pruitt, 2001) or who may not receive them until their behavioral pattern is quite severe.

Third, research suggests that a student's perceived connection to school (Mulvey & Cauffman, 2001), as well as the presence of a charismatic adult outside the home (i.e., oftentimes an educator), are strong predictors of well-being in adolescence (Werner & Smith, 1982). Thus, the way that educators respond to a child who demonstrates challenging behavior plays a critical role in determining the trajectory of that child's behavior.

Finally, children with disruptive behavior problems often divert class attention from educational tasks. Thus, the educator who attempts to address the emotional and behavioral needs of the student with ODD performs a great service not only for the student but also for the class as a whole. More specifically, by removing the behavioral barriers to learning (i.e., oppositional and defiant behaviors), the student and the teacher can more effectively engage in the learning process, resulting in elevated student productivity, work accuracy, grades, and test scores.

AVOIDING COERCIVE EXCHANGES: WHAT CAN EDUCATORS DO?

When parents bring their child to a mental health clinic for treatment of disruptive behavior problems, they are often surprised to learn that instead of recommending individual therapy for their child, mental health professionals often recommend that the parents attend weekly sessions to learn to use behavior modification strategies to alter their children's behavior. Research suggests that working with the parents of inattentive and disruptive children is more effective than working with the child alone (e.g., Pelham, Wheeler, & Chronis, 1998). Indeed, evidence from over 100 studies indicates that behavioral parenting programs that teach parents skills such as praise, giving effective instructions, time-out procedures, and active ignoring improve child compliance (e.g., Pisterman et al., 1989; Pisterman et al., 1992), reduce disruptive behaviors (e.g., Anastopoulos, Shelton, DuPaul, & Guevremont, 1993; Firestone, Kelly, & Fike, 1980), and improve parent-child interactions (e.g., Pisterman et al., 1989; Wierson & Forehand, 1994).

Thus, it follows logically that teaching educators how to employ the same strategies would lead to improvements in child behavior in the school setting and would foster consistency and collaboration across home and school settings. Changing oppositional and defiant behaviors in children often requires change in adult discipline behaviors. Furthermore, maximal change can occur when both parents and teachers are receptive to new strategies and actively involved in implementing them. Thus, in what follows, the specific techniques most likely to be effective in reducing children's oppositional and defiant behavior in the classroom are highlighted. Many of the techniques discussed are those taught in most evidence-based parenting programs (Barkley, 1997; Cunningham, Bremner, & Secord, 1996; Forehand & McMahon, 1981; Patterson, 1976; Rayfield, Monaco, & Eyberg, 1999; Webster-Stratton, 1984, 1996).

Strategy 1: Don't Take It Personally

To avoid falling into coercive exchanges with children with ODD, it is critical that educators remember that the child with ODD, as a function of his or her temperament and previous experiences, routinely engages in coercive interactions with others. The oppositional and defiant behavior is not directly related to you, personally (although it may feel as if this is the case). Rather, this child has learned what behaviors produce anger and frustration in others and that producing this emotional reaction can lead to benefits for him or her. This pattern of behavior has been consistently, although unintentionally, reinforced and has become a habitual means of interacting with others. When you remember that the disrespectful behavior is not a direct personal attack but, rather, behavior that would likely be directed toward any authority figure, you will likely experience less negative emotion toward the child, and subsequently be more likely to engage in calm, effective discipline (see Strategies 2 through 8 below). It is recognized that this process can be very challenging, even for the experienced educator.

Research (Brophy, 1985) has demonstrated that when a teacher interprets the child's disrespectful behavior as a personal attack (i.e., teacher-owned problems) rather than as a behavioral management problem, the teacher's typical response is to use harsh punishment or criticize the child. In contrast, when a teacher views the child as having behavior problems that are out of his control (i.e., student-owned problems), the teacher's typical response to the child's disruptive behavior is to attempt to redirect the behavior and problem solve with the child. Thus, it is important for educators to keep in mind that despite the oppositional and disrespectful exteriors presented by children with ODD, their underlying behavioral disturbances (i.e., student-owned problems) and associated disruptive behaviors can be modified through consistent use of effective behavioral management techniques.

Strategy 2: Stay Calm

The behavior of children with ODD easily elicits anger and frustration from adults. It is important for educators to stay calm in response to children's oppositional behaviors. Again, this is easier said than done. However, research has demonstrated that when adults are stressed and emotionally aroused, they are less likely to use effective discipline strategies (Smith & O'Leary, 1995) and more likely to use harsh punishments (e.g., yelling, humiliation). This applies to educators and parents. Thus, calm is effective, whereas angry is ineffective and coercive, and perpetuates the very cycle you are trying to break.

In addition, there are other benefits of remaining emotionally neutral in response to children's disruptive behavior. For example, research has demonstrated that both the "mood of the discipline situation" and the quality of the relationship between a child and his or her disciplinarian affect the degree of child compliance (Bergin & Bergin, 1999, p. 196). Although it is not likely that the ODD child's mood will be positive during a discipline situation, if the child's disciplinarian responds, in turn, with hostility, the negative behaviors exhibited by the child are likely to escalate, and compliance will not be achieved. In contrast, if the disciplinarian remains calm, not only is he or she more likely to achieve compliance but that person also models self-control for the child and the rest of the class (Bergin & Bergin, 1999).

Managing the stress of educating a child with ODD can be difficult. Thus, it is important for educators to monitor their own stress levels and make use of their social support networks. Educators can seek out assistance from aides and other support staff when they notice that their interactions with certain children are becoming coercive so that they get a break and return to a calmer state. Finally, educators are encouraged to start each day with a "clean slate," which is beneficial for both the educator and the child. Rarely are there benefits to transitioning yesterday's arguments into today's interactions. Indeed, in doing so, adults are more likely to maintain the negative cycle they are trying to break.

Strategy 3: Find a Way to Praise

One of the most basic, yet effective tools for use with all children is positive reinforcement or praise. Providing positive attention in response to children's positive behaviors increases the likelihood that they will display these behaviors in the future. It is not uncommon for a frustrated educator to state that the child rarely engages in positive or appropriate behavior. Indeed, Barkley (1997) indicates that adults have to "catch them being good," suggesting that with disruptive children, adults need to be vigilant and seize opportunities, no matter how brief, to praise the children (p. 226).

To illustrate the importance of positive attention, Barkley (1997) suggests that you imagine the worst and the best supervisors or bosses that you have ever had. Think about their different characteristics, as well as the differences in how they responded to you. For many individuals, this exercise leads to the conclusion that the best supervisor was a person who recognized and praised their positive achievements and efforts, whereas the worst supervisor focused more heavily on mistakes. Also, many find that their level of motivation to be productive was higher when working for the best supervisor compared with the worst supervisor. Thus, when adults recognize children's positive achievements and behaviors, children are motivated by this attention to repeat the praised behavior.

Strategy 4: Positive Interactions Must Outweigh Negative Interactions

Monitoring the ratio of positive to negative attention that you give a child is critical. As a rule of thumb, educators are encouraged to provide two positive or praise statements to the child for every reprimand or negative statement (2-to-1 ratio of positive statements to negative statements) that they make toward the child. You are encouraged to imagine your most disruptive student. Think about how many times in a given day you redirected, reprimanded, and spoke negatively to this student. Now, think of how many positive statements you would have to give that student to outweigh the negative or to achieve the 2-to-1 ratio. Educators may wonder how they could possibly achieve this with such a disruptive student.

There are many opportunities for children to earn positive attention in the classroom, although some children take more advantage of these opportunities than others. To achieve the 2-to-1 ratio, it may be necessary to reinforce the most basic acts of compliance. Indeed, any time a child follows your direction (e.g., puts away his book, begins to work, lines up), praise him. This reinforcement can come in a variety of forms: verbal statements (e.g., "thank you," "I appreciate that you did what I told you to," "good job following directions"), physical gestures (e.g., a thumbs-up signal, a high-five, a pat on the back, a smile), privileges (e.g., line leader, office runner, time on the computer at the end of class), or tokens (e.g., stickers, tickets) that eventually can be traded in for a prize or privilege. However, educators are encouraged to refrain from making praise statements that are backhanded comments (e.g., I'm glad to see you *finally* turned in your homework). Praise that is genuine and enthusiastic is most effective.

When educators effectively use *at least* a 2-to-1 ratio, the adult-student relationship is characterized by more positive interactions than negative interactions. The child with ODD may have few other adults with whom this is true. Thus, the child may be less drawn to engage in coercive interactions with this adult. When an educator provides opportunities for the child to break the coercive cycle, the educator becomes a trusted and influential adult in the life of this child. Therefore, effective and consistent use of positive attention that begins early in the school year is likely to keep the negative behaviors (e.g., attention-seeking, noncompliance) of the child with ODD to a minimum.

Strategy 5: Active Ignoring

Despite an educator's best preventative efforts, it is likely that the child with ODD will display negative and disruptive behaviors in the classroom at some point. When this occurs, teachers are encouraged to withdraw all attention from (i.e., ignore) the child; the child with ODD may prefer negative attention (e.g., reprimands) from teachers to no attention at all. Indeed, in some cases, the child may not have much experience with positive attention and may therefore thrive on or seek out negative attention. In other words, negative attention often serves to reinforce negative behaviors. Active and planned ignoring of mildly disruptive or annoying behaviors (e.g., eye rolling, foot stomping) is effective in reducing their reoccurrence, although it is often difficult to do.

To send a clear message to children that they will not receive attention for their behavior, educators are encouraged to remove eye contact and turn their body posture away from the child. Also, if possible, educators should detract peers' attention away from the child, perhaps by directing the attention of the class to another student who is behaving appropriately. Furthermore, it is very important for educators to ignore the child until the negative behavior has ceased and then subsequently and immediately praise the child for the alternative behavior that occurs following the negative behavior. For example, if the child has left his or her seat without permission and has approached you for an inappropriate reason, you might calmly state, "I have not given you permission to be out of your seat. I will speak with you when you return to your seat," and then ignore all subsequent attempts by the student to engage the educator in discussion (e.g., the student may say "But you helped Jack, can't you help me?"). If you argue, lecture the child about being out of his or her seat, or threaten the child, you reinforce the child's defiant behavior and increase the likelihood that it will continue. Thus, it is imperative that you avoid engaging the child in an argument, because this may be perceived as a victory for a child with ODD.

Once the student makes a motion back toward his or her seat, the educator should immediately praise the student ("I like how you're going back to your seat. I'll be there to help you in a moment"). In this instance, the educator has ignored the inappropriate behavior and has praised the appropriate behavior rather than inadvertently reinforcing the negative behavior by arguing or threatening. Indeed, the educator has "caught the student being good."

Another important time to use active ignoring is when a child is *behaviorally* doing what he was told, yet is *verbally* refusing. For example, an educator may tell a fourth-grade student to put away the art supplies because it is time for math. The fourth grader then begins to put the markers in the box; however, at the same time he states, "I don't want to, I hate math." If the educator responds to this offer to engage in a coercive dialogue (argument), the educator will likely interfere with completion of the task and will inadvertently reinforce (by providing adult attention) verbal complaints. In contrast, if the educator ignores the verbal complaint but praises the physical behavior ("Good job putting the markers away"), the educator will seize the opportunity to reinforce positive behavior and will provide the opportunity to break the cycle of coercive interactions. Furthermore, the child will continue to comply with the instruction, and both the child and the educator will move on to the next activity without a negative interaction. When educators successfully ignore the negative behaviors of the child with ODD, they are avoiding accidental reinforcement of the child's negative behavior. In addition, they are avoiding the coercive trap that the child has set for them.

Strategy 6: Time-Out in the Classroom

Although active ignoring is strongly recommended as a response to mildly disruptive behaviors, undoubtedly there will be times when children with ODD will display more severe behaviors that cannot be ignored. Consider this example of a coercive exchange in the classroom. The class is instructed to line up, and they begin to do so; however, a child with ODD continues to play with materials from the previous activity. The child is told again to get in line, and he irritably responds by saying, "I will in a minute!" The teacher then raises her voice, ordering the child to get in line. The child replies, "Okay, I am" but still refuses to stop playing with the materials. The teacher, now increasingly frustrated and irritated that the child is rendering the entire class late for lunch, yells at the child to get in line. The child throws his materials down and slowly saunters over to join the group while muttering under his breath. In this example, the teacher accidentally reinforces the child for his noncompliance by providing continued attention to him and his behaviors. Furthermore, the teacher is negatively reinforced for using coercion (yelling) to get what she wants because the child finally complied once she raised her voice. Thus, this coercive interaction is likely to be repeated until the teacher recognizes the ineffectiveness of her responses and ends the battle for control. In these instances, a strategy other than ignoring is warranted.

In these cases, the traditional consequence of time-out is recommended. Time-out is short for "time-out from positive reinforcement" (Pelham, 1996, p. 126). As such, time-out is similar to ignoring; however, time-out is a punishment of boredom, is more aversive to the child, and is thus an appropriate consequence for more severe behaviors. It is recommended that behaviors such as physical aggression, destruction of property, and repeated noncompliance (i.e., not following directions after being told twice) result in an immediate time-out (Pelham).

When using time-out in the classroom, educators may find it useful to use a stoplight analogy. When an educator gives an instruction, the child is on green-light status ("all systems go"). If the child complies with the instruction, he or she remains on green-light status. If the child does not comply with the educator's instruction, the child moves to the yellow-light status (caution). The educator should provide a neutral warning (e.g., "If you do not do what I told you, you will earn a time-out") and should restate the original instruction. If the child then complies, he or she returns to green-light status, and the educator should praise the child for making a good choice. If the child fails to comply following this second instruction (repeated noncompliance), the child moves to red-light status (stop) and earns a time-out.

When instructing a child to go to the time-out location (e.g., chair, carpet square), it is important to use a neutral tone of voice so that the child is not reinforced for his or her behavior as described above. There should be an established length (e.g., 5–10 minutes) and location for the time-out. In terms of the location, it is often helpful to keep the child in the classroom so that learning is not interrupted but preferably in a location in which he or she cannot be easily observed by peers (e.g., perhaps to the side of the classroom and away from the door). This allows the educator to continue monitoring the child, who may continue to learn while also observing what he or she is missing (i.e., positive attention from the educator). Time-out will be particularly effective if the educator can maintain positive interactions with other students while the child is in time-out. Thus, the child will observe the positive attention that he or she is not receiving.

Rules for time-out should be posted at the designated time-out location. Common time-out rules include (a) no negative behaviors during time-out (e.g., whining, attracting peers' attention, playing inappropriately with materials) and (b) remain in the time-out area. Furthermore, it should be clear that any violation of the time-out rules will result in an extra 5 minutes of time-out. Following completion of the time-out, it is crucial for teachers to quickly engage the child in a positive interaction through praise so that "time-in" is more reinforcing than time-out. Otherwise, time-out may not be viewed as a punishment, and the child may revert to using oppositional and defiant behavior in an attempt to attract attention to himself or herself.

Strategy 7: Use Effective Instructions

The time-out sequence typically begins when an educator gives an instruction. Thus, we encourage educators to "set the child up for success" and "set yourself up for success" by using effective instructions. In a sense, an instruction is the foundation on which other discipline strategies (e.g., time-out) are built. To set the child up for success and thus reduce the need for time-out, it is important to make sure that your expectations of students are clear. First, before giving an instruction, it is necessary to have the attention of the child or group of children to whom you are speaking. If you do not have their attention, the likelihood that they follow your instruction the first time decreases dramatically. In fact, obtaining their attention is half the battle. Second, make your instructions as specific as possible and state them one at a time so that the child is not overwhelmed. Telling the child to "put the art supplies on the shelf" is more specific than telling him or her to "clean up." You can create success for both yourself and the child by being specific about what you want. Third, give the instruction using positive statements so the child knows *what to do* (e.g., "put your hands flat on your desk") rather than simply *what not to do* (e.g., "stop playing with the scissors"). Finally, give instructions in the form of a statement rather than a question. When you ask a child (rather than tell him or her) to do something, you are providing the opportunity for the child to say "no." By stating your instruction clearly the first time, you can immediately begin to implement the time-out sequence if the child does not comply (i.e., proceed to yellow-light status).

Strategy 8: Daily Report Card

When used in combination, the preceding seven strategies should effectively reduce the disruptive behaviors of many children in your classroom; however, as noted earlier, the behavioral patterns of children with ODD can be particularly resistant to change. Remember, these oppositional and defiant behaviors have worked for the child in the past and are also likely to be long-term, habitual behaviors. Thus, it may be necessary to implement a daily report card intervention for children with severe behavior problems so that they receive more intensive and individualized feedback about their behavior. The daily report card procedure is a behavioral contract between the teacher, the parents, and the child. It is an evidence-based intervention used to identify, monitor, and change individualized target behaviors; provide daily communication between home and school; and provide a positive context that motivates children to improve their behavior (O'Leary & Pelham, 1978; O'Leary, Pelham, Rosenbaum, & Price, 1976; Pelham, 1996).

First, target behaviors are identified and agreed on by the parents, teacher, and child. For example, the goals for one child may be to increase math productivity and decrease class disruptions. Second, parents, teachers, and the child must identify the behavioral criterion that the child must achieve to receive a reward (or avoid a consequence) for that target behavior each day (e.g., 70% completion of math work, five or fewer class disruptions during morning work stations). The criterion should initially be set at a level that will lead to success for the child at least 3 out of 5 days. Although this may result initially in a low behavioral expectation for the child, if the child experiences early success, he or she will be more motivated by the intervention.

Once the target behaviors and their criteria are established, the teacher provides the child with feedback about these behaviors on a daily basis. For example, the teacher may remind the child of the goal at the start of math class and tell the child whether or not he or she met the goal at the end of math class. The teacher will record this on the child's daily report card. Each time the child is disruptive during the morning, the teacher will acknowledge the disruption (stating in a neutral tone of voice, "That was your third disruption") and make a notation on the report card. At the end of the day, the child delivers the report card to the parents, who should implement a home-based privilege-and-consequence system contingent on the child's performance with regard to his target behaviors. When a home-based privilege system is not possible, school-based reward programs should be implemented. Regardless of the rewards used, educators can enhance the effectiveness of the daily report card intervention by asking children about their receipt of rewards on a daily basis, which serves to make the rewards salient in the child's mind.

Detailed descriptions for implementing the daily report card procedure are available online (http://summertreatmentprogram.com/ctadd/index.html). Included in the downloadable packet are instructions for establishing the report card, sample report card target behaviors, sample daily report cards, sample home and school rewards, tracking sheets, and troubleshooting guidelines. We now offer a brief case vignette to illustrate the use of some of the strategies described above.

Nick is a 7-year-old, first-grade, Caucasian male living in a rural community. He was initially brought to the attention of the school social worker at his school by his teacher, who reported that Nick was often argumentative and disrespectful when given instructions, was intentionally provocative toward peers, and had difficulty controlling his anger when upset. He often kicked walls or isolated himself when angry. An interview with Nick's mother revealed that he was frequently argumentative and defiant toward her as well and made comments indicating that he had low self-esteem (e.g., "I can't do this!" "I'm just stupid."). His mother further reported that Nick's behavior problems had been a concern since he was approximately 5 years old. School records revealed that, although Nick was reading at a first-grade level, he had yet to fully master many of the reading, math, and writing skills for his grade level.

Nick's developmental history revealed that he was a product of a teenage pregnancy. His mother reported that when she was 7 months pregnant with Nick, she was placed on bed rest due to medical complications. Nick was born 3 weeks early and weighed 6 pounds. His mother reported that he was a "good baby." He was walking by 13 months and was talking shortly thereafter. She further reported that Nick has not experienced any significant medical problems.

During the first several years of his life, Nick lived in the same neighborhood as several of his older cousins, and he spent most of his time with older boys who "played rough" with Nick from the time he was an infant, because they enjoyed wrestling for fun. Nick's father reportedly encouraged this. When Nick was 4 years old, his parents divorced. The family experienced many stressors during this time. For example, Nick's father experienced job loss related to clinical depression, which created financial stress for the family. Over the course of the next 2 years, Nick moved five times. Furthermore, Nick witnessed his mother being verbally abused by her boyfriends. In terms of her parenting practices, his mother stated that when Nick engaged in disrespectful behavior, she directed him to sit on the couch for a "time-out" (often in front of the TV). Other times, particularly when stressed, she reported responding to Nick's behavior by spanking him or sending him to bed. Many characteristics of Nick's early childhood and family functioning are consistent with stressors found in families of children with ODD.

Prior to establishing behavioral strategies to address Nick's educational and behavioral needs, the school social worker conducted an assessment of Nick's academic, emotional, and behavioral functioning. Information was gathered through an interview with Nick's mother, an interview with Nick's teacher, parent and teacher rating scales, and a behavioral observation of Nick in the classroom. Data from these sources provided evidence that Nick met criteria for ODD. Observations of Nick's behavior in the classroom strongly suggested that he had learned he could get what he wanted (e.g., attention from the teacher or class, avoidance of assignments that were difficult for him) through coercion and was adept at eliciting coercive behaviors (e.g., yelling) from his teacher. Nick's disrespectful behavior did not diminish as a result of his teacher's coercive behavior; it appeared that he was reinforced by it. Thus, Nick's teacher unintentionally often fell victim to his coercive traps.

Following the assessment, the school social worker and the teacher met to collaboratively discuss the results of the assessment and to identify strategies to address Nick's needs. Once the teacher better understood the nature of Nick's behavioral problems (e.g., ODD as a student-owned problem), she became more willing to change the way she interacted with Nick. The teacher and the school social worker established bi-weekly meetings *to monitor and modify his behavior using the agreed-on strategies. Nick's teacher made great efforts to give Nick as much* positive reinforcement *as possible whenever he was displaying appropriate behaviors in her classroom. She stated that she felt that she was "killing him with kindness." For example, when she noticed him concentrating on his work at his desk, she* caught him being good *by providing genuine and specific praise for this behavior. Initially, Nick did not respond well to the teacher's praise, but* she persisted. *Nick's teacher eventually reported that the* continual positive reinforcement *seemed to be effective, as Nick seemed to take greater interest in completing his work and would bring his completed work to her desk to show her what he had accomplished. It was evident by his smile that Nick began to enjoy this type of attention.*

Nick's teacher also began to address his noncompliance in a different way. Remarkably, she became skilled at calmly ignoring his mildly disrespectful comments *that had earlier guaranteed him attention, not only from her but also from the entire class. These comments steadily decreased. Furthermore, Nick's teacher instituted a* time-out intervention, *not only for Nick but for the entire class. Nick was frequently placed in time-out in the early stages of this intervention; however, he seemed to quickly learn that time-out was not enjoyable; thus, it was no longer worth it for him to behave in a coercive manner—especially when he could earn positive attention through other behaviors. There were times, of course, when Nick would revert to his old habits, and his teacher responded by calmly placing him in time-out. When Nick had "served his time," his teacher granted him a "clean slate" as demonstrated by her kind words toward him when he rejoined the rest of the class. Nick's teacher stated that after implementing these strategies for several months, she became* less personally affected *when Nick reverted to engaging in disrespectful behavior.*

By the end of the school year, it became apparent that Nick had a more positive relationship with his teacher. For example, on a field trip, Nick was quick to volunteer to hold her hand as they walked around the park. As a result of his teacher's persistence and caring, Nick seemed to have formed a strong connection not only to his teacher but also to school in general. Furthermore, his academic functioning, as well as his self-esteem, seemed to improve. Even his mother reported that Nick had a smile on his face when he got home from school, and he no longer whined about completing his homework. Although Nick's attitude continues to be disrespectful toward adults at times, his authority figures have learned not to reinforce his negative behavior. With persistence and consistency in ignoring Nick's milder oppositional and defiant behaviors, *additional improvements are expected. In addition, Nick's behavior will continue to be monitored to determine if a* daily report card intervention *is also warranted.*

Strategy 9: Think Prevention: Create a Positive School Culture

As we present our last two strategies, we encourage educators to recognize that oppositional and defiant behaviors occur on a continuum. Thus, in a given classroom you will likely see children who demonstrate mildly oppositional behavior, children who demonstrate severe oppositional behavior, and children who do not demonstrate any oppositional behavior at all. Regardless of the presence or absence of this disruptive behavior pattern, educators and their students will benefit from use of the strategies outlined above. For example, you may remember that in the case of Nick, the teacher began to implement praise strategies, active ignoring, and time-out with the entire classroom.

Indeed, when schools adopt a universal, schoolwide approach to teaching social, emotional, and behavioral skills, many mild-to-moderate oppositional and defiant behaviors can be prevented and modified. There is increasing evidence that schoolwide and classwide programs that teach these skills in a positive and proactive manner improve academic performance and social adjustment and reduce office referrals and disruptive behavior problems (e.g., Nelson, Martella, & Marchand-Martella, 2002; Scott & Barrett, 2004; Zins, Weissberg, Wang, & Walberg, 2004). Therefore, educators are strongly encouraged to create a school culture that focuses on building social, emotional, and behavioral competence by implementing evidence-based behavioral strategies in a schoolwide approach. In this manner, we can prevent (rather than respond to) potential problems. Two school-based models of universal social and behavioral programs that are emerging are positive behavior support (PBS; see www.pbis.org) and social and emotional learning (SEL; see www.casel.org).

PBS programming includes primary, secondary, and tertiary prevention approaches that address the educational and behavioral needs of all children. Primary prevention interventions are employed schoolwide to address both classroom and nonclassroom settings. Secondary prevention interventions are for students who are at risk for developing challenging or chronic problem behaviors. These students need extra instruction and practice to learn appropriate school-related and social behaviors. Tertiary intervention strategies are necessary for students with existing problem behaviors that are more severe. These strategies are highly specialized and require collaborative teams who conduct functional behavior assessments and implement evidence-based behavioral interventions, as described in the case of Nick. The PBS program teaches educators to be proactive (rather than reactive), to make data-based decisions, and to engage in team-based problem solving. Schools interested in receiving professional development training for PBS are encouraged to contact their local special education regional resource center (SERRC), which may have a certified PBS trainer. Additional information is available at www.pbis.org.

The Collaborative for Academic, Social, and Emotional Learning (CASEL) is an interdisciplinary organization that seeks to promote children's academic and life success by providing them with SEL in the classroom setting. The SEL curriculum teaches children the skills necessary to make good choices, manage emotions, demonstrate care for others, and behave in an ethical and responsible manner (Elias et al., 1997). SEL can be integrated into the regular academic curriculum or can be provided as part of an informal curriculum (e.g., at recess or lunch when peer interactions are frequent). Recent research conducted by CASEL (2003) indicates that both approaches can have positive effects on children's academic performance, particularly when educators themselves are directly involved in teaching the SEL curriculum. Furthermore, SEL programs have been shown to result in reduced school dropout and truancy (Wilson, Gotfredson, & Najaka, 2001).

Strategy 10: Think Collaboration

Finally, as mentioned earlier, there is a clear and direct link between children's mental health and their school success. This link renders schools an ideal location for collaborative efforts among educators, parents, mental health professionals, and other children's service agencies. The movement to jointly address children's mental health and educational needs in a coordinated and collaborative manner is gaining momentum at the state and federal levels (New Freedom Commission on Mental Health, 2003; Paternite, Rietz, Garner, Johnston, & Leigh, 2003; U.S. Department of Health and Human Services, 2001).

When you notice that a student in your classroom is demonstrating a pattern of oppositional or defiant behavior, take action sooner rather than later. As you are learning from this chapter, children are not likely to grow out of the coercive exchange pattern. Be proactive rather than reactive. For example, you may talk to other teachers to brainstorm effective reactions to the child's behavior. When discussing a child's behavior with your colleague, it can be helpful to vent your frustrations; however, it is equally, if not more, important to also focus the discussion on finding an active solution to the problem, such as initiating communication with the child's parents or implementing a combination of the above-described strategies. Again, when developing a collaborative relationship with parents, educators are encouraged to solicit the parents' views, share concern for the child's educational needs, and work as a team toward identifying and implementing a solution. In addition, you may choose to consult with a behavioral intervention specialist, school counselor, or other mental health professional within the school district who may have additional ideas for behavioral intervention strategies. This professional may also be able to facilitate communication between the school and the parents when teachers are unable to reach parents because of multiple competing demands (e.g., busy daily schedules, grading, class planning). Finally, teachers are encouraged to inquire whether the child is seeing a mental health professional outside the school district. Because this professional likely knows the child and family well, working collaboratively with this professional can lead to powerful behavioral changes as well.

SUMMARY

In summary, the behavior of children with ODD can be particularly difficult to manage in the classroom. It is our hope that educators have a better understanding of the nature of oppositional and defiant behavior, the associated factors, and the adult-child cycle of coercive exchanges that is often present when working with these children. Educators receive training related to recognizing individual differences in learning styles as well as strategies for adapting the lesson or the classroom environment to meet the needs of many different types of learners. Likewise, there are many individual differences in behavioral control styles. Thus, if educators apply such a framework to children with ODD, they may acquire a better understanding of the unique educational and behavioral needs of these children. Clearly, the behavioral style demonstrated by the child with ODD requires a unique set of strategies. Educators play a significant role in leading the child with ODD down the pathway to school success. The pathway to success involves active ignoring of provocative statements and gestures, consistent praise of behaviors that are often taken for granted in other students, use of choice-based discipline strategies that decrease emotional arousal in the child and the educator, and collaborative efforts with the child's parents and mental health professionals. When these strategies are implemented, many of the noncognitive barriers to learning are removed or reduced, leaving the educator in a position to do what he or she enjoys most: teach! Furthermore, when these strategies are used consistently, the educator begins to dismantle a negative interaction pattern that has become habitual and routine for the child. As this process unfolds, the educator becomes an adult whom the child can trust, respect, and emulate. The child learns to trust and respect authority, gains a sense of healthy control and independence, and builds competencies that will facilitate additional success in the future.

The next time you feel angry or resentful toward an oppositional and defiant student who challenges your authority, it is our hope that you recognize this negative emotion and use it as a reminder that there are many effective actions you can take to help yourself and the student in your classroom. It is particularly important for you to remember that the child's behavior is reflective of a mental health disorder, a student-owned behavioral control problem, and to refrain from becoming emotionally aroused, which helps neither you nor the child. Clearly, there are many competing demands on your attention, and you may find it difficult to make a change in your own behavior or to continue to engage in evidence-based behavioral strategies consistently across the year. However, if you invest the time and energy, you will reap the benefits. The child's mental health problem can be a chronic barrier to your reaching the child educationally, or it can be an obstacle that you, working in collaboration with parents and colleagues, can effectively remove. The choice is yours.

DISCUSSION QUESTIONS

1. Think about the case of Nick. Identify how positive reinforcement and response-cost were incorporated into the classroom intervention for him.
2. How can the use of behavior modification strategies contribute to improved academic performance? Discuss the relationship between oppositional behavior and academic productivity.
3. How does Oppositional Defiant Disorder impair the child's daily functioning? Consider multiple domains of functioning (e.g., academic, social, behavioral).
4. What role can teachers play in helping parents engage in communication strategies that would decrease oppositional behavior at home?

FOR ADDITIONAL HELP

	Organization	*Web Address*	*Description*
Oppositional Defiant Disorder	Comprehensive Treatment for ADD (CTADD)	www.summertreatmentprogram.com	Provides information relating to implementing a daily report card
	Positive Behavioral Intervention and Support	www.pbis.org	This center was established by the Office of Special Education Programs, U.S. Department of Education to give schools capacity-building information and technical assistance for identifying, adapting, and sustaining effective schoolwide disciplinary practices.

REFERENCES

American Psychiatric Association. (2000). *Diagnostic and statistical manual of mental disorders* (4th ed., text revision). Washington, DC: Author.

Anastopoulos, A. D., Shelton, T. L., DuPaul, G. J., & Guevremont, D. C. (1993). Parent training for attention-deficit hyperactivity disorder: Its impact on parent functioning. *Journal of Abnormal Child Psychology, 21*(5), 581–596.

Angold, A., & Costello, E. J. (1996). Toward establishing an empirical basis for the diagnosis of oppositional defiant disorder. *Journal of the American Academy of Child and Adolescent Psychiatry, 35*(9), 1205–1212.

Barkley, R. A. (1997). *Defiant children: A clinician's manual for assessment and parent training* (2nd ed.). New York: Guilford Press.

Bergin, C., & Bergin, D. A. (1999). Classroom discipline that promotes self-control. *Journal of Applied Developmental Psychology, 20*(2), 189–206.

Biederman, J., Faraone, S. V., Milberger, S., Jetton, J. G., Chen, L., Mick, E., et al. (1996). Is childhood oppositional defiant disorder a precursor to adolescent conduct disorder? Findings from a four-year follow-up study of children with ADHD. *Journal of the American Academy of Child and Adolescent Psychiatry, 35*(9), 1193–1204.

Brestan, E. V., & Eyberg, S. M. (1998). Effective psychosocial treatments of conduct-disordered children and adolescents: 29 years, 82 studies, and 5,272 kids. *Journal of Clinical Child Psychology, 27*(2), 180–189.

Brophy, J. (1985). Teachers' expectations, motives, and goals for working with problem students. In R. Ames & C. Ames (Eds.), *Research on motivation in education: The classroom milieu* (Vol. 2, pp. 175–214). Orlando, FL: Academic Press.

Burke, J. D., Loeber, R., & Birmaher, B. (2002). Oppositional defiant disorder and conduct disorder: A review of the past 10 years, Part II. *Journal of the American Academy of Child and Adolescent Psychiatry, 41*(11), 1275–1293.

Burke, J. D., Loeber, R., & Lahey, B. B. (2003). Course and outcomes. In C. A. Essau (Ed.), *Conduct and oppositional defiant disorders: Epidemiology, risk factors, and treatment* (pp. 61–94). Mahwah, NJ: Erlbaum.

Carlson, C. L., Tamm, L., & Gaub, M. (1997). Gender differences in children with ADHD, ODD, and co-occurring ADHD/ODD identified in a school population. *Journal of the American Academy of Child and Adolescent Psychiatry, 36*(12), 1706–1714.

Carlson, C. L., Tamm, L., & Hogan, A. E. (1999). The child with oppositional defiant disorder and conduct disorder in the family. In H. C. Quay & A. E. Hogan (Eds.), *Handbook of disruptive behavior* (pp. 337–352). New York: Kluwer Academic/Plenum.

Cohen, P., & Flory, M. (1998). Issues in the disruptive behavior disorders: Attention deficit disorder without hyperactivity and the differential validity of oppositional defiant and conduct disorders. In T. A. Widiger, A. J. Frances, H. J. Pincus, et al. (Eds.), *DSM-IV sourcebook* (Vol. 4, pp. 455–463). Washington, DC: American Psychiatric Press.

Collaborative for Academic, Social, and Emotional Learning. (2003). *Safe and sound: An educational leader's guide to evidence-based social and emotional learning programs.* Chicago: Author.

Cunningham, C. E., Bremner, R., & Secord, M. (1996). *COPE: The Community Parent Education Program. A school-based family systems oriented workshop for parents of children with disruptive behavior disorders.* Hamilton, Ontario, Canada: COPE Works.

Elias, M. J., Zins, J. E., Weissberg, R. P., Frey, K. S., Greenberg, M. T., Haynes, N. M., et al. (1997). *Promoting social and emotional learning: Guidelines for educators.* Alexandria, VA: Association for Supervision and Curriculum Development.

Firestone, P., Kelly, M. J., & Fike, S. (1980). Are fathers necessary in parent training groups? *Journal of Clinical Child Psychology, 9,* 44–47.

Flaherty, L. T., Weist, M. D., & Warner, B. S. (1996). School-based mental health services in the United States: History, current models and needs. *Community Mental Health Journal, 32*(4), 341–352.

Forehand, R., & McMahon, R. (1981). *Helping the noncompliant child: A clinician's guide to parent training.* New York: Guilford Press.

Frick, P. J., Lahey, B. B., Loeber, R., Stouthamer-Loeber, M., Christ, M. A. G., & Hanson, K. (1992). Familial risk factors to oppositional defiant disorder and conduct disorder: Parental psychopathology and maternal parenting. *Journal of Consulting and Clinical Psychology, 60*(1), 49–55.

Loeber, R., Burke, J. D., Lahey, B. B., Winters, A., & Zera, M. (2000). Oppositional defiant and conduct disorder: A review of the past 10 years, Part I. *Journal of the American Academy of Child and Adolescent Psychiatry, 39,* 1468–1484.

Mulvey, E. P., & Cauffman, E. (2001). The inherent limits of predicting school violence. *American Psychologist, 56,* 797–802.

Nelson, J. R., Martella, R. M., & Marchand-Martella, N. (2002). Maximizing student learning: The effects of a comprehensive school-based program for preventing problem behavior. *Journal of Emotional and Behavioral Disorders, 10,* 136–148.

New Freedom Commission on Mental Health. (2003). *Achieving the promise: Transforming mental health care in America: Final report* (DHHS Pub. No. SMA03-3832). Rockville, MD: U.S. Department of Health and Human Services.

Ohio Department of Mental Health & Ohio Department of Education. (2003). *Legislative forum on mental health and school success: Fact sheet.* Retrieved November 3, 2005, from www.units.muohio.edu/csbmhp/resources/resourcessagenda/FinalFacts10-6-03.pdf

O'Leary, S. G., & Pelham, W. E. (1978). Behavior therapy and withdrawal of stimulant medication with hyperactive children. *Pediatrics, 61,* 211–217.

O' Leary, S. G., Pelham, W. E., Rosenbaum, A., & Price, G. (1976). Behavioral treatment of hyperkinetic children: An experimental evaluation of its usefulness. *Clinical Pediatrics, 15,* 510–515.

Paternite, C., Rietz, K., Garner, T., Johnston, T., & Leigh, D. (2003, October). *Enhancing existing collaborations to promote a mental health-schools-families shared agenda for children's mental health: Ohio's experience.* Paper presented at the 8th annual Conference on Advancing School-Based Mental Health, Portland, OR.

Patterson, G. R. (1976). *Living with children: New methods for parents and teachers* (revised). Champaign, IL: Research Press.

Patterson, G. R., Reid, J. B., & Dishion, T. J. (1992). *Antisocial boys.* Eugene, OR: Castalia.

Pelham, W. E. (1996). *Children's summer treatment program: 1996 program manual.* Unpublished manuscript.

Pelham, W. E., Wheeler, T., & Chronis, A. (1998). Empirically supported psychosocial treatments for attention deficit hyperactivity disorder. *Journal of Clinical Child Psychology, 27,* 190–205.

Pisterman, S., Firestone, P., McGrath, P., Goodman, J. T., Webster, I., Mallory, R., & Goffin, B. (1992). The role of parent training in treatment of preschoolers with ADHD. *American Journal of Orthopsychiatry, 62,* 397–408.

Pisterman, S., McGrath, P. J., Firestone, P., Goodman, J. T., Webster, I., & Mallory, R. (1989). Outcome of parent-mediated treatment of preschoolers with attention deficit disorder with hyperactivity. *Journal of Consulting and Clinical Psychology, 57,* 628–635.

Rayfield, A., Monaco, L., & Eyberg, S. M. (1999). Parent-child interaction therapy with oppositional children. In S. W. Russ & T. H. Ollendick (Eds.), *Handbook of psychotherapies with children and families* (pp. 327–343). New York: Kluwer Academic/Plenum.

Rey, J. M., Bashir, M. R., Schwarz, M., Richards, I. N., Plapp, J. M., & Stewart, G. W. (1988). Oppositional disorder: Fact or fiction? *Journal of the American Academy of Child and Adolescent Psychiatry, 27*(2), 157–162.

Rowe, R., Maughan, B., Pickles, A., Costello, E. J., & Angold, A. (2002). The relationship between *DSM-IV* oppositional defiant disorder and conduct disorder: Findings from the Great Smoky Mountains Study. *Journal of Child Psychology and Psychiatry, 43*(3), 365–373.

Schachar, R., & Wachsmuth, R. (1990). Oppositional disorder in children: A validation study comparing conduct disorder, oppositional disorder and normal control children. *Journal of Child Psychology and Psychiatry, 31*(7), 1089–1102.

Scott, T. M., & Barrett, S. B. (2004). Using staff and student time engaged in disciplinary procedures to evaluate the impact of school-wide PBS. *Journal of Positive Behavior Interventions, 6,* 21–27.

Simonoff, E., Pickles, A., Meyer, J. M., Silberg, J. L., Maes, H. H., Loeber, R., et al. (1997). The Virginia Twin Study of Adolescent Behavioral Development: Influences of age, sex, and impairment on rates of disorder. *Archives of General Psychiatry, 54,* 801–808.

Smith, A. M., & O'Leary, S. G. (1995). Attributions and arousal as predictors of maternal discipline. *Cognitive Therapy & Research, 19*(4), 459–471.

Society of Clinical Child and Adolescent Psychology. (2003). *Oppositional defiant and conduct disorders: Evidence-based treatment options.* Retrieved March 10, 2004, from www.clinicalchild psychology.org

Stevens, J., Quittner, A. L., & Abikoff, H. (1998). Factors influencing elementary school teachers' ratings of ADHD and ODD behaviors. *Journal of Clinical Child Psychology, 27,* 406–414.

U.S. Department of Health and Human Services. (2001). *Report of the Surgeon General's conference on children's mental health: A national action agenda.* Retrieved March 20, 2004, from www .surgeongeneral.gov/topics/cmh

Webster-Stratton, C. (1984). Randomized trial of two parent training programs for families with conduct-disordered children. *Journal of Consulting and Clinical Psychology, 52,* 666–678.

Webster-Stratton, C. (1996). Early intervention with videotape modeling: Programs for families of children with oppositional defiant disorder or conduct disorder. In E. S. Hibbs & P. S. Jensen (Eds.), *Psychosocial treatments for child and adolescent disorders: Empirically-based strategies for clinical practice* (pp. 435–474). Washington, DC: American Psychological Association.

Weist, M. D., Lowie, J. A., Flaherty, L. T., & Pruitt, D. (2001). Collaboration among the education, mental health, and public health systems to promote youth mental health. *Psychiatric Services, 52*(10), 1348–1351.

Werner, E. E., & Smith, R. S. (1982). *Vulnerable but invincible.* New York: McGraw-Hill.

Wierson, M., & Forehand, R. (1994). Parent behavioral training for child noncompliance: Rationale, concepts, and effectiveness. *Current Directions in Psychological Science, 3,* 146–150.

Wilson, D. B., Gotfredson, D. C., & Najaka, S. S. (2001). School-based prevention of problem behaviors: A meta-analysis. *Journal of Quantitative Criminology, 17,* 242–272.

Zins, J. E., Weissberg, R. P., Wang, M. C., & Walberg, H. J. (Eds.). (2004). *Building academic success through social and emotional learning: What does the research say?* New York: Teachers College Press.

Part III

Mental Health Issues Involving Significant Risks to Self and Others

Chapter 9

Anorexia Nervosa, Bulimia Nervosa, and Obesity

Laura L. Myers

PREREADING QUESTIONS

As you read this chapter, reflect on the following issues and questions:

1. What can teachers do to encourage healthy eating habits and healthy exercise habits among their students?
2. What are the signs that a student is suffering from Anorexia Nervosa?
3. What are the signs that a student is suffering from Bulimia Nervosa?
4. What can we do to help prevent childhood obesity?

Children and adolescents are bombarded today with the message that they should be extremely thin and fit. At the same time, they often live a sedentary lifestyle and consume a diet of fast foods and junk foods. These trends have led to a society of children and adolescents who, from a very young age, are unhappy with their shape and weight. In one study, 55% of girls and 35% of boys want to be thinner than they are (Herrin & Matsumoto, 2002), and anecdotally, teachers report hearing *preschool* children express dissatisfaction with their weight and their body image.

The result is that many children and adolescents are dieting from a very early age. Herrin and Matsumoto (2002) use the following statistics from recent surveys to emphasize our society's problem with eating disorders among children and adolescents:

> - More than 70% of adolescents are dissatisfied with their bodies and want to lose weight.
> - On any given day, approximately two thirds of all teenage girls and one fifth of all teenage boys are dieting.
> - Among *preadolescents,* 60% of all girls and 25% of all boys report having dieted recently.
> - One study found that 13% of the girls surveyed and 7% of the boys surveyed binged and purged a few times a week or more.
> - Recent findings indicate that girls who smoke to suppress their appetite are the highest group of new nicotine addicts. (p. xx)

As a result of early yo-yo dieting habits and other disordered eating habits, many children and adolescents find themselves developing severe body image problems, leading to an eating disorder or obesity. Based on this unfortunate combination of phenomena, we are currently living in a society where obesity and eating disorders are considered epidemics by many researchers. Teachers, because they see many children and adolescents who otherwise would not come into contact with other professionals, may be in a unique position to help children who find themselves suffering from these devastating disorders.

Fairburn and Harrison (2003) make the following statement in a recent review of the current clinical and research advances in the field of eating disorders:

> Eating disorders are of great interest to the public, of perplexity to researchers, and a challenge to clinicians. They feature prominently in the media, often attracting sensational coverage. Their cause is elusive, with social, psychological, and biological processes all seeming to play a major part, and they are difficult to treat, with some patients actively resisting attempts to help them. Nevertheless, there is progress to report both in terms of their understanding and treatment. (p. 407)

ORGANIZATION OF CHAPTER

In this chapter, the current definitions and research regarding **Anorexia Nervosa**, **Bulimia Nervosa**, and **obesity** are presented. First, Anorexia Nervosa and Bulimia Nervosa are considered; these are mental disorders currently defined in the *Diagnostic and Statistical Manual of Mental Disorders (DSM-IV-TR*; American Psychiatric Association, 2000). The diagnostic criteria for each, prevalence data, causes and risk factors, symptoms and early warning signs, and effective treatments are presented. Next, obesity is discussed, including definitions, causes and risk factors, physical and emotional complications, and treatment of childhood obesity. Finally, the chapter deals with the difficult question of what teachers can do to help with these major problems among children and adolescents. Because these disorders are difficult to treat, the emphasis of this section is on what teachers can do to help children and adolescents prevent the onset of obesity and eating disorders.

ANOREXIA NERVOSA

Anorexic children refuse to maintain even a minimally normal body weight. They are intensely afraid of gaining weight, a fear fueled by a distorted perception of their body shape and size. No matter how thin they get, they see themselves as fat and unattractive, and this distortion in perception usually becomes more severe the more weight they lose (Herrin & Matsumoto, 2002, p. 4).

The distinctive core psychopathology for both Anorexia Nervosa (AN) and Bulimia Nervosa (BN) is a person's constant concern and evaluation of his or her shape and weight. Although most people assess themselves on a variety of domains (i.e., academics, sports, relationships, work, parenting skills), people with eating disorders judge their own self-worth almost exclusively or, in extreme cases, exclusively on their shape and weight. Fairburn and Harrison (2003) argue that the differences between AN and BN are secondary to this psychopathology and its consequences. One could argue that the main difference between individuals with AN and individuals with BN is how successful the person has been in his or her goal of weight loss because part of the criteria for AN is weight loss of 15% of total body weight. Others might perceive the difference as a matter of severity, with individuals with AN having a more severe body image disturbance, and therefore continuing to feel overweight even at extremely low weights.

The prevalence of eating disorders is difficult to ascertain; people who suffer from them are usually secretive until the physical and medical consequences make it impossible for them to hide their problem. Indeed, many individuals with eating disorders who have lost a great deal of weight are envied by friends and family members for their great self-control. Therefore, unless the psychological or physical symptoms become extreme, many eating disorders remain undiagnosed. Research has, however, estimated the prevalence of AN in young women at 1%, affecting females 10 to 1 over males. It has also been estimated that 10% of those who suffer from AN die as a result of complications of the disorder (Hall & Ostroff, 1998).

Definitions

The operational definitions of AN and BN are still in a state of flux, changing significantly with each new edition of the American Psychiatric Association's (APA) diagnostic manual. The names of the eating disorders, the criteria, and the distinction between AN and BN have changed. The current criteria for AN, as defined by the APA in the fourth edition of the *Diagnostic and Statistical Manual of Mental Disorders* (*DSM-IV-TR,* 2000), include (a) refusal to maintain body weight at or above a minimally normal weight for age and height (weight loss leading to maintenance of body weight less than 85% of that expected or failure to make expected weight gain during a period of growth, leading to body weight less than 85% of that expected); (b) intense fear of gaining weight or becoming fat, even though underweight; (c) disturbance in the way in which one's body weight or shape is experienced, undue influence of body weight or shape on self-evaluation, or denial of the seriousness of the current low body weight; and (d) in postmenarcheal females, absence of at least three consecutive menstrual cycles.

There are two subtypes of AN. A person with the restricting type of AN attempts to lose weight by reducing his or her intake of calories, exercising excessively following food intake, and frequent fasting. A person with the second type of AN also restricts food intake but, usually as a result of the starvation, participates in periods of binge eating and purging. The purging may involve self-induced vomiting or the abuse of laxatives, diuretics, or enemas. Sometimes purging is used after only small amounts of food are eaten (Herrin & Matsumoto, 2002).

Causes and Risk Factors

Research has shown that the cause of eating disorders is a complex phenomenon, with genetic predispositions, environmental risk factors, and personality traits implicated. Probably the most widely studied environmental cause of AN and BN is today's extreme social pressure, particularly on women, to be slim. This has led to a society-wide obsession with dieting for the main purpose of weight loss.

Counselors have found that AN is often brought on by a stressful life event, including leaving home for college or summer camp; parental divorce; an insensitive comment or being teased about one's weight or shape by a parent, friend, coach, or sibling; breaking up with a boyfriend; or failing to get picked for a sports team (Herrin & Matsumoto, 2002). These events may encourage a person's self-doubt regarding his or her weight and shape and lead to a period of dieting in an effort to be slimmer, more attractive, or more athletic. Dieting in general has been shown to be the most common predecessor for the development of an eating disorder. Herrin and Matsumoto (2002) conclude, "Dieting *is* a form of disordered eating, and it does put the dieter, especially if that dieter is a child or an adolescent, at risk for an eating disorder" (p. 22).

General risk factors for all eating disorders include living in a Western society; being female; adolescence and early adulthood; adverse parenting (especially low contact and high expectations); sexual abuse; family dieting; critical comments about eating, shape, or weight from family and others; and a family history of dieting, eating disorders, and depression (Fairburn & Harrison, 2003). Other risk factors found to be particularly common in people with AN include well-educated parents, affluence, an overprotective mother, and a personality that is overly sensitive, moody, or fearful (Herrin & Matsumoto, 2002). Two personality traits that are particularly common antecedents for AN are perfectionism and low self-esteem (Fairburn, Cooper, Doll, & Welch, 1999).

Warning Signs and Symptoms

The main warning signs of AN are very rapid weight loss, extreme weight loss, or both. Individuals with AN practice a severe and extreme restriction of food intake. They generally avoid all foods considered fattening. In an effort to compensate for even small amounts of food eaten, individuals with AN might participate in a compulsive exercise regime, use self-induced vomiting, or misuse laxatives or diuretics to rid their bodies of extra pounds (Fairburn & Harrison, 2003). They may turn to vegetarianism in an effort to avoid extra fat. Most individuals with AN eat only a limited number of foods, and they may develop other rituals around food intake to help reduce their calorie intake, such as cutting their food into tiny bites, chewing each bite of food a certain number of times, or constantly drinking water or diet soda (Herrin & Matsumoto, 2002). These types of behaviors can sometimes be observed in a school setting, with students eating little or nothing during snack time or lunch-time, exercising constantly during recess times, or regularly going to the restroom after ingesting any amount of food or drink.

Psychological symptoms of AN include depression, anxiety, irritability, mood swings, impaired concentration, loss of sexual desire, and obsessive thoughts. Individuals with AN often withdraw from friends and family and become very isolated as obsession with their weight and body shape increases. As part of their obsession with food, some people with AN will spend a great deal of time shopping for and preparing food for family and friends but will eat only small amounts or none at all (Herrin & Matsumoto, 2002).

Physical symptoms may include heightened sensitivity to cold; constipation; fullness or bloatedness after eating; dizziness; fainting; absence of menstruation; dry skin; hair loss; crying without tears caused by dehydration; fine downy hair, called *lanugo,* on the back, forearms, and side of the face; cold hands and feet; cardiac arrhythmias; and muscle weakness (Fairburn & Harrison, 2003). Herrin and Matsumoto (2002) add, "Among girls who have not yet reached puberty, menstruation may be delayed or completely inhibited by anorexia" (p. 4). More serious signs that AN may be affecting a person's heart include fatigue, lightheadedness, bluish, splotchy hands and feet, slowed or irregular heartbeat, shortness of breath, chest pain, leg pain, rapid breathing, and low blood pressure. Another serious complication of AN is osteoporosis, caused by the reduction of estrogen, which leads to bone loss. During adolescence, when bones are still developing, this bone loss can be particularly devastating (Herrin & Matsumoto, 2002).

Prognosis and Treatment

The onset of AN most often occurs during the midteen years and usually begins with dieting, which then develops into extreme and unhealthy food restriction. Some people with AN grow out of the disorder naturally as they mature through adolescence. Others get entrenched in their compulsions toward weight loss and require intensive treatment to overcome the disorder. In a small percentage of individuals with AN (10%–20%), the disorder proves to be intractable (Steinhausen, 2002). The mortality rate among people with AN is 12 times the normal rate, usually resulting from starvation, suicide, or extremely low potassium levels (Herrin & Matsumoto, 2002).

Compared with BN, the treatment of AN has been the subject of surprisingly little research. Of course, one of the problems with all eating disorders is that as long as the person is successful in controlling his or her shape and weight, he or she often does not consider the behavior a problem and will not seek help. Because research has not had any significant findings regarding the treatment of AN, Fairburn and Harrison (2003) offer four components of the treatment of AN that summarize the opinions of many professionals working with this disorder. The first is to motivate the person to accept that he or she needs help. Second, the person's weight needs to be restored. Reversing the effects of malnutrition usually results in a significant improvement of the person's overall state. This step may have to be completed in a hospital, especially if there are indications of suicide risk, severe and rapid weight loss, or medical complications, such as edema, severe electrolyte imbalance, hypoglycemia, or infection.

The third component of the treatment of AN involves the person's distorted thinking regarding his or her weight and shape, disordered eating habits, and overall psychosocial functioning. Family-based treatment has shown to be helpful with younger adolescent individuals with AN (Lock, le Grange, Agras, & Dare, 2001; Russell, Szmukler, Dare, & Eisler, 1987). The final issue in the treatment of AN is the question of compulsory treatment. Many individuals with AN do not feel that weight loss is a problem and therefore do not seek or want treatment. These individuals are sometimes admitted to a hospital against their wishes and fed intravenously to ward off the extreme effects of starvation, including death. The decision to treat a person with AN against his or her wishes should never be taken lightly (Fairburn & Harrison, 2003; Russell, 2001).

BULIMIA NERVOSA

Instead of the self-starvation characteristic of anorexics, bulimics engage in periodic bouts of binge eating. These are always followed by a period of contrition during which the bulimic tries to undo the effects of the binge, either by purging, abusing diuretics or laxatives, or fasting or exercising to the extreme (or both) (Herrin & Matsumoto, 2002).

Since it was recognized by the APA as a diagnostic entity in 1980, BN has become a widespread clinical problem. Many people who suffer with BN are secretive about their dieting and eating behaviors and avoid discussing them with even their closest friends. Because of the prevalence of this disorder in middle and high schools, teachers are in a unique position to recognize and reach young people who suffer from this serious disorder. The prevalence rates of BN offered by researchers vary significantly from study to study. In general, the percentages are higher when a younger female population is studied and when earlier, less stringent, criteria are used, such as those defined in the *DSM-III* (APA, 1980). In studies that looked at middle and high school populations, the prevalence rates for females ranged from 1.2% (Whitaker et al., 1989) to 16% (VanThorre & Vogel, 1985) using the *DSM-III* (1980) criteria and 2.2% (Gross & Rosen, 1988) using the more stringent *DSM-III-R* (APA, 1987) criteria. Males ranged from 0% (Maceyko & Nagelberg, 1985) to 4.4% (Lachenmeyer & Muni-Brander, 1988) using the *DSM-III* (1980) criteria and 0.1% (Gross & Rosen, 1988) using the *DSM-III-R* (1987) criteria.

Definitions

Although individuals with AN generally restrict their calorie intake to lose a significant amount of weight, individuals with BN may be attempting the same goal, but experience frequent episodes of binge eating, or uncontrolled overeating. These are usually followed by some type of purging behavior to help get rid of the unwanted calories. These individuals sometimes describe themselves as failed anorexics (Fairburn & Harrison, 2003). As with AN, there are two subtypes of BN—the purging type and the nonpurging type. The purging type uses self-induced vomiting or the abuse of laxatives or diuretics to control weight gain, and the nonpurging type uses fasting and excessive exercise to compensate for binge eating (Herrin & Matsumoto, 2002).

The current criteria for BN, as defined in the *DSM-IV* (APA, 1994), include (a) recurrent episodes of binge eating; (b) recurrent inappropriate compensatory behavior to prevent weight gain, such as self-induced vomiting, misuse of laxatives, diuretics, or other medications, enemas, fasting, or excessive exercise; (c) these behaviors have occurred, on average, at least twice a week for 3 months; (d) self-evaluation is unduly influenced by body shape and weight; and (e) the disturbance does not occur exclusively during episodes of AN (p. 549). If the person meets the criteria for both BN and AN, binge-eating/purging type, only the diagnosis for AN is made. The distinguishing factors between BN and AN are the presence of significant weight loss and the absence of menstrual cycles in the criteria for AN.

Defining the terms used in the criteria for BN has prompted numerous debates, including the presence and frequency of binging, the size of the binge, the presence and frequency of purging activity, and the presence of distorted body image. Binging is defined in the criteria for BN as being characterized by both of the following: (a) eating, within any 2-hour period, an amount of food that is definitely larger than most people would eat during a similar period of time and under similar circumstances and (b) a sense of lack of control over eating during the episode, such as feeling that one cannot stop eating or control what or how much one is eating (*DSM-IV,* 1994).

Schlundt and Johnson (1990), believing that the classification of food intake as a binge is subjective and differs from person to person, define a binge as "the ingestion of any food substance or quantity that violates the individual's idea of dieting and thereby increases anxiety regarding weight gain" (p. 4). They argue that for different individuals, a binge may involve the consumption of thousands of calories, a normal-sized meal, or even a single doughnut. The frequency of binging can also differ greatly between individuals, ranging from infrequently to 15 times a day. Myers (1996) offers a more complete discussion of the variations in binging and purging behaviors that occur in the client population.

Causes and Risk Factors

As with to AN, many causes and risk factors have been associated with the onset of BN. General risk factors include being female, adolescence or early adulthood, and living in Western society. Childhood sexual abuse, childhood obesity, parental obesity, early onset puberty and menarche, and parental alcoholism are a few factors that seem to predispose young people to BN. Family dieting, adverse parenting, and critical comments by parents and siblings regarding weight and shape are often seen in the histories of people who develop BN (Fairburn & Harrison, 2003).

Counselors have found that certain triggers may encourage the onset of BN. The extreme hunger brought on by constant dieting is probably the most common trigger for binge eating among people with BN and others. Sometimes a depressed mood or a traumatic or stressful event will precede the onset of this disorder. Stressful events can include leaving home for the first time, a death or illness in the family, breaking up with a boyfriend, starting high school, starting to menstruate, a first sexual experience, an abortion, or being criticized for being fat (Herrin & Matsumoto, 2002).

Warning Signs and Symptoms

Individuals with BN attempt to restrict their food intake and are often quite successful at keeping a low body weight. However, this extreme dieting is interrupted by episodes of eating in which there is a sense of loss of control, and large amounts of food are eaten in short periods of time. Herrin and Matsumoto (2002) point out that "such a 'failure' is perfectly normal behavior after a period of self-starvation, although the bulimic does not see this" (p. 10). During these binges, an average of 1,000 to 2,000 calories is ingested. To compensate for this large intake of calories, individuals with BN use a variety of purging techniques. If the compensatory techniques lead to an extreme loss of weight, then the person moves from a diagnosis of BN to a diagnosis of AN. Usually, however, individuals with BN maintain a fairly average weight (Fairburn & Harrison, 2003).

The most obvious warning sign for BN that a teacher might observe in a student is a fluctuating pattern of extreme food intake restriction and large amounts of food consumption. For example, a student might never eat sweets or fattening foods at snack time or lunchtime, but at a Christmas party or Valentine's party might seem to lose control and have several cookies, two pieces of cake, lots of M&Ms, and several cups of punch. If the student has BN, he or she will almost certainly attempt to compensate for this food intake after the food is ingested. The teacher might notice a long restroom break and may notice the student develop a renewed vigor in food intake restriction over the following days.

Sandra is an excellent seventh-grade student, and has always maintained a weight within the normal range. The teacher has noticed that Sandra's eating habits have fluctuated significantly throughout the school year. Some days, Sandra eats only raw vegetables and diet sodas for lunch and snack. Other days, she purchases several snack cakes or other unhealthy snacks from the school's vending machine and eats these at lunchtime or snack time. On these days, Sandra seems very agitated after eating and always spends a significant amount of time in the restroom after eating.

Recently, Sandra's eating has increased. Now, most days she eats a big lunch, including sweets, as well as a very high-calorie, high-sugar snack during snack time. She religiously goes to the restroom every time she eats. Despite her heavy eating, the teacher has noticed that her weight has dropped significantly over the past 6 weeks. She is worried that Sandra may be developing an eating disorder.

Some people who suffer with BN complain of stomach flu symptoms or complain that certain foods do not digest well. Many show signs of depression, anxiety disorders, and compulsive behaviors, and a smaller group abuse substances (including appetite suppressants), and possibly injure themselves. People who vomit regularly might suffer from heartburn, chronic sore throat, hoarseness, difficulty swallowing, swollen cheeks, redness or calluses on the backs of their hands from using their fingers to induce vomiting, redness around the mouth due to exposure to stomach acid, red blood spots around the eyes from the pressure of vomiting, and large numbers of cavities (Fairburn & Harrison, 2003; Herrin & Matsumoto, 2002).

Prognosis and Treatment

The average age of onset for BN is slightly later than for AN. BN usually starts with dieting, much like AN. In about 25% of the cases of BN, the criteria for AN are met for a period of time before developing into BN. Extreme food restriction and the resulting weight loss are interrupted by repeated binge-eating episodes until the weight returns to near-normal levels (Sullivan, Bulik, Carter, Gendall, & Joyce, 1996).

Cognitive-Behavioral Therapy

Research has found that cognitive-behavioral therapy (CBT) focusing on the specific eating behaviors and the distorted thinking that maintains the disorder is the most effective treatment for individuals with BN. Treatment usually involves 20 individual sessions stretching over 5 months, with 30% to 50% of the individuals making a complete and lasting recovery (Fairburn & Harrison, 2003). Components involved in CBT include self-monitoring, reducing environmental cues to binge, meal planning, introducing forbidden foods, problem-solving skills, relaxation training, nutrition education, and cognitive restructuring (Fairburn, 1988).

Several CBT group and individual programs have been developed for individuals with BN, and in general, research studies suggest that these programs

> produce substantial improvements in both eating behavior (including, in episodes of overeating, a reduction in the use of other methods of weight control and in the level of dietary restraint), as well as an improvement in attitude about body shape and weight. (Kennedy & Garfinkel, 1992, p. 311)

Nutrition education and therapy has proven to be an extremely important component of most cognitive-behavioral treatment models for both AN and BN. The purpose of nutrition education and therapy is "to educate eating-disordered patients about basic principles of good nutrition, and to help them use this information in planning healthy and appropriate patterns of food intake" (Schlundt & Johnson, 1990, p. 321). One research study suggests that nutritional counseling may be effective as a sole form of treatment for individuals with BN who show little evidence of other underlying psychopathology (O'Connor, Touyz, & Beumont, 1987).

More advanced research has shown CBT to be as effective or more so in treating BN as supportive psychotherapy, focal psychotherapy, exposure with response prevention, behavior therapy, and treatment with antidepressants (Fairburn, Marcus, & Wilson, 1993). Although antidepressant drugs result in a quick decline in the frequency of binging and purging behavior, the effect is not generally sustained and the improvement is not as great as that obtained with CBT. Combining antidepressant drugs with CBT provided few consistent benefits over CBT alone (Fairburn & Harrison, 2003).

OBESITY

During the past two decades, the prevalence of obesity in children has risen greatly worldwide. Obesity in childhood causes a wide range of serious complications and increases the risk of premature illness and death later in life, raising public health concerns. Results of research have provided new insights into the physiological basis of body weight regulation. However, treatment for childhood obesity remains largely ineffective (Ebbeling, Pawlak, & Ludwig, 2002).

In addition to the obvious effects on the children, there are also economic effects of childhood obesity. The American Academy of Pediatrics Committee on Nutrition (2003) states, "The potential future health care costs associated with pediatric obesity and its co-morbidities are staggering, prompting the surgeon general to predict that preventable morbidity and mortality associated with obesity may exceed those associated with cigarette smoking" (p. 425).

Strauss and Knight (1999) report that obesity affects 20% to 30% of children and adolescents in the United States. Research (Flegel & Troiano, 2000) has also found that the heaviest children, who are already at the greatest risk for negative medical and psychological consequences, are getting even heavier. Although prevalence rates among the white population has increased by 2 to 3 times over the past 25 years, the prevalence among some minority groups has risen more than twice as fast, making the difference, in prevalence between these groups even greater than they already were (Ebbeling et al., 2002; Strauss & Pollack, 2001).

Definitions

The most commonly used definition of overweight and obesity used in research is based on the **body mass index (BMI).** BMI is calculated by taking one's height in inches, dividing it by weight in pounds squared, and multiplying it by 703. **Overweight** is defined in many studies as having a BMI at or above the 85th percentile based on an appropriate reference population, and **obesity** is defined as having a BMI at or above the 95th percentile. In a longitudinal study, Kimm and others (2002), using these definitions, found that 31% of black 9-year-old girls and 22% of white 9-year-old girls were overweight, and 18% of black 9-year-old girls and 8% of white 9-year-old girls were obese. Between the ages of 9 and 19 years, the rate of overweight and obese girls in both racial groups approximately doubled.

Another common definition for overweight and obesity is based on BMI scores rather than percentiles. Overweight is often defined as a BMI between 25 and 30, and obesity is defined as a BMI above 30 (National Heart, Lung, and Blood Institute, 1998). Unfortunately, because the BMI was developed for use by adults, it does not take into consideration the child's natural rate of growth, body build, or genetic predisposition; thus it is not an ideal method of determining whether a youth is overweight or obese (Herrin & Matsumoto, 2002). Another definition of obesity is weight that is 20% above the ideal based on the growth charts developed by the National Center for Health Statistics (Dunn, 2000).

Causes and Risk Factors

Causes and risk factors leading to obesity have been identified in the areas of genetics, exercise, diet, and family lifestyle choices.

Genetics

Research has shown that genetic factors make certain individuals more likely to be overweight than others. Five genetic mutations, all presenting during childhood, have been identified as predisposing an individual for obesity (Farooqi & O'Rahilly, 2000). These were reported to account for a very small number of cases of obesity. More recent research on the predisposition to obesity has suggested a complex interaction between at least 250 obesity-associated genes (Rankinen et al., 2002).

Prenatal overnutrition may increase the chance of childhood and adult obesity. Maternal obesity is clearly linked to birth weight and obesity later in life, although it is difficult to distinguish which effects are genetic, which are passed through the uterus, and which are environmental (Whitaker & Dietz, 1998). The largest increases in body weight occur at the beginning of puberty and at menarche, and early onset puberty and menarche have been linked to an increased risk of obesity (Kimm & Obarzanek, 2002).

Exercise

Lack of physical activity and an inactive lifestyle, particularly excessive television viewing, may cause obesity in children (Ebbeling et al., 2002). One national survey (Andersen, Crespo, Bartlett, Cheskin, & Pratt, 1998) found that 20% of children in the United States reported participation in two or fewer vigorous activities per week, and over 25% of children watched at least 4 hours of television a day. These researchers also found that children who watched the most hours of television or participated in the least amount of vigorous activity were the most overweight. Hernandez et al. (1999) found that the risk of obesity increased by 12% for every hour of daily television viewing and decreased by 10% for every hour of daily physical activity. Robinson (1999) speculated that television viewing promotes weight gain in children not only by decreasing the amount of energy expended but also by encouraging the intake of energy-dense foods (junk foods) while watching television. In addition, television advertising may be adversely affecting the eating patterns of children, encouraging the intake of fast foods, soft drinks, sweets, and sugar-sweetened breakfast cereals.

Diet

The preferred diet for children has been cause for great debate over the past decade. The Food Guide Pyramid developed by the United States Department of Agriculture (USDA), released in 1992, encouraged eating carbohydrates and discouraged eating fats (Willett & Stampfer, 2003). Despite a decrease in the amount of fat in the diets of children in the United States, the occurrence of obesity among children has increased (Troiano, Briefel, Carroll, & Bialostosky, 2000). Current research suggests that the type of fat may be more significant than the total amount of fat consumed. Saturated fats, found in red meat and dairy products, raise the levels of unwanted cholesterol (LDL, or low-density lipoprotein) and increase the risk of heart disease. Transunsaturated fats, or trans fats, found in margarines, baked goods, and fried foods, are particularly bad because they raise the unwanted cholesterol (LDL) and lower the desired cholesterol (HDL, or high-density lipoprotein). Conversely, studies have shown that monounsaturated and polyunsaturated fats, found in olive and other vegetable oils, fish, and nuts, tend to lower the rates of heart disease (Willett & Stampfer, 2003).

A new food pyramid, recently introduced by the USDA (http://mypyramid.gov), attempts to solve some of the problems of the original pyramid. Unfortunately, the pyramid itself does not display any recommended amounts for the different categories of foods. The categories of foods, including grains, vegetables, fruits, milk, and meat and beans, are shown by different-colored stripes making up the pyramid. You have to read additional information to get detailed information on how much of each type of food is recommended.

The new pyramid improves in some areas. For example, it specifically points out that our bodies need some oils for good health. It also shows a person running up the side of the pyramid, indicating the importance of exercise. It does not improve in other areas. For example, all carbohydrates are still in one category rather than dividing the whole grains from the processed carbohydrates. Sugar and butter and oleo (the bad carbohydrates and the bad fats) are not even on the pyramid, making the recommendation unclear unless you read the additional information. Although the information presented with the pyramid is more accurate and reflects some of the current research, the pyramid itself seems less clear and provides less guidance. Because children see the picture of the pyramid displayed throughout their schools and doctors' offices, the information that we want the children to receive needs to be clear, direct, and easy to understand. It seems the new pyramid fails to meet these needs.

Diet tendencies among adults clearly affect the diets of children, as children generally eat what they are given by their parents and schools. Although people in the United States have decreased their fat intake, they have increased their intake of carbohydrates, particularly refined carbohydrates such as breads, ready-to-eat cereals, potatoes, white rice, soft drinks, cakes, and bagels (Subar, Krebs-Smith, Cook, & Kahle, 1998). Research (Ludwig et al., 1999) has shown that eating these refined carbohydrates actually stimulates hunger, increases the appetite, and causes overeating in adolescents. One study (Ludwig, Peterson, & Gortmaker, 2001) indicated a 60% increase in risk of obesity for each sugar-sweetened soft drink consumed daily. Ebbeling and others (2002) point out that fast food generally incorporates all the dietary factors that seem to encourage obesity, including high saturated and trans fats, high refined carbohydrates, and large portion sizes. A large fast-food meal (double cheeseburger, french fries, soft drink, and dessert) contains about 2,200 calories. As the consumption of fast food rises, one may expect to see a corresponding rise in childhood and adolescent obesity.

Popular low-carbohydrate diets, most notably the Atkins diet (Atkins, 2002), may be altering the high-carbohydrate trend in our country. Many people have lost weight successfully on the Atkins diet. However, the diet calls for extreme reduction in carbohydrate intake, including all fruits and most vegetables at the weight-reduction portion of the diet. This restriction makes the diet suspect to many, especially those dealing with obesity issues with children. Ideally, as adults become more aware of the dangers of carbohydrate-rich diets, this will affect the way children are fed at home and in their school and day-care environments.

Environment

Certainly a child's home environment also influences the risk of obesity. Strauss and Knight (1999) found that maternal obesity was the most consistent predictor of childhood obesity. Low family income and low cognitive stimulation in the home were also found to be significant predictors. Another study (Whitaker, Wright, Pepe, Seidel, & Dietz, 1997) found that the chances of becoming obese are 3 times greater if a child has one obese parent, and the chances are increased to over 10 times if both parents are obese. During infancy, children who were breast-fed seem to be at less risk for obesity than those who were bottle-fed (Gillman et al., 2001). Eating out more, particularly fast foods, is seen as a greater risk than eating meals cooked at home. Eating dinner together as a family has been shown to decrease television viewing and improve diet quality (Gillman et al., 2000).

Consequences of Obesity

There are many medical complications caused by obesity, including hypertension and other cardiovascular disease risk factors. Type 2 diabetes is a condition attributed almost entirely to the epidemic of childhood and adolescent obesity (Ludwig & Ebbeling, 2001). Complications caused by Type 2 diabetes include heart disease, stroke, limb amputation, kidney failure, and blindness. According to Dean and Flett (2002), 10% of children with Type 2 diabetes develop renal failure, requiring dialysis or even resulting in death at an early age. Pulmonary complications include sleep apnea, asthma, and exercise intolerance. The presence of asthma and exercise intolerance can reduce a child's activity level, leading to further weight gain (Ebbeling et al., 2002).

The psychosocial consequences of childhood and adolescent obesity can also be very serious. Obese children are often stereotyped as lazy, socially inept, academically slow, unhealthy, and having poor hygiene (Hill & Silver, 1995). These children experience early and systematic discrimination in our society (Dietz, 1998). As a result of society's negative view of obesity, children and adolescents who are overweight experience low self-esteem, negative self-image, loneliness, and nervousness and display high-risk behaviors (Davison & Birch, 2001; Strauss, 2000). These adverse psychosocial effects seem to be more severe in Caucasian children, particularly girls, than in other ethnic and racial groups (Kimm et al., 1997).

Based on these serious consequences of obesity, Jerum and Melnyk (2001) point out that the "estimates of the costs of society related to obesity are more than 99 billion dollars per year due to physical complications, negative mental health outcomes, increased use of medical services, and loss of productivity" (p. 606). They further urge professionals "to develop, test, and translate evidence-based interventions for the treatment and prevention of child and adolescent obesity into practice" (p. 606).

Prognosis and Treatment

Obese children can develop serious medical and psychological complications and are at a greatly increased risk for early mortality. Ebbeling et al. (2002) point out that the key to the prevention and treatment of obesity is to encourage children and adolescents to eat less and be more active. Although this sounds fairly straightforward, the treatment of obesity has proven to be very difficult. Many interventions for childhood obesity have been based on family and parental support, but a review of controlled studies (Epstein, Myers, Raynor, & Saelens, 1998) of family interventions concluded that most obesity interventions have led to little weight loss and high relapse rates. One group of researchers (Haddock, Shadish, Klesges, & Stein, 1994), conducting a meta-analysis of interventions to reduce obesity in children, concluded that interventions that incorporated knowledge, behavioral, and exercise components were more likely to result in weight loss than those interventions that did not include these components. Involvement of at least one parent was also found to produce better weight loss outcomes than interventions that did not involve parents (Epstein, Coleman, & Myers, 1996). .

School-based interventions have concentrated on prevention rather than treatment of childhood and adolescent obesity. One intervention (Robinson, 1999) aimed at reducing television viewing and video game playing reported a significant reduction in BMI, a decrease in the amount of time watching television, and a decrease in the number of meals eaten in front of the television. A school-based program, Planet Health (Gortmaker et al., 1999), attempted to decrease dietary fat consumption, increase consumption of fruits and vegetables, increase physical activity, and decrease television viewing. Over 2 years, the prevalence of obesity among girls in the school decreased, one of very few programs that resulted in an effect on obesity prevalence. A possible weakness of many of these school-based prevention programs is the emphasis on fat reduction. With the new research pointing toward a reduction in refined carbohydrates and an increase in unsaturated fats, this emphasis on fat reduction may have actually made weight loss more difficult (Ebbeling et al., 2002).

WHAT CAN TEACHERS DO?

If a student is obese, there is probably very little a teacher can do to directly help that child. Obviously, the parents are aware of their child's problem and may respond negatively if the teacher suggests that something must be done for their child. However, if a teacher suspects, based on the signs and symptoms discussed earlier, that a student is suffering from an eating disorder, he or she should refer the student to the school counselor who in turn may refer the student to a therapist who specializes in eating disorders. For many reasons, parents may fail to recognize an eating disorder, even one that is fairly obvious to other people who come in contact with the child. Having a teacher or counselor point out the obvious, or not so obvious, problem could possibly save a child's life. Where teachers may have tremendous influence is in the prevention of eating disorders and obesity.

PREVENTION OF EATING DISORDERS

Herrin and Matsumoto (2002) challenge parents and teachers to help strengthen children and adolescents in three areas to help protect them from developing eating problems.

Arm Children Emotionally and Socially

First, parents and teachers can arm children "emotionally and socially to help protect [them] from the specific personality traits, stressful life events, physical changes, and peer pressures that can put [them] at risk for eating problems" (Herrin & Matsumoto, 2002, p. 37). Specific suggestions include these (from Herrin & Matsumoto, 2002):

- *Work on building the child's self-esteem.* "Try to foster in her a sense of autonomy, or the feeling that she has control over important aspects of her life" (p. 37).
- *Seek help for depressed children.* "The depressed child is more vulnerable to disordered eating as well as to eating disorders" (p. 38).
- *Teach healthier coping mechanisms.* "Show your child healthier ways to cope with anxiety, fear, anger, disappointment, or depression. Be careful not to encourage your child to use food to calm, soothe, or reward herself" (p. 38).

- *Watch for early signs of perfectionism, compulsiveness, or obsessiveness.* "Encourage your perfectionistic child to aim to achieve in more productive arenas than changing her body size, such as sports, academics, art, theater. . . . Obsessiveness is reflected in a preoccupation with orderliness at the expense of flexibility and spontaneity. . . . Obsessiveness is often expressed as a constant worry that he has consumed too much fat or too many calories. . . . Compulsiveness is often expressed in the form of counting calories and fat grams" (p. 39).
- *Be watchful if a child is moody, has problems with impulse control, often overdoes things, or tends to get overinvolved in fun activities.* This may be particularly true with a child who is sensitive to peer and cultural messages.
- *Be watchful around the onset of puberty.* "Hormonally induced changes in mood, body size and shape, and especially body fat can trigger eating problems among adolescents. . . . make it clear that these changes are normal and expected" (p. 40).
- *Encourage families to eat together as much as possible.* "By preparing and enjoying healthy meals together as a family, you are helping to lay down a strong protective defense against eating problems. . . . Young adolescents who eat most meals alone or with friends are more likely to diet, skip meals, and make unhealthy choices" (p. 42).

Arm Children With Knowledge and Information

Second, parents and teachers can arm children with "information and critical thinking abilities that will help protect [them] from the powerful and sometimes destructive cultural messages that saturate our modern-day lives" (Herrin & Matsumoto, 2002, p. 37). Specific suggestions include the following (from Herrin & Matsumoto, 2002):

- *Promote media literacy.* "It is our job to teach our children to think critically about the influence of the media, to understand the power of magazines, movies, popular music, and television to influence the way we think and behave" (p. 46). This is one area where teachers may have a significant impact, particularly if this critical thinking skill is taught to students from a very young age.
- *Show indifference to the cultural ideal of thinness.* "Through your words and actions . . . demonstrate that you care little for the incessant messages our culture bombards us with promoting the thinness ideal" (p. 47).

Arm Children With Positive Attitudes

Finally, parents and teachers can arm children with "positive attitudes toward food, size, and shape" (Herrin & Matsumoto, 2002, p. 37). Specific suggestions include the following:

- Give children the freedom to choose food, while encouraging them to eat well.
- Provide regular meals and snacks.
- Encourage picky eaters to try a wide variety of foods, but don't pressure them to eat.
- Model body self-acceptance by not discussing your dieting attempts and by not making negative comments about your own body size or shape.
- Model healthy attitudes toward eating and exercise.

- Be aware of food and exercise attitudes that are inappropriate for a child's age.
- Explain to children that different children have different body types. Concentrate on keeping the body healthy and functioning well.
- Do not buy magazines that glorify thinness.
- Do not allow your children to tease other people about their body size or shape.
- Avoid overly purist attitudes toward food. Forbidding the consumption of certain foods can make these foods seem even more attractive to a child.
- Do not instill a fear of fat in children by counting calories or fat grams.
- Be very careful about restricting your child's eating. Dieting can precede both obesity and eating disorders.
- Do not tell children they must clean their plates. They must learn to control their own food intake and learn to trust their own sense of being full. Do not allow children to eat dessert only after they have cleaned their plates. They may eat dessert even though they are full, because it may not be available to them at the next meal.

PREVENTION OF OBESITY

Several researchers and organizations offer suggestions to help prevent childhood obesity (American Academy of Pediatrics Committee on Nutrition, 2003; American Obesity Association, 2002; Ebbeling et al., 2002). Many of these suggestions require parental involvement, but in some cases, teachers can challenge the children in a variety of ways to influence their out-of-school behaviors:

- Limit television and video time to a maximum of 2 hours per day.
- Promote healthy eating patterns by offering nutritious snacks, such as vegetables and fruits, low-fat dairy food, and whole grains.
- Make time for the entire family to participate in regular physical activities.
- Assign active chores to every family member.
- Enroll children in structured physical activities.
- Implement the same healthy diet for your entire family, not just selected individuals.
- Prepare food together with your children.
- Eat meals together at the dinner table at regular times.
- Do not rush to finish meals.
- Do not engage in other activities (such as TV viewing) during mealtimes.
- Avoid large serving sizes.
- Limit the frequency of fast foods to no more than once per week.
- Do not use food as a reward or the lack of food as punishment.
- Model healthy food choices, set appropriate limits on food choices, and encourage your child's autonomy in self-regulation of food intake.

Although these suggestions are most relevant to the home environment, teachers can often influence children's behavior at home through assignments, challenges, and education. Other suggestions are clearly school based and require commitments from school boards, teachers, principals, and school-based parent organizations:

- Establish healthy standards for school lunches (i.e., eliminate availability of unhealthy foods, such as fast foods and soft drinks).
- Fund mandatory physical education.
- Provide adequate time for eating and physical activity during the school day.
- Encourage teachers not to use candy or other unhealthy treats as a reward.

Finally, there are community-wide actions that can help promote healthy eating and activities:

- Protect open spaces in your community.
- Build sidewalks, bike paths, parks, and playgrounds in your community.
- Improve insurance coverage for obesity treatment.
- Consider a tax on fast food and soft drinks, subsidize healthy foods, such as fruits and vegetables, require nutrition labels on fast foods, prohibit food advertisement directed at children, and increase funding for campaigns to prevent obesity.

There are many recommendations here that may help prevent obesity and eating disorders in our children and adolescents. Clearly, no teacher can be involved in all these prevention efforts. However, if teachers could select one of these challenges that is particularly appropriate to the age-group they teach, they have a tremendous opportunity to affect change in the eating behaviors and self-image of today's children and adolescents.

SUMMARY

Eating disorders and obesity are severe problems among youths in our society today. There is clearly a link between our society's ideal of extreme thinness, today's trend toward a sedentary lifestyle, and the current epidemics of obesity, Anorexia Nervosa, and Bulimia Nervosa among our children and adolescents. Dieting from an early age leads children and adolescents into disordered eating patterns that, in some young people, lead to the development of obesity and eating disorders. Teachers, because they are in a very influential position with children, are poised to help prevent the development of unrealistic body image, unhealthy eating habits, and potentially ruinous dieting habits from an early age.

DISCUSSION QUESTIONS

1. How does today's society influence our children and adolescents in their eating habits, exercise habits, and body image?
2. What are your views of dieting? How can dieting influence the development of Anorexia Nervosa, Bulimia Nervosa, and obesity?
3. Consider some of the consequences of obesity both to individuals and to society.
4. After reading the case study, do you think Sandra is developing an eating disorder? What are the signs that helped you reach this conclusion? What do you think the teacher should do?

FOR ADDITIONAL HELP

	Organization	*Web Address*	*Description*
Anorexia Nervosa, Bulimia Nervosa, and Obesity	National Eating Disorders Association (NEDA)	www.nationaleatingdisorders.org	NEDA is dedicated to expanding public understanding of eating disorders and promoting access to quality treatment for those affected along with support for their families through education, advocacy, and research.
	Eating Disorders Association (EDA)	www.edauk.com	You will find information and help on all aspects of eating disorders, including Anorexia Nervosa, Bulimia Nervosa, Binge Eating Disorder, and related eating disorders.
	Planet Health—Harvard Prevention Research Center on Nutrition and Physical Activity	www.hsph.harvard.edu/prc/proj_planet.html	Planet Health is an interdisciplinary curriculum focused on improving the health and well-being of sixth- through eighth-grade students. Through classroom and physical education (PE) activities, Planet Health aims to increase activity, improve dietary quality, and decrease inactivity.
	American Obesity Association	www.obesity.org/subs/childhood	The American Obesity Association is focused on changing public policy and perceptions about obesity.

REFERENCES

American Academy of Pediatrics Committee on Nutrition. (2003). Prevention of pediatric overweight and obesity. *Pediatrics, 112,* 424–430.

American Obesity Association. (2002). *Childhood obesity.* Retrieved March 17, 2004, from http://obesity.org/subs/childhood

American Psychiatric Association. (1980). *Diagnostic and statistical manual of mental disorders* (3rd ed.). Washington, DC: Author.

American Psychiatric Association. (1987). *Diagnostic and statistical manual of mental disorders* (3rd ed., Rev.). Washington, DC: Author.

American Psychiatric Association. (1994). *Diagnostic and statistical manual of mental disorders* (4th ed.). Washington, DC: Author.

American Psychiatric Association. (2000). *Diagnostic and statistical manual of mental disorders* (4th ed., text revision). Washington, DC: Author.

Andersen, R. E., Crespo, C. J., Bartlett, S. J., Cheskin, L. J., & Pratt, M. (1998). Relationship of physical activity and television watching with body weight and level of fatness among children: Results from the Third National Health and Nutrition Examination Survey. *JAMA, 279,* 938–942.

Atkins, R. C. (2002). *Dr. Atkins' new diet revolution.* New York: Avon Books.

Davison, K. K., & Birch, L. L. (2001). Weight status, parent reaction, and self-concept in five-year-old girls. *Pediatrics, 107,* 46–53.

Dean, H., & Flett, B. (2002). Natural history of Type 2 diabetes diagnosed in childhood: Long term follow-up in young adult years. *Diabetes, 51,* A24.

Dietz, W. H. (1998). Health consequences of obesity in youth: Childhood predictors of adult disease. *Pediatrics, 101,* 518–525.

Dunn, A. M. (2000). Nutrition. In C. E. Burns, M. A. Brady, A. M. Dunn, & N. B. Starr (Eds.), *Pediatric primary care: A handbook for nurse practitioners* (pp. 243–302). Philadelphia: W. B. Saunders.

Ebbeling, C. B., Pawlak, D. B., & Ludwig, D. S. (2002). Childhood obesity: Public-health crisis, common sense cure. *Lancet, 360,* 473–482.

Epstein, L. H., Coleman, K. J., & Myers, M. D. (1996). Exercise in treating obesity in children and adolescents. *Medical Science Sports Exercise, 28,* 428–435.

Epstein, L. H., Myers, M. D., Raynor, H. A., & Saelens, B. E. (1998). Treatment of pediatric obesity. *Pediatrics, 101,* 554–570.

Fairburn, C. G. (1988). The current status of the psychological treatments for bulimia nervosa. *Journal of Psychosomatic Medicine, 32,* 635–645.

Fairburn, C. G., Cooper, Z., Doll, H. A., & Welch, S. L. (1999). Risk factors for anorexia nervosa: Three integrated case-control comparisons. *Archives of General Psychiatry, 56,* 468–476.

Fairburn, C. G., & Harrison, P. J. (2003). Eating disorders. *Lancet, 361,* 407–416.

Fairburn, C. G., Marcus, M. D., & Wilson, G. T. (1993). Cognitive-behavioral therapy for binge eating and bulimia nervosa: A comprehensive treatment manual. In C. G. Fairburn & G. T. Wilson (Eds.), *Binge eating: Nature, assessment, and treatment* (pp. 361–404). New York: Guilford Press.

Farooqi, I. S., & O'Rahilly, S. (2000). Recent advances in the genetics of severe obesity. *Archives of Disabled Children, 83,* 31–34.

Flegel, K. M., & Troiano, R. P. (2000). Changes in the distribution of body mass index of adults and children in the US population. *International Journal of Obesity, 24,* 807–818.

Gillman, M. W., Rifas-Shiman, S. L., Camargo, C. A., Jr., Berkey, C. S., Frazier, A. L., Rockett, H. R., et al. (2001). Risk of overweight among adolescents who were breastfed as infants. *JAMA, 285,* 2461–2467.

Gillman, M. W., Rifas-Shiman, S. L., Frazier, A. L., Rockett, H. R., Camargo, C. A., Jr., Field, A. E., et al. (2000). Family dinner and diet quality among older children and adolescents. *Archives of Family Medicine, 9,* 235–240.

Gortmaker, S. L., Peterson, K., Wiecha, J., Sobol, A. M., Dixit, S., Fox, M. K., et al. (1999). Reducing obesity via a school-based interdisciplinary intervention among youth. *Archives of Pediatric and Adolescent Medicine, 153,* 409–418.

Gross, J., & Rosen, J. C. (1988). Bulimia in adolescents: Prevalence and psychosocial correlates. *International Journal of Eating Disorders, 7,* 51–61.

Haddock, C. K., Shadish, W. R., Klesges, R. C., & Stein, R. J. (1994). Treatments for child and adolescent obesity. *American Behavioral Medicine, 16,* 235–244.

Hall, L., & Ostroff, M. (1998). *Anorexia nervosa: A guide to recovery.* Carlsbad, CA: Gurze Books.

Hernandez, B., Gortmaker, S. L., Colditz, G. A., Peterson, K. E., Laird, N. M., & Para-Cabrera, S. (1999). Association of obesity with physical activity, television programs and other forms of video viewing among children in Mexico City. *International Journal of Obesity, 23,* 845–854.

Herrin, M., & Matsumoto, N. (2002). *The parent's guide to childhood eating disorders.* New York: Henry Holt.

Hill, A. J., & Silver, E. K. (1995). Fat, friendless and unhealthy: 9-year-old children's perception of body shape stereotypes. *International Journal of Obesity, 19,* 423–430.

Jerum, A., & Melnyk, B. M. (2001). Effectiveness of interventions to prevent obesity and obesity-related complications in children and adolescents. *Pediatric Nursing, 27,* 606–610.

Kennedy, S. H., & Garfinkel, P. E. (1992). Advances in diagnosis and treatment of anorexia nervosa and bulimia nervosa. *Canadian Journal of Psychiatry, 37,* 309–315.

Kimm, S. Y., Barton, B. A., Berhane, K., Ross, J. W., Payne, G. H., & Schreiber, G. B. (1997). Self-esteem and adiposity in black and white girls: The NHLBI Growth and Health Study. *Annals of Epidemiology, 7,* 550–560.

Kimm, S. Y. S., Barton, B. A., Obarzanek, E., McMahon, R. P., Kronsberg, S. S., Waclawiw, M. A., et al. (2002, November). Obesity development during adolescence in a biracial cohort: The NHLBI Growth and Health Study. *Pediatrics, 110*(5).

Kimm, S. Y. S., & Obarzanek, E. (2002). Childhood obesity: A new pandemic of the new millennium. *Pediatrics, 110,* 1003–1007.

Lachenmeyer, J. R., & Muni-Brander, P. (1988). Eating disorders in a nonclinical adolescent population: Implications for treatment. *Adolescence, 23,* 303–312.

Lock, J., le Grange, D., Agras, W. S., & Dare, C. (2001). *Treatment manual for anorexia nervosa: A family-based approach.* New York: Guilford Press.

Ludwig, D. S., & Ebbeling, C. B. (2001). Type 2 diabetes mellitus in children: Primary care and public health considerations. *JAMA, 286,* 1427–1430.

Ludwig, D. S., Majzoub, J. A., Al-Zahrani, A., Dallal, G. E., Blanco, I., & Roberts, S. B. (1999). High glycemic index foods, overeating, and obesity. *Pediatrics, 103,* e26.

Ludwig, D. S., Peterson, K. E., & Gortmaker, S. L. (2001). Relation between consumption of sugar-sweetened drinks and childhood obesity: A prospective, observational analysis. *Lancet, 357,* 505–508.

Maceyko, S. J., & Nagelberg, D. B. (1985). The assessment of bulimia in high school students. *Journal of School Health, 55,* 135–137.

Myers, L. L. (1996). Bulimia nervosa: What social workers need to know. *Journal of Applied Social Sciences, 20,* 63–75.

National Heart, Lung, and Blood Institute. (1998). Clinical guidelines on the identification, evaluation, and treatment of overweight and obesity in adults: The evidence report. *Obesity Research, 6*(Suppl. 2), 51S-209S.

O'Connor, M. A., Touyz, S. W., & Beumont, P. J. V. (1987). Nutritional management and dietary counseling in bulimia: Some preliminary observations. *International Journal of Eating Disorders, 7,* 657–662.

Rankinen, T., Perusse, L., Weisnagel, S. J., Snyder, E. E., Chagnon, Y. C., & Bouchard, C. (2002). The human obesity gene map: The 2001 update. *Obesity Research, 10,* 196–243.

Robinson, T. (1999). Reducing children's television viewing to prevent obesity: A randomized controlled trial. *JAMA, 282,* 1561–1567.

Russell, G. F. M. (2001). Involuntary treatment in anorexia nervosa. *Psychiatric Clinics of North America, 24,* 337–349.

Russell, G. F. M., Szmukler, G. I., Dare, C., & Eisler, I. (1987). An evaluation of family therapy in anorexia nervosa and bulimia nervosa. *Archives of General Psychiatry, 44,* 1047–1056.

Schlundt, D. G., & Johnson, W. G. (1990). *Eating disorders: Assessment and treatment.* Boston, MA: Allyn & Bacon.

Steinhausen, H. C. (2002). The outcome of anorexia nervosa in the 20th century. *American Journal of Psychiatry, 159,* 1284–1293.

Strauss, R. S. (2000). Childhood obesity and self-esteem. *Pediatrics, 105,* e15.

Strauss, R., & Knight, J. (1999). The influence of the home environment on the development of obesity in children. *Pediatrics, 103,* 1278–1279.

Strauss, R. S., & Pollack, H. A. (2001). Epidemic increase in childhood overweight, 1986–1998. *JAMA, 286,* 2845–2848.

Subar, A. F., Krebs-Smith, S. M., Cook, A., & Kahle, L. L. (1998). Dietary sources of nutrients among US children, 1989–1991. *Pediatrics, 102,* 913–923.

Sullivan, P. F., Bulik, C. M., Carter, F. A., Gendall, K. A., & Joyce, P. R. (1996). The significance of a prior history of anorexia in bulimia nervosa. *International Journal of Eating Disorders, 20,* 253–261.

Troiano, R. P., Briefel, R. R., Carroll, M. D., & Bialostosky, K. (2000). Energy and fat intakes of children and adolescents in the United States: Data from the National Health and Nutrition Examination Surveys. *American Journal of Clinical Nutrition, 72*(Suppl.), 1343S–1353S.

VanThorre, M. D., & Vogel, F. X. (1985). The presence of bulimia in high school females. *Adolescence, 20,* 45–51.

Whitaker, A., Davies, M., Shaffer, D., Johnson, J., Abrams, S., Walsh, B. T., & Kalikow, K. (1989). The struggle to be thin: A survey of anorexic and bulimic symptoms in a non-referred adolescent population. *Psychological Medicine, 19,* 143–163.

Whitaker, R. C., & Dietz, W. H. (1998). Role of the prenatal environment in the development of obesity. *Journal of Pediatrics, 132,* 768–776.

Whitaker, R. C., Wright, J. A., Pepe, M. S., Seidel, K. D., & Dietz, W. H. (1997). Predicting obesity in young adulthood from childhood and parental obesity. *New England Journal of Medicine, 337,* 869–873.

Willett, W. C., & Stampfer, M. J. (2003). Rebuilding the food pyramid. *Scientific American, 288,* 64–71.

Chapter 10

Conduct Disorder

Raymond J. Waller

Katherine S. Waller

Michelle Madden Schramm

Diane J. Bresson

PREREADING QUESTIONS

As you read this chapter, reflect on the following questions and issues:

1. What responsibilities do schools have to students who engage in behaviors that are illegal?
2. Are you more empathetic toward students who have behavior problems for a reason than you are toward students who are just "bad"?
3. How would you handle being afraid of a student in your classroom?
4. Why do some students engage in aggressive behavior?
5. Does aggressive or antisocial behavior suggest the presence of a personality flaw?

Students with Conduct Disorder present one of the most difficult philosophical and practical concerns to classroom educators. These students may engage in behaviors that are ostracizing, harmful, oppositional, or frightening. It is important to know that, although these are challenging behaviors, we as educators can make a crucial difference in the outcomes for students with Conduct Disorder.

CONDUCT DISORDER

Definition

Conduct Disorder (CD) refers to an enduring, habitual pattern of behavior involving violating the rights of other people or violating serious societal norms. Behaviors that you might observe in children with CD include, but are not limited to, bullying, stealing, threatening, intimidating, fighting, and vandalism. If these behaviors sound familiar but you recognize them by a different label, CD can also be referred to within some school settings as **social maladjustment** and within the legal system as **juvenile delinquency**. The onset of CD can manifest in the preschool years, but it is much more common for it to appear in middle childhood through middle adolescence. Estimates of the prevalence of CD range greatly but may affect anywhere between 1% and 10% of the school-age population (*DSM-IV-TR*; American Psychiatric Association, 2000), and the prevalence may be as high as 25% in some higher-risk subgroups—for example, children living in poverty (Rimm-Kaufman, Pianta, & Cox, 2000). Whatever the actual prevalence rate, the teacher observing the behaviors associated with CD knows how disruptive and disturbing these behaviors can be even to the veteran teacher. In fact, these behaviors in students are often cited as one of the primary reasons that teachers leave the field of education ("Behave, or Else," 2004).

ETIOLOGY

A variety of factors have been implicated in the expression of CD, including genetics (Seligman, 1993); difficult childhood temperament (Kanchanska, 1993); social learning (Eddy, Reid, & Curry, 2002); coercive, ineffective, or inconsistent parenting (Patterson, DeGarmo, & Knutson, 2000); and difficulty and lack of success in the educational setting (Kazdin, 1998). There are two primary types of CD: early onset and late onset. Early onset CD manifests prior to age 10, and late onset appears after age 10. This chapter concentrates on early onset CD for four specific reasons. First and most obvious, early onset CD affects the school setting for a much longer period of time. Second, although the prognosis for early onset CD *without intervention* is poor (Walker, Ramsey, & Gresham, 2004), conduct-related problems in young children appear to be malleable and responsive to effective intervention (Webster-Stratton, Reid, & Hammond, 2004). Third, the interventions for early onset CD are more treatment oriented, and many can be put into practice in the school setting. Conversely, interventions for late onset CD are more likely to involve the juvenile justice system, which yields a high level of **recidivism.** In fact, some studies (e.g., Snyder, 1998) report the rate of recidivism for child and adolescent criminal offenders to be as high as 90%. Finally, the behaviors associated with the manifestation of CD can become entrenched behavior patterns in children at a young age, which may begin a downward spiraling combination of school and social failure concurrent with disruptive behavior that has been particularly difficult to address once children enter adolescence (Ruma, Burke, & Thompson, 1996). Therefore, early intervention is clearly the preferred option.

Intervention

Intervention for children with CD can be a difficult proposition. As noted, the behaviors associated with CD can be, by definition, amazingly disruptive in the classroom. Contrasted with an **internalizing disorder** such as depression, CD is categorized as an **externalizing disorder**, so the symptoms are likely to be patently obvious. The good news is that there are both general strategies that can moderate disruptions in the classroom and specific approaches to addressing CD that have shown **efficacy** in intervening with students with CD.

General Classroom Strategies

Strategy 1: Get Help

Some problems confronted in the classroom can be effectively attended to in the classroom by you alone. However, CD represents a serious problem, and you need as much help as is reasonably available. Intervention planning is best done within the context of a team approach. Viable team members include you, the school counselor, the school social worker, the school psychologist, school administrators, and the child's parents or guardians. One function of the team is to develop a **behavior intervention plan** that includes contingencies for a variety of disruptive behavior situations. For example, in the most extreme circumstances, you may have a student with CD who loses control. In a case such as this, it might be wise to have a contingency plan that allows you to clear the other students out of the room or to have an alternative location where the student with CD can go to regain composure. This is difficult to do if you are alone in the classroom, but it is easier if there is a teacher assistant in your room. If you are alone, you might want to strategize with the office staff to have help come in a swift but inconspicuous way. Perhaps there is a school counselor or school social worker to whom the student could go for a cool-down period. *Always keep in mind that safety is the primary concern.* The most effective behavior intervention plans are those built on data obtained from a **functional behavior assessment** (FBA). An FBA is a powerful set of procedures that can involve interviewing, completion of paper-and-pencil measures, direct observation, or preferably some combination of these. The purpose of conducting an FBA is to determine the *function* of a behavior. Once you have identified the function of a behavior, it is much easier to design interventions that will be effective. An FBA is required by federal law under certain circumstances for some students receiving special education services, so it is almost ensured that the procedures and expertise needed to conduct an FBA already exist in your school system. Talk to your administrator to find out how to access help with this.

Strategy 2: Avoid Power Struggles

The student with CD may be more likely to engage in challenging you directly than will other students. This is likely a pattern of behavior that has been effective in some settings. Directly challenging you can also serve other purposes. For example, it can allow the student to get attention from you. Although it may seem illogical that a student would seek negative attention from you, it may be that students with CD get primarily negative attention from adults, and any kind of attention is better than none. Also, challenging your authority can serve the purpose of helping the student avoid academic tasks that he or she finds unpleasant. If a student can engage you in an argument, he or she can put off attempting the assignments that you have given. The student might get sent to the office and avoid the work altogether. Another possibility, particularly with older students, is that challenging your authority provides the student with a degree of popularity or peer respect that he or she has not been successful at achieving in more prosocial ways, such as academic success. Some steps in assisting with avoiding power struggles are to (a) remain calm, (b) have plans in place to implement if behavioral escalation occurs, (c) communicate your expectations to the student, and (d) be consistent.

Strategy 3: Be Honest With Yourself

Many of us who engage in the process of educating educators emphasize the need to base your work on research-based "best practices," but we also acknowledge that there is a time and a place for philosophizing and reflection. If you are to effectively engage students with disruptive behavior disorders such as CD, you must determine if you are more inclined to think that such students (a) should receive interventions to address their problematic behaviors or (b) should be punished for their disruptive behaviors. Do you think that children who engage in behaviors that are illegal should be served in a school setting, or should these behaviors be addressed by the juvenile courts? We frequently hear of children who manifest behaviors associated with CD as described as being B-A-D, contrasted with having a disability, such as having an emotional/behavior disorder or a diagnosed mental health problem. Labeling a child as *bad* does not help serve the best interests of the child, classroom, school, or community. Although it is true that students with CD can be turned off of school and pushed out of school, the outcomes for students in this situation tend to be poor. Moreover, the assumption that students with CD are simply bad is not supported by evidence. In fact, most students with CD are **comorbid** for other problems as well. Common comorbities seen in children with CD include Attention Deficit Hyperactivity Disorder (Barkley, Guevremont, Anastopoulos, DuPaul, & Shelton, 1993) and internalizing disorders such as depression and anxiety (Angold, Costello, & Erkanli, 1999). Furthermore, children with CD are much more likely than other children to have the following:

- Parents experiencing a high level of overall stress (Pinderhughes, Dodge, Bates, Pettit, & Zelli, 2000)
- A mother with depression or a father who abuses drugs (Beauchaine, Webster-Stratton, & Reid, 2005)
- Parents who are experiencing psychological difficulty, such as marital discord and poor family relationships; a family history of **psychopathology**; and residing in poverty (Kazdin, 1998)
- Parents who are more likely to use harsh and inconsistent forms of discipline and to be less nurturing to their children (Patterson, Reid, & Dishon, 1992)

Thus, most children with CD experience emotional duress, much like a child who has clinical depression or an anxiety disorder. The belief that children with CD are just B-A-D is unfounded and does not facilitate effective intervention planning. Please keep in mind that, for even the most severe behaviors associated with CD such as aggressive behaviors, a variety of interventions have been found to be helpful for most children (Johnson & Waller, in press).

Strategy 4: Reframe Your Perceptions

One of the most common of human responses is to avoid things that we find too different or unsettling. It is, therefore, paramount when we have students who engage in behaviors that we find disconcerting or frightening that we take the time to reframe our initial distaste or fear and concentrate on the understanding that all behavior serves a function. Children do not engage in behaviors because they are "bad" but because those behaviors have served an effective purpose for that student at some point and in some environment. This is also true for aggressive and violent behavior and other behaviors associated with CD. Considering the example of aggressive behavior, think about some of the potential functions of aggressive behavior. One of the first things that should be acknowledged about aggressive behavior is that it *works,* in that it often gets the aggressor what he or she wants (at least in the short term). A powerful component of aggression is that it instills fear in other people, and fear can inspire us to give other people what they want (again, at least in the short term). Some children have systematically learned that fear can be very effective in helping them avoid unpleasant situations and in getting them things, both tangible and intangible, that they want from other people. You must make the effort to reframe your views on aggressive behaviors. Although fear is a natural response, fear will not change aggressive behavior for the better, and it tends to cause us to make negative assumptions about the aggressor or label him or her as a "bad" student. Aggression is actually a functional behavior, and we can best intervene or change this behavior by making the behavior irrelevant or ineffective. However, the safety of all students must be of utmost concern.

Strategy 5: Develop a Positive Relationship With Your Students

The effectiveness of your behavior management plan with students with CD depends, at least in part, on your ability to market it to your students. Your ability to market your behavior management plan will depend in part on your ability to develop and maintain a positive relationship with your students. The mechanics and implementation of the behavior management plan can be tailored to suit your individual classroom and your own creativity. The more that you can get them invested in what is happening in the classroom, the more effective it is likely to be. Your plan is less likely to be successful, particularly for students with disruptive behavior disorders such as Attention Deficit Hyperactivity Disorder, Oppositional Defiant Disorder, and CD, if students perceive that you are attempting to force rules onto them. Students with CD can be particularly resistant to what they see as imposed control. Whether you choose a token economy, a point system, or other preferred behavior management plan, you will greatly enhance the effectiveness of it by getting your students to buy into it.

Strategy 6: Become a Consistent Source of Positive Reinforcement

When confronting a student with considerable disruptive behaviors, it can be challenging to train yourself to interact with that student in a positive way. It is easy to get into a pattern of correcting students rather than reinforcing the things that they are doing well. If you have children of your own, think about how parents can unintentionally reinforce argumentative behavior in children. If you have more than one child, when your children are playing together quietly, you are less likely to attend to what they are doing. This is a good opportunity for you to breath, without serving as referee. However, as soon as the sibling rivalry or disagreements begin, we are often forced to intervene. By doing so, we are unintentionally giving our attention to our children when they are behaving in ways that we *don't* want them to behave, unintentionally reinforcing behaviors that are less preferable. The same situations can easily arise in the classroom; we unintentionally ignore, or pay less attention to, students who are quietly progressing in their assignments and give *more* of our attention to students who are not progressing or who are being disruptive. We can avoid this misbehavior trap by teaching ourselves to be, in essence, a continuous source of positive reinforcement. This involves attending to the positive things that most of our students are doing much of the time rather than giving our attention primarily to negative issues. In some difficult cases, it is challenging to find a student doing *anything* to reinforce. When this happens, sometimes it is helpful to contrive a situation or circumstance for which the student may be reinforced. It can also be very helpful to reinforce the behavior of other students in the classroom who are adhering to classroom rules. This can frequently provide the impetus for other students to engage in the desired behavior. Therefore, when you say, "I like the way Damien is working quietly," other children often rapidly follow the model that Damien has set. Sometimes with a very disruptive student, just your making such a statement can break a chain of disruptive behavior long enough to create a situation to reinforce a child, such as "and now Billy is standing quietly." A small breakthrough can create the opportunity for additional positive attention, and positive interactions within the classroom have been found to reduce the behaviors associated with CD (Sprott, 2004).

Strategy 7: Use Your Creativity Positively

Teachers, as a group, are among the most creative people on earth. Although many educators are comfortable expressing their creativity in instructional ways, some are less relaxed about employing their creativity in the area of behavior management. What some teachers find is that the behavior management plan that worked last year may be ineffective this year. One reason is that a classroom may operate adequately with a substandard behavior management plan if there are no students in that classroom with substantial behavioral issues. However, the introduction into that classroom of a student with disruptive behaviors will almost invariably necessitate the induction of an effective behavior management plan. A classroom full of students with no behavioral or emotional difficulties may respond to the mild threats, intimidations, and disapproval that some educators use to exert influence in the classroom. Students with CD are unlikely to respond favorably to this. The frustration that teachers can experience based on the ineffectiveness of previously used techniques can be exacerbated by the additional frustration of the disruptive behaviors themselves, and the result can be desperation. This desperation may then result in a spiral of doing ineffective things *more,* because they worked in the past. Additional threats and mild punishments from the teacher are likely to result in an escalation of disruptive behavior, resulting in more attempts from the teacher to punish the disruptive behaviors into annihilation. Some teachers have used their considerable creativity to try to devise more effective punishments, effectively doing more of what doesn't work, much like the thirsty consumer who, after loosing money in a soda machine, escalates from pushing the drink button to punching the button, to rocking the machine, to getting squashed under the weight of the machine that now rests on top of him or her. Even if punishment would work, you may find that you are unable to compete with the harsh and inconsistent punishment that many children with CD have experienced.

Better instead to turn your creative verve toward finding positive ways to reinforce the behaviors that you desire. Indeed, the ways that you can reinforce behavior are limited only by your imagination. One good example of this is when one of us (KSW) had a student who engaged in frequent, screaming tantrums. Although the teacher attempted, she could not determine a function of the tantrums, and no outside help was available. One day, the student was having more tantrums than usual, and he appeared to have a cold. The teacher took the student to have his temperature taken by the school nurse. The student's temperature was normal, but the nurse noted that the child had some nasal congestion. While in the clinic he dropped to the floor and began to scream and have another tantrum. The teacher said to the student, "Would you like some clinic water? It might make you feel better." The student nodded, and he was given "clinic water" from a small paper cup. From that point on, anytime that the student began a tantrum, he would ask if he could have some "water" (from a paper cup) to make himself feel better. Amazingly, the tantrums decreased from several a day to about two per week. Allow yourself to be creatively positive.

Corey D. is a 16-year-old, 10th-grade, Caucasian male living in a rural community. He was initially referred for an evaluation by his regular education teacher, who reported that Corey had made several threatening comments toward his peers. Corey would often throw objects at walls and cuss when he felt his classmates were ignoring him. Corey's mother, Mrs. Horton, confirmed his teacher's concerns about Corey's aggressive behavior. She also commented that he has made threatening comments toward her and her husband.

Corey's developmental history revealed that his mother took medication to prevent premature labor, but despite the doctor's attempt to prolong her pregnancy, Corey was born 4 weeks early, weighing 5 pounds, 9 ounces. Mrs. Horton reported that Corey was a happy baby. He walked at 14 months and talked around 18 months. Mrs. Horton also reported that aside from a brief hospital stay for pneumonia when Corey was 19 months old and an operation to insert tubes into Corey's ear when he was 24 months old, Corey was a healthy child.

According to Mrs. Horton, she had recently relocated in an attempt to provide a new environment for her son. Mrs. Horton reported that her son's friends had begun to participate in illegal behaviors, such as shoplifting. In addition, Mrs. Horton explained that Corey's home life has been filled with ups and downs. She reported that Corey's father was in and out of prison when Corey was younger. She divorced Corey's father when Corey was 5 years old. She remarried when Corey was 10 years old. Corey has never accepted the fact that his mother remarried. Mrs. Horton explained that Corey and her husband have verbally argued in the past, but recently Corey's comments have become threatening. For example, in a recent disagreement Corey threatened to smash his stepfather's face in.

Mrs. Horton reported that she responded to the disagreements by begging Corey to stop and agreeing to talk to her husband for Corey. Ultimately, this resulted in Corey turning his aggression toward her.

After a referral from Corey's regular education teacher, an assessment of Corey's academic, emotional, and behavioral functioning was conducted. As part of the assessment process, an FBA was also conducted. Information was gathered through an interview with Corey's mother, his stepfather, and his teacher. In addition to the interviews, direct observations of Corey's interactions within the classroom were taken over a period of 10 days. Data from these sources provided evidence that Corey met the criteria for CD. The FBA suggested that Corey had learned how to avoid classroom assignments through inappropriate comments and actions (e.g., cussing and/or making threatening comments to the point of getting out of his seat to stand over a peer in a form of intimidation). Furthermore, Corey's actions resulted in his being removed from the classroom to talk with his teacher or a member of the support team. When talking to the teacher or a member of the support team did not help, Corey would spend a class period in In-School Suspension (ISS). While in ISS, his work points were based on completing assignments that revolved around materials that interested Corey. Corey always managed to work his way out of ISS by following the rules and completing his assignments in time for physical education, Corey's favorite subject. Thus, the information from the FBA led the team to the hypothesis that the functions of his behavior were to seek attention and to escape from academic tasks.

Following the assessment, the school social worker met with the teacher and the support team to discuss the findings and to identify strategies to address Corey's needs. They agreed that Corey's aggressive behavior was reinforced by the teacher and the support team each time they removed Corey from class to talk with him at length about his behavior. In addition, they agreed that Corey's behaviors would improve dramatically right before his favorite subject. With this information, the school social worker, the teacher, and the support team set up a plan that provided peer assistance for Corey. This would provide Corey with academic assistance and the opportunity for positive interaction and attention. Corey was reluctant to work with a peer to complete his assignments. He expressed concern that he would appear "stupid" in front of his classmates. To remedy this situation, the teacher worked with Corey to establish rules for effectively working with another classmate to complete an assignment and offered the opportunity to everyone in the class to work with a peer to complete assignments. Corey seemed very receptive to this idea. He even thanked his teacher for including him in the decision process. As Corey began to spend more time in the classroom completing assignments and less time in ISS avoiding assignments, he quickly completed his assignments on his own so he could "help" his classmates who were struggling. This helpful attitude spilled over into other areas in his school career. For example, he began to encourage his classmates in physical education through positive praise instead of insults.

Corey's teacher also set up a token economy system for the class. The system allowed each student to receive tokens for coming prepared to class and starting to work on time and for respectful behavior toward everyone in the class in a

20-minute increment. The tokens could be traded in for activities that were decided on by the teacher and the students, including extra time to talk, extra computer time, or short breaks to play Nintendo. Corey enjoyed the extra privileges, but he became very argumentative the first time he did not receive tokens, claiming that the teacher was trying to make his life miserable. Over a few days, however, with the teacher consistently applying the token economy, Corey responded favorably to the system. He was still upset when he did not receive tokens, but his argumentative behavior lessened.

Corey's teacher and the support team also changed their response to his outbursts by developing a 1-2-3 plan. This plan involved placing a check on the board by his name each time that he engaged in disruptive behavior. The 1-2-3 plan proved to be very effective by drastically cutting down on the amount of individual attention Corey received from the teacher and the support team after his disruptive behavior occurred while providing him with a cue that he was being disruptive. The plan also reduced the opportunity for arguing between Corey and his teacher. In addition, during ISS Corey was expected to complete the same assignments his classmates were completing before returning to class instead of an easier assignment. He was given the opportunity to ask for assistance three times during his ISS stay. According to his teacher, this plan removed the extra attention Corey was receiving after an outburst, but it did not provide the escape from assignments that Corey often sought. It also removed the extra attention that he had been getting in ISS. Corey's teacher also commented that she felt more at ease in dealing with Corey's behaviors and that within a week, she was able to redirect Corey's behavior before his behavior turned aggressive by commenting on Corey's positive behaviors (e.g., "Corey, thank you for getting a pencil for Johnny").

By the end of the school year, Corey began to complete 90% of his assignments within the allotted time. He began to raise his hand more frequently to answer questions, and he began to ask for extra-credit opportunities. Corey's teacher provided extra-credit opportunities that revolved around subjects of interest to Corey, thus increasing his excitement about school. Corey began to engage in conversations with his teacher before and after class. Even Corey's mother reported that Corey seemed excited about school. She also reported that the relationship between Corey and his stepfather had improved. They were spending more time talking out their differences and less time yelling.

SPECIFIC STRATEGIES FOR INTERVENING WITH CONDUCT DISORDER

Beyond these general suggestions to help with disruptive behaviors associated with CD, specific programs can be purchased and implemented in classrooms and in schools. The following are curricula and activities that show promise in reducing disruptive behavior in the classroom. This is not intended to provide you with an exhaustive list of possible resources but to provide you with some examples of research-based programs that have shown efficacy when used in the classroom environment.

The PAX Good Behavior Game

The Good Behavior Game (GBG) has been used and improved for over 35 years. The GBG was originally invented by a first-year, fourth-grade teacher, Muriel Saunders, who had a very difficult group of students. The success of the GBG was first scientifically studied by Barrish, Saunders, and Wolf (1969). Since that time, more than 30 studies have reported on the power of the GBG (e.g., Darveaux, 1984; Kellam, Mayer, Rebok, & Hawkins, 1998; Medland & Stachnik, 1972; Tingstrom, 1994; van Lier, Muthen, van der Sar, & Crijnen, 2004; Warner, Miller, & Cohen, 1977). The newest and most researched permutation of the GBG is the PAX GBG. GBG is a response-cost activity for teams of students that rewards self-control over behaviors associated with CD. In very broad terms, GBG has been divided into six steps by Embry (2002):

1. Students are taught the definitions and rules of the game.
2. Students are taught which behaviors will interfere with desired outcomes. These behaviors are called "fouls."
3. Verbal and physical examples are demonstrated for students.
4. The teacher explains that the game is played in "innings," or time intervals decided on by the teacher. The game is not played for the entire day.
5. The teacher divides the class into teams and explains that the team with the fewest fouls wins.
6. The teacher maintains a prominently displayed scoreboard, like a baseball or football scoreboard.

Embry (2002) describes the GBG as a sort of "behavioral vaccine" that teaches self-control. Embry and his colleagues have added additional teacher-friendly components to make the GBG more powerful and quick acting and to improve time for teaching, which is why it is called the PAX Good Behavior Game.

Brief Summary of the GBG

We recommend the GBG for many reasons. First, it has demonstrated efficacy. This means that research findings support its use (see Figure 10.1). Indeed, GBG has been identified as a suggested strategy for youths with CD in the surgeon general's report on youth violence (2001). Second, the GBG is easy to implement in a classroom setting. Third, the GBG fits in well with other established classroom or schoolwide behavior management plans. Fourth, the GBG can be implemented and used successfully in your classroom even if your school does not have a schoolwide behavior management plan that has been successful for you or your students. Fifth, the GBG helps build delay of gratification and ability to regulate attention, which is likely to foster student self-management. Sixth, the GBG is relatively inexpensive, and all the materials needed to fully implement the game are available for about $250, which can be paid for by many sources of funds from special education funds, parent teacher associations, mental health collaborative efforts, gifts from parents, or

Figure 10.1 Results of One Study Showing Decreases in Disruptive Behaviors after Implementing the GBG

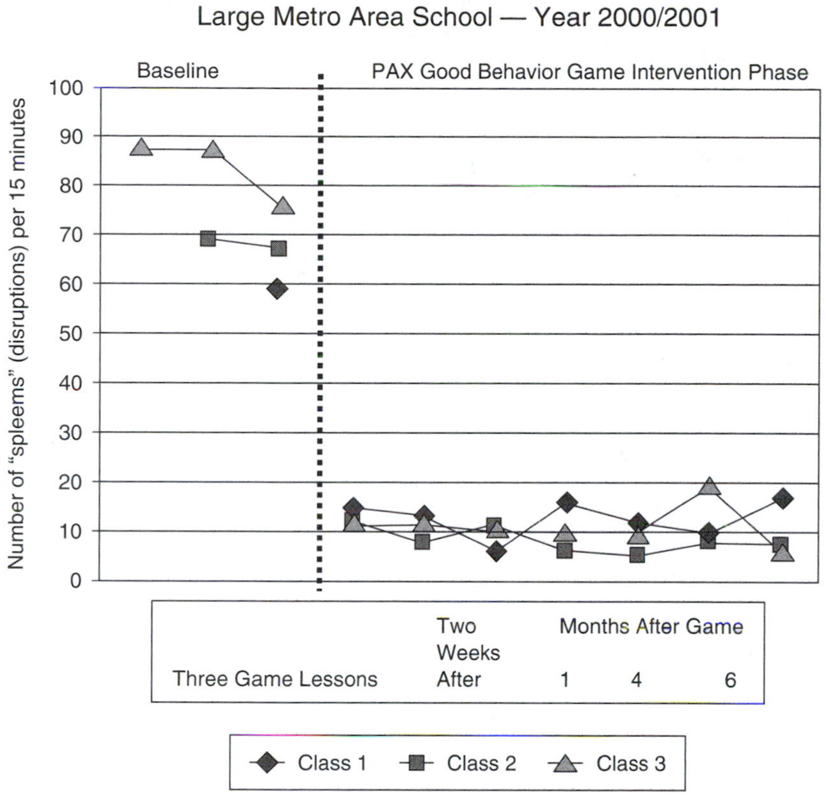

SOURCE: www.hazelden.org/HAZ_MEDIA/gbg_research.pdf. Reprinted with permission of the Praxis Institute.

NOTE: These data are from three teachers' classrooms in the Chicago area. Before they used the PAX Good Behavior Game, rates of student disruptions (spleems) were 60 to 90 every 15 minutes. After learning and using the game, the classes developed much more PAX (good)—with only 10 or so disruptions, or spleems, per 15 minutes. Other data collected in this study show that the game can be implemented anytime during the year with positive effects.

regular school funds. Seventh, the game is not a curriculum, so it will not interfere with any state academic performance standard. Finally, the GBG has demonstrated utility in helping to reduce a variety of problematic childhood behaviors (Kellam, Ling, Merisca, Hendricks, & Ialango, 1998), including Attention Deficit Hyperactivity Disorder and common conduct problems that result in special education referrals or 504 plans (van Lier et al., 2004). The game is unique in that it can be used with and can be successful for individual teachers, grade-level teams, or whole schools. The GBG has documented positive effects across a wide range of cultures, ethnic backgrounds, and grade levels. In the PAX Good Behavior Game iteration, all students are put on a level playing field of learning two basic new words: *PAX* (for good) and *spleems* (for fouls) (additional information about the GBG can be found at http://hazelden.org/OA_HTML/hazAuthor.jsp?author_id=84&section=null&item=657).

The Incredible Years Classroom Social Skills and Problem-Solving Curriculum

The Incredible Years Classroom Social Skills and Problem-Solving Curriculum (IY) is a comprehensive program specifically developed to address behavioral difficulties seen in children with Oppositional Defiant Disorder and CD, but it has more recently been adapted to serve as a prevention curriculum for use in preschool and elementary-age students to help avoid and reduce externalizing behaviors in classroom settings (Webster-Stratton & Reid, 2004). IY represents a significant investment from the school system if implemented completely because it involves a multitiered approach to intervention, including parent education, teacher training, and child training. It should be noted that, although the investment is substantial, the objectives that are addressed by IY are extensive, as well. For a brief introduction to the objectives addressed by IY, see Table 10.1.

Parent Training

Parent training has been reported to be paramount in intervention planning for children with CD (Brestan & Eyberg, 1998) and has been shown in numerous studies to improve outcomes for children (Barkley, 1997). The IY parent training programs for adult caregivers of children with CD emphasize teaching parents to be more positive and nurturing in their relationships with children and less harsh and inconsistent with their discipline. The IY parenting program focuses also on accentuating home-school relationships. The program is conducted in 2-hour, group weekly sessions that last from 22 to 24 weeks and include instruction in praise, ignoring, use of logical consequences, and encouragement (Reid & Webster-Stratton, 2001).

Teacher Training

Training teachers to use more effective behavior management strategies is another intervention approach that has been shown to be useful for children with CD. Many studies (e.g., Pfiffner & Barkley, 1998) support the implementation of such programs. The IY teacher training program is four daylong seminars that include sessions on building relationships with students, proactive teaching strategies designed to prevent problems from occurring in the first place, effective use of reinforcement, and the importance of praise and positive attention (Reid & Webster-Stratton, 2001).

Child Training

Child training is the final component of the IY training series. This program is administered in group sessions conducted while caregivers are in parent training meetings. Child training includes topics such as anger management, problem solving, and making friends (Reid & Webster-Stratton, 2001). Teaching prosocial skills to children is a widely adopted strategy. Although outcomes for children who receive *only* social skills training have been mixed (Barkley et al., 2000), the child social skills training component of IY has been found to reduce aggression and improve social problem solving and peer relationships in three randomized controlled studies (e.g., Webster-Stratton et al., 2004).

Table 10.1 Content and Objectives of the Incredible Years Teacher Training Program

Content	*Objectives*	*Content*	*Objectives*
PROGRAM ONE: The Importance of Teacher Attention, Encouragement, and Praise	• Using praise and encouragement more effectively. • Building children's self-esteem and self-confidence by teaching children how to praise themselves. • Understanding the importance of general praise to the whole group as well as individual praise. • Knowing the importance of praising social and academic behaviors. • Recognizing common traps. • Using physical warmth as a reinforcer. • Providing nonverbal cues of appreciation. • Doubling the impact of praise by involving other school personnel and parents. • Helping children learn how to praise others and enjoy others' achievements.	PROGRAM TWO: Motivating Children Through Incentives	• Understanding why incentives are valuable teaching strategies for children with behavior problems. • Understanding ways to use an incentive program for social problems such as noncompliance, inattentiveness, uncooperativeness, and hyperactivity as well as for academic problems. • Setting up individual incentive programs for particular children. • Using group or classroom incentives. • Designing programs that have variety and build on the positive relationship between the teacher, child, and parent. • Using incentives in a way that fosters the child's internal motivation and focuses on the process of learning rather than the end product. • Providing unexpected rewards. • Appreciating the importance of involving parents in incentive programs.
PROGRAM THREE: Preventing Behavior Problems—The Proactive Teacher	• Preparing children for transitions. • Establishing clear, predictable classroom rules.	PROGRAM FOUR: Decreasing Students' Inappropriate Behavior	• Knowing how to redirect and engage children. • Knowing how and when to ignore inappropriate responses from children.

(Continued)

Table 10.1 (Continued)

Content	*Objectives*	*Content*	*Objectives*
PROGRAM THREE Continued	• Using guidelines for giving effective commands or instructions. • Identifying unclear, vague, and negative commands. • Understanding the value of warnings and helpful reminders, especially for distractible and impulsive children. • Engaging children's attention. • Using nonverbal signals and cues for communication. • Recognizing the need for ongoing monitoring and positive attention.	PROGRAM FOUR Continued	• Using verbal and nonverbal cues to reengage off-task children. • Understanding the importance of reminders and warnings. • Using guidelines for setting up Time-Out in the classroom. • Avoiding common mistakes in using Time-Out. • Handling common misbehaviors such as impulsivity, disengagement, noncompliance, tantrums, and disruptive behaviors. • Using the color cards system. • Recognizing when to use logical consequences or removal of privileges as discipline.
PROGRAM FIVE: Building Positive Relationships With Students	• Building positive relationships with difficult students. • Showing students you trust and believe in them. • Fostering students' sense of responsibility for the classroom and their involvement in other students' learning as well as their own. • Giving students choices when possible. • Teaching students how to ask for what they want in appropriate ways.	PROGRAM SIX: How to Teach Social Skills, Problem Solving, and Anger Management in the Classroom	• Helping increase children's awareness of different feelings and perspectives in social situations. • Building children's emotional vocabulary. • Understanding how to help children identify a problem and to generate possible solutions. • Helping children learn to think ahead to different consequences and to different solutions and how to evaluate the most effective solutions.

Content	*Objectives*	*Content*	*Objectives*
PROGRAM FIVE Continued	• Fostering listening and speaking skills between students. • Teaching students how to problem solve through role-plays and examples. • Promoting positive self-talk. • Implementing strategies to counter students' negative attributions. • Promoting positive relationships with students' parents.	PROGRAM SIX Continued	• Helping children recognize their anger and learn ways to manage it successfully. • Using puppets to present hypothetical problem situations such as being teased, bullied, or isolated by other children. • Providing small-group activities to practice friendship, group entry, play, and problem-solving skills. • Helping children learn how to use friendly talk such as giving compliments, providing suggestions, offering apologies, asking for help, and sharing ideas and feelings. • Helping children learn classroom behavior such as listening, quiet hand up, cooperating, and following teacher's directions.

SOURCE: © The Incredible Years (www.incredibleyears.com). Reprinted with permission of Incredible Years.

Brief Summary of IY Series

We recommend IY for many reasons. First and foremost, it, like the GBG, has demonstrated efficacy and has strong supportive research findings. It has been studied intensively with international application. In fact, the research base supporting IY is so substantial that it could legitimately be called a **best practice**. Second, IY requires a significant investment from the school system. If you get the system approval to implement IY, it demonstrates strong evidence that the community is committed to serving the best interests of students. Third, IY is supported by a large variety of training and implementation materials, including hours of videotapes. Fourth, IY is a comprehensive program, including training components for teachers, parents, and students that, together with the manuals and videotapes, will lead to high fidelity of program delivery and the likelihood of obtaining results for children similar to those found in the research. Additional information about IY can be found at www.incredibleyears.com.

CONCLUSION

One criterion used to determine whether or not a person has a mental health problem is suffering (Seligman, Walker, & Rosenhan, 2001). That is, if a person is suffering, he or she may be experiencing emotional duress that could be ameliorated by successful behavioral or psychosocial interventions. The evidence suggests that children with CD are suffering, even as the people around them can suffer as a result of their outward behavior. Responding to children with this problem from the spirit of retribution for disruptive behaviors has not been found to help children over the long term. It is much more helpful to conceptualize CD as a problem of skill deficits. Skill deficits fall soundly into the purview of educators. The students themselves have not learned to behave in a way that you find conducive to the classroom. Some of the parents have not learned parenting skills that foster healthy emotional growth and acquisition of prosocial behavior. And sometimes teachers have skill deficits in the behavior management strategies most likely to modify disruptive behaviors. Although some of these skill deficits are beyond your control, some are not.

The behaviors associated with CD will be seen in all children occasionally. Behaviors such as biting, hitting, lying, and stealing are not limited to children with significant disruptive behaviors. In fact, any or all these behaviors may be seen in a 2-year-old child. However, these behaviors usually disappear with teaching and socialization. Fortunately, most educators are trained in human development and thus are able to formulate educated opinions about whether behaviors observed in children in their classes are developmentally appropriate or not. Furthermore, most educators have access to other professionals within the schools who can help with making such determinations, including school social workers, school counselors, and school psychologists.

Although the behaviors associated with CD can challenge the patience of even experienced teachers, the evidence is quite clear that you can effectively intervene to ensure that school is a positive and successful experience for all students. Also, the outcome for students with CD is much more likely to be optimistic if they develop the skills needed to succeed in school rather than have their behaviors addressed by the juvenile justice system. The behaviors associated with CD have served a function for these students; however, you can effectively make those behaviors irrelevant with effective behavior management strategies, fostering positive relationships with your students, and patience.

DISCUSSION QUESTIONS

1. What are some skill deficits that you can successfully address for students with CD?
2. Considering the evidence presented in this chapter, do you consider CD to be a mental health issue or a personality flaw? Why?
3. Which of the listed suggestions for general classroom management do you already use? What are some general strategies that you have used effectively that were not listed in this chapter that you think should be added to the list?
4. Does your school use a practical and effective approach to intervening with children with CD?
5. How do you think that you can balance the necessity of maintaining a safe school environment for all students while applying the strategies outlined in this chapter?

FOR ADDITIONAL HELP

	Organization	*Web Address*	*Description*
Conduct Disorder	Parent Advocacy Coalition for Educational Rights (PACER Center)	www.pacer.org/index.htm	The mission of PACER Center is to expand opportunities and enhance the quality of life of children and young adults with disabilities and their families, based on the concept of parents helping parents.
	ConductDisorders.com	ConductDisorders.com	ConductDisorders.com is a group of parents who are raising challenging children.

REFERENCES

American Psychiatric Association. (2000). *Diagnostic and statistical manual of mental disorders* (4th ed., text revision). Washington, DC: Author.

Angold, A., Costello, E., & Erkanli, A. (1999). Comorbidity. *Journal of child psychology and psychiatry, 40,* 57–97.

Barkley, R. A. (1997). *Defiant children: A clinician's manual for assessment and parent training* (2nd ed.). New York: Guilford Press.

Barkley, R. A., Guevremont, D. C., Anastopoulos, A. D., DuPaul, G. J., & Shelton, T. L. (1993). Driving-related risks and outcomes of attention deficit hyperactivity disorder in adolescents and young adults: A 3- to 5-year follow-up survey. *Pediatrics, 92,* 212–218.

Barkley, R. A., Shelton, T. L., Crosswait, C., Morehouse, M., Fletcher, K., Barrett, S., et al. (2000). Multi-method psycho-educational intervention for preschool children with disruptive behavior: Preliminary results at post-treatment. *Journal of Child Psychology and Psychiatry, 41,* 319–332.

Barrish, H., Saunders, M., & Wolf, M. M. (1969). Good Behavior Game: Effects of individual contingencies for group consequences on disruptive behavior in a classroom. *Journal of Applied Behavior Analysis, 2,* 119–124.

Beauchaine, T. B., Webster-Stratton, C., & Reid, M. J. (2005). Mediators, moderators, and predictors of one-year outcomes among children treated for early-onset conduct problems: A latent growth analysis. *Journal of Consulting and Clinical Psychology, 73,* 371–388.

Behave, or else. (2004). *The Economist, 373,* 55.

Brestan, E. V., & Eyberg, S. M. (1998). Effective psychosocial treatments of conduct-disordered children and adolescents: 29 years, 62 studies, and 5272 kids. *Journal of Clinical Child Psychology, 27,* 180–189.

Darveaux, D. X. (1984). The Good Behavior Game plus merit: Controlling disruptive behavior and improving student motivation. *School Psychology Review, 13,* 510–514.

Eddy, J. M., Reid, J. B., & Curry, V. (2002). The etiology of youth antisocial behavior, delinquency, and violence and a public health approach to prevention. In M. R. Shinn, H. M. Walker, & G. Stoner

(Eds.), *Interventions for academic and behavior problems II: Preventative and remedial approaches* (pp. 27–52). Bethesda, MD: National Association of School Psychologists.

Embry, D. E. (2002). The Good Behavior Game: A best practice candidate as a universal behavioral vaccine. *Clinical Child and Family Psychology Review, 5,* 273–297.

Johnson, M., & Waller, R. J. (in press). A review of effective interventions for youth with aggressive behavior who meet diagnostic criteria for conduct disorder or oppositional defiant disorder. *Journal of Family Psychotherapy.*

Kanchanska, G. (1993). Toward a synthesis of parental socialization and child temperament in early development of conscience. *Child Development, 64,* 325–347.

Kazdin, A. E. (1998). Conduct disorder. In R. J. Morris & T. R. Kratchowill (Eds.), *The practice of child therapy* (3rd ed., pp. 199–230). Boston: Allyn & Bacon.

Kellam, S., Ling, X., Merisca, R., Hendricks, B. C., & Ialongo, N. (1998). The effects of the level of aggression in first grade classrooms on the course and malleability of aggressive behavior in middle school. *Development and Psychopathology, 10,* 165–185.

Kellam, S. G., Mayer, L. S., Rebok, G. W., & Hawkins, W. E. (1998). Effects of improving achievement on aggressive behavior and improving aggressive behavior through achievement through two prevention interventions: An investigation of causal paths. In B. P. Dohrenwend (Ed.), *Adversity, stress, and psychopathology* (pp. 486–505). New York: Oxford University Press.

Medland, M. B., & Stachnik, T. J. (1972). Good Behavior Game: A replication and systematic analysis. *Journal of Applied Behavior Analysis, 5,* 45–51.

Patterson, G. R., DeGarmo, D. S., & Knutson, N. (2000). Hyperactive and antisocial behaviors: Comorbid or two points in the same process? *Development and Psychopathology, 12,* 91–106.

Patterson, G. R., Reid, J. B., & Dishon, T. J. (1992). *A social learning approach: Vol. 4. Antisocial boys.* Eugene, OR: Castalia.

Pfiffner, L., & Barkley, R. A. (1998). Educational management. In R. A. Barkley (Ed.), *Attention deficit hyperactivity disorder: A handbook for diagnosis and treatment* (pp. 438–539). New York: Guilford Press.

Pinderhughes, E. E., Dodge, K. A., Bates, J. E., Pettit, G. S., & Zelli, A. (2000). Discipline responses: Influences of parent's socioeconomic status, ethnicity, beliefs about parenting, stress, and cognitive processes. *Journal of Family Psychology, 14,* 380–400.

Reid, M. J., & Webster-Stratton, C. (2001). The Incredible Years Parent, Teacher, and Child intervention: Targeting multiple areas of risk for a young child with conduct problems using a flexible, manualized treatment program. *Cognitive and Behavioral Practice, 8,* 377–386.

Rimm-Kaufman, S. E., Pianta, R. C., & Cox, M. J. (2000). Teachers' judgments of problems in the transition to kindergarten. *Early Childhood Research Quarterly, 15,* 146–160.

Ruma, P. R., Burke, R. V., & Thompson, R. W. (1996). Group parent training: Is it effective for children of all ages? *Behavior Therapy, 27,* 159–169.

Seligman, M. E. P. (1993). *What you can change and what you can't: The complete guide to successful improvement.* New York: Knopf.

Seligman, M. E. P., Walker, E. F., & Rosenhan, D. L. (2001). *Abnormal psychology* (4th ed.). New York: W. W. Norton.

Snyder, H. N. (1998). Juvenile arrests 1996. *Juvenile Justice Bulletin.* Washington, DC: U.S. Department of Justice, Office of Juvenile Justice and Delinquency Prevention.

Sprott, J. B. (2004). The development of early delinquency: Can classroom and school climates make a difference? *Canadian Journal of Criminology and Criminal Justice, 46,* 553–682.

Tingstrom, D. H. (1994). The Good Behavior Game: An investigation of teachers' acceptance. *Psychology in the Schools, 31,* 57–65.

U.S. Surgeon General. (2001). *Youth violence: Report of the surgeon general.* Washington, DC: U.S. Department of Health and Human Services.

van Lier, P. A. C., Muthen, B. O., van der Sar, R. M., & Crijnen, A. A. M. (2004). Preventing disruptive behavior in elementary schoolchildren: Impact of a universal classroom-based intervention. *Journal of Consulting & Clinical Psychology, 72*(3), 467–478.

Walker, H. M., Ramsey, E., & Gresham, F. M. (2004). *Antisocial behavior in school: Strategies and best practices* (2nd ed.). Pacific Grove, CA: Brooks/Cole.

Warner, S. P., Miller, F. D., & Cohen, M. W. (1977). Relative effectiveness of teacher attention and the Good Behavior Game in modifying disruptive classroom behavior. *Journal of Applied Behavior Analysis, 10,* 737.

Webster-Stratton, C., & Reid, M. J. (2004). Strengthening social and emotional competence in young children: The foundation for early school readiness and success: Incredible Years Classroom Social Skills and Problem-Solving Curriculum. *Journal of Infants and Young Children, 17,* 96–113.

Webster-Stratton, C., Reid, M. J., & Hammond, M. (2004). Treating children with early onset conduct problems: Intervention outcomes for parent, child, and teacher training. *Journal of Clinical Child and Adolescent Psychology, 33,* 105–124.

Chapter 11

Bullying Behavior and School Violence

W. Sean Newsome

Michael Kelly

PREREADING QUESTIONS

As you read this chapter, reflect on the following questions and issues:

1. What is the prevalence of bullying behavior and school violence in the United States?
2. Why is bullying behavior and school violence such a vital issue facing kindergarten through Grade 12 (K–12) educational settings?
3. What are the warning signs school personnel should be aware of when addressing bullying behavior and school violence?
4. How can teachers begin to address the issue of bullying behavior and school violence?

Although schools are still one of the safest places for America's children, acts of bullying behavior and school-related violence have become pervasive problems (Leff, Kupersmidt, Patterson, & Power, 1999; Nansel et al., 2001). In fact, although recent data suggest a downturn in the amount of violence committed by young people in school settings, exposure to violence and victimization at school remains high for many school-age youths (Kaufman et al., 2000). As such, issues of bullying behavior and school violence remain a significant health problem facing this country's educational system.

The growing awareness and concerns over bullying behavior and school violence are well founded. It is estimated that nearly 30% of American children and adolescents are regularly involved in bullying behavior, either as bullies, victims, or both (Nansel et al., 2001). Moreover, research confirms that bullying behavior and school-related violence pose serious risks to children and adolescents and may seriously affect the climate of schools (Limber & Small, 2003). In addition, violence among children and adolescents remains much higher in the United States than in most developed countries (U.S. Surgeon General, 2001).

The perplexing issues of bullying behavior and school-related violence have resulted in many youths feeling unsafe and threatened at school (Josephson Institute on Ethics, 2001). Issues such as depression, low self-esteem, psychosomatic complaints, bed-wetting, poor school performance, and social isolation are but a few of the emotional and behavioral results of being victimized by bullies and witnessing school violence (Hawker & Boulton, 2000; O'Moore & Kirkman, 2001; Williams, Chamgers, Logan, & Robinson, 1996).

With such aforementioned considerations, bullying behavior and school violence are receiving increased attention at school board meetings, in the media, and in state legislatures. Strict policies and procedures addressing school violence have been initiated by schools, and 15 states have passed laws addressing bullying among schoolchildren (Limber & Small, 2003). However, for many school-based practitioners, bullying behavior and school violence are not new phenomena. What is new is the growing awareness that bullying behavior and school violence have serious mental health and social consequences for both students and schools.

Therefore, this chapter begins with a discussion concerning the prevalence of bullying behavior and school violence followed by the warning signs and symptoms educators should be aware of. As such, research over the last decade has paid particular attention to the individual characteristics of students in an attempt to better prepare and support educators in combating the issue of bullying behavior and school violence. For example, educators need to know the distinctions, outlined later in this chapter, that research has focused on as potential warning signs and correlates. In addition, many authors have also cited the complexities of individual, family, school, and community factors that may influence or act as warning signs for educators attempting to reduce and prevent bullying behavior and school violence.

Next, the chapter provides descriptions of current practices regarding research on violence and bullying prevention practices in schools. A discussion of current intervention techniques to address bullying behavior and school violence is then presented. This component of the chapter is divided into three major sections. The first section details for school educators the possible approaches and programs that current research shows to be effective in combating bullying behavior and school violence. As will be shown, preventive programs addressing the complex issues of bullying behavior and school violence may be best addressed at the collective level rather than the individual level. Finally, particular emphasis in the third and final section of the chapter is given to how two of the key stakeholders in schools (i.e., teachers and school-based mental health professionals) can use current research to design effective interventions for their schools.

SCHOOL VIOLENCE, VICTIMIZATION, AND BULLYING BEHAVIOR

Over the past 20 years or so, the issue of school-related violence has received considerable attention. Much of this attention was fueled by the ever-increasing trends of violent crime committed by children and adolescents during the mid-1980s and 1990s. During this time, acts of bullying behavior; intimidation; school and community vandalism; school fighting; sexual harassment; gang violence; carrying weapons to school; violence directed toward school staff; hate crimes against ethnic and religious groups, gay, lesbian, bisexual, and transsexual students; dating violence; rape; and murder received widespread public attention. As a result, school-related violence in many schools during the mid-1980s and the 1990s presented a serious threat to the structure of K–12 education across the United States.

Although conclusive numbers on the prevalence of school-related violence are hard to generate, evidence from several large studies in the midwestern and southeastern United States suggest that school-related violence is quite common (Espelage, Bosworth, & Simon, 2000; Limber et al., 1997). During the 1990s, national school-based data indicated that violence was prevalent in many schools across the country. In fact, in 1993 the Youth Risk Behavior Survey indicated that 42% of adolescents were in a physical fight during the 12 months preceding the survey and 22% carried a weapon during the 30 days preceding the survey (Kann, 1995). In another national study, the Centers for Disease Control and Prevention (CDC; 1992) found that 50% of boys and 25% of girls reported being physically attacked by someone at school. Even more alarming, however, was that the National Center for Education Statistics (NCES; 1998) found that more than half of public schools experienced some crime during the 1996–97 school year and that 1 in 10 schools reported at least one serious violent crime such as a rape or robbery during that year.

Victimization also appears to be a growing concern for many students in K–5 educational settings. In a national study of children attending kindergarten, approximately half the children reported experiencing some form of victimization (Kochenderfer & Ladd, 1997). In a national study of third graders, it was found that the prevalence of victimization was similar, with approximately 40% of the students reporting being the victims of physical or verbal aggression (Silvernail, Thompson, Yang, & Kopp, 2000). Even more alarming during the mid-1990s was that almost 2.6 million youths between the ages of 12 and 17 were victims of violent crime. Despite such figures, however, current research suggests that school-related violence is down. Empirical data suggest a steady decline in the rate of school violence over the past 4 years (U.S. Departments of Education and Justice, 2000; U.S. Department of Health and Human Services, 2001).

Despite the downturn in K–12 violence, schools present a prime location for bullying behavior. As a result, many students are being bullied in the classroom or lunchroom or on the playground (Craig & Pepler, 1997; Craig, Pepler, & Atlas, 2000). Over the years, such behaviors were often ignored or viewed as simply part of the "growing up" process. However, research has found that students repeatedly victimized by bullies display (a) a reluctance to attend school, (b) a sudden drop in grades, (c) nightmares or difficulty sleeping, (d) fear of meeting new people or trying new things, (e) apprehension when another child approaches, (f) withdrawal from social events, or (g) some combination of these (Sheras & Tippins, 2002).

Adding to this problem is that many adults, including those in K–12 settings, do not know how to intervene in bullying situations. However, given the complexity and occurrences of bullying behavior, there appears to be growing concern for teachers, staff, administrators, parents, and school-age youths in K–12 educational settings. Similarly, given that bullies and victims of bullying behavior experience a wide range of academic, social, behavioral, and emotional difficulties as they get older, effective prevention programs are essential to their well-being (Moffitt, Caspi, Dickson, Silva, & Stanton, 1996).

One of the most challenging aspects of understanding bullies and their behavior has to do with reaching a consensus on a definition. However, what is clear is that bullying behavior is a subset of physical or verbal aggression that is systematic and carried out by an individual or group of individuals to gain power, prestige, or goods (Espelage & Swearer, 2003). As such, bullying behavior has taken on the following definitions over the last 15-plus years:

> A person is being bullied when he or she is exposed, repeatedly over time, to negative actions on the part of one or more other students. (Olweus, 1993, p. 319)
>
> A student is being bullied or picked on when another student says nasty and unpleasant things to him or her. It is also bullying when a student is hit, kicked, threatened, locked inside a room, sent nasty notes, and when no one ever talks to him [or her]. (Smith & Sharp, 1994, p. 1)
>
> Bullying is longstanding violence, physical or mental, conducted by an individual or group and directed against an individual who is not able to defend himself [or herself] in the actual situation. (Roland, 1989, p. 143)

Bullying and/or intimidation of others includes (a) any aggressive or negative gesture; (b) any written, verbal, or physical act that places another student in reasonable fear of harm to his or her person or property; or (c) any act that has the effect of insulting or demeaning any student in such a way as to disrupt or interfere with the school's educational mission or the education of any student. Bullying most often occurs when a student asserts physical or psychological power over, or is cruel to, another student perceived to be weaker. Such behavior may include but is not limited to pushing, hitting, threatening, name-calling, or other physical or verbal conduct of a belittling or browbeating nature (McDonald, Fineran, Constable, & Moriarty, 2002; Zuehl, Dillon, Schilling, & Oltmanns, 2002).

Although the prevalence of bullying behavior is difficult to gauge in K–12 settings across the United States, it appears to peak in the middle school years and declines as children approach their high school years (Haynie et al., 2001; Nansel et al., 2001). However, every school day, 160,000 children miss school because they are afraid (Fried & Fried, 1996). Studies on bullying in the United States have shown rates from 10% for victims of severe bullying (Perry, Kusel, & Perry, 1988) to 75% for school-age children who report being bullied at least once during the school year (Hoover, Oliver, & Hazler, 1992). More recently, a nationally representative sample coordinated by the World Health Organization and supported by the National Institute of Child Health and Human Development revealed that 30% of students in Grades 6 through 10 reported bullying others, being victims of bullies, or as being both bullies and victims (Nansel et al., 2001).

Studies have also found that children in elementary school are committing acts of bullying behavior. In fact, Limber et al. (1997) found that 25% of elementary school-age students in fourth through sixth grade admitted to bullying another student with some regularity. Even more alarming are the statistics on bullying behavior for junior high and high school students. Recently, Haynie et al. (2001) found that 31% of middle school-age youths reported being victimized by bullies. In a national study of 15,686 students in Grades 6 through 10, it was found that a total of 29.9% reported frequent involvement in bullying behavior—either as bullies, victims, or both (Nansel et al., 2001).

In response to the problems of bullying behavior and school-related violence, most schools have implemented strategies, policies, or programs to prevent and reduce such acts. Still others, however, have focused on the psychological and individual characteristics of bullies to better curtail and combat the issues of such behavior. Through such work, potential correlates, warning signs, and factors have materialized that help to indicate why some school-age youths commit acts of bullying behavior and school-related violence.

POTENTIAL CORRELATES, WARNING SIGNS, AND FACTORS CONTRIBUTING TO BULLYING BEHAVIOR AND SCHOOL-RELATED VIOLENCE

Recently, much of the focus on addressing the issue of bullying behavior has been on making a distinction based on the following:

- Diagnostic categories (Nansel et al., 2001; Wolke, Woods, Blomfield, & Karstadt, 2000)
- Gender (Callagan & Joseph, 1995; Craig, 1998; Endresen & Olweus, 2001)
- Race/ethnicity (Graham & Juvonen, 2002; Juvonen, Nishina, & Graham, 2001; Nansel et al., 2001)
- Age (Loeber & Stouthamer-Loeber, 1998; Pellegrini & Bartini, 2001)
- Anger (Bosworth, Espelage, & Simon, 1999; Espelage et al., 2000)
- Depression (Austin & Joseph, 1996; Slee, 1995; Swearer, Song, Cary, Eagle, & Mickelson, 2001)
- Anxiety (Craig, 1998; Duncan, 1999; Roth, Coles, & Heimberg, 2002)
- Empathy (Borg, 1998; Endresen & Olweus, 2001)

Each characteristic has been looked at by practitioners and researchers alike as potential correlates educators should be aware of in addressing the complex issue of bullying behavior.

In addition to the potential correlates related to bullying behavior, many researchers and practitioners have also increased their understanding of the possible warning signs displayed by bullies. In fact, students who bully others are likely to have some general characteristics in common. Research has found that many bullies display greater than average aggressive behavior patterns, the desire to dominate peers, the need to feel in control, no sense of remorse for hurting another child, and a refusal to accept responsibility for their behavior (Heinrichs, 2003). Students who bully other students may also be described as being hot tempered, impulsive, oppositional, defiant, average to above average in popularity and academic performance, and good at talking their way out of difficult situations (Olweus, 1993; Schwartz, 2000).

Beyond some of the common characteristics shared by those who bully others, school-age youths committing acts of school violence also display warning signs that educators must be aware of. Recognizing such warning signs are imperative given that in 2002 the number of juvenile arrests for violent crimes was 92,160, which made up 14.9% of all violent crimes, as indicated and tracked by the FBI's Violent Crime Index. Specifically, the FBI Violent Crime Index reported that 1,360 juveniles were arrested for murder and nonnegligent manslaughter; 4,720 for forcible rape; 24,500 for robbery; and 61,600 for aggravated assault (Snyder, Puzzanchera, & Kang, 2005). Despite the steady decrease in the number of juvenile arrests for violent crimes since the mid-1990s, the shocking and excessive nature of these rates still have many wondering if these school-age youths "snapped" violently, without any apparent warning. The interested reader may want to refer to http://ojjdp.ncjrs.org/ojstatbb for the latest statistics from the Office of Juvenile Justice and Delinquency Prevention, released in 2005.

Contrary to earlier speculation in the school community during the mid- to late 1980s, it appears that school-age youths committing such horrific acts of violence display certain warning signs. Studies have found that such acts can be attributable to many individual, family, school, and community factors that may influence violent behavior. However, one of the most important considerations one must keep in mind is that although these warning signs have been identified, the causal relationship between these factors and the act of committing horrific, school-related violence is far from clear. With such considerations in mind, the following warning signs and factors contributing to school violence have been identified.

- *Individual* warning signs and factors such as neurological, hormonal, and physiological issues; impaired cognitive functioning and low academic achievement; issues related to poor impulse control; poor peer relations and problem-solving skills; reinforcement for violence and aggression; emotional deprivation and biases and deficits in cognitive processing; belonging to a gang; abusing alcohol and drugs

- *Family* warning signs and factors such as inadequate management skills, coercion, noncompliance, harsh or inconsistent discipline, limited supervision, parental distance and lack of involvement, parental pathology and stressful external events, family history of criminal violence, history of being abused

- *School* warning signs and factors such as witnessing verbal and physical violence, availability of weapons, availability of illegal drugs, racial conflict, gang/cult/group influences, association with defiant peers, exposure to classrooms or social network groups with normative beliefs supporting aggressive and violent behavior, schoolwide discipline policies, the lack of prosocial classroom instruction, classroom management procedures

- *Community* warning signs and factors such as poverty, neighborhood violence, social disorganization, and a noncollective approach to community social order (Schneider-Denenberg, Denenberg, & Braverman, 1998)

Given such considerations, it is essential that interventions addressing bullying behavior and school violence contain components that work at multiple levels. Foremost, such components must contain the ultimate goal of creating a new social environment in schools where bullying behavior and school violence are not acceptable. The challenge, therefore, is to develop and use innovative programs and preventive measures—some of which we present below—that successfully create a classroom and school community of respect and empowerment for all students.

WHAT EDUCATORS CAN DO TO ADDRESS BULLYING BEHAVIOR AND SCHOOL VIOLENCE AT THE SCHOOLWIDE LEVEL

In addressing bullying behavior and school-related violence, Tolan, Guerra, and Kendall (1995) have identified three different levels of interventions that schools can choose from to try to prevent bullying behavior and school violence:

1. *Universal interventions:* schoolwide interventions that focus on curriculum change as well as community programs and involvement for parents and other community stakeholders
2. *Selective interventions:* programs that focus on specific at-risk students, often employing classroom or group therapy interventions that focus on a group for students in a self-contained behavior disorder classroom or mentoring programs for students who have limited family support
3. *Indicator interventions:* programs directed at students and families who are already showing some signs of having a specific problem, such as a student who has already been suspended for fighting or for threatening another student with a weapon (Neace, Munoz, Olson-Allen, Weber, & Johnson, 2003; Tolan et al., 1995)

Currently, much of the practice addressing bullying behavior and school-related violence in K–12 educational settings uses more selective and indicated interventions that focus on at-risk students. In addition, many selective and indicator interventions are being marketed to educators as comprehensive when they are largely focused on a few "damaged individuals" (Erickson, Mattaini & McGuire, 2004). As Astor, Vargas, O'Neil-Pitner, and Meyer (1999) point out, a number of ineffective interventions and programs are characterized by a focus on a single hypothesized source of the problem, a view that individuals are the source of the problem, hypothesized deficits or pathologies of individuals or subpopulations of youths, and the underuse of contextual strategies. Some of the most promising universal programs to prevent bullying behavior and school violence are listed in the Reference section of this chapter. It should be noted that the programs referenced do not focus on individual pathologies, but rather, they approach bullying behavior and school violence from a universal, schoolwide collective. Although the programs do not represent an exhaustive list of the universal, schoolwide programs available, they do represent many of the programs that have been evaluated or applied in K–12 educational settings.

Although all the programs referenced have shown some strong initial results in decreasing behavior problems, they have not been conclusively shown to be effective with all schools and all settings. Like much of the literature on applied, school-based practice, the empirical evidence for universal interventions to address bullying behavior and school violence is still in its early stages. Some of these programs have been shown to help some students, but none of them have looked at their overall impact on bullying behavior and school-related violence at the larger school level (Erickson et al., 2004; Reinke & Herman, 2002). In addition, no large-scale studies have been conducted comparing universal, selective, and/or indicator approaches in one school to address issues of bullying behavior and school violence, thus making it hard to know if a universal approach would yield the best results (Astor, Benbenishty, & Marachi, 2004;

Collaborative for Academic, Social, and Emotional Learning [CASEL], 2003; Greenberg et al., 2003).

Despite such considerations, there do appear to be some core ideas that educators can derive from current universal schoolwide approaches addressing bullying behavior and school violence. The literature reveals that the most effective universal school violence and bullying prevention programs require in-service training of teachers, manualized lessons, and a consistent implementation across an entire building. The most wide-ranging of these programs also recommend conducting needs assessment surveys and holding community/parent meetings at night to involve all the adult stakeholders in the community in their violence prevention efforts (Astor et al., 2004; CASEL, 2003; Cantor et al., 2002; Erickson et al., 2004; Greenberg, Domitrovich, & Bumbarger, 2001).

WHAT TEACHERS CAN DO TO ADDRESS BULLYING BEHAVIOR AND SCHOOL VIOLENCE AT THE CLASSROOM LEVEL

School-related violence and bullying behavior are major problems affecting K–12 educational settings, but limited research exists addressing the role of teachers. Studies that have been conducted have found that teachers (a) tend to report lower rates of bullying activities than do students, (b) do not always identify who the bullies are in their schools, and (c) do not feel confident in their abilities to intervene with bullies (Boulton, 1997; Leff et al., 1999; Stockdale, Hangaduambo, Duys, Larson, & Sarvela, 2002). As a result, teachers might not only be unaware of the bullying behavior and school-related violence occurring around them; they may be uncertain of how to intervene when such behavior takes place.

Given the aforementioned considerations as well as the limited research that documents the necessary techniques for teachers to use in their classrooms to address bullying behavior and school violence, it must seem inevitably frustrating to many educators. After all, if there are no definite techniques that work, what can educators do to make their schools and classrooms safer? Fortunately, in regard to the larger questions of what works to prevent bullying behavior and school violence, there are some practices for teachers and educators that appear to have growing empirical support. Although these approaches do not guarantee that classrooms or schools will become bully and violence free, they increase the likelihood that students, parents, and teachers will be able to recognize and respond proactively to situations that threaten school climate. The National Resource Center for Safe Schools (NRCSS; 2000) lists the following six strategies for teachers hoping to prevent bullying and violence in their schools:

1. Teach violence prevention throughout the year, working lessons about conflict resolution and social skills into the curriculum.
2. Employ consistent positive classroom discipline, realizing that if teachers do not model peaceful nonaggressive discipline, it will be hard to expect students to behave differently in their interactions with each other.
3. Respond quickly and decisively to reports of bullying and hazing from students.

4. Establish a climate in your class where students feel that teachers really "know" them, making them more likely to share problems or situations that might become violent.

5. Involve parents in classroom rules, making sure that they know, understand, and support the rules.

6. Learn and understand how to notice the "warning signs" of students who might be prone to bullying or other forms of violence.

Such aforementioned practices, as asserted by the NRCSS, have been shown to greatly affect bullying behavior and school violence in a classroom setting. In addition to the NRCSS practices, the References section of this chapter also includes a variety of classroom-based interventions for teachers to teach violence and bullying prevention.

Along these same lines, we wish to highlight two curricula that we have worked with. These two programs have focused on making classroom climates more prosocial and positive and appear to be showing some strong empirical results in increasing prosocial behavior in the classroom. Positive Action (Flay, Allred, & Ordway, 2001) and the Responsive Classroom (Elliot, 1999; Rimm-Kaufman, 2003) are curricula that emphasize daily social skills and ongoing communication between students and teachers. Both programs have shown some promising results in helping teachers reduce disruptions, improve social interactions between peers, and increase student achievement. More important, establishing safe, regular communication with students seems to be a strong predictor of whether teachers will be able to respond proactively in their classrooms to conflicts between students. In addition, one of the most popular ways to establish this sort of classroom environment appears to be the use of "class meetings" where students can share concerns and brainstorm solutions with the teacher acting in a facilitator role. Such an approach, when done by a teacher who feels comfortable with facilitating discussions on bullying behavior and school-related violence, can produce a classroom climate of safety and positive problem solving.

WHAT SCHOOL-BASED MENTAL HEALTH PRACTITIONERS CAN DO TO ADDRESS BULLYING BEHAVIOR AND SCHOOL VIOLENCE

School-based mental health practitioners bring a wealth of practice wisdom on how to work with issues related to school violence and students who are bullied and/or who bully others. In this endeavor, there is a growing body of literature that shows a variety of clinical interventions (cognitive-behavioral, solution-focused, and interpersonal therapies) can make a difference in helping students learn social skills, reduce their anger, and improve their own sense of well-being (Gillham, Reivich, Jaycox, & Seligman, 1995; Newsome, 2005; Pedro-Carroll, Sutton, & Wyman, 1999). Table 11.1 describes some of the school-based interventions and techniques that have had a positive impact on prosocial behavior, social skill development, anger management, and conduct disorders with populations in schools. The best of these interventions show modest but positive change on reducing a student's likelihood of committing an act of bullying behavior and/or school-related violence in K–12 educational settings.

Table 11.1 Individual and Group Treatment Addressing Social Skill Development

Practice Approaches	*Examples of Interventions*	*Outcomes of Empirical Research*
Cognitive-behavioral therapy (CBT)	Anger Coping Program (Lochman, 1985); Brainpower Program (Hudley & Graham, 1995); Penn Prevention Program (Gillham, Reivich, Jaycox, & Seligman, 1995); Queensland Early Intervention and Anxiety Prevention Project (Dadds et al., 1999); anger management programming in a residential school facility (Whitfield, 1999)	Evidence shows that CBT approaches decrease hostile attributions of thoughts by students to others, theoretically decreasing their likelihood of becoming violent; CBT has also been shown to help with depression and anxiety in students. Although individual students can be relieved of some Conduct Disorder symptoms, limited research exists that shows the effect of CBT on decreasing school violence and/or bullying behavior.
Solution-focused brief therapy (SFBT)	Middle school SFBT with special education students (Diehlman & Franklin, 1999); Group SFBT counseling (Newsome, 2005); SFBT training for all school staff (Franklin & Streeter, 2004)	Initial studies of SFBT practice in schools indicate that SFBT can positively affect student self-concept and teachers' perceptions of student's disruptive behavior, and improve academic achievement. No evidence thus far exists that SFBT alone can improve overall school climate and prevent school violence and bullying.
Social skills training	First Steps Program (Walker, Stiller, Severson, Feil, & Golly, 1998); Earlscourt Social Skills Group (Pepler, King, Craig, Byrd, & Bream, 1995)	By training students in prosocial behaviors, social skills programs have shown that students can learn new behaviors and practice them in treatment groups. It is still unclear whether treatment effects from these groups last very long beyond group treatment and whether these treatments affect overall school climate.
Family therapy/ family-centered programs	Multisystemic therapy (Henggeler, Melton, Brondino, Scherer, & Hanley, 1997); functional family therapy (Barton, Alexander, Waldron, Turner, & Warburton, 1985); Families and Schools Together (FAST) (Fischer, 2003)	Students and their parents engage in intensive family treatment and group sessions to help both students and parents learn new behaviors. Families seem to get better with these treatments; no evidence that effects from treatment generalize to school climate.

However, despite the interventions presented in Table 11.1, the reality of bullying behavior and school-related violence (and the growing research base about the effectiveness of school-wide preventive programs) is that clinical, selective, and indicator interventions are not enough to help schools become safer places for all students. Although many of the interventions presented in Table 11.1 can and do positively affect a student's individual behavior, they are not equipped to deal with the larger issues of what may precipitate, produce, or expand bullying behavior and violence in K–12 educational settings. More important, the larger contextual factors are absent from many selective and indicator interventions; consequently, their claims of curtailing or combating bullying behavior or school-related violence should be tempered.

In addition, most selective or indicator interventions are focused on specific students and do not address the complexity of school culture or school climate. As Erickson et al. (2004) points out, the trend in school-based interventions still appears to be one of "fixing" the violent kids, with less attention being paid to the social and structural components of youth and school-related violence. As a result, bullying behavior and school-related violence is a multifaceted phenomenon that may necessitate a larger schoolwide approach to combat or curtail the problem (Astor et al., 2004; Cantor et al., 2002).

We now offer a brief case example to demonstrate the importance of designing interventions for students being bullied that help them solve their problems but that also address some systemic causes of school bullying and potential school violence.

Carl is a 9-year-old African American youth who is a new student this year at a mostly white K–5 elementary school. Currently, he is doing well academically, and his teacher has had no problems with him behaviorally, but his mother called the principal one day in January to tell her that she is considering pulling her son out of the school. She said, "He isn't safe at your school; he's telling me every day that kids are picking on him. He's afraid to come to school most days, and if this doesn't change, I'm going to have to tell him to fight back and defend himself." The principal was stunned, having seen Carl playing happily on the playground just the day before. The principal referred the situation to the school social worker who meets with Carl. Carl says that he likes the school fine, except when "those fifth graders bother me." Carl tells the school social worker that these older boys cut in on games on the playground during recess and change the rules. When Carl complains, they threaten him and push him away. Carl is scared of the boys because they are much bigger and also because all the other third-grade boys around him don't step up to tell the older boys to stop. Despite reporting to the playground supervisors that this has happened four or five times, he can't tell the social worker who the boys are and says that he feels like they are "out to get him." Together, the school social worker and principal discuss how to proceed. The school social worker suggests going out to the playground to notice who interacts with Carl and to intervene, if necessary, with the other students who are bullying him. They also decide to set up an initial focus group with all the third- to fifth-grade classrooms to discuss playground activities. Last, the principal states that she will also venture outside sometime later that day to see if there are any other changes that need to take place around the playground area.

During his playground observation, the school social worker notices a few interesting things about Carl and the playground climate. First, there is minimal adult supervision next to the basketball court and kickball diamond, two places that the majority of the older boys are playing. The staff members who are currently out there are seated nearer to the playground equipment and are conversing with each other as much as they are observing the children playing. Second, although Carl is right that other kids are telling him how to play, it's clear that Carl isn't clear about the rules for a basketball shooting game called "knock-out." He keeps getting into arguments with other boys who tell him that he isn't playing right. It turns out that Carl has brought his own ball and is claiming that because it's "my ball," he can decide what game(s) to play. Finally, there are some older boys who begin to make a move toward the basketball hoop but quickly change direction and go to the field to play when they see the school social worker. Later that day, the principal and school social worker meet with all the third- to fifth-grade classrooms and conduct focus groups discussing playground activities. They hear that many kids are frustrated about how older kids push younger kids around and that they wind up arguing a lot about who got there first when they want to play basketball or kickball. They also hear that there appears to be a lot of disagreement as well about how kickball, knock-out, and other basketball games should be played, which results in a lot of arguments between students. The students also say that they don't tell the lunch supervisors because they usually just tell them to stop arguing and tell them to go work it out themselves. Toward the end of the day, and as part of the plan initiated by the principal and school social worker, the principal walks the playground and discovers that there are stations for five basketball rims but that, usually, only two basketball rims are put up each day. She asks the custodian to put up all five rims to increase the options for the kids. In addition, she assigns different grade levels to each one, so that all first through fifth graders have the chance to play at a rim with their classmates. She meets with the playground staff, gives them the feedback from the students, and discusses ways to spread out the supervisors over the whole playground to better monitor students playing. Through weekly announcements on the intercom, she also reminds students that no games at the school are "locked" (meaning that anyone who wants to play is allowed, as long as they follow the rules). A few weeks later, the playground issue for Carl and many others becomes less and less of a problem. In fact, a month later, Carl tells the school social worker and his mom that the older boys have stopped picking on him and he doesn't mind the new games he's learning at school. His mother is pleased as well, and also grateful that the school took such strong action to help her son.

This vignette illustrates the power of intervening with school bullying on multiple levels. By interviewing Carl, the school social worker was able to establish both what Carl knew about the bullying and what he wanted to see changed about the situation. By respecting his wishes to not talk to the boys directly, Carl was empowered to feel part of the solution rather than potentially being revictimized by the older boys. In addition, their observations told the principal and school social worker that poor adult supervision on the playground combined with limited play equipment had made the situation combustible for many students. Observation of playground activity also told school staff that Carl himself was not blameless in the situation, because he was very intense about advocating for games to be played his way.

Another key factor in the intervention occurred at the classroom level. By moving the discussion out of the venue of "victim Carl" and "older bullies," the staff was able to learn about other potential problems on the playground—issues such as poor supervision, a lack of trust in adults who were expected to intervene, and a general disagreement over how to handle the limited playground equipment. Although the matter of adult supervision was serious and took some extensive work and discussion, the last problem was relatively easy to solve, because the principal was able to put out more basketball hoops and to encourage different grades to use different hoops. She also was able to clarify the rules of the popular playground games with Carl and the other students who either didn't understand or didn't agree with the rules. By making the problem one that had many potential causes as discussed earlier, the school staff was able to come up with solutions to Carl's complaint that allowed him to feel safe without ever having to directly confront the bullies. Conversely, the older students were not labeled as "bad kids" or removed from the playground for intensive treatment but, rather, were successfully redirected into more positive play.

Given the success of the intervention addressing this problem on the playground, school-based mental health practitioners are presented with a future challenge. Specifically, school practitioners are faced with the challenge of either choosing the use of individual-based programming, which, according to current research, will likely have minimal impact on the larger school culture and school climate, or look to integrate all three levels of interventions (i.e., universal, selective, and indicator) in developing a comprehensive program that meets the needs of all stakeholders. Some have asserted that school-based mental health practitioners (i.e., school social workers) must be willing to adopt new roles in their schools (McDonald et al., 2002). Such new roles might encompass the following:

- Create, implement, and manage a schoolwide, universal bullying and school violence program
- Perform a functional assessment of places and relationships located in the school that are likely to stimulate or provoke violence
- Develop a referral network for students who are considered to be engaged in bullying behavior or school-related violence or who are being victimized in the school
- Become need assessors, public speakers, and community organizers in their schools to lead the kinds of programs that are showing positive results in making schools safer
- Act as consultants
- Contribute to the mission statement and policy development at their school (McDonald et al., 2002)

As can be surmised from these roles asserted by McDonald and colleagues (2002), effective school intervention and prevention must contain components that work at the individual, classroom, school, and community level. Such components ultimately have the goal of creating a new social environment where bullying behavior and school violence are not accepted by students or school personnel. Creating a new social environment, however, will require a long-term effort by many school-based professionals. Such efforts on the part of school-based mental health practitioners as well as other school personnel, however, are critical to the intervention and subsequent prevention of bullying behavior and school violence.

SUMMARY

In this chapter, we have attempted to document the importance of addressing and treating bullying behavior and school violence. We began with a discussion concerning the prevalence of bullying behavior and school violence, which was then followed by potential warning signs and factors that educators should be aware of. Particular attention in this section was paid to the individual, family, school, and community factors that may influence or act as warning signs for educators who are attempting to reduce or prevent bullying behavior and school violence in K–12 educational settings. Specifically, an attempt was put forth that recognized the importance of contextual influences in understanding bullying behavior and school violence.

Next, attention was given to some of the current intervention techniques to address bullying behavior and school violence. Particular emphasis was given to addressing bullying behavior and school violence from a collective, schoolwide level rather than the individual level. Finally, a discussion was provided on how two of the key stakeholders in schools (i.e., teachers and school-based mental health professionals) might go about using current research to design effective interventions for their schools.

With such considerations and despite the persistent concerns in the larger culture about bullying behavior and school violence, K–12 educational settings continue to be one of the safest places for children to spend their day. On the other hand, although a child may not risk serious physical harm on a daily basis at his or her school, our review of the literature shows that a steady if not growing number of students are victimized in many K–12 educational settings across the United States. Even more alarming is that many of these same children report significantly poorer perceptions of school climate than students who are not victimized (Nansel et al., 2001).

It must also be acknowledged, however, that bullying behavior and school violence are not just problems associated with school culture and the school environment. American society as a whole has an intimidating, aggressive, "Darwinian" nature that inevitably comes with students to school. Such an approach ultimately makes K–12 educational settings a complex community when addressing bullying behavior and school violence.

Last, we must always keep in mind that as educators and school-based practitioners many of us started our careers working with aggressive, violent, and at-risk students. For many of us, such students still form the core of our practice, consume much of our day, and need the best help we can provide. By uncovering and using schoolwide approaches and by working together in partnership as educators, we are accepting the challenge of addressing bullying behavior and school violence. More important, we are extending our hands to the victims as well as the perpetrators of such acts.

DISCUSSION QUESTIONS

1. What contextual issues potentially influence bullying behavior and victimization in K–12 educational settings?
2. Considering the three different levels of interventions addressing bullying behavior and school violence, which approach might work best in urban or rural school districts? Why might one choice be better than another in the context of urban or rural school districts?

3. Should school practitioners and community agencies partner together in addressing bullying behavior and school violence? What are some of the benefits and pitfalls of such collaborative efforts?

4. Is it more important to address the issue of bullying behavior and school violence from a schoolwide perspective or from an individual perspective? Given the school context, why might one approach be more vital than the other?

FOR ADDITIONAL HELP

	Organization	*Web Address*	*Description*
Bullying Behavior and School Violence	Responsible Classroom (RC)	www.responsiveclassroom.org	Teacher curriculum focused on improving teacher efficacy and classroom behavior through a variety of techniques.
	Positive Action (PA)	www.positiveaction.net	A cognitive and behaviorally based program, PA contains daily lessons for teachers to use to teach students that their self-concepts are influenced and shaped by their actions and that students who make positive choices have better behavioral and academic outcomes.
	Peace Builders	www.peacebuilders.com	Using a mixture of schoolwide programming as well as classroom and community meetings, five universal principles are taught. The program is intended to be implemented schoolwide to be effective.
	Promoting Alternative Thinking Strategies (PATHS)	www.preventionscience.com	Teacher curriculum, divided into lessons that emphasize (a) self-control and self-esteem, (b) emotional understanding, (c) good peer relationships, and (d) interpersonal problem solving.

REFERENCES

Astor, R. A., Benbenishty, R., & Marachi, R. (2004). Violence in schools. In P. Allen-Meares (Ed.), *Social work services in schools* (pp. 149–182). Boston: Pearson Education.

Astor, R. A., Vargas, L. A., O'Neil-Pitner, R., & Meyer, H. A. (1999). School violence: Research, theory, and practice. In J. M. Jensen & M. O. Howard (Eds.), *Youth violence: Current research and recent practice innovations* (pp. 139–171). Washington, DC: National Association of Social Workers Press.

Austin, S., & Joseph, S. (1996). Assessment of bully/victim problems in 8 to 11 year olds. *British Journal of Educational Psychology, 66,* 447–456.

Barton, C., Alexander, J. F., Waldron, H., Turner, C. W., & Warburton, J. (1985). Generalizing treatment effects of functional family therapy: Three replications. *American Journal of Family Therapy, 3,* 16–26.

Borg, M. G. (1998). The emotional reactions of school bullies and their victims. *Educational Psychology, 18,* 433–443.

Bosworth, K., Espelage, D. L., & Simon, T. (1999). Factors associated with bullying behavior in middle school students. *Journal of Early Adolescence, 19,* 341–362.

Boulton, M. J. (1997). Teachers' views on bullying: Definitions, attitudes, and ability to cope. *British Journal of Educational Psychology, 67,* 223–233.

Callagan, S., & Joseph, S. (1995). Self-concept and peer victimization among school children. *Personality and Individual Differences, 18,* 161–163.

Cantor, D., Crosse, S., Hagen, C. A., Mason, M. J., Siler, A. J., & Von Glatz, A. (2002). *A closer look at drug and violence prevention efforts in American schools: Report on the study on school violence and prevention.* Washington, DC: U.S. Department of Education Editorial Publication Center.

Centers for Disease Control and Prevention. (1992). *Proceedings of the third national injury control conference.* Atlanta, GA: Author.

Collaborative for Academic, Social, and Emotional Learning. (2003, March). *Safe and sound: An educational leader's guide to evidence-based social and emotional learning (SEL) programs.* Chicago: Author.

Craig, W. M. (1998). The relationship among bullying, victimization, depression, anxiety, and aggression in elementary school children. *Personality and Individual Differences, 24,* 123–130.

Craig, W. M., & Pepler, D. J. (1997). Observations of bullying and victimization in the schoolyard. *Canadian Journal of School Psychology, 13,* 41–59.

Craig, W. M., Pepler, D. J., & Atlas, R. (2000). Observations of bullying in the playground and in the classroom. *School Psychology International, 21,* 22–36.

Dadds, M. R., Holland, D. E., Laurens, K. R., Mullins, M., Barrett, P. M., & Spence, S. H. (1999). Early intervention and prevention of anxiety disorders in children: Results at two-year follow-up. *Journal of Community Psychology, 20,* 200–214.

Diehlman, M., & Franklin, C. (1998). Brief solution-focused therapy with parents and adolescents. *Social Work in Education, 20*(4), 261–268.

Duncan, R. D. (1999). Maltreatment by parents and peers: The relationship between child abuse, bully victimization, and psychological distress. *Child Maltreatment, 4,* 45–55.

Elliot, S. N. (1999). *A multi-year evaluation of the responsive classroom approach: Its effectiveness and acceptability in promoting social and academic competence.* Retrieved November 5, 2005, from www.responsiveclassroom.org/PDF_files/FINAL_REPORT.pdf

Endresen, I. M., & Olweus, D. (2001). Self-reported empathy in Norwegian adolescents: Sex differences, age trends, and relationships to bullying. In A. C. Bohart, C. Arthur, & D. J. Stipek (Eds.), *Constructive & destructive behavior: Implications for family, school, and society* (pp. 147–165). Washington, DC: American Psychological Association.

Erickson, C., Mattaini, M., & McGuire, M. (2004). Constructing nonviolent cultures in schools: The state of the science. *Children & Schools, 26,* 102–116.

Espelage, D. L., Bosworth, K., & Simon, T. R. (2000). Examining the social context of bullying behaviors in early adolescence. *Journal of Counseling and Development, 78,* 326–333.

Espelage, D. L., & Swearer, S. M. (2003). Research on school bullying and victimization: What have we learned and where do we go from here. *School Psychology Review, 32,* 365–383.

Fischer, R. L. (2003). School-based family support: Evidence for an exploratory field study. *Families in Society, 84,* 339–347.

Flay, B. R., Allred, C. G., & Ordway, N. (2001). Effects of the Positive Action program on achievement and discipline: Two matched-control comparisons. *Prevention Science, 2,* 71–89.

Franklin, C., & Streeter, C. (2004). *Solution-focused alternatives for education (SAFED).* Retrieved June 2, 2004, from www.utexas.edu/research/cswr/projects/pj0181.html

Fried, S., & Fried, P. (1996). *Bullies and victims: Helping our children survive the schoolyard battlefield.* New York: M. Evans.

Gillham, J. E., Reivich, K. J., Jaycox, L. H., & Seligman, M. (1995). Prevention of depressive symptoms in schoolchildren: Two-year follow-up. *Psychological Science, 6,* 343–351.

Graham, S., & Juvonen, J. (2002). Ethnicity, peer harassment, and adjustment in middle school: An exploratory study. *Journal of Early Adolescence, 22,* 173–199.

Greenberg, M. T., Domitrovich, C., & Bumbarger, B. (2001). The prevention of mental disorders in school-aged children: Current state of the field. *Prevention and Treatment, 4,* 135–146.

Greenberg, M. T., Weissberg, R. P., O'Brien, M. U., Zins, J. E., Fredericks, L., Resnik, H., et al. (2003). Enhancing school-based prevention and youth development through coordinated social, emotional, and academic learning. *American Psychologist, 58*(6–7), 466–474.

Hawker, D. S., & Boulton, M. J. (2000). Twenty years' research on peer victimization and psychosocial maladjustment: A meta-analytic review of cross-sectional studies. *Journal of Child Psychology and Psychiatry, 41,* 441–455.

Haynie, D. L., Hansel, T., Eitel, P., Crump, A. D., Saylor, K., Yu, K., et al. (2001). Bullies, victims and bully/victims: Distinct groups of at-risk youth. *Journal of Early Adolescence, 21,* 29–49.

Heinrichs, R. R. (2003). A whole-school approach to bullying: Special considerations for children with exceptionalities. *Intervention in School & Clinic, 38,* 195–205.

Henggeler, S. W., Melton, G. B., Brondino, M. J., Scherer, D. G., & Hanley, J. H. (1997). Multisystemic therapy with violent and chronic juvenile offenders and their families: The role of treatment fidelity in successful dissemination. *Journal of Consulting and Clinical Psychology, 65,* 821–833.

Hoover, J. H., Oliver, R., & Hazler, R. J. (1992). Bullying: Perceptions of adolescent victims in midwestern U.S.A. *School Psychology International, 13,* 5–16.

Hudley, C., & Graham, S. (1995). School-based interventions for aggressive African American boys. *Applied & Preventative Psychology, 4,* 185–195.

Josephson Institute on Ethics. (2001). *2000 report card: Violence and substance abuse.* Retrieved April 2002, from www.josephsoninstitute.org/Survey2000/violence2000-commentary.htm

Juvonen, J., Nishina, A., & Graham, S. (2001). Self-views versus peer perceptions of victim status among early adolescents. In J. Juvonen & S. Graham (Eds.), *Peer harassment in school: The plight of the vulnerable and victimized* (pp. 105–124). New York: Guilford Press.

Kann, L. (1995). Youth risk behavior surveillance: United States. *MMWR, 44*(SS-1), 1–56.

Kaufman, P., Chen, X., Choy, S., Chandler, K., Chapman, C., Rand, M. R., et al. (2000). *Indicators of school crime and safety, 1998* (NCES 98-251/NCJ-172215). Washington, DC: U.S. Departments of Education and Justice.

Kochenderfer, B. J., & Ladd, G. W. (1997). Victimized children's responses to peers' aggression: Behaviors associated with reduced versus continued victimization. *Developmental and Psychopathology, 9,* 59–73.

Leff, S. S., Kupersmidt, J. B., Patterson, C. J., & Power, T. J. (1999). Factors influencing teachers identification of peer bullies and victims. *School Psychology Review, 28,* 505–517.

Limber, S. P., Cunningham, P., Florx, V., Ivey, J., Nation, M., Chai, S., et al. (1997, June/July). *Bullying among school children: Preliminary findings from a school-based intervention program.* Paper presented at the Fifth International Family Violence Research Conference, Durham, NH.

Limber, S. P., & Small, M. A. (2003). State laws and policies to address bullying in schools. *School Psychology Review, 32,* 445–455.

Lochman, J. E. (1985). Effects of different treatment lengths in cognitive-behavioral intervention with aggressive boys. *Child Psychiatry and Human Development, 16,* 45–56.

Loeber, R., & Stouthamer-Loeber, M. (1998). Development of juvenile aggression and violence: Some common misconceptions and controversies. *American Psychologist, 53,* 242–259.

McDonald, S., Fineran, S., Constable, R., & Moriarty, A. (2002). Creating safe and responsive schools: Bullying and peer sexual harassment. In R. Constable, S. McDonald, & J. P. Flynn (Eds.), *School social work: Practice, policy, and research perspectives* (pp. 458–480). Chicago: Lyceum Books.

Moffitt, T. E., Caspi, A., Dickson, N., Silva, P., & Stanton, W. (1996). Childhood-onset versus adolescent-onset antisocial conduct problems in males: Natural history from ages 3 to 18 years. *Development and Psychopathology, 8,* 399–424.

Nansel, T. R., Overpeck, M., Pilla, R. S., Ruan, W. J., Simons-Morton, B., & Scheidt, P. (2001). Bullying behaviors among U.S. youth: Prevalence and association with psychosocial adjustment. *Journal of the American Medical Association, 285,* 2094–2100.

National Center for Education Statistics. (1998). *Violence and discipline problems in U.S. public schools: 1996–97.* Washington, DC: U.S. Department of Education.

National Resource Center for Safe Schools. (2000). *What teachers can do about violence* (Fact sheet No. 6). Washington DC: Author.

Neace, W. P., Munoz, M. A., Olson-Allen, S., Weber, J., & Johnson, K. (2003, April). *Pushing the boundaries of education: Evaluating the impact of research-based social service programs with educational performance indicators.* (ERIC Document Reproduction Services No. ED479023)

Newsome, W. S. (2005). The impact of solution-focused brief therapy with at-risk junior high school students. *Children & Schools, 27*(2), 83–90.

Olweus, D. (1993). Bully/victim problems among school children: Long-term consequences and an effective intervention program. In S. Hodgins (Ed.), *Mental disorder and crime* (pp. 317–349). Thousand Oaks, CA: Sage.

O'Moore, M., & Kirkman, C. (2001). Self-esteem and its relationship to bullying behavior. *Aggressive Behavior, 27,* 269–283.

Pedro-Carroll, J. L., Sutton, S. E., & Wyman, P. A. (1999). A two-year follow-up evaluation of a preventive intervention for young children of divorce. *School Psychology Review, 28,* 467–476.

Pellegrini, A. D., & Bartini, M. (2001). Dominance in early adolescent boys: Affiliative and aggressive dimensions and possible functions. *Merrill-Palmer Quarterly, 47,* 142–163.

Pepler, D., King, G., Craig, W., Byrd, B., & Bream, L. (1995). The development and evaluation of a multisystem social skills group training program for aggressive children. *Child and Youth Care Forum, 24*(5), 297–313.

Perry, D., Kusel, S., & Perry, L. (1988). Victims of peer aggression. *Developmental Psychology, 24,* 807–814.

Reinke, W. M., & Herman, K. C. (2002). A research agenda for school-violence prevention. *American Psychologist, 57,* 796–797.

Rimm-Kaufman, S. (2003). *Preliminary findings on the study of social and academic learning.* Retrieved November 5, 2005, from www.responsiveclassroom.org/PDF_files/SALS_Prelim.pdf

Roland, E. (1989). A system oriented strategy against bullying. In E. Roland & E. Munthe (Eds.), *Bullying: An international perspective* (pp. 143–151). London: David Fulton.

Roth, D. A., Coles, M. E., & Heimberg, R. G. (2002). The relationship between memories for childhood teasing and anxiety and depression in adulthood. *Journal of Anxiety Disorders, 16,* 149–164.

Schneider-Denenberg, T., Denenberg, R. V., & Braverman, M. (1998). Reducing violence in U.S. schools. *Dispute Resolution Journal, 53,* 28–35.

Schwartz, D. (2000). Subtypes of victims and aggressors in children's peer groups. *Journal of Abnormal Child Psychology, 28,* 181–192.

Sheras, P. L., & Tippins, S. (2002). *Your child: Bully or victim? Understanding and ending schoolyard tyranny.* New York: Fireside.

Silvernail, D. L., Thompson, A. M., Yang, Z., & Kopp, H. J. P. (2000). *A survey of bullying behavior among Maine third graders.* Gorham, ME: Maine Center for Educational Policy, Applied Research and Evaluation, University of Southern Maine. Retrieved November 5, 2005, from http://lincoln.midcoast.com/~wps/against/execsummary.html

Slee, P. T. (1995). Peer victimization and its relationship to depression among Australian primary school students. *Personality & Individual Differences, 18,* 57–62.

Smith, P. K., & Sharp, S. (1994). *School bullying: Insights and perspectives.* London: Routledge.

Snyder, H., Puzzanchera, C., & Kang, W. (2005). *Easy access to FBI Arrest Statistics 1994–2002 Online.* Retrieved November 16, 2005, from http://ojjdp.ncjrs.org/ojstatbb/ezaucr

Stockdale, M. S., Hangaduambo, S., Duys, D., Larson, K., & Sarvela, P. D. (2002). Rural elementary students', parents', and teachers' perceptions of bullying. *American Journal of Health Behavior, 26,* 266–277.

Swearer, S. M., Song, S. Y., Cary, P. T., Eagle, J. W., & Mickelson, W. T. (2001). Psychosocial correlates in bullying and victimization: The relationship between depression, anxiety, and bully/victim status. *Journal of Emotional Abuse, 2,* 95–121.

Tolan, P. H., Guerra, N. G., & Kendall, P. C. (1995). A developmental/ecological perspective on antisocial behavior in children and adolescents: Toward a unified risk and intervention framework. *Journal of Consulting and Clinical Psychology, 63,* 579–584.

U.S. Department of Health and Human Services. (2001). *Youth violence: A report of the Surgeon General.* Rockville, MD: U.S. Department of Health and Human Services; Centers for Disease Control and Prevention, National Center for Injury Prevention; Substance Abuse and Mental Health Services Administration, Center for Mental Health Services; and National Institutes of Health, National Institute of Mental Health.

U.S. Departments of Education and Justice. (2000). *2000 Annual report of school safety.* Washington, DC: Author.

U.S. Surgeon General. (2001). *Youth violence: A report of the surgeon general.* Washington, DC: U.S. Department of Health and Human Services.

Walker, H. M., Stiller, B., Severson, H. H., Feil, E. G., & Golly, A. (1998). First step to success: An early intervention approach to preventing school antisocial behavior. *Journal of Emotional & Behavioral Disorders, 6,* 66–80.

Whitfield, G. W. (1999). Validating school social work: An evaluation of a cognitive-behavioral approach to reduce school violence. *Research on School Violence, 9,* 399–426.

Williams, K., Chamgers, M., Logan, S., & Robinson, D. (1996). Association of common health symptoms with bullying in primary school children. *British Medical Journal, 313,* 17–19.

Wolke, D., Woods, S., Blomfield, L., & Karstadt, L. (2000). The association between direct and relational bullying and behavior problems among primary school children. *Journal of Child Psychology & Psychiatry & Related Disciplines, 41*(8), 989–1002.

Zuehl, J. J., Dillon, E., Schilling, J. L., & Oltmanns, J. K. (2002). *Student discipline issues.* Unpublished manuscript.

Chapter 12

CHILDHOOD SEXUALITY AND SEXUAL BEHAVIOR

Ramona M. Noland

PREREADING QUESTIONS

As you read this chapter, please reflect on the following questions and issues:

1. What do you know about normal childhood sexual development?
2. What do you know about atypical childhood sexual development?
3. How important is it for teachers to communicate with parents regarding a child's sexuality development?
4. Which professionals within the school setting are available to support teachers if they have concerns about a child's sexual development?
5. How important is sexuality education for children? At what age should it begin? What topics should be covered?

It is probably safe to say that sex and childhood sexuality are not easy topics of discussion for most people. Although a few lucky individuals had parents who maintained open lines of communication with them, the majority most likely remember "talks" that, if they were held, contained misinformation in youth (i.e., the stork story) and little information in adolescence (i.e., don't have sex), and were too late because our friends had already been schooling us for several years. Our sexuality continues to be shrouded in mystery, misinformation, and myth. There are probably more sexually related urban legends than any other type, and these stories born out of ignorance promote a continued cycle of misunderstanding.

Within the past 60 years, we have truly been influenced by a sexual revolution in terms of the increased prevalence and acceptance of sexual behaviors within the media and our everyday lives. Behaviors and lifestyles are now prevalent in society that were not acknowledged 60 years ago, thus broadening our understanding of what is "normal" in terms of our human sexuality. As teachers and education professionals, you are likely to encounter behaviors or situations that might require a better understanding of human sexuality and its development. Anecdotal information from teachers and caregivers supported a hypothesis that professionals who work with children often observed sexual activities that made them uncomfortable and that they believed were problematic (Ryan, 2000). It is often difficult to recognize what is normal and to differentiate what is problematic. The teachers who participated in the Essa and Murray (1999) research study reflected this ambiguity. They were not sure they could distinguish between appropriate and inappropriate behaviors of children, they felt uncertain about what standards to follow, and they were ambivalent about their own feelings concerning sexuality in relation to young children.

This chapter has been developed in an effort to address concerns held by education professionals regarding children's expressions of sexuality. Educators are provided a brief overview of major theoretical constructs regarding general development during childhood and how a child's sexuality might fit in with overall development. Normal sexual behaviors and sexual exploration are discussed, along with suggestions to potentially handle situations that fall within the typical range of sexual behaviors. Finally, the readers are provided with a frank discussion of those behaviors that could be considered deviant and suggestions for action related to these types of behaviors.

This year I had a student named Julie, a pretty girl and very capable in class, but she always settled for average grades because she was very distracted by (and was distracting to) the boys in class. All year long, when Julie appeared to be listening during a lesson, I could walk by her desk and find her involved in note writing to various boys in class. She really seemed to need their attention. She was never upset to be caught or to receive whatever consequence she had earned. That was never as important as keeping an ongoing communication with boys.

Our school may be more conservative than most in behavior expectations and in our dress code. Each morning after the "Moment of Reflection" and the "Pledge of Allegiance," my students were reminded over the intercom to "Please stand for the dress code check." Only a few students had to be sent out to the hall during the year to be checked and possibly written up by an administrator, but Julie was a regular. She was sent out for dress code violations such as "too-tight shirts, midriff exposed, shirts hanging off the shoulders, and too-short skirts." Julie would regularly have to call home for someone to bring her another shirt or other piece of clothing, but she would most often borrow something from a box of clothes in the office. She would very pleasantly return to the office in the afternoon to return the borrowed item. The type of dressing described as a problem above may have been all attention-getting behavior, but I often wondered if anybody was checking on and guiding Julie at home. The clothes she wore were often wrinkled and dirty and she commented to me once that she really liked the school sweatshirt she had had to wear that day; she had never realized how comfortable they were!

It was difficult to reach Julie's parents for a conference to discuss her grades and behavior. Even when her mother requested a conference after report cards went home in the fall, all the contact numbers except her mother's work number had been disconnected. Later in the year, her mother wanted me to set up a conference for the dad and the assistant principal about the dress code issue, but no one could furnish me with a phone number for the dad. When we did have a conference with Julie, her mom, and the two of us that taught her, we didn't get very far. The mother seemed very proud of her beautiful daughter and laughed through most of our concerns. Julie seemed to have the upper hand with her mother because she excused her way through any problems and really seemed like the adult of the two of them. There also seemed to be a lot that was unsaid, but understood, between the two of them. We emphasized to the mother that we thought Julie was wonderful, too, but she was focused on boys and not her schoolwork. We made a plan to send notes home to the mother in Julie's agenda to keep her up-to-date, and we gave Julie's name to the guidance counselor as someone to meet with occasionally.

The off-task behavior continued throughout the year—talking, note writing to boys, flirting, and blowing kisses across the room. I changed the seating chart frequently. One morning near the end of the school year, I was checking the roll and noticed that a boy, Josh, was out of his assigned seat and sitting next to Julie. As I told Josh to take his seat I noticed that he was sitting too close to Julie and at a funny angle. Not wanting to draw the class's attention to them I kept checking the roll. My eyes dropped down below their desktops and I noticed that he had a hand between Julie's legs near the crotch area. I didn't think my students would handle this very well so I looked directly at Josh and said, "You need to take your books and step outside right now." An administrator would be walking down the hall for dress check any minute and could walk Josh to the office. Josh quietly walked out and Julie did not even blush. Josh was given two weeks out-of-school suspension and would be allowed to go to in-school suspension to finish his work and take final exams. He had a record in the office of inappropriate touching (touching, hitting, slapping) girls. He will be recommended for the alternative school in August when we return to school. Julie was given one day out-of-school suspension and two days in-school. Her greatest offenses prior to this were dress code violations, talking, and note writing.

With the history of these two students, I shouldn't have been surprised by this incident, but I was greatly upset at having seen this and to know that this is going on in an environment where students should be positively influenced by those around them. Also, I am greatly concerned about where Julie and Josh are headed if they are this knowledgeable and casual about sexual behavior in the seventh grade.

NORMAL CHILDHOOD SEXUALITY DEVELOPMENT

From birth onward, children are developing the skills and experiences they need to further their growth and provide a foundation for behavior throughout their adult life. This is true for sexual development just as it is true for physical development (i.e., crawling, walking, and running), cognitive development (i.e., acquisition of language and nearly constant learning of new information that will ultimately lead to critical thinking), and all other areas of development. Children begin by building behavioral repertoires and then practicing these learned behaviors, often in a trial-and-error fashion. Babies explore their bodies just as they explore everything else, and in the process usually discover that touching their genitals feels good. Some masturbation throughout childhood is common (Couchenour & Chrisman, 1996). A child explores the environment individually but is also influenced by others interacting within that environment as well. During the first year of life, there are significant events that contribute to the child's erotic or sexual capacity, including an attachment or bond that becomes the basis of later capacity for intimacy and an appreciation of and practice in the aspects of physical and emotional attachment and intimacy (i.e., hugging, kissing, gazing, stroking) (Martinson, 1991). Later, because it is the time when language and labeling occur, toddlerhood is a significant period of bodily exploration, developing relationships, and psychological awareness (Frayser, 1994). The parents and family play the primary role in a child's early development, including the child's conceptualization of sexuality. How parents, family members, and caregivers react to a child's actions and questions can encourage further exploration, satiate curiosity, or potentially indicate to the child that certain topics or body areas are mysterious or even "bad." It must be kept in mind that sexual exploration is normal and necessary for appropriate development, even though normal sexual exploration may cause some concerns for teachers, parents, and other caregivers. Some examples of appropriate sexual exploration are listed in Table 12.1.

The earliest influences on sexuality come from the parents, family, and early caregivers, but soon children begin to gain access to peers as cooperative explorers. As part of their information gathering, children explore each other's bodies by looking and touching, by which they begin to build an understanding of what the body looks like, what differences exist between boys and girls, and what it feels like to touch another's body (Johnson, 1999). This is a time of general innocence and intrigue, where children will offer trades of body touching ("you can touch mine if I can touch yours") and develop games that allow for physical exploration (i.e., playing doctor). They experiment in play with adult roles in games such as "house" and "school," and their social interactions mimic relationship roles when they claim another as a "boyfriend" or "girlfriend." The information gathered through early childhood and preadolescence and the experimentation with various roles and social expectations is critical in allowing the child to make a reasonable transition into adolescence and young adulthood. Children are slowly able to build the cognitive and emotional backbone that will help to steer them once their biological "urges" emerge.

Table 12.1 What Is *Healthy* Sexual Exploration?

Autostimulation	• Discovered in children as early as *in utero.* • Can occur in both boys and girls. • Purposeful for pleasure, but not always to achieve orgasm. • Masturbation is more common in boys and frequency increases with advancing age.
Sexual behaviors	• Occur mainly between children who have an ongoing mutual play or friendship. • Children are generally of similar age, size, and developmental level. • Normal exploration is usually without pressure. • If "caught," the behaviors will decrease or stop, at least in *the sight of adults.*

SOURCE: Adapted from Frayser (1994) and Johnson (1999).

The behaviors and level of interest observed during infancy, toddlerhood, early childhood, and preadolescence are likely to fall somewhere along a continuum that ranges from negligible to high. Just as a child reaches developmental milestones during a range of time and similar to our adult levels of interest and desire for sexual fulfillment, each child will vary in the onset of behaviors and the amount of interest he or she takes in the topic of sexuality. What seems like one child's more frequent behavior or interest may not necessarily indicate anything more than a typical, but high, level of sexual exploration. Likewise, what appears to be a child's complete lack of behavior and interest may also fall within normal limits for sexuality development.

A sexual awakening is experienced by many children in preadolescence as their puberty occurs (Martinson, 1991). Recent data provided by Petersen, Leffert, and Graham (1995) indicated that girls begin puberty as early as 8 years old and as late as 13, whereas boys begin puberty approximately 1.5 to 6 years later than girls, generally between the ages of 9.5 and 14.5 years of age. In addition, the duration of puberty ranges from 1 to 6 years with an average of 4 years. An 8-year-old would generally be in the second to third grade, and a 14-year-old would be in the eighth to ninth grade. This is an amazing range in ages for the onset of puberty! Some children clearly have more time than others to hone their sexuality both cognitively and emotionally. Again, it is important to emphasize that there is a continuum of sexual behavior exhibited by growing children. Some things that are normal prior to puberty become problematic if they continue later, whereas other behaviors that were less expected among younger children become normal among adolescents (Ryan, 2000). One thing is certain: Adolescents have a distinct social disadvantage because they are more likely than older age-groups to be involved in situations in which they lack experience (Petersen et al., 1995). Adolescents need to be allowed increasingly independent social opportunities that will support their gaining the needed experiences to help them expand into increasingly adult roles while keeping their risk of vulnerability to a minimum.

A concept with which all children must grapple throughout their youth is gender. There are many facets of gender concept development (see Box 12.1 for some definitions in regard to gender development), and children progress from the most basic to complex over time. By the age of 2.5 or 3 years, most children can answer correctly the question, "Are you a boy or a girl?" Nevertheless, it is not until several years later that children attain gender constancy—that is, understand that their sex remains invariant across time and changes in surface appearance

Box 12.1 Some Helpful Definitions

- *Gender role*: One's social role to fulfill societal expectations based on our sex
- *Gender identity*: Psychological characteristics considered masculine/feminine
- *Sexual orientation*: Defined by the gender of the individual who is one's sexual interest
- *Intersexual*: Individual who is born with mixed sexual characteristics, or generally some mixture of male and female sexual organs and/or characteristics
- *Gender dysphoria*: A feeling of incongruity with an experienced disparity between one's biological sex and one's inner experience of gender identity
- *Gender identity disorder*: A clinical condition that may result when gender dysphoria disrupts social, occupational, or other areas of functioning

SOURCE: Adapted from American Psychiatric Association (2000), Baker (2002), and Petersen et al. (1995).

(e.g., hair length) (Egan & Perry, 2001). Understanding gender roles provides an area of high exploration.

Children are intrigued by both male and female roles, and they are drawn to games and activities that allow for play-based acceptance of a variety of roles, both within- and cross-gender. Exploring other gender roles and clothing styles has become culturally more acceptable for little girls but remains controversial for boys (Johnson, 1999). Adults are far more noticeably uncomfortable when children want to cross gender "lines" in their playful exploration, and they continue to reinforce gender stereotypes. However, playing dress-up in early childhood is not equivalent to adult cross-dressing or homosexuality (Couchenour & Chrisman, 1996). One of the best ways for children to gain a concrete understanding of what it means to fulfill a **gender role** is to actively participate in that role. In fact, it is unclear in the wealth of research and discussions about sexuality what, if anything, gender nonconforming behavior in childhood means (Gottschalk, 2003), but hindering children's ability to fully explore clearly leaves them with unanswered questions.

Although rare, there are two types of children who might be encountered who exhibit atypical **gender identity** development. Children who are categorized as intersexuals have been born with some form of indiscriminate sexual characteristics that have made distinguishing biological gender difficult. This biological confusion can occur based on a number of medical conditions, and until very recently doctors would often advise parents to determine the sex of their infant surgically soon after birth. However, several **intersexed** individuals have come forward in recent years describing extremely painful childhoods and adolescent experiences stemming from having one sex and concurrent gender role and "feeling" that they were the other. In other words, they were experiencing **gender dysphoria** because a decision had been made regarding their sexual and gender identity that in the end did not fit their inner experience of their own gender. There is a strong push currently to allow children who are intersexed to develop and mature into adolescence prior to making any decisions related to gender determination. Although intersexuals have a medical basis for their experiences of gender dysphoria, experiencing gender dysphoria is not limited to only intersexual individuals. Some children who have no biological malady at birth and are clearly born as one sex or the other can also experience gender dysphoria. These children show a strong and continuing desire to take on the role of the opposite gender in both dress and action well into preadolescent development.

Adolescence is the defining period of time when all individuals struggle to establish their identity, including their **sexual identity.** This is not an easy endeavor, as any parent of an adolescent would attest. Dating is the preferred means of relationship exploration for youths in the United States. Although the majority of teens will ultimately develop a heterosexual, or opposite-sex, orientation, there are other possible **sexual orientation** outcomes. These alternative sexual orientations, although they describe a minority of individuals, are still considered to fall within the range of normal sexuality development. Today we are all becoming increasingly aware of sexual orientation, particularly the development of a same-sex orientation. With prevalence rates for gay, lesbian, bisexual, transgendered, and "questioning" individuals being offered by gay and lesbian rights groups that are as high as 1 in 10, the likelihood that educational personnel will encounter children who are at least questioning their sexual orientation is fairly high.

Just as it is likely for an educator to come into contact with a child who is potentially developing a homosexual sexual orientation, it is also possible for an educator to be working with parents who identify with a sexual orientation other than heterosexual. Statistics vary, but it is thought that approximately 4 to 6 million gay, lesbian, transgendered, or bisexual individuals parent around 8 to 10 million children (Meadows, 2001). Educators should be aware that research has shown the most common concern for gay, lesbian, and transgendered parents and parents-to-be is that their children will be teased or bullied, followed by a concern that discussion about lesbian or gay families would not be included in the school and preschool curriculum (Ray & Gregory, 2001).

Homosexuality has become more prevalent in our culture, achieving representation on several television shows and in a number of popular movies. However, full acceptance of alternative sexuality and the rights of these individuals has yet to be achieved within the United States. Regardless of one's personal views, it is important for educators to know the facts rather than the myths (Frieman, O'Hara, & Settel, 1996). Baker (2002) addresses several common myths of homosexuality, making it possible to conclude that all individuals who do not demonstrate the traditional heterosexual orientation (a) are *not* mentally ill, (b) *cannot* be cured, (c) are *not* making a choice, (d) are *not* sexual molesters, and (e) will *not* attempt to convert children to an alternative sexual lifestyle.

DEALING WITH NORMAL CHILDHOOD SEXUALITY DEVELOPMENT

Ryan (2000) conducted a small study to gain insight into the behavioral observations and concerns of education professionals. The results of this survey have been summarized in Box 12.2. The most frequently reported behaviors observed within the school setting clearly fell within normal expectations for childhood sexuality development. As was indicated earlier, some masturbation throughout childhood is normal. However, masturbation that is compulsive and continues throughout the day is not normal and can indicate great stress, an infection in the urethra or the genital region, that a child has been exposed to explicit adult sexual activity or pornography, or that sexual abuse has occurred (Honig, 2000). When a child demonstrates a sexual behavior that should be addressed, it is often best to start with the simplest solution first and then work toward the increasingly complex. I say this because I recall on more than one occasion great alarm being raised because of self-stimulation behavior in the classroom,

Box 12.2 School Personnel Survey Results

- Highest reported behaviors
  - Children rubbing genitals during class
  - Sexual talk
- Most frequent descriptors of restroom and playground behavior
  - Secrecy
  - Giggling
- Highest reported complaints
  - Children grabbing others
  - Name-calling
- Most frequent reported reaction
  - Redirection of the behavior
  - Prohibiting the behavior
- Most frequently reported concern
  - When to suspect sexual victimization
- Number whose teacher training covered childhood sexuality
  - Less than 30%

SOURCE: Adapted from Ryan (2000).

and later it was discovered that no one had taken the time to talk with the children and tell them not to perform that action in public. If children are discovered rubbing their private areas in the classroom during story time or nap time or whenever, an adult should speak with them about the behavior. "Some behaviors we can do anytime and anywhere, while there are other behaviors that are not to be done around other people." Parents should be contacted and delicately informed of the school's concern, and plans should be made in terms of who will talk with the child and what steps might be taken if the behavior should continue. When more compulsive masturbation is evident, it again is appropriate to contact the parents and inform them of the concern. There may be a medical or psychological reason for the behavior that is not related to sexual abuse, but the parents' help must be enlisted to rule this out. If the behavior and your concerns continue, then it would be appropriate to seek assistance from the school's counselor or psychologist or even outside agencies. Start with the simplest solution first (in other words, do *not* always assume the worst initially), but also maintain documentation of behaviors and conversations and carefully consider all the things you are observing. An estimated 1.5% of children are confirmed victims of child abuse (all types) each year, and it is quite certain that this is an underestimate of the actual occurrence because this is only what comes to the attention of the authorities (Johnson, 1999).

When children are overheard talking about sexual topics, educators are encouraged to consider the context in which the behavior occurred as well as the content of the conversation. Some discussion of sexual topics is to be expected, but there are, of course, appropriate times and places and less appropriate times and places. If language used in a conversation between children seems age appropriate and noncoercive, this is probably the time to provide the child

Box 12.3 Providing Information

Accurate information

- It is important to fully answer questions yet not overdisclose.
- Children need names for sexual parts; avoid euphemisms because they are confusing to young children.
- Share current information on gender roles (i.e., ways to dress, traditional and nontraditional employment, etc.) so that children can understand similarities as well as differences.

Corrective information

- Children may need to be told that certain behaviors are best not done while at school or in a public place around other people.
- Try to avoid communicating that some body parts are "bad" or that the child is "naughty" because of an action or word.
- Help children have the words needed to interact with peers regarding sexuality and give them the ability to refuse interactions.

Supportive information

- React calmly when children bring up a sexual topic.
- Listen carefully and openly to their concerns; respond when appropriate or tell them their parents might be better suited to answer this particular concern.
- Acknowledge sexual feelings of adolescents and the difficulty of the situation they are facing, yet encourage them to delay action until more maturity has been accumulated.

SOURCE: Adapted from Chrisman and Couchenour (2002), Couchenour and Chrisman (1996), Honig (2000), and Petersen et al. (1995).

with information (see Box 12.3). If the content of the sexual language seems too advanced for the child's age or if any derogatory or threatening overtones or statements are evident, then that child's behavior is moving away from normal expectations and is falling more within the realm of deviant sexual behavior. As the behavior is increasingly deviant, providing the child information may simply not be enough. You will want to enlist the help of the parents and school support personnel to develop a plan of action to be taken.

In the study conducted by Ryan (2000), the highest reported complaint to educators was rough play and children grabbing others. The next highest complaint was name-calling. "He touched me" and "Mr. N., Shawna called me a dweeb" and the endless list of similar complaints can certainly become old very quickly. However, when the touching and name-calling begin to include sexual connotations, this can move typical play behavior toward harassment. Educators are encouraged to take all reports of student-to-student harassment very seriously. It is possible that the children were not aware that they were crossing a line of acceptable behavior. If this is true, then the behavior will cease following an intervention. It seems as though the curriculum today will burst with the expectations placed on teachers and topics that should be covered each school year. Nevertheless, infusing an understanding of diversity within lessons, encouraging tolerance of those who are different, and accepting no discriminatory or derogatory comments from children may help to reduce teasing behaviors and office

Box 12.4 Take Action: How to Support Healthy Sexuality Development

- Honestly evaluate and recognize any biases you may have.
- Examine the words and actions you habitually use and take steps to ensure that they reflect inclusiveness and respect for each family.
- Maintain a classroom focus on diversity, including sexual diversity.
- Challenge negative remarks made about gay people, other minority groups, or anytime children use derogatory terms to describe people who are different.
- Understand that complaints of student-to-student harassment need your serious consideration and attention.
- Act immediately on reports of student-to-student harassment and abuse.
- Ensure that your actions have lasting effects and are not merely halting the behavior for that moment or day.
- Attempt to find resources for families or put them in touch with individuals who can, such as the school's counselor, psychologist, or school social work.
- Be familiar with some of the issues that may be of concern to students and families with individuals whose sexuality is nontraditional.
- Seek professional development that will support you in educating students and challenging false ideas about people whose sexuality is nontraditional.

SOURCE: Adapted from Frieman et al. (1996), Meadows (2001), and Ray and Gregory (2001).

referrals and ultimately provide peace of mind as the school year progresses. Most educators should be prepared to address bias toward different races, cultures, and even obesity, but it is possible that some educators may have difficulty understanding *sexuality* that appears so different from their own. For some, these types of sexuality differences could represent actions or lifestyles that go against their religious or moral belief systems. Educator actions identified in Box 12.4 include starting with a personal analysis of possible biases and reflecting on how these biases could be represented in everyday classroom language. Because of the increasing potential for encountering individuals whose sexuality falls within our culture's minority, educators who have carefully examined their thoughts, feelings, and actions will be better prepared when the time for accommodating sexual diversity arrives.

Gender dysphoria in children does not necessarily represent sexual *deviancy* for a child but instead might best be included in our ever-expanding understanding of the human sexuality continuum. Although certainly not common among developing children, it is a period of heightened gender exploration and an attempt to accommodate biology with psychology related to one's gender. As children grow, they may move into adulthood and have their gender dysphoria resolved or they may move into adulthood with **Gender Identity Disorder** and later identify as a transsexual. In terms of gender and the developing child,

> it is felt pressure for gender conformity, not a perception of the self as gender typical, that is harmful. Thus, children's adjustment is optimized when they (a) are secure in their conceptions of themselves as typical members of their sex yet (b) feel free to explore cross-sex options when they so desire. (Egan & Perry, 2001, p. 459)

A small, rural community in western Colorado actively dealt in a proactive way with an elementary-age boy who was clearly experiencing gender dysphoria. The boy sought often to wear girls' clothing and makeup and to practice cross-gender play. Parents and educators supported the child in his choices to explore and supported his peers in their understanding and acceptance of his differences. The boy's opportunity to develop in a supported environment will obviously lead to a less troubled development of sexuality and gender, no matter what the ultimate outcome of his childhood exploration.

Similar to gender identity development, it is also advisable for educators to encourage and support sexual identity development during adolescence, understanding that some children will want to explore alternative sexual orientations. Although some schools are taking a proactive stance and establishing student alliances, many, if not most, schools still pretend that sexuality other than heterosexuality does not exist among youths—silence is the response of many schools to the issue of gay students (Baker, 2002). Therefore, educators working with "questioning" youths are encouraged to be available to these students for individual conversations or by assisting in the development of a student organization. The school's counselor or psychologist may be asked to develop a small student group that could focus on their concerns and possible ways to resolve conflicts or difficulties being encountered.

DEVIANT CHILDHOOD SEXUAL BEHAVIOR

Deviancy, in its broadest sense, refers to any quality, conduct, or thought that significantly diverges from a standard or norm and may be determined by the laws, customs, or standards of any group and may refer to appearances, behaviors, or beliefs (Steele & Ryan, 1991). For the purposes of this chapter, deviant childhood sexual behaviors are defined as those that are clearly maladaptive with the capacity to lead to increasingly negative patterns of sexually relating with others. Student-to-student harassment, sexually precocious knowledge and behavior, sexual abuse victims, potentially sexually abusive behaviors, and juvenile sexual offenders will all be addressed below.

In our schools, harassment is pervasive and problematic. Estimates of this problem's prevalence range from just under one half to slightly more than three quarters of high school students experiencing at least one incidence of sexual harassment (Grube & Lens, 2003). This statistic is limited to high school students, but this is not to imply that harassing behaviors are limited in any way to only the high school setting. It is difficult for children to clearly identify when harassment has occurred, and adults have difficulty distinguishing behaviors that are teasing from those that approach student-to-student harassment. The Supreme Court decision in 1999 in *Davis v. Monroe County Board of Education* is the only case to date that addresses a school's liability for student-to-student harassment, and in essence, the court created no standard for when schoolyard taunts become sexual harassment (Grube & Lens, 2003). In terms of sexual harassment, "What is illegal or intolerable in the workplace is often ignored or trivialized in the schoolyard, with adult women afforded more protection than young girls from sexual harassment" (p. 173).

Sexually precocious knowledge, dress, and behaviors all fall within the category of "red flags" for possible sexual abuse and should be observed and documented very carefully by educators. Young children should not be able to describe or playfully demonstrate advanced sexual acts reserved for experience in adulthood. In addition, children should not be dressing or behaving in ways that are more advanced for their age. Of course, one must take into account cultural differences and influences on dress and behavior. However, children who consistently seek older peers or adults of either sex and maintain too little interpersonal distance, rub up against others, or demonstrate other sexually suggestive behaviors should be viewed with concern.

One of the major reasons to carefully monitor behavior that could be considered sexually precocious is that sexually abused children are at risk for repeated sexual victimization, as they seek further sexual contact as a vehicle for obtaining pleasure and as a means of mastering the original trauma (Green, 1988). Hypersexual behavior, including compulsive masturbation and promiscuity, has been described in the sexual abuse literature, but it is also possible to see phobic reactions and sexual inhibition as immediate and long-term consequences to incest or sexual abuse (Green, 1988). Thus, child sexual abuse victims may demonstrate either extreme (hypersexuality or sexual inhibition or even fear) in response to the abuse they have experienced. The short-term impact of sexual abuse on the victims may be evidenced in their emotional reactions (unexplained and/or sudden anger or crying), psychological functioning (demonstrating anxiety, depression, or possibly a flat or emotionless affect), and behavioral change (misbehaving or withdrawing). In all reactions to trauma and stress, males are more inclined to externalize reactions or act out, whereas females are more likely to internalize their reactions or withdraw and be quiet (Ryan, 1991). Although adolescent and adult survivors of childhood sexual abuse are overrepresented in many dysfunctional populations, educators cannot assume that every victim's experience is the same or that the impact or outcome will be the same (Ryan, 1991).

Because we tend to believe in our society that children are innocent, it is generally very difficult to conceptualize them as abusers, and the difficulties of conceptualizing young people as abusers and of developing appropriate responses to them may be further compounded when *sexual* abuse is involved (Green & Masson, 2002). It *is* possible for children, even very young children, to demonstrate sexually abusive behaviors toward others. As children move from developmentally appropriate sexual behaviors to increasingly more deviant and abusive sexual behaviors (see Table 12.2), there is an increased chance that they themselves have been abused and an increase in need of therapeutic intervention to address the behaviors. Parents and educators will need to evaluate observed behaviors within the unique context in which they were demonstrated. Ryan (2000) identified three main elements useful in defining abusive behaviors: (a) there is a lack of consent, (b) there is a lack of equality, and/or (c) there is some type of coercion in the interaction. Anytime any one of these elements is present there is cause for adults to be concerned that the behaviors are approaching deviance rather than falling within the typical expectations for children. Ryan also conducted interviews with sexually abusive youth, and their descriptions of their own behavior included use of force, abuse of power, intimidation, manipulation, trickery, and bribes associated with both memories and *fantasies.* It is possible that a child has up to the present time demonstrated only slightly deviant sexual behavior, but his or her described fantasies can be indicators of problems related to sexual and psychological development. Also, links have been established between sexually abusive behaviors and fireplay and/or sadistic physical abuse of pets or siblings (Ryan, 2000). Children who have the potential to become or who are already identified as juvenile sexual offenders tend to move in progressive steps with their chosen victims rather than attempting to sexually assault on the first encounter. The progression from less intrusive

Table 12.2 Sexual Behavior Classification

Behavior Category	*Teacher/Parent Response*	*Example Behaviors*
Group 1: developmentally acceptable	Requires adult supervision	Playing house or doctor Occasional masturbation Looking at and/or touching each other
Group 2: clearly advanced, with emotionality	Requires adult response	Precocious sexual knowledge, talk about sexual acts May feel anxious, guilty, or ashamed of sexuality Act in overly sexual ways around adults
Group 3: advanced, lacking emotional affect	Requires adult correction, possibly intervention	Sexual act participation is consensual, but highly secretive Compulsive masturbation Sexually explicit conversation, significant age difference
Group 4: coercive, with or without aggression	Requires therapeutic intervention for the children	Touching another's genitals without permission Forced exposure of another's genitals Sexually explicit proposals that include threats

SOURCE: Adapted from Essa and Murray (1999) and Ryan (2000).

to more intrusive behaviors on the part of the perpetrator is called **grooming** (Crosson-Tower, 2002). It is possible during grooming for the victims to become confused about their consent for participation or not understand that they are being coerced. The behavioral examples provided here and in Table 12.2 are not exhaustive but should be useful in helping educators identify occasions when it is appropriate to be concerned.

DEALING WITH WHAT IS DEVIANT

It goes without saying that all educators play a valuable role in the development of children. They can have a positive impact in many ways, and one of the most important of these is that teachers represent a "first line of defense" in recognizing potential problems and bringing help to children in need. In their daily interactions with children, educators build a special rapport with the children they serve, and this relationship makes possible both positive influence and ability to provide assistance. By building and maintaining a good relationship with all children in their classes, teachers are most likely to be the adults sought out when children experience any type of difficulty and want help. In terms of student-to-student harassment, children are likely to bring both minor complaints and more serious issues to the attention of their teacher. It is important that their concerns be heard and adequately addressed, whether minor or major, so that the child will be encouraged to bring other concerns to the teacher in the future. Because the Supreme Court in *Davis v. Monroe County Board of Education* placed the burden on the student to come forward with a complaint, it is essential that students feel comfortable in doing so (Grube & Lens, 2003).

Student-to-student harassment can range from taunts, teasing, and name-calling to hazing activities such as pulling down another child's pants or touching or grabbing another child in an inappropriate manner. Whether or not the harassment is sexual in nature, it is important for the educator in charge to act immediately in addressing the behavior as was discussed earlier. Because of the confusion about what constitutes consent for willing participation in various behaviors, student instruction regarding school behavior should place emphasis on defining expectations for appropriate school behavior (Grube & Lens, 2003).When the harassment is clearly sexual in nature, additional steps should be taken to address the potential needs of the child exhibiting the behavior, the family of this child, and the child who was harassed. It is preferable that your school have an established policy regarding reporting such behaviors within the administrative hierarchy, and of course, everyone is advised to follow those procedures already established within your school or school district. However, if there is no identified procedure for reporting, educators are encouraged to (a) report the behavioral incident to their principal, (b) identify the person who will contact the families of the involved children and inform them of the concern, (c) determine if the behavior meets criteria for abuse and therefore requires a report being made to the appropriate authorities for your state (see the following discussion on suspected abuse), (d) seek additional support available from your school's counselor or psychologist as needed, and (e) inasmuch as it is possible, involve the parents and the children in developing immediate and extended intervention services.

As stated previously, sexually precocious dress, behavior, and conversation are all "red flags" or warning signs of premature exposure to sexual material (a potential form of sexual abuse), sexual victimization, or even possible sexual offending. It is easier for teachers and principals to address sexually precocious dress because most schools have an established dress code for all students. The teacher or school counselor may want to be available for conversations related to clothing styles, socialization, and any other topic of concern for the student. Educators will need to evaluate all instances of sexually precocious language and behavior to determine the best course of action. Depending on the level of the behavior (see behavior classifications in Table 12.2), educators could follow a similar procedure to that outlined for dealing with sexually harassing behavior.

Children who are victims of physical and/or sexual abuse need to feel supported. "When our society fails to address the abuse issue with a victim, it is reinforcing the 'secret' and perpetuating the silence that contributes to the pattern of abuse" (Good, 1996, p. 84). It is believed that incidence rates of both physical and sexual abuse of children continue to be underestimates, and all educators are encouraged to be aware of common behavioral symptoms of victimization (see Box 12.5) and to know their state's laws and professional responsibilities related to the reporting of abuse. In many states, mere suspicion is enough to warrant a report to child protective services. Of course, prior to making a report, one needs to carefully consider all information, gather more if needed, and document the sources of the information. For example, two true cases of "children with bruises" can have two very different endings. In each of the examples, the children had bruises on their bodies—some visible, some hidden by their clothing, some very recent, and others a week or more old. One child was never asked about the bruises and a report was made to child protective services. Following an investigation, it was determined that the child had acquired her significant

Box 12.5 Sexual Abuse "Red Flag" Warnings and Behaviors

- Fearfulness of being touched
- Ability to describe or mimic adult sex acts
- Compulsive masturbation
- Inflammation of genital or anal areas
- Frequent urinary tract infections or yeast infections
- Pain in urination
- Excessive sore throats
- Early pregnancy
- In younger children, more sexual knowledge than would be expected
- Excessive fear of males (or females)
- Extremely seductive behavior, dress, or both
- A sudden decline in school performance or withdrawal in activity participation
- Extreme aggressive and inappropriate behaviors

SOURCE: Adapted from Crosson-Tower (2002) and Essa and Murray (1999).

bruises in practicing her twirling for the high school marching band. The other child had only one unusual visible bruise on his chin, and his teacher asked him how he had come to be bruised in such an unusual place. His response that his mother had "accidentally" hit him with a suitcase did not satisfy the teacher's curiosity and suspicion, and while he talked with the teacher and the principal he showed them his back, which was covered with large bruises; a report was made, and that afternoon he left school no longer in his mother's custody.

"If abuse is confirmed, teachers should advise parents to seek professional help for their child from a counselor or child psychologist" (Good, 1996, p. 84). Also, it may be beneficial to advise them to seek resources of support for themselves and siblings of the victim(s) as well. There may be times when a family's cultural values or practices are not in line with the values and behaviors promoted by this culture and, potentially, are even considered against the laws of the state. When cultural values conflict with the laws of the states and country, it is usually the practice of child protection agencies to try to educate the parents about the laws and **mores** of their newly adopted land (Crosson-Tower, 2002).

Educators in both urban and rural school settings could be called on to provide services to children who are in the process of being identified or who have previously been identified as sexual offenders. These children can be identified very young (I personally worked with an offender who was a 5-year-old and identified at the age of 3) and can be found at the elementary, middle, and high school levels. Teachers are the professionals most likely to see behaviors that are indicative of a child who is becoming more deviant. In fact, Ryan (2000) concluded that adults must recognize the relationship between fantasy and behavior and respond to fantasy material and play as potential precursors of future behavior. Children can demonstrate their thoughts, fantasies, and experiences through their drawing, painting, and writing in addition to their social behaviors with other children and adults. Schools should develop an education policy that will allow service provision to meet the educational needs of students who pose a threat to other children, and may ultimately be identified as sexual offenders that meets their educational needs while continuing to maintain the safety of all children in the educational environment. Their education may be appropriately provided within the regular education setting, within a setting modified by special education services, at an alternative school placement, or at a treatment facility. All educators should be prepared to meet the needs of sexual offenders as they move along this service continuum to progressively more specialized therapeutic treatment and then ultimately back again to the least restrictive educational environment.

"Aftercare" is that portion of comprehensive sexual perpetrator treatment intervention that takes place in the community after the offender is released from an institutional treatment program (Greer, 1991). Aftercare should be established during a cooperative collaboration among representatives of the treatment program, receiving public school, child protective services workers, family members, and, as appropriate, the juvenile offender. Educators are cautioned to remember that those offenders who have been able to master adequate behavior management techniques to lessen their risks to others are simply *lower-risk offenders* (Greer, 1991). Thus, the needs of a sexual offender transitioning back into the community school setting should not be underestimated. Without adequate therapeutic and behavioral supports in place, a program developed for juvenile offenders is increasing the likelihood of their reoffending.

TAKE A PROACTIVE STANCE TOWARD HEALTHY CHILDHOOD SEXUALITY DEVELOPMENT

Sadly, educators are often left alone to seek information related to healthy sexuality development of children. As Couchenour and Chrisman (1996) point out, obtaining information about the best educational practices in the area of healthy sexuality is difficult because teacher preparation programs, if they cover the topic of sexuality development at all, typically introduce human sexuality during the study of adolescent development rather than implementing an approach that would more fully cover sexuality development across the life span. So childhood sexuality has traditionally been an unsavory topic for discussion, and educators have entered their profession less than adequately prepared to meet the challenges presented to them by the increasingly complex needs of their students. Too often, we in the field of education wait to develop policies and procedures for action until we are face-to-face with a daunting "situation." With the support of the school's principal, even a small group of educators within the school can organize professional development training for all school faculty and staff.

Each individual reading this chapter is challenged to find a few other colleagues who are also interested in proactively addressing children's sexuality needs. Once you've identified a core group, work collectively to help organize professional development experiences that can meet the needs of your school's faculty and staff. Chrisman and Couchenour (2002) identify several possible topics for professional development of early educators. These topics were generalized for all educators and have been summarized in Box 12.6.

Any efforts made to establish school policies and teacher expectations that adequately address the healthy sexuality development of all children prior to the development of a "situation" will go a long way toward alleviating anxiety and stress among faculty, parents, and children. The knowledge of what behaviors constitute normal, as opposed to deviant, childhood sexuality development provides educators a foundation for adequately dealing with

Box 12.6 Suggestions for Professional Development Related to Childhood Sexuality

1. Obtain knowledge on typical childhood development, including sexuality development.
2. Promote discussion among faculty and staff related to sexuality development.
3. Develop or update policy to clearly specify guidelines for staff and parent handbooks.
4. Allow personnel the opportunity to rehearse professional responses and reactions.
5. Give opportunities to role-play potential conversations and situations with families.

SOURCE: Adapted from Chrisman and Couchenour (2002).

those behaviors as well as providing support to all children and families. All education professionals and parents are encouraged to follow the suggestion made by Meadows (2001) in that everyone should be open to dialogue and willing to cut through natural defenses. After all, both professionals and parents ultimately have the same goal: a positive outcome for the children.

DISCUSSION QUESTIONS

1. Human sexuality has traditionally been a difficult subject for most of us to discuss. How might you as a teacher open this topic for discussion in a proactive way? How would you approach parents when you have a specific concern?

2. How was sexuality addressed within your family when you were a child? Would you want your children introduced to the topic in a different way? If so, how would their experiences be different?

3. The author, a psychologist, includes differences in sexual orientation and gender identity within the section on normal sexuality development. This is consistent with her training and with current positions within her field. However, for many individuals in our country, these differences are seen as deviant and perhaps unacceptable. What complications are presented when sexual orientation and gender identity differences are viewed so differently? How might you address them within your classroom?

4. Is your school district addressing the needs of children with regard to their healthy sexual development? Do bullying and sexual harassing behaviors occur routinely on your campus?

5. Work cooperatively with your school's principal to conduct a simple analysis of behavioral referrals within the last year. How many of these referrals held some form of sexual content or implication?

FOR ADDITIONAL HELP

	Organization	*Web Address*	*Description*
Childhood Sexuality and Sexual Behavior	Sexuality Information and Education Council of the United States (SIECUS)	www.siecus.org	The national voice for sexuality education, sexual health, and sexual rights

REFERENCES

American Psychiatric Association. (2000). *Diagnostic and statistical manual of mental disorders* (4th ed., text revision). Washington, DC: Author.

Baker, J. M. (2002). *How homophobia hurts children: Nurturing diversity at home, at school, and in the community.* Binghamton, NY: Harrington Park Press.

Chrisman, K., & Couchenour, D. (2002). *Healthy sexuality development: A guide for early childhood educators and families.* Washington, DC: National Association for the Education of Young Children.

Couchenour, D., & Chrisman, K. (1996). Healthy sexuality development in young children. *Dimensions of Early Childhood, 24*(4), 30–36.

Crosson-Tower, C. (2002). *When children are abused: An educator's guide to intervention.* Boston: Allyn & Bacon.

Egan, S. K., & Perry, D. G. (2001). Gender identity: A multidimensional analysis with implications for psychosocial adjustment. *Developmental Psychology, 37*(4), 451–463.

Essa, E. L., & Murray, C. I. (1999). Sexual play: When should you be concerned? *Childhood Education, 75*(4), 231–234.

Frayser, S. G. (1994). Defining normal childhood sexuality: An anthropological approach. *Annual Review of Sex Research, 5,* 173–217.

Frieman, B. B., O'Hara, H., & Settel, J. (1996). What heterosexual teachers need to know about homosexuality. *Childhood Education, 73,* 40–42.

Good, L. A. (1996). When a child has been sexually abused: Several resources for parents and early childhood professionals. *Young Children, 51*(5), 84–85.

Gottschalk, L. (2003). Same-sex sexuality and childhood gender non-conformity: A spurious connection. *Journal of Gender Studies, 12*(1), 35–50.

Green, A. H. (1988). Child maltreatment and its victims. *Psychiatric Clinics of North America, 11*(4), 591–610.

Green, L., & Masson, H. (2002). Adolescents who sexually abuse and residential accommodation: Issues of risk and vulnerability. *British Journal of Social Work, 32*(2), 149–168.

Greer, W. C. (1991). Aftercare: Community integration following institutional treatment. In G. D. Ryan & S. L. Lane (Eds.), *Juvenile sexual offending: Causes, consequences, and correction* (pp. 377–390). Washington, DC: Lexington Books.

Grube, B., & Lens, V. (2003). Student-to-student harassment: The impact of Davis v. Monroe. *Children and Schools, 25*(3), 173–185.

Honig, A. S. (2000). Psychosexual development in infants and young children. *Young Children, 55*(5), 70–77.

Johnson, T. C. (1999). *Understanding your child's sexual behavior.* Oakland, CA: New Harbinger.

Martinson, F. M. (1991). Normal sexual development in infancy and early childhood. In G. D. Ryan & S. L. Lane (Eds.), *Juvenile sexual offending: Causes, consequences, and correction* (pp. 57–81). Washington, DC: Lexington Books.

Meadows, M. (2001). Gay, lesbian, transgendered and bisexual families: The teacher or caregiver's role in the development of positive relationships. *Journal of Early Education and Family Review, 8*(3), 24–29.

Petersen, A. C., Leffert, N., & Graham, B. L. (1995). Adolescent development and the emergence of sexuality. *Suicide and Life-Threatening Behavior, 25*, 4–17.

Ray, V., & Gregory, R. (2001). School experiences of the children of lesbian and gay parents. *Family Matters, 59,* 28–34.

Ryan, G. (1991). Consequences for the victim of sexual abuse. In G. D. Ryan & S. L. Lane (Eds.), *Juvenile sexual offending: Causes, consequences, and correction* (pp. 175–181). Washington, DC: Lexington Books.

Ryan, G. (2000). Childhood sexuality: A decade of study. Part I: Research and curriculum development. *Child Abuse and Neglect, 24*(1), 33–48.

Steele, B., & Ryan, G. (1991). Deviancy: Development gone wrong. In G. D. Ryan & S. L. Lane (Eds.), *Juvenile sexual offending: Causes, consequences, and correction* (pp. 83–101). Washington, DC: Lexington Books.

Chapter 13

Child Abuse and Neglect

Julie Roberts Palmour

Diane J. Bresson

Raymond J. Waller

Miriam Johnson

PREREADING QUESTIONS

As you read this chapter, reflect on the following questions and issues:

1. What are some physical signs or behavioral indications that a child may be the victim of child abuse and neglect?
2. What are your legal responsibilities if you suspect child abuse or neglect?
3. What procedures does your school have in place to help recognize and prevent child abuse or neglect? Has your school provided training on these procedures?
4. What are some ways that you might help after a report has been made?
5. How can your school be proactive in the prevention of child abuse and neglect?

The United States of America is the most affluent country in the world, yet every 10 seconds a child is abused or neglected (Crosson-Tower, 2002). The National Clearinghouse on Child Abuse and Neglect Information (U.S. Department of Health and Human Services [DHHS], 2005) publishes an annual report titled *Child Maltreatment.* This report contains data submitted from state **Child Protective Services** (CPS). The report, citing data collected in 2003, stated that nationally, an estimated 906,000 children were victims of abuse or neglect, and more than 1,500 children died as a result of these incidents. Approximately 63% of those children suffered **neglect** (including medical neglect), 19% were **physically abused**, 10% were **sexually abused**, and 5% were **emotionally abused**. Together, these types of abuse fall under an umbrella term that many researchers and practitioners call **child maltreatment**. There were an estimated 2.9 million referrals received by CPS agencies, which involved approximately 5.5 million children. Educators filed the most reports—16.3% of the total. This is most likely because school-age children spend a great deal of their day in school; thus, it is important that educators be well informed and remain proactive in dealing with issues of substantiated or suspected cases of child abuse and neglect.

This chapter provides you with an overview of (a) how to recognize physical signs and behavioral indications that a child may be the victim of child abuse and neglect, (b) your role as an educator and how to report suspected crimes, (c) what you can do to provide support for a child who has been a victim of child abuse and neglect, and (d) how you and your school can be proactive in preventing child abuse and neglect in your community.

DEFINITIONS

Federal guidelines that states must use in defining child abuse and neglect are contained in the Child Abuse Prevention and Treatment Act (CAPTA), which was last amended in 2003. CAPTA provides the following minimum federal definition of child abuse and neglect: "Child abuse means, at a minimum, any recent act or failure to act on the part of a parent or caretaker, which results in death, serious physical or emotional harm, sexual abuse or exploitation or an act or failure to act which presents an imminent risk of serious harm." Each state is required to further define child abuse and neglect and to stipulate the grounds for state intervention on behalf of the child. Teachers need to be aware of their state's definitions and specific laws relating to the reporting of suspected cases of child abuse and neglect. The following Web site maintained jointly by the National Clearinghouse on Child Abuse and Neglect Information and the National Information Clearinghouse[1] contains current individual state definitions of child abuse and neglect: http://nccanch.acf.hhs.gov/general/legal/statutes/define.pdf.

Regardless of formal definitions, all forms of child abuse and neglect cause pain and suffering for the victim as well as for those who support the victim. Teachers should be aware that included in the various forms of abuse and neglect are physical abuse, physical neglect, sexual abuse, and emotional abuse. Each of these types of abuse and neglect will be covered in further detail in this chapter.

CAUSATION

There is no specific causation for child abuse and neglect. Most adults may not intend to hurt the children they care for, but because of loss of control, lack of knowledge, or stress, some adults do inflict harm on children. Reasons that appear to contribute to child abuse and neglect include the following:

- Adults or caregivers lose their tempers when thinking about their own problems.
- There is a lack of skill on the part of the adult or caregiver regarding discipline.
- Unrealistic expectations for behavior relative to a child's age or ability are held by the adult or caregiver.
- The adult or caregiver was abused by a parent or partner.
- The adult or caregiver is experiencing financial problems.
- The adult or caregiver is experiencing job stress.
- The adult or caregiver is coping with a family member's illness or death.
- The adult or caregiver is experiencing marital problems.
- The adult or caregiver is using or abusing drugs and alcohol. (American Psychological Association, 2003)

Teachers and school personnel are consistent observers of children. Indications of child abuse and neglect may be easily identified or may be hidden behind unusual behaviors. No one sign or symptom definitively indicates abuse or neglect. Educators should not attempt to make diagnostic or definitive judgments about whether or not abuse or neglect has occurred but should always report cases of suspected abuse.

PHYSICAL SYMPTOMS AND BEHAVIORAL INDICATIONS

A number of physical symptoms and behavioral indicators may be present in cases of child abuse and neglect. Table 13.1 may be used as a guideline to help educators recognize child potential abuse and neglect.

Physical Abuse

Physical abuse occurs when there is physical injury that is intentional or unintentional, allowed and repeated, that results in serious harm or endangerment to a child. Physical abuse is often the result of harsh or extreme discipline. Cultural differences in child rearing exist, and some cultures have practices that would by most legal standards be considered abusive in the United States. The legal definition of abuse is often entangled with the individual rights of parents and caregivers. However, educators should not allow those cultural differences or individual rights to obscure their responsibility to recognize and report suspected instances of child abuse or neglect (Crosson-Tower, 2002).

Children may cover up for their abusive parents and caregivers, and may not reveal abuse even when questioned. Excuses such as "I don't remember" or "It was an accident" are often presented in an attempt to conceal physical abuse. In fact, the child may not perceive that "abuse" has occurred at all but may consider the things that he or she has experienced to be normal reactions from caregivers. Disclosure of harmful events is more likely when the child has developed a trusting relationship with an adult. This frequently occurs in the relationships that children form with their teachers. Therefore, it is essential that teachers be alert to the signs and symptoms of physical abuse so that recognition comes when the necessity arises.

Table 13.1 Physical Symptoms and Behavioral Indications of Child Abuse and Neglect

Type of Child Abuse or Neglect	*Physical Symptoms*	*Behavioral Indications*
Physical abuse	✓ Bruises and welts – on head, face, abdomen, forearm, back – in the shape of handprint, hangar marks, electrical cord, belt – in different colors, indicating various stages of healing – on multiple parts of the body, indicating blow from different directions ✓ Burns – especially from objects such as cigarettes, irons, and other objects ✓ Other – unexplained abdominal bleeding observed as discoloration under the skin or blood-filled lumps – complaints or soreness or stiffness and awkward movements as if caused by pain – bald spots from severe hair pulling – adult-sized bite marks – injuries for which the explanation given is inadequate	✓ Acting out, displaying aggressive or disruptive behavior ✓ Wary of adults ✓ Destructive to self or others ✓ Comes to school early or not wanting to leave school (this may indicate fear of going home) ✓ Fearlessness or extreme risk taking ✓ Described as "accident-prone" ✓ Cheats, steals, or lies (may be related to too-high expectations at home) ✓ Low achiever (to learn, children must convert aggressive energy into learning; children in conflict may not be able to do this) ✓ Unable to form healthy peer relationships ✓ Wears clothing that covers the body and that is inappropriate for warmer weather ✓ May be regressive or less mature ✓ Dislikes physical contact ✓ Reports injury by parents
Neglect	✓ Consistently hungry ✓ Poor hygiene ✓ Inappropriate dress ✓ Listless and tired with little energy, possibly due to no structure for bedtime at home ✓ Unattended medical and dental problems ✓ May seem emaciated or have a distended stomach (malnutrition) ✓ Difficulty with language comprehension and expression ✓ Diagnosed with a conduct disorder	✓ Stealing, hoarding food ✓ Vandalism, stealing, or other delinquent behavior ✓ Frequent school absences or tardiness ✓ Reports always caring for younger siblings ✓ Poor peer relationships ✓ Withdrawn ✓ Craves attention due to low self-esteem (even eliciting negative responses to gain it) ✓ Has difficulty problem solving or coping
Sexual abuse	✓ Difficulty walking or sitting ✓ Pain or bleeding in genital or anal area ✓ Frequently vomit without normal cause ✓ Eating disorder ✓ Self-mutilation ✓ Suicide thoughts or attempts ✓ Sudden onset of bedwetting or wetting or soiling of pants	✓ Frequent psychosomatic illnesses ✓ Exceptional secrecy ✓ Sexual knowledge that is beyond age ✓ Extreme compliance or withdrawal, low self-esteem ✓ Overt aggression ✓ Fear of males (or females)

Type of Child Abuse or Neglect	*Physical Symptoms*	*Behavioral Indications*
	✓ Pregnancy ✓ Sexually transmitted disease	✓ Cruelty to animals ✓ Frequent runaway ✓ Sudden drop in school performance ✓ Extremely seductive behavior or dressing much older than peers ✓ Sleep problems or fears ✓ Crying without any apparent reason
Emotional abuse	✓ Rocking, thumb sucking, head banging ✓ Enuresis (wetting pants) or soiling after an age when behavior is inappropriate ✓ Eating disorders ✓ Frequent stomachaches, headaches, or unexplained weight loss or gain ✓ Self-destructive behavior	✓ Extreme in behavior—manically happy or very depressed ✓ Withdrawn (no verbal or physical communication with others) ✓ Vandalism, stealing, cheating ✓ Delinquent and destructive behavior ✓ Difficulty concentrating or learning new material or compulsive attention to detail ✓ Inappropriately turns negatives into jokes and laughs when in pain

SOURCE: Crosson-Tower (2003).

In addition, teachers might notice unusual or questionable behaviors on the part of the parent or caregiver that may be responsible for the physical abuse. No single indicator ensures that abuse is taking place, but combinations or extreme displays of the indicated behaviors should be considered worthy of report.

Neglect

Child neglect is characterized by failure to provide for the child's basic needs. Neglect can be physical, educational, emotional, or medical in nature. Because neglect can often be seen as "less dramatic" (Crosson-Tower, 2002), it is often underreported or reported in a less timely manner than other forms of abuse. As a general rule, our society holds parents or caregivers responsible for providing adequate food, shelter, clothing, medical care, education, supervision, and protection to their minor children. The conscious inattention to these needs by a parent or caregiver indicates neglect. Furthermore, some legal advocates have suggested that definitions of neglect that focus only on the behavior of the parent or caretaker are insufficient. They strongly advocate that the parents' behavior must result in some specific physical damage or impairment or some identifiable symptoms of emotional damage to a child resulting from the parents' behavior or failure to act (Wald, 1976).

The U.S. Department of Health and Human Services (DHHS) (Gaudin, 1993, pp. 5–6; DHHS, 2003a) suggests that the various forms of child neglect can be defined as follows:

Physical Neglect

Refusal of Health Care	Failure to provide or allow needed care in accord with recommendations of a competent health care professional for a physical injury, illness, medical condition, or impairment.
Delay in Health Care	Failure to seek timely and appropriate medical care for a serious health problem which any reasonable layman would have recognized as needing professional medical attention.
Abandonment	Desertion of a child without arranging for reasonable care and supervision. This category includes cases in which children were not claimed within 2 days, and when children were left by parents/substitutes who gave no (or false) information about their whereabouts.
Expulsion	Other blatant refusals of custody, such as permanent or indefinite expulsion of a child from the home without adequate arrangement for care by others, or refusal to accept custody of a returned runaway.
Other Custody Issues	Custody-related forms of inattention to the child's needs other than those covered by abandonment or expulsion. For example, repeated shuttling of a child from one household to another due to apparent unwillingness to maintain custody, or chronically and repeatedly leaving a child with others for days or weeks at a time.
Other Physical Neglect	Conspicuous inattention to avoidable hazards in the home; inadequate nutrition, clothing, or hygiene; and other forms of reckless disregard of the child's safety and welfare, such as driving with the child while intoxicated, leaving a young child unattended in a motor vehicle, and so forth.

Supervision

Inadequate Supervision	Child left unsupervised or inadequately supervised for extended periods of time or allowed to remain away from home overnight without the parent/substitute knowing (or attempting to determine) the child's whereabouts.

Emotional Neglect

Inadequate Nurturance/Affection	Marked inattention to the child's needs for affection, emotional support, attention, or competence.
Chronic/Extreme Abuse or Domestic Violence	Chronic or extreme spouse abuse or other domestic violence in the child's presence.
Permitted Drug/Alcohol Abuse	Encouraging or permitting drug or alcohol use by the child; cases of the child's drug/alcohol use were included here if it appeared that the parent/guardian had been informed of the problem and had not attempted to intervene.
Permitted Other Maladaptive Behavior	Encouragement or permitting of other maladaptive behavior (e.g., severe assaultiveness, chronic delinquency) in circumstances in which the parent/guardian had reason to be aware of the existence and seriousness of the problem but did not attempt to intervene.
Refusal of Psychological Care	Refusal to allow needed and available treatment for a child's emotional or behavioral impairment or problem in accord with competent professional recommendation.

Delay in Psychological Care	Failure to seek or provide needed treatment for a child's emotional or behavioral impairment or problem which any reasonable layman would have recognized as needing professional psychological attention (e.g., severe depression, suicide attempt).
Other Emotional Neglect	Other inattention to the child's developmental/emotional needs not classifiable under any of the above forms of emotional neglect (e.g., markedly overprotective restrictions which foster immaturity or emotional overdependence, chronically applying expectations clearly inappropriate in relation to the child's age or level of development.

Sexual Abuse

CAPTA offers the following as a definition of child sexual abuse:

> a. the employment, use, persuasion, inducement, enticement, or coercion of any child to engage in, or assist any other person to engage in, any sexually explicit conduct or simulation of such conduct for the purpose of producing a visual depiction of such conduct; or
> b. the rape, molestation, prostitution, or other form of sexual exploitation of children, or incest with children. (CAPTA of 1974, as amended in 1984)

Any form of direct or indirect sexual contact between a child and an adult is abusive because it is motivated purely by adult needs and involves a child who, by virtue of his or her age and position in life, is unable to give consent (Central Agencies Sexual Abuse Treatment Program, 1997). It is believed that boys are almost as likely as girls to be sexually abused and that the incidence among boys is highly underreported (Mulryan, Cathers, & Fagin, 2004).

Child sexual abuse is also underreported. This may be due to the secrecy and conspiracy often embedded in the abuse (DHHS, 2003a). Although this chapter is devoted to the issue of child abuse and neglect, it is worth noting that sexual offenses perpetrated by individuals other than the child's parent or caretaker are also a federal offense and fall under the legal domain of sexual assault. Educators should be aware of their school policies and procedures for reporting these crimes as well.

Emotional Abuse

Emotional abuse is the most difficult type of abuse or neglect to define. Emotional abuse goes beyond physical trauma. Emotional abuse implies a psychological or mental injury, including actions or lack of action that has or could have caused serious behavioral, cognitive, emotional, or mental disorders (see www.yesican.org/CAPTA.htm). Emotional abuse is typically a symptom of uncontrolled and unhealthy desires to gain power and control. Persons who emotionally abuse children constantly reject, ignore, belittle, dominate, and criticize their victims. Emotional abuse may occur with or without physical abuse, but there is frequently an overlap (Stevens, 1996). Although emotional abuse does not occur in the physical realm, physical symptoms may be present in a child suffering this type of maltreatment.

ROLE OF EDUCATORS

Enormous responsibility is placed on classroom teachers in schools today. No longer are teachers accountable for just the academic development of their students. Rather, teachers must attend to, be educated in, and be supportive of the social, emotional, and physical needs of children and adolescents (see DHHS, 2003b). The Texas Department of Family and Protective Services (2005) suggests that the following roles may help teachers bridge into the lives of their children and make a difference in their lives.

Observer

Teachers can help to identify and report suspected child abuse and neglect by assuming the role of observer. Awareness of the physical and behavioral signs of abuse and neglect is the essential foundation for reporting. Teachers naturally observe the children in their classrooms, and through that observation, they notice that which is "different." Teachers should be attuned to the differences in children, and when something either does not "feel right" or is blatantly disclosed, teachers have a responsibility to report their suspicions or findings.

Listener

Teachers, as a matter of routine, listen to what children say. Messages of abuse and neglect are often not as apparent as answers to math questions or comments about content being covered in class. Children may speak directly to teachers or they may convey messages through what they say to others, through their play, in their writing, or in reaction to what they are learning.

Role Model

Children learn by what they observe. Teachers have the unparalleled opportunity to model the importance of self-worth for children. By demonstrating actions and behaviors that reinforce the need to value one's self, body, spirit, and place in the community, teachers can provide children a foundation for learning about acceptable behavior. Through modeling, teachers can reinforce a child's self-worth and create a positive environment in which a child feels safe. In that sense of safety and atmosphere of trust, children are more likely to disclose abuse and neglect.

Advocate

Children often feel helpless in finding solutions to problems involving adults. Teachers must act as advocates for children and adolescents by remaining informed of and maintaining connections with local and state services for children who are abused and neglected. Child abuse and neglect is a community issue. Maintaining relationships within the community such that there is mutual support for children in need is essential in the drive to improve the conditions of their lives.

REPORTING ABUSE AND NEGLECT

Teachers are placed in a difficult situation when signs of abuse and neglect arise. It is necessary for educators to recognize that although there are specific cultural and racial groups who have varying percentages of documented cases of abuse and neglect, incidences of maltreatment can and do occur in all socioeconomic, cultural, and regional areas of our society.

As previously stated, teachers in all states have some form of mandated reporting of suspected or known abuse and neglect. Generally, a report must be filed when you suspect or have reason to suspect that a child has been abused or neglected. It is crucial that teachers keep in mind that the decision to involve the legal system in child abuse and neglect situations is the responsibility of the CPS agency in their locality. Common names of such service agencies include Department of Social Services and Department of Family and Children Services. Individual school districts should have a protocol for reporting suspected cases of maltreatment, and it is very important that teachers be trained in and follow that protocol to avoid penalty for failure to follow mandated reporting. Often, this penalty is a misdemeanor, which may include a fine, but in some states, failure to properly report abuse and neglect can result in imprisonment. Suspected cases of child abuse and neglect are commonly very complicated and may involve persons who are friends, family members, or business acquaintances. Therefore, hotlines are available in many communities to provide help and advice. In addition, the U.S. Department of Health and Human Services provides the following national hotline number:

Childhelp USA National Child Abuse Hotline

1-800-4-A-CHILD (1-800-422-4453)

TDD: 1-800-2-A-CHILD

Childhelp is a nonprofit agency that can provide local reporting numbers and maintains counselors who can provide assistance with referrals.

If a child discloses abuse or neglect to a teacher it is important for the teacher to remain calm and supportive. Because disclosures may happen in the midst of instruction, it is important that the teacher acknowledge the disclosure but maintain strict confidentiality in the discussion and action of the disclosure. In the circumstance of suspicion due to physical or behavioral signs, teachers should not press a child with questions but should simply report what they have observed. Regardless of the situation leading to reporting, teachers should remember the following:

- Follow your school's protocol for reporting.
- Remain calm, keep an open mind, and don't make judgments.
- Support the child with active listening.
- Find a quiet, private place to talk to the child.
- Reassure the child that he or she has done the right thing by telling someone.
- Listen to the child *without interruption;* let him or her talk openly about the situation and record concrete information.
- Tell the child that there is help available.
- Reassure the child that you will do your best to protect and support him or her.

- Let the child know you must report the abuse to someone who has helped other children like him or her and their families.
- Report the incident to the proper authorities.
- Let the child know what will happen when the report is made (if you have appropriate information).
- Seek out your own support person(s) to help you work through your feelings about the disclosure (if needed).
- Be aware of personal issues and how they affect your perception.

Because abuse and neglect is often shocking and may result in many difficult emotions within individuals who are confronted with the possibility that a child is in danger, teachers should avoid what may be instinctual but detrimental reactions to the abuse. Teachers should be careful *not* to promise confidentiality, express panic or shock, or convey anger or impatience if the child is not ready to discuss the abuse, disclose the information indiscriminately, or make negative comments about the perpetrator. Tell only those adults who need the information to protect and support the child. School personnel should not investigate the allegation or suspicion. Remember that investigation is the job of CPS or law enforcement.

AFTER A REPORT HAS BEEN FILED

Once a report has been made to the proper authorities, it is important that the teacher continue to provide support in the classroom for the child. The teacher will sometimes be made aware of the progress of the report and may have limited information about services that the child, family, or both are receiving. Many times, however, the communication is limited, vague, and even withheld. This frustration can cause feelings of distrust in or apathy for the process. It is important that teachers do not hesitate to report suspected cases of child abuse and neglect because of feelings that "nothing will happen." Systems are in place to deal with these issues, and although not perfect, they are the only secure way in which children's needs are addressed. Frequently, teachers acknowledge that they were treated with professionalism and courtesy when following appropriate child abuse reporting protocol. Unfortunately, some teachers have an experience that leaves them uninformed and, sometimes, violated or threatened, such as the example provided by the following teacher.

This is my first year teaching a self-contained class for students with mild mental retardation. Even though I have been a special education teacher for 6 years, this year has been full of new experiences. One of the unexpected problems I have faced this year is the number of child abuse cases that I have suspected and reported. My first child abuse situation (of six reports I have made during the first 100 days of school) occurred in the first few months of the school year.

Tyler G. is a kindergarten student being served in my classroom most of the day. He has exhibited a lot of difficult behaviors this year, including refusing to do work, crying for his mother, sleeping for hours each day, and tantrumming. Tyler has an active imagination, and he is able to imitate characters from movies that he has seen. His speech articulation problems make him difficult to understand at times, but he says many words clearly with little or no regional dialect. One afternoon, Tyler began telling one of his unusual stories. I was trying to understand what movie he was talking about when I realized he was actually describing a violent scene. He was talking about someone walking through his house with a large knife as he imitated the motions. Then he described in detail his mother being choked with a telephone cord. I couldn't understand all of the words he used, but he went through all of the motions as though we were playing charades. When I asked him who was doing this, he stopped acting out the scene. His facial expression became solemn as he stated his father's name, Tommy G., with perfect enunciation. I really didn't know whether I should make a report or not. I had seen no signs on Tyler of physical abuse, and I knew that he was quite the storyteller. But something about his tone and expression when he said his father's name concerned me. I also wondered how a 5-year-old with mental retardation would know about such violence. While my aide continued with class, I quickly went to the office to talk with the counselor about the incident.

Before speaking to the counselor, I really wasn't sure if the incident Tyler described, even if true, was actually child abuse that should be reported. The counselor assured me that this was an incident that needed to be reported immediately. I wrote down all of the details, and she called the Department of Family and Children Services (DFCS). The next morning, Tyler was called to the counselor's office to talk with a worker from DFCS. After my initial conversation with the counselor, I was no longer involved with the investigation. I was given no information about the case.

The next day, I was in the middle of teaching a lesson when I noticed Tyler's mother, Mrs. G., at the door. When I stepped into the hallway to see why she was there, I saw that she had her husband with her as well. I checked to see that they were wearing visitor's tags showing that they had signed in at the front office before entering the building. Even though they had signed in, no one in the office alerted me that the parents were on their way to my room. I felt very intimidated since I was alone with them. Mrs. G. asked if I was the person who called DFCS. I told her (truthfully) that the counselor and administrators handle communication with DFCS. After I evaded several more questions, Mrs. G. began explaining the incident Tyler described. She said that she had used a knife to open a door with a broken lock, and Tyler must have made up the details. Mrs. G. said that Mr. G. had moved out of the house several weeks earlier, and Tyler was having difficulty adjusting to his father's absence. A week later, Mrs. G. told me that the case had been dismissed and that the investigator believed that Tyler had made up the story.

Even though DFCS workers are supposed to keep the identity of reporters confidential, I'm certain that Mrs. G. knows that I am the person that initiated the child abuse report. Tyler spent most of his time at school with me. No other person would have had the opportunity to speak with Tyler at length without his mother present. Fortunately, Mrs. G. does not appear to harbor resentment. She told me that she knew I was only doing my job.

Since Tyler's case, I have made five other reports of child abuse. One other student reportedly witnessed her parent being strangled, and two students had suspicious bruises. I have little or no involvement with DFCS, so I don't know if any of the reports have led to substantiated cases. It's a little disconcerting to think that these parents could come to the school to confront me about the report at any time. I am concerned that the next parent at my classroom door may be less understanding than Mrs. G. Even after the investigation, regardless of the outcome, I must continue to work with the students and their parents on a daily basis.

After a report is filed, CPS staff, law enforcement, or both make the decision as to the substantiation of the abuse or neglect. A determination as to whether the child should remain in the home is made and a plan for protecting the child from future abuse and neglect is put in place if needed. In some cases, the courts are involved automatically. Additional criminal charges may be filed, particularly in cases of death or extreme abuse. Occasionally, educators are asked to appear in court as witnesses. When this happens, it is important to remember that teachers are not the ones on trial but are there to provide help and support to the child. Children who have experienced maltreatment may be monitored by the courts or CPS and other social service agencies, placed in foster care or remanded to the custody of another relative or friend, or returned to their own home situation. In cases where the abuse was not perpetrated by a custodial member of the child's family, restraining orders may be filed to protect the child.

PROVIDING SUPPORTS FOR CHILDREN WHO ARE VICTIMS OF ABUSE AND NEGLECT

Teachers are often uncomfortable and uncertain about interacting with an abused child when he or she returns to or enters school. The classroom teacher can play a significant role in the rehabilitation of an abused child by acknowledging, but not dwelling on, the situation and then creating a supportive and safe environment for the child. It is important to remember that the experience of abuse or neglect can result in a wide range of psychological problems, including anxiety disorders, depression, Posttraumatic Stress Disorder, substance abuse, and increased levels of suicidal ideation (Sadock & Sadock, 2003). Therefore, students who have experienced abuse may continue to need a high level of support and understanding from their teachers and other supportive adults. This can be accomplished by providing the child with the following.

Security

A most basic need for all people, particularly children, is the need to feel safe. Children need to know that there are adults who can be trusted. Talk to the child, one-on-one, share something about yourself, and use eye contact. Avoid using touch when working with a child who has been an abuse victim because a touch may cause the child to feel threatened. Let the child know that you are there to help in any way you can. Follow the child's lead as to the depth and breadth of discussion. Try to create as normal and stable an environment as possible. Refer the case to appropriate personnel, such as the school counselor, school social worker, or school psychologist for help.

Structure

Initially, structure may increase the child's sense of security. The child may need very clear instructions. All children feel more comfortable when the adults around them provide consistency and a moderate amount of control. By providing structure, you create an atmosphere in which the child can begin to know what to expect, which ultimately leads to the child's feeling safer and more secure.

Positive Feedback

Give the child positive personal feedback. "You are someone who makes friends easily," or "You are someone who really tries hard on difficult problems." Let the child express feelings, whether they are of grief, fear, loss, or relief, without offering advice.

Consistency and Predictability

The child who has been abused has experienced a great deal of upheaval in his or her family life. The child needs to be able to predict your behavior and to be clear about your expectations regarding behavior and academic performance. It is important to share information about new situations as they arise. In addition, it is important that the classroom teacher not tolerate inappropriate behavior. If the child who has been maltreated exhibits inappropriate behavior, the teacher should respond immediately, as with any student. This helps the child to know that you maintain respect for him or her and that you know he or she is capable of acting appropriately.

Sense of Belonging

Be sure the child's work is displayed and that he or she has belongings in the room and a place to store them. The child should be seated where a feeling of inclusion can be gained. Reinforce the child's association with other children.

PREVENTION OF CHILD ABUSE AND NEGLECT

Just as teachers are in a unique position regarding the ability to recognize and report suspected cases of child abuse and neglect, they are also in a strategic position for initiating prevention programs. Effective prevention programs reduce the number of victims, while educating a broader cross section of the public. Teachers can advocate for abuse prevention education and student assistance. Programs and curricula that provide children with the understanding of appropriate and inappropriate behavior, that incorporate information on sex and sexual health, and that share resources such as access to clinics and support groups are useful in the prevention of child abuse and neglect.

In addition, teachers and their students can work for public awareness by sharing statistics on child abuse and neglect, creating resources for delivering messages about abuse and neglect and who should be held responsible, and lobbying in an effort to influence public policy regarding the protection of children. Comprehensive training for school employees, parents, and other professionals on recognizing and reporting abuse and neglect, the importance of sensitivity to disclosure, and how to talk to and educate children on this issue are essential in the battle against child abuse and neglect. Many such programs are in place or are available to schools, often at no charge, and should be reviewed and recommended to school administration for implementation. Finally, school systems should have written policies on reporting suspected child abuse that are easily accessible to all school employees, and faculty and staff members should be trained on school policies relating to child maltreatment at least annually.

SUMMARY

The role of educator is quite different today than in decades past. It is vital that educators, no matter what the age of their students, be knowledgeable and proactive in dealing with issues of child abuse and neglect. It is only through commitment, training, and action that we can begin to break the cycle of abuse and neglect.

DISCUSSION QUESTIONS

1. How does your state define child abuse and neglect, and what are your reporting responsibilities under this statute?
2. What are your school's reporting procedures for suspected cases of child abuse and neglect?
3. Have you ever known a child who was removed from his or her home because of abuse or neglect? What was the outcome?
4. Is your school district engaged in any initiatives to improve parenting skills in the community? Is this something that you would be willing to participate in?

FOR ADDITIONAL HELP

	Organization	*Web Address*	*Description*
Child Abuse and Neglect	Childhelp USA	www.childhelpusa.org	Childhelp USA® exists to meet the physical, emotional, educational, and spiritual needs of abused and neglected children. Efforts are focused on the areas of treatment, prevention, and research.
	American Professional Society on the Abuse of Children (APSAC)	http://apsac.fmhi.usf.edu	APSAC is dedicated to serving professionals who work in child abuse and neglect and thereby improve the quality of services to maltreated children and the adults who share and influence their lives.

Organization	Web Address	Description
National Clearinghouse on Child Abuse and Neglect Information	http://nccanch.acf.hhs.gov	The National Clearinghouse on Child Abuse and Neglect Information and the National Adoption Information Clearinghouse are services of the Children's Bureau, Administration for Children and Families, U.S. Department of Health and Human Services. The mission of the clearinghouses is to connect professionals and concerned citizens to practical, timely, and essential information on programs, research, legislation, and statistics to promote the safety, permanency, and well-being of children and families.

NOTE

1. The clearinghouses are services of the Children's Bureau Administration for Children and Families, U.S. Department of Health and Human Services. See http://nccanch.acf.hhs.gov.

REFERENCES

American Psychological Association. (2003). *Protecting our children from abuse and neglect* [pamphlet]. Washington, DC: Author.

Central Agencies Sexual Abuse Treatment Program. (1997). *When a child is sexually abused* [online handbook].Toronto, Ontario. Retrieved November 9, 2005, from www.casat.on.ca/handindx.htm

Child Abuse Prevention and Treatment Act (CAPTA) of 1974 as Amended by Pub. L. No. 98-457, 98th Congress (1984).

Child Abuse Prevention and Treatment Act (CAPTA), including Adoption Opportunities and the Abandoned Infants Assistance Act, as amended by the Keeping Children and Families Safe Act of 2003 (2003).

Crosson-Tower, C. C. (2002). *Understanding child abuse and neglect.* Boston, MA: Allyn & Bacon.

Crosson-Tower, C. C. (2003). *The role of educators in preventing and responding to child abuse and neglect* (DHHS Publication No. ACF 92-30172). Washington, DC: U.S. Department of Health and Human Services, Administration for Children and Families, Administration on Children, Youth and Families, National Center on Child Abuse and Neglect.

Gaudin, J. M., Jr. (1993). *Child neglect: A guide for intervention.* Washington, DC: U.S. Department of Health and Human Services, Administration for Children and Families, Administration on Children, Youth and Families, National Center on Child Abuse and Neglect.

Mulryan, K., Cathers, P., & Fagin, A. (2004). How to recognize and respond to child abuse. *Nursing, 34*(10), 52–55.

Sadock, B. J., & Sadock, V. A. (2003). *Kaplan & Sadock's synopsis of psychiatry* (9th ed.). New York: Lippincott Williams & Wilkins.

Stevens, C. (1996). *Preventing emotional abuse.* National Association for Regulatory Administration. Retrieved November 9, 2005, from www.nara-licensing.org/displaycommon.cfm?an=1&subarticlenbr=43

Texas Department of Family and Protective Services. (2005). *Your role regarding child abuse.* Retrieved November 13, 2005, from www.dfps.state.tx.us/it's_up_to_you/HTML/CAP2005-SectionI.html#yourrole

U.S. Department of Health and Human Services. (2003a). *A coordinated response to child abuse and neglect: The foundation for practice.* Retrieved November 13, 2005, from http://nccanch.acf.hhs.gov/pubs/usermanuals/foundation/foundationj.cfm

U.S. Department of Health and Human Services. (2003b). *Recognizing child abuse and neglect: Signs and symptoms.* Retrieved November 9, 2005, from http://nccanch.acf.hhs.gov/pubs/factsheets/signs.cfm

U.S. Department of Health and Human Services, Administration on Children, Youth and Families. (2005). *Child maltreatment, 2003.* Retrieved November 16, 2005, from www.acf.dhhs.gov/programs/cb/publications/cm03/cm2003.pdf

Wald, M. S. (1976). State intervention on behalf of neglected children: Standards for removal. *Stanford Law Review, 28,* 625–706.

Chapter 14

Self-Injury and Suicide

Steve Knotek

Sarah Hamel

Rachel Schoolman

Natalie Siegel

PREREADING QUESTIONS

As you read this chapter, please reflect on the following questions and issues:

1. What causes a child to commit suicide?
2. What can teachers do to help prevent their students from committing suicide?
3. What obligations do teachers have when it comes to working with suicidal students?
4. Which school personnel in particular should be involved with suicide prevention efforts?

Suicide, the ultimate outward expression of despair and hopelessness, is increasing among our nation's children and adolescents. Thought by many parents and teachers to be a nonexistent threat to our students, suicide is becoming an increasingly frequent occurrence and ranks as the third leading cause of death among young people (Spirito & Donaldson, 1998). It is an equal opportunity act occurring across ethnicity, gender, and socioeconomic status. Over the course of a teacher's career, at least one student will likely attempt or actually commit suicide. It is a difficult, yet very real part of the school experience. Therefore, it is imperative that people who serve youths further their efforts to identify and provide support for children who may be at risk for suicide. In this chapter, we discuss theories about the causes of youth suicide, highlight risk factors, and identify ways that teachers can help prevent suicide.

WHY ON EARTH?

As far back as William Shakespeare's time, parents and educators have tragically found themselves dealing with the aftermath of youth suicide and belatedly asking, "Why did this happen?" In the play *Romeo and Juliet,* the Montagues and the Capulets were dumbfounded over the deaths of two of their town's brightest teenage lights. It seemed incomprehensible to the adults that two young people with so much to live for could take the ultimate step over a challenge to a first love. Suicide can happen to youths, and those who are charged with caring for and educating them need to have an understanding of what could cause a student to take this step. Although it is important to note that any single suicide may have many causes or perhaps even seem beyond reason, there are four broad theories under which youthful suicide is studied: biological, psychological, social, and ecological (Henry, Stephenson, Hanson, & Hargett, 1993).

Biological

Increasingly, our theories about human behavior include some acknowledgment of our physical being as we realize that our feelings, attitudes, and thoughts are influenced by the complex biochemistry of our brains. From this biological perspective, suicide can be viewed as a symptom of a mental disorder, a medical disorder, a biological predisposition to suicide, or hormone changes.

Psychological

Psychological theories of youth suicide concentrate on personality development and are exemplified by the theorists Sigmund Freud and Erik Erikson. Freud's **psychoanalytic theory** of suicide suggests that a delay in "ego development" causes anger, which may lead to an unconscious death wish that evolves into destructive and suicidal behaviors (Henry et al., 1993; Lees & Stimpson, 2002). Another major psychological theory of suicide is based on Erikson's model of development. In this theory, the child does not construct a healthy identity. As a result, the child feels intolerable distress, and because he or she has not developed adequate coping skills either, the child chooses to end his or her life. This result is often attributed to immaturity as well; many children and adolescents commit suicide because they cannot project their minds into the future and imagine that things can get better (Henry et al., 1993; Portes, Sandhu, & Longwell-Grice, 2002). One common example of this is an adolescent committing suicide because he or she has broken up with a boyfriend or girlfriend. In some cases, even the loss of a family pet has provoked suicidal behaviors.

Social

Another class of theories includes social psychological theories. The two most popular are based on Bandura's (1986) "social learning theory" and the "family systems theory." Social learning theory posits that children learn maladaptive coping skills from the environment in which they are raised. These coping strategies elicit attention from others because of their harmfulness, and the resulting attention reinforces the maladaptive behaviors. Family systems theory views suicide as resulting from a symptom dysfunction and lack of communication within families. A child may commit suicide to avoid talking about an issue because he or she does not want to bring up hurtful and negative emotions. Sociological theory, proposed by Durkheim, has also gained popularity. This theory looks at larger sociological factors, such as religion, government, family structure, and societal values, which may combine to form motives for suicidal behavior (Durkheim, 1952).

The biological, psychological, and social theories are all useful in understanding some aspect of the development of suicidal behaviors in youths. However, the particular emphasis of these theories on the body, mind, and family do not provide educators with an accessible and manageable approach to suicide prevention in schools. What can the classroom teacher do to assuage a child's delayed ego development or boost his or her **neurotransmitters**? The ecological theory offers a means to better understand and conceptualize suicide in a way that lends itself to providing support in a school environment.

Ecological

Bronfenbrenner's (1979) model of human development, ecological theory, is an approach to understanding suicide that has appeared in the literature of school psychologists, counselors, and social workers (Ayyash-Abdo, 2002; Henry et al., 1993; Jackson & Nuttall, 2001). The previously described theories have their strengths and are useful in understanding some aspects of suicide. However, the other theories focus on just one aspect of an individual's functioning—the person or the environment. Bronfenbrenner's theory is considered by many the most valued because it views behavior as a function of the person in his or her environment. Both the person and the environment are taken into consideration, as well as the interaction between the two. Consequently, this theory allows educators to attain a more comprehensive understanding of suicide.

A child's development is influenced by and interconnected with the many places that make up his or her world. Home, community, and school all support and detract from a child's healthy development, and occurrences in one setting likely affect outcomes in another. Teachers are very familiar with the reality that bad news at home may show up as withdrawn or acting-out behavior at school. However, the opposite effect also occurs; prosocial coping skills learned by children at school may find expression at home and in the community.

Ecological theory, with its emphasis on the interconnectedness of development across settings, may be most aligned with the framework of governmental agencies that deal with suicide prevention. According to the interagency National Strategy for Suicide Prevention Web site, "Suicidal behaviors in young people are usually the result of a process that involves multiple social, economic, familial, and individual risk factors with mental health problems playing an important part in its development" (Substance Abuse and Mental Health Services Administration, n.d., para. 3). That is, suicide doesn't usually result from interactions in a single realm of a child's life; it develops in multiple settings, including the home, school, and community. Although educators may not have influence on a student's functioning in the community or even a child's home, they do have influence over how a child functions while he or she is at school. Children spend over 6 hours each weekday in school, sometimes more if they are involved in after-school programs.

SCHOOL SETTING

Schools have the opportunity to encourage and model healthy coping behaviors for children, so that even if they are not experiencing these positive interactions at home, schools may still have an impact on students' abilities and decisions. Parents and relatives may themselves be too involved with an emotionally distressed child to be able to objectively identify suicidal warning signs; however, teachers often have comparably better emotional distance and may be able to more clearly recognize relevant signs and symptoms. Helsel (2001) states, "Faculty members should be encouraged to remember that the suicidal child wants to discuss the subject of suicide openly and frankly" (p. 92). Teachers who recognize symptoms of suicide can serve as the first line of suicide prevention for students by detecting and then immediately referring children who exhibit warning signs.

RISK FACTORS AND WARNING SIGNS OF SUICIDE

Although the reasons or forces that drive a student to attempt suicide are not always readily apparent, it is important to note that suicide does not randomly happen to students; there are risk factors and associated warning signs that students often display prior to committing suicide (Lieberman & Davis, 2002). Risk factors include the presence of mental illness (especially depression), family stress, environmental risks, and situational crises (Poland & Lieberman, 2003). These risk factors seldom exist alone in an individual and are usually "comorbid"; that is, they are jointly present in a person's life circumstances. The mere presence of a risk factor does not guarantee that a person will attempt suicide but rather that youths who have these factors are at a higher risk for attempting suicide.

Warning signs are explicit symptoms and include loss of appetite, suicidal threats, preoccupation with death, prior suicidal behavior, planning a suicide, giving away prized possessions, and changes in a student's thoughts, feelings, and/or behaviors (Lieberman & Cowan, 2004). Gaining familiarity with these risk factors and their warning signs can enhance an educator's ability to detect and refer students who may be suicidal and can reduce the misunderstandings and misperceptions that can easily occur when behaviors associated with suicide are observed.

Susan Franks is a 13-year-old, seventh-grade, Caucasian female who lives in a rural, eastern seaboard community. She is the oldest of four children and resides with both of her parents in a middle-class neighborhood. Her teachers know her as a serious student who can be hard on herself when she does not perform up to her own high academic expectations. In addition, Susan is known for her slender frame and her involvement with ballet.

Administrators and teachers were surprised when they received a call in mid-January from Susan's parents indicating that she had attempted suicide and would be in a residential treatment program for the remainder of the month. Consensus among the staff was that no one saw her suicide attempt coming and that Susan was the last student anyone would expect to attempt suicide. Three weeks after Susan was hospitalized, her parents called the principal to say that she would be returning to school, that arrangements had been made for her to be medically supervised by a psychiatrist, and that the family would be engaging in family counseling. Other than the principal's informing Susan's guidance counselor of her return, no planning for school mental health services was made.

Susan's first few days back in school were uneventful; however, she then started to "pass out" during school, and several times was taken by ambulance to a hospital. The school principal's position was that this was unacceptable behavior that was detracting from other students' schoolwork. The case was brought to the attention of the school psychologist when the guidance counselor asked him to review a letter that the principal intended to send home to the parents. The letter outlined the rules of good conduct at the school and included a strongly worded section on the importance of ensuring that Susan have a diet that consisted of "nutritious and nourishing foods." Finally, the letter addressed the need for the parents to stop their daughter's attention-seeking behaviors. Ms. Page, the counselor, related that she was mostly trained as an academic counselor and would welcome any input on how to address the student's mental health needs in the school setting. Together, the counselor and the psychologist agreed that the school should have a formal plan in place to monitor Susan's day-to-day emotional functioning and to assist her in managing her academic responsibilities.

The school's first formal response was to contact Susan's parents and ask for permission to conduct a psychoeducational evaluation to assess what Susan's mental health needs were in relation to her schooling and to get permission to speak to her psychiatrist about coordinating Susan's care. A resulting behavioral/emotional/academic evaluation suggested that Susan had a strong tendency for self-criticism, felt alienated from and harshly judged by her parents, and possessed a poor academic self-concept. In addition, she met the diagnostic criteria for anorexia and depression.

The results of the evaluation allowed the school to focus its response on three critical areas: educating the school's staff about suicide and school personnel's role as gatekeepers, creating collaborative links between the school and the local mental health agencies, and increasing Susan's sense of connectedness at school. The counselor and the school psychologist held an in-service training to both further individual awareness about the dynamics and symptoms of suicide and to formalize a schoolwide policy on referral and intervention. The in-service included a video on suicide in students, written materials and referral forms, a role play, and discussion. Interagency collaboration was furthered during a meeting chaired by the school psychologist. Representatives from all the local mental health providers attended, and the group discussed means to coordinate service delivery and increase suicide prevention awareness in parents and teachers.

Susan's direct service plan was developed to monitor her behavior for symptoms of suicide and to foster her sense of belonging and competence in school. A weekly progress conference was held between Susan's parents and the school counselor in which the counselor related teachers' comments and the parents discussed their concerns and observations. In addition, the counselor talked with Susan's psychiatrist weekly to coordinate treatment. Susan also received teacher monitoring and frequent support, as well as weekly academic counseling that focused on addressing her distortions of her academic abilities, her performance anxiety, and her punishing self-judgments.

Depression

Some adults have difficulty believing that youths experience "real" depression because it conflicts with their vision of the trouble-free existence that is supposed to characterize childhood. However, like suicide, depression is a very real fact for some students (Phares, 2003). Depression is one of the major risk factors associated with suicide (Fremouw, Deperczel, & Ellis, 1990). Warning signs associated with depression include loss of interest in everyday activities, crying, agitation, a sense of hopelessness, feeling out of control, withdrawal from friends, changes in sleeping and eating, and a preoccupation with death and suicide, including a suicide plan (Spirito & Donaldson, 1998).

A suicide plan is obviously the most critical warning sign of a suicidal student. The details of the plans may differ by students' gender, but they usually include methods and times. Boys generally prefer more lethal methods such as guns, whereas girls typically prefer less lethal means such as pills. Children who communicate that they have a suicide plan (e.g., through talking, notes, drawing, behavior) should immediately be referred to the school counselor or mental health administrator on site.

Anxiety

Anxiety has also been found to be a risk factor for suicide. In one study, Rudd, Joiner, and Rumzek (2004) found that people who attempted suicide multiple times were twice as likely to have an early onset Anxiety Disorder as those who only attempted suicide once. In addition, it was found that multiple attempters were almost three times more likely to have an early diagnosis of major depression. Clearly, anxiety is a risk factor for suicide and teachers need to be aware of anxiety and depression as predispositions for suicide. Some warning signs for anxiety include social problems, inconsistent test performance, low activity involvement, low self-esteem, excessive worrying, irritability, restlessness, and being easily fatigued (American Psychiatric Association [APA; *DSM-IV-TR*], 2000). Teachers are well advised to be alert for suicidal students when such behaviors are frequently displayed.

Other Psychiatric Disorders

Many other psychiatric disorders, in particular bipolar, conduct, and eating disorders, have been found to place adolescents at high risk for suicide. Kelley, Cornelius, and Lynch (2002) found that Bipolar Disorder was the non-substance-related disorder that put adolescents at the greatest risk for attempted suicide. The warning signs for Bipolar Disorder may be a concern if the following occurs: The person appears to be manic (extremely hyper) and depressed alternately and social functioning is impaired. Conduct Disorder was found to be twice as prevalent among teens who had attempted suicide. Conduct Disorder is illustrated by low empathy for others, aggression, lack of guilt, bullying (indicative of low self-esteem), irritability, violating rules, and high frustration (*DSM-IV-TR*, 2000). Adolescents with bulimia and anorexia have also been found to be more likely to attempt suicide.

Substance Abuse

Teens who use alcohol, cocaine, opiates, inhalants, and hallucinogens are at an increased risk for attempting suicide (De Man & Leduc, 1995). Substance abuse can lead to a depressed mood, rigid thinking, lack of impulse control, and paranoia. Each of these issues can contribute to a person's likelihood of attempting suicide. Some signs that may be indicative of substance abuse are disturbances of perception, hyperactivity or sleepiness (depending on the drug), lack of attention, poor judgment, and deteriorating interpersonal relationships (*DSM-IV-TR*, 2000).

Sexual Orientation

Many gay, lesbian, and bisexual adolescents feel depressed about being different and choose to hide their sexuality. Those who do choose to reveal their sexual orientation are sometimes rejected, ridiculed, or both and may feel suicide is the only way to escape. Sometimes these youths turn to alcohol or drugs as a means of coping, which in turn is a risk factor for suicide (McFarland, 1998). Although homosexuality is a controversial and uncomfortable issue for many teachers and parents, it is a fact that teens who report same-sex orientation have a higher risk for suicide (Russell & Joyner, 2001). Specifically, homosexual youths have been found to be twice as likely to attempt suicide as heterosexual youths. In addition, homosexual adolescents reported higher levels of alcohol use, depression, and hopelessness (all signs of suicide). Finally, it was found for all teens that victimization for any reason (such as bullying) might place individuals at a high risk for suicide. As a teacher, it is extremely important to provide support, or access to a support system, to counteract the stress that gay adolescents often feel.

Social Support, Friends, and Family

The situations that students find themselves in may also increase the risk of suicide. Paulson and Everall (2001) have found evidence that situational factors such as a major negative life event like sexual abuse, a series of daily stresses, and/or few social supports put teenagers at an increased risk for attempting suicide. When combined with the stress of simply growing up and going through puberty, a negative life event can feel overwhelming, and a strong urge to escape the situation can occur. Students experiencing stressful events and struggling to maintain a sense of control need to have access to outside resources.

Social Support

Students exposed to situational risk factors benefit from having a social support as a buffer from the stressful situation. Social support can be defined as "an individual's perception of general support or specific supportive behaviors (available or enacted on) from people in their social network, which enhances their functioning or may buffer them from adverse outcomes" (Demaray & Malecki, 2002, p. 215). This process is important because students' social networks can overlap settings and include home, peers, and school. Effective social support in school settings can offset a lack of support in some other environment. For example, it is known that levels of perceived social support decrease as students progress from elementary school to high school, and students with low perceived support also have lower self-concepts, whereas those with the highest self-concept have the highest level of perceived support (Demaray & Malecki, 2002). Given this knowledge, combined with the finding that suicide rates increase as students get older, proactive middle and high schools may want to consider means to programmatically encourage social support among students (e.g., buddy teams).

Solitary Activity

Mazza and Eggert (2001) found that adolescents at risk for suicide were more likely to engage in solitary activities than other peers. Solitary activities may be risk factors for some students because they can lead to depression, hopelessness, or low levels of perceived social support. Interestingly, the study showed there was less of a discrepancy between suicidal and nonsuicidal teens on weekends, indicating families often integrated their kids into activities. The major difference occurred during the week; because after-school activities take place during this time, it is extremely important that school personnel take measures to ensure that all teens get involved.

School personnel have the opportunity to decrease the risk of suicide by assessing their students' perceived social support and providing opportunities for students to engage in meaningful interactions. Prevention efforts should focus on programs, such as study buddies, that increase levels of perceived social support.

Family Turmoil

Mothershead, Kivlighan, and Wynkoop (1998) reported that family dysfunction is significantly correlated with interpersonal distress and attachment to other family members. As family dysfunction increases, parental attachment to their children may decrease, which can lead to corresponding interpersonal distress in the family's children. Parental attachment must be high to keep interpersonal distress from occurring in children. This relationship has important implications for teens whose parents are divorced, abuse drugs, or simply are not a strong presence in the lives of their children. For these adolescents, it is important to find an alternative role model or source of support. Although a teacher cannot replace a parent, teachers can provide a great source of support for students.

Factors in the World at Large

According to the ecological model of development, students face additional risk factors in settings that they are not active in but that influence their lives. Referred to as the *exosystem*, these settings include the parent's workplace, the local school board, and the media. The following examples illustrate this point: (a) A student who started a new school in the middle of the academic semester, whose family happens to be migrant agricultural workers, who is in a low socioeconomic category, and who has no system of external social support has increased risk for suicide. (b) A student whose local school board adopts policies that do not promote openness about suicide and do not offer children crisis services may be at a greater risk for suicide than a student whose district has a well-run crisis program. (c) Media may pose a risk for adolescent suicide when the suicides of celebrities are excessively covered or glorified (Ayyash-Abdo, 2002; Henry et al., 1993).

Culture

Another setting considered by ecological theory is the *macrosystem*, which consists of ideas, thoughts, beliefs, and practices common throughout groups of people, including cultures and subcultures. An example of the protective possibility of the macrosystem is the relatively low suicide rate in Spanish-speaking, Roman Catholic populations. It is hypothesized that because suicide is a sin in Catholicism, coupled with the Church's belief that humans should not control life and death, people of the Catholic faith commit fewer suicides.

PROTECTIVE FACTORS

Most research on the causes of suicide in children and adolescents focus on negative risk factors. Previous studies have examined the characteristics and experiences of those who have attempted suicide. Some recent studies have taken an opposite view; to fully understand what causes suicide, research must also examine the characteristics of people who do not attempt suicide. During the development of the *Reasons for Living Inventory for Adolescents,* Osman and colleagues (1998) found five protective factors that decrease the likelihood of an adolescent's attempting suicide: future optimism, suicide-related concerns (e.g., scared to commit suicide), family alliance, peer acceptance and support, and self-acceptance. One can see how these protective factors might inversely correlate with risk factors, such as hopelessness and family turmoil. However, appropriate intervention will not only focus on risk factors, but also attempt to build on strengths children already possess. In addition, teachers must realize that it is not always actual life experiences that put children at risk for suicide; how each individual child subjectively interprets the situation and internalizes the experience is sometimes what makes the difference (Malone et al., 2000).

Tragically, suicide occurs in adolescents and children. However, suicide is not a random event and is usually preceded by warning signs related to risk factors in students' interpersonal traits, environmental settings, family life, support systems, community life, and culture. Risk factors may predispose a student to be at risk for suicide. However, protective factors, such as social support, can reduce this risk. Because of the nature of overlapping influence from one setting (e.g., school) to another (e.g., home), teachers have the ability to promote practices in school that reduce the effects of students' exposure to risk factors. Teachers do not have to be mental health practitioners to make an important and meaningful impact on lessening a student's risk for suicide.

YOU CAN HELP PREVENT SUICIDE

The Right Stuff

Teachers are often the right people at the right time in the right place to provide early warning and referral of students at risk for suicide. Two factors make the involvement of teachers critical to reducing the occurrence of suicide: Teachers are trained in child and adolescent development, and besides the student's primary caregivers, teachers are often the adults who interact with children the most.

Training and Contact

Schools, being staffed by highly trained teachers, are an ideal organization from which to engage in suicide prevention. As mentioned previously, it is not uncommon for teachers to be the first adults to notice that a student is exhibiting suicide warning signs. By taking action at an early stage, the teacher can be instrumental in preventing suicide. The first author of this chapter has seen many teachers initiate the process that brought support and professional care to students who were suicidal. Teachers are encouraged to immediately contact the mental health staff in their school if they observe any of the suicide warning signs discussed in this chapter.

Right Place

It is likely that school personnel might have concerns about how parents will react to a schoolwide suicide prevention program. Understandably, parents will have a variety of reactions. Some parents will be pleased the school is being proactive in creating prevention programs, but others might be uncomfortable with their children being exposed to such material. The fact of the matter is, however, that schools do have an ethical obligation to create prevention programs targeted at the entire student body. While being sensitive to parents' concerns, teachers can and should do everything possible to establish prevention programs designed to decrease the occurrence of suicide.

PREVENTION PROGRAMS

Teachers do not have to wait until a student is "on the edge" and actively contemplating suicide before they can help prevent this act. Prevention programs directed toward helping the entire school community are one of the best defenses against suicide. These programs mainly emphasize creating a greater awareness of suicide, identifying students who may be suicidal, providing information about mental health resources, and improving individuals' coping skills. Potter and Stone (2003) identified a variety of principles of effective suicide prevention that apply to nearly all programs. Specifically, suicide prevention programs should work to enhance protective factors and reverse or reduce risk factors. Programs should be long term; one simple presentation to students is not enough to prevent suicide. In addition, whenever possible, families should be involved in suicide prevention. Finally, programs should be developmentally appropriate, age specific, and culturally sensitive.

Although prevention programs vary from one school to another, a variety of researchers have discussed critical elements of effective comprehensive programs (Gould & Kramer, 2001; Kalafat, 2003; Kalafat & Lazarus, 2002; King, 2001; Potter & Stone, 2003). These components include administrative consultation (including developing a school or district policy for suicide prevention), establishing a school crisis intervention team, educating school employees about suicide, encouraging collaboration among all school employees, including suicide prevention education in the curriculum, developing a peer assistance program, screening for suicide risk, implementing activities to increase school connectedness, and parent training (including developing supportive school-family partnerships).

Administrative Consultation

Before a school can have an effective primary suicide prevention program, it is essential that administrators ensure that policies and procedures relating to suicide are in place. All schools should have a suicide intervention and prevention policy that is updated at least once a year. This plan should emphasize that suicide prevention is a school priority. In addition, effective plans should include information such as procedures that faculty and staff should take if they believe a student is at risk for suicide, procedures to take if a student threatens or attempts suicide, and procedures to take following a suicide (King, 2001). It is the administrator's responsibility to see that all faculty and staff are aware of and understand this policy.

Establishing a School Crisis Intervention Team

When a student commits suicide or another school crisis takes place, having a crisis intervention team in place can help survivors deal with the situation and prevent further tragedy from occurring. From the ecological perspective, microsystem factors such as negative life events are definite risk factors for suicide. Learning of a classmate who has committed suicide can create a variety of reactions among survivors, including considering committing suicide. By having a crisis intervention team in place before a crisis occurs, school personnel are better prepared to help students cope with the crisis and prevent a future crisis from occurring.

Every school should have a crisis intervention team made up of a diverse group of professionals. This team works with the administrators to create (and revise) a school suicide prevention and intervention policy. This team may also be responsible for helping to coordinate prevention programs in the school.

Educating School Employees About Suicide

Given the proper training, teachers will often be the first individuals to become aware of a suicidal student. The expertise to provide this training may already be possessed by school social workers, school psychologists, and school counselors within the school system. If not, the school system may choose to bring trainers in or develop a team that can be sent out of the school system to obtain training. It is essential that training be given to all faculty and staff members, providing them with information on the identification of, initial response to, and methods of referral for potentially suicidal students. This training should include information about risk factors and warning signs of suicide, myths about suicide, and available school and community resources to help employees deal with a potential suicide. School personnel must understand the proper steps to take to refer a potentially suicidal student. Just recognizing the signs is not enough if a teacher or staff member does not feel comfortable or does not know the appropriate way to report what he or she suspects is going on. Moreover, it is useful to provide information on school policies and legal issues so that personnel understand what their responsibilities are when it comes to reporting suspected suicidal students.

Encouraging Collaboration Among All School Employees

School employees should be encouraged to collaborate with one another to prevent a student from committing suicide. For instance, teachers should refer students suspected of being suicidal to school social workers, counselors, or psychologists. Counselors might visit various classes to provide suicide prevention programs. Psychologists and school social workers often lead workshops for all school employees about the risk factors of suicide. These professionals should be readily accessible to classroom educators and should actively cultivate collaborative relationships with teachers. By working with one another, there is a greater likelihood that suicide will be prevented.

Including Suicide Prevention Information in the Curriculum

Although the content varies, lessons for students dealing with suicide-related issues should be presented at all grade levels. For elementary school students, programs on problem solving and self-esteem can help enhance protective factors that will be beneficial throughout their lives. These classes should not focus on suicide but, rather, should teach children help-seeking skills and resources. For students in junior high and high school, classes should focus on teaching suicide risk factors so that students can better recognize a suicidal peer. These classes should also provide the students with resources so they know where to turn when suicide issues arise. In addition, the classes should continue to emphasize issues such as problem solving and self-esteem to further enhance protective factors. When designing these lessons, it is recommended that consideration be given to parents' reactions to such programming. All students need to receive suicide prevention education, but care should be taken to address parents' concerns in the best way possible.

Develop a Peer Assistance Program

Even though teachers may be the first adults to observe behaviors associated with suicide, research has demonstrated that adolescents are more likely to confide in friends than parents or teachers, especially when it comes to suicide (Brock & Sandoval, 1999; King, 2001; Sandoval & Brock, 1996). Given this, prevention programs involving peer counselors who have been trained in suicide awareness and proper referral steps can be effective. One critical component of peer programs is discussing confidentiality and helping the students understand when they must share information pertaining to suicide. If a child or adolescent confides in another person that he or she has contemplated suicide, it may be under a strict promise that the confidant tell no one else. However, part of a peer assistance program would include teaching peers that when a person is in danger, telling someone else is the right thing to do. Although the mental health professions are tightly bound by confidentiality, there are a few exceptions to even these strict standards, and protecting a person from harming himself or herself is one of these exceptions.

As mentioned previously, a risk factor for suicide is lack of social support. When students perceive that they do not have the support of others, they might have suicidal thoughts. By creating peer assistance programs to help students from the moment they feel alone, it is more likely that such suicidal thoughts can be prevented.

Screen for Suicide Risk

One way to prevent suicide is to try to screen students to determine who is suicidal, and intervene before it is too late. Screening programs typically have two stages (Sandoval & Brock, 1996). First, students are given a psychological questionnaire specifically designed to screen for suicide. At this point, screening is given to all students and thus is ethical. After looking at the results of these questionnaires, all students at risk are given a clinical evaluation, typically involving a combination of interviews and additional questionnaires. One downside of such programs is that for them to be effective, they must be conducted multiple times a year.

Although screening might seem like a lot of work for teachers, the bottom line is that screening is a tremendously effective suicide prevention technique. Taking the time to regularly screen students (both formally and informally) can really make a difference in identifying students who are having some difficulties before it is too late.

Implement Activities to Increase School Connectedness

Research has shown that the more connected students feel to their school, the less likely they are to consider suicide (King, 2001). Again, one big risk factor for suicide is lack of perceived social support. When students are connected to their school, they feel social support. Consequently, all school professionals should work to create an environment where students have ties to their school community. In addition, an emotionally supportive environment where students feel cared for and comfortable turning to someone for help when needed can help prevent students from committing suicide during difficult times.

Parent Training

Parents should be provided with training opportunities similar to what school personnel receive. In addition, they should be given information regarding prevention strategies. Specifically, information should be given to parents regarding steps they can take to prevent their child from attempting suicide. These include things as simple as limiting the means by which their child might commit suicide, such as not having a gun accessible. Without training in this area, parents might not understand how, for instance, experiencing a negative life event can put a student at risk for suicidal thoughts. By learning about the specific risk factors, parents can become more attuned to their children's needs and become better equipped to get help for their child if the need arises. Because parents often do not see the relevance of suicide training (thinking their own child would never commit suicide), it is suggested that the training be incorporated with another event. In addition, schools should try to provide opportunities for parents to become involved in prevention programs at school.

SUMMARY

Although suicide prevention might seem beyond the scope of what a teacher can do on a typical day, teachers can have a tremendous impact on preventing suicide. Being on the lookout for students exhibiting signs of suicidal behavior and taking the appropriate follow-up steps can have one of the greatest impacts on prevention efforts. Popenhagen and Qualley (1998) outline a variety of concrete steps that teachers can take to facilitate suicide prevention. In the classroom, teachers can work to dispel myths students might have about suicide. Teachers can provide extra support to students just by listening to them and providing positive reinforcement and by helping them to see there is a trusted adult they can turn to. Teachers should also be aggressive in initiating prevention programs and can contact teachers' organizations to sponsor seminars on this topic.

The bottom line is that teachers and other school employees can make a difference when it comes to suicide prevention. Educators know their students' personalities and daily moods well and consequently are in a unique position to identify, refer, and support students who exhibit warning symptoms associated with suicide.

DISCUSSION QUESTIONS

1. How can the ecological model be used to help us understand suicide?
2. What are some warning signs for anxiety and depression?
3. How can conduct disorder and bipolar disorder be recognized?
4. How might a student be acting if he or she is abusing alcohol or drugs?
5. How can school staff collaborate on increasing social support for at-risk students?
6. Specifically, what can a teacher do to support an at-risk student?
7. What are the key elements of most prevention programs?
8. What are some things teachers can do to help prevent their students from committing suicide?
9. What steps can school administrators take to help prevent suicide?

FOR ADDITIONAL HELP

	Organization	Web Address	Description
Suicide	Prevent Suicide Now	www.preventsuicidenow.com/teen-suicide-and-youth-suicide.html	Prevent Suicide Now has a variety of stated goals, but the primary mission is to prevent as many suicides as possible.
	Healthy Place	www.healthyplace.com/communities/depression/related/suicide_2.asp	Healthy Place provides self-help and mutual support. The intent is to provide a safe space for asking questions, sharing advice and resources, telling our stories, and being heard.

REFERENCES

American Psychiatric Association. (2000). *Diagnostic and statistical manual of mental disorders* (4th ed., text revision). Washington, DC: Author.

Ayyash-Abdo, H. (2002). Adolescent suicide: An ecological approach. *Psychology in the Schools, 39*(4), 459–475.

Bandura, A. (1986). *Social foundations of thought and action.* Englewood Cliffs, NJ: Prentice Hall.

Brock, S. E., & Sandoval, J. (1999). Suicidal ideation and behaviors. In A. S. Canter & S. A. Carrol (Eds.), *Crisis prevention and response: A collection of NASP resources* (pp. 137–153). Bethesda, MD: National Association of School Psychologists.

Bronfenbrenner, U. (1979). *The ecology of human development.* Cambridge, MA: Harvard University Press.

De Man, A. F., & Leduc, C. P. (1995). Suicidal ideation in high school students: Depression and other correlates. *Journal of Clinical Psychology, 51,* 173–181.

Demaray, M. K., & Malecki, C. K. (2002). Critical levels of perceived social support associated with student adjustment. *School Psychology Quarterly, 17*(3), 213–241.

Durkheim, E. (1952). *Suicide, a study in sociology.* London: Routledge & Kegan Paul.

Fremouw, W. J., Deperczel, M., & Ellis, T. E. (1990). *Suicide risk: Assessment and response guidelines.* New York: Pergamon Press.

Gould, M. S., & Kramer, R. A. (2001). Youth suicide prevention. *Suicide and Life-Threatening Behavior, 31,* 6–31.

Helsel, D. C. (2001). Does your school track the suicidal student? *The Clearing House, 75*(2), 92–95.

Henry, C. S., Stephenson, A. L., Hanson, M. F., & Hargett, W. (1993). Adolescent suicide and families: An ecological approach. *Adolescence, 28*(110), 291–308.

Jackson, H., & Nuttall, R. L. (2001). Risk for preadolescent suicidal behavior: An ecological model. *Child and Adolescent Social Work Journal, 18*(3), 189–203.

Kalafat, J. (2003). School approaches to youth suicide prevention. *American Behavioral Scientist, 46,* 1211–1218.

Kalafat, J., & Lazarus, P. J. (2002). Suicide prevention in schools. In S. E. Brock, P. J. Lazarus, & S. R. Jimerson (Eds.), *Best practices in school crisis prevention and intervention* (pp. 211–224). Bethesda, MD: National Association of School Psychologists.

Kelley, T. M., Cornelius, J. R., & Lynch, K. (2002). Psychiatric and substance use disorders as risk factors for attempted suicide among adolescents: A case control study. *Suicide and Life-Threatening Behavior, 32*(3), 301–310.

King, K. A. (2001). Developing a comprehensive school suicide prevention program. *Journal of School Health, 71*(4), 132–137.

Lees, J., & Stimpson, Q. (2002). A psychodynamic approach to suicide: A critical and selective review. *British Journal of Guidance & Counseling, 30*(4), 373–382.

Lieberman, R., & Cowan, K. C. (2004). Save a friend: Tips for teens to prevent suicide. *NASP Communique, 33*(2).

Lieberman, R., & Davis, J. (2002). Suicide intervention. In S. E. Brock, P. J. Lazarus, & S. R. Jimerson (Eds.), *Best practices in school crisis prevention and intervention* (pp. 531–551). Bethesda, MD: National Association of School Psychologists.

Malone, K. M., Oquendo, M. A., Haas, G. L., Ellis, S. P., Li, S., & Mann, J. J. (2000). Protective factors against suicidal acts in major depression: Reasons for living. *American Journal of Psychiatry, 157*(7), 1084–1088.

Mazza, J. J., & Eggert, L. L. (2001). Activity involvement among suicidal and nonsuicidal high-risk and typical adolescents. *Suicide and Life-Threatening Behavior, 31*(3), 265–279.

McFarland, W. P. (1998). Gay, lesbian, and bisexual student suicide. *Professional School Counseling, 1*(3), 26–30.

Mothershead, P. K., Kivlighan, D. M., & Wynkoop, T. F. (1998). Attachment, family dysfunction, parental alcoholism, and interpersonal distress in late adolescence: A structural model. *Journal of Counseling Psychology, 45*(2), 196–203.

Osman, A., Downs, W. R., Kopper, B. A., Barrios, F. X., Baker, M. T., Osman, J. R., et al. (1998). The Reasons for Living Inventory for Adolescents (RFL-A): Development and psychometric properties. *Journal of Clinical Psychology, 54*(8), 1063–1078.

Paulson, B. L., & Everall, R. D. (2001). The teen suicide research project. *Alberta Journal of Educational Research, 67*(1), 91–94.

Phares, V. (2003). *Understanding abnormal child psychology.* Hoboken, NJ: John Wiley.

Poland, S., & Lieberman, R. (2003). Questions and answers: Suicide intervention in the schools. *NASP Communique, 31*(7).

Popenhagen, M. P., & Qualley, R. M. (1998). Adolescent suicide: Detection, intervention, and prevention. *Professional School Counseling, 1*(4), 30–36.

Portes, P. R., Sandhu, D. S., & Longwell-Grice, R. (2002). Understanding adolescent suicide: A psychological interpretation of developing and contextual factors. *Adolescence, 37*(148), 805–814.

Potter, L., & Stone, D. M. (2003). Suicide prevention in schools: What can and should be done. *American Journal of Health Education, 34*(5), S35–S41.

Rudd, M. D., Joiner, T. E., & Rumzek, H. (2004). Childhood diagnoses and later risk for multiple suicide attempts. *Suicide and Life-Threatening Behavior, 34*(2), 113–123.

Russell, S. T., & Joyner, K. (2001). Adolescent sexual orientation and suicide risk: Evidence from a natural study. *American Journal of Public Health, 91*(8), 1276–1282.

Sandoval, J., & Brock, S. E. (1996). The school psychologist's role in suicide prevention. *School Psychology Quarterly, 11*(2), 169–185.

Spirito, A., & Donaldson, D. (1998). Suicide and suicide attempts during adolescence. In T. Ollendick (Ed.), *Comprehensive clinical psychology* (Vol. 5, pp. 463–485). Oxford, UK: Elsevier Science.

Substance Abuse and Mental Health Services Administration, Center for Disease Control, National Institute of Health, Health Resources and Services Administration, & Indian Health Services. (n.d.). *At a glance: Suicide among the young.* Retrieved November 10, 2005, from www.mentalhealth.samhsa.gov/suicideprevention/young.asp

Part IV

Moving Beyond the Classroom

Chapter 15

The Role of the Educator in Early Identification, Referral, and Linkage

Dawn Anderson-Butcher

PREREADING QUESTIONS

As you read this chapter, reflect on the following questions and issues:

1. Think about the symptoms and risk factors that you have read about in previous chapters. How many students in your school exhibit problems like the ones that you have read about?
2. If you thought that a student was burdened by a number of the risk factors that you have read about, what would you do? Are there systems in place in your school, community, or both where you may refer students and their families?
3. Discuss the way that your school system addresses mental health among students. How effective are schoolwide prevention programs? Does your school have staff members on site to support student mental health (e.g., school counselors, social workers, etc.)? In what ways does the school support students with mental or emotional disturbances? Do you consider your school's approach to be proactive or reactive?
4. Is there support available to help you with problems that you see in the students that you teach?
5. What processes for early identification, referral, and linkage exist within schools where you work? How is information about these systems communicated to educators?

Many students are coming to school with unmet needs and issues. More than 25% are at risk of school failure and related issues such as depression, aggression, and suicide (Ellickson, McGuigan, Adams, & Bell, 1996; Kashani et al., 1987). Between 8% and 30% meet the criteria for Conduct Disorder, and between 5% and 27% have substance dependence or substance abuse issues (Stiffman, Chen, Elze, Dore, & Cheng, 1997). In relation to social and emotional well-being, estimates suggest that at any given time, approximately 15% to 30% of youths have diagnosable mental health problems (Costello, 1989; Lynn, McKay, & Atkins, 2003; Stephens, Dulberg, & Joubert, 1999; Stiffman et al., 1997) and that 54% of all youth access the mental health system at some point in their lives (Farmer, Burns, Phillips, Angold, & Costello, 2003). These and other social, emotional, and physical health problems interfere with students learning, educators teaching, and overall school success.

Evidence suggests, however, that many students who need more intensive supports often do not receive the additional services they need (Costello, Burns, Angold, & Leaf, 1993; Ruffolo, 1998; Stiffman et al., 1997; U.S. Surgeon General, 2001). Oftentimes, **gateway providers** are ineffective at identifying mental health problems and related issues (Early, Anderson-Butcher, & Burke, 2004; Stiffman et al., 1997). It is clear that more can be done within schools to identify, refer, and link students and their families to the needed supports both in schools and in communities.

Schools and educators are central to this process. Although identification of mental health problems and other issues by gateway providers is low (Early et al., 2004; Stiffman et al., 1997), schools are the most common point of entry into the mental health system for youths without formal diagnoses (Farmer et al., 2003). In fact, the majority of youths receiving mental health services receive their treatment in schools (Farmer et al., 2003; Greenberg et al., 2003; Rones & Hoagwood, 2000).

The reality is this: Educators see youths every weekday, both formally and informally assessing and responding to identified academic, social, and emotional learning needs. Few people outside family systems know youths better than educators. With appropriate tools and training, educators can and should be integral players who contribute to academic achievement as well as the overall social and emotional development of youths. As Paternite (2004) suggests, "Through their day-to-day interactions with students, educators are the linchpins of school-based efforts to encourage healthy psychological development of youth" (p. 18).

This chapter explores the role of the educator in identifying early indicators of risk, building assets and strengths, and referring and linking students and their families to supportive services existing within schools and neighborhoods. A comprehensive mental health continuum, starting with prevention and early intervention in the classroom and ending with important school linkages to intervention systems in communities, is overviewed. Furthermore, a template is provided for educators, allowing them to better examine and respond to the various nonacademic barriers that interfere with school success. Barriers and systems-related challenges correlated to educator referral and the provision of expanded mental health models in schools are also discussed.

MENTAL HEALTH IN SCHOOLS

One might wonder how it is that educators become pivotal in addressing mental health in schools. Schools are in the education business, not the mental health business, right? The importance of educators becomes critical when schools adopt an expanded definition of mental health. In essence, *mental health* is different from mental health problems or diagnosed disorders (Adelman & Taylor, 2003; Paternite, 2004). More specifically, mental health involves how students feel about themselves, how they get along with others, how well they function academically and socially, and how they navigate their environmental systems.

Defined in this way, mental health programs in schools cover an expansive continuum of care (Adelman & Taylor, 1998, 2000a, 2000b; Browne, Gafni, Roberts, Byrne, & Majumdar, 2003; Paternite, 2004). They begin with primary prevention, health promotion, and youth development strategies targeted at the entire student population. Expanded mental health programs also include early intervention services directed toward targeted youths through the use of student assistance teams, school counselors, social workers, psychologists, and other support staff. Last, programs involve more intensive interventions for youths with more critical problems and needs and, thus, rely on important linkages to outside social and health service providers located in the community (particularly in relation to coordinated case management, accommodation plans, and individualized instruction). Several models for school mental health and comprehensive reform incorporate these various strategies into their system designs, including Comer's School Development Program, full-service schools, community schools, and the school mental health movement (e.g., Anderson-Butcher et al., 2004). Essentially, expanded mental health programs support the needs of *all* youths and involve assessment, referral, support, and intervention at many stages within the school system. The role of educators and other school staff members in all levels of this expanded mental health continuum, particularly in promoting healthy youth development and providing early identification, referral, and linkage is discussed in the following.

PRIMARY PREVENTION, HEALTH PROMOTION, AND YOUTH DEVELOPMENT

Expanded mental health programs involve schoolwide primary prevention, health promotion, and youth development strategies targeting the entire student population. Such activities build social and emotional competencies as well as provide protective factors (also called "developmental assets"), which are known to promote healthy development and reduce problem behaviors among youths (Anderson-Butcher et al., 2004; Benson, 1997; Dryfoss, 1990; Hawkins, Catalano, & Miller, 1992; Jessor, Van Den Bos, Vanderryn, Costa, & Turbin, 1997; Lawson & Anderson-Butcher, 2001; Payton et al., 2000). A comprehensive list of these various youth development strengths is provided in Table 15.1. These assets are attributes that all youths need to succeed and, thus, become important qualities that all adults working with youths, including educators, should target and strengthen.

As outlined, strengths and assets exist within various contexts for youths and include interpersonal skills, family qualities, school characteristics, community-related factors, and opportunities for youths to be engaged in prosocial activities. In essence, these strengths and assets work somewhat on a "banking system." In other words, the more one has banked, the better one is equipped to deal with daily life challenges and stressors. The key is to help all youths develop and experience these strengths and assets, preparing them on the "front end" with the skills and supports they need to be successful in school and life. Educators are pivotal in helping youths navigate this banking system.

Table 15.1 Youth Development Strengths and Assets

A. Interpersonal

Positive self-esteem and identity
Strong sense of competence
Optimistic; sees the positive
Aspirations for the future; sense of purpose
Feels empowered; feels control over what happens
Feels safe and secure
Values for honesty, integrity, caring, responsibility
Easygoing, flexible
High expectations for self
Sense of humor
Accepts personal responsibility
Able to identify emotions
Has effective social skills (relates to others, friendship skills)
Able to ask for help when needed
Able to resist pressures; has refusal skills
Able to problem solve nonviolently
Gets along well with others
Able to create and sustain relationships with others
Able to see things from other people's perspective
Shows respect and concern for others (empathy)
Peers are involved in prosocial activities
Identifies with a prosocial peer group

B. School Related

Engaged in school
Sees importance of education for later in life
Motivated to do well in school
Connected with teachers and school
Experiences a sense of belonging to school
School has high expectations for youth
Positive school climate

C. Family Related

Family support and engagement in schooling
Bonded to family with prosocial values and beliefs
Strong supportive family
Family provides reinforcement for prosocial involvement
Receives recognition for prosocial involvement

D. Community Related

Positive neighborhood norms and supports
Opportunities for healthy youth development
Youth experiences a sense of community
Youth experiences belonging to the community
Community sees youth as valuable assets
Community laws and norms are prosocial
Community has high expectations for youth

E. Opportunities for Prosocial Involvement

Connected to a faith-based organization, spirituality
Involvement in prosocial activities
Involvement in leadership activities
Has opportunities for skill building, active learning
Has a positive job or vocational experience
Has hobbies and other self-interests
Involvement in community service
Experiences a sense of belonging to a prosocial institution
Strong relationships with caring adults, in general

F. Others

Specifically, each school day, educators have the opportunity to positively engage youths in ways that build strengths and assets. Their most obvious contributions relate to building interpersonal, family, and school-related strengths and assets. Foremost, educators are key role models, providing ongoing support, guidance, and nurturance to students on a daily basis. They attempt to instill the value of education and learning among students. They use proactive classroom practices that build school climate by establishing clear rules, organizing routines, reinforcing positive behaviors, and providing consistent consequences for inappropriate behavior (Hawkins & Lam, 1987). They assign homework that builds a sense of responsibility and accountability. Educators also structure lesson plans that allow youths to practice active listening, perspective taking, and refusal skills (Payton et al., 2000), thereby building social skills, interpersonal relationships, and related social competencies.

Other educators approach their role even more expansively. They reach out to families in culturally sensitive ways, attempting to engage parents in the lives of their children and in the schools. They invite parents and other volunteers (adults and older youths) into their classrooms to provide more individualized instruction, lower adult-to-student ratios, and strategic role modeling. Others develop strong peer networks through cooperative learning contexts or set up peer mentoring or buddy systems that promote connections, teamwork, and sense of community.

Still others are even more creative. More specifically, educators who truly understand their role in promoting an expansive model of mental health often provide youths with more strategic referrals designed to build assets and strengths in areas where youths may be missing them. For instance, educators refer students to school-based extracurricular activities and programs (our research has shown that this is a primary reason for students' initial attendance in these programs; Lawson & Anderson-Butcher, 2001; Lawson, Anderson-Butcher, & Barkdull, 2002). They encourage involvement in leadership and service-learning activities at the school and in their communities (some may even be the advisers or leaders of these groups). Others refer students to outside youth development organizations such as Boys & Girls Clubs, Big Brothers & Big Sisters, and local community recreation centers. They may even provide referrals to parents and adult caregivers related to specific community resources and supports (e.g., family support and education activities, advocacy groups, community organizations, etc.). Some also incorporate effective collaboration skills into their practice, building effective, trusting relationships with individuals both within and outside of the school to enhance strategic linkages for students and families within their schools.

The key is this: Educators need to focus on mental health promotion among their students and their families. This means educators need to examine what strengths and assets their students have, as well as the ones that still need developing, and provide strategic supports and referrals in response to their assessments. As educators periodically explore where students are in relation to these strengths and assets and respond with primary prevention activities and referrals, they help students fill their "banks" with additional supports and skill sets. Frameworks such as the one outlined in Table 15.1 can help. Referrals are endless as all youths are guided toward positive contexts and supports that promote healthy youth development and overall student success. Assessment and referral does not stop here, however; certain students will display risk factors that may call for early intervention via early identification, assessment, and referral. Referrals to early intervention services in schools become pivotal at this point.

EARLY INTERVENTION, IDENTIFICATION, AND ASSESSMENT

Expanded mental health programs in schools include early intervention services directed toward targeted youths through the use of prereferral processes and school supportive service personnel (i.e., school counselors, social workers, psychologists, etc.). These early intervention services are essential to supporting students before chronic problems develop. For these early interventions to work, however, there must be the *early* identification and assessment of needs, risk factors, and problems. Educators are critical to this process because they often are the first professionals to encounter symptoms among youths (Paternite, 2004).

One obvious way in which educators engage in this early identification and intervention system is through the use of prereferral processes. Prereferral processes involve collaborative teams called child study teams, student support teams, or teacher assistance teams (Chalfant, Pysh, & Moultrie, 1979). These intraschool teams, which are required or recommended in at least 34 of 50 states (Carter & Sugai, 1989), provide opportunities for professionals working in schools to brainstorm ways to solve student problems early, ideally limiting the number of mild issues that develop into severe ones (Neisler, McInnis-Dittrich, & Mooney, 1999). The successful implementation of these teams and their response plans have been shown to reduce the overall number of special education placements (Chalfant & Pysh, 1989; Sindelar, Griffin, Smith, & Watanabe, 1992) as well as provide supports to youths who do not and most likely never will be eligible for special education (Pugach & Johnson, 1995).

Essentially, educators observe and document concerns among youths and refer these students to prereferral teams. The collaborative team composed of other educators and school supportive services staff then works with the referent to identify the underlying causes of the problem and develop solutions to address the situation. The team then comes up with potential teaching strategies and techniques, classroom accommodations, and student interventions to support the student and the educator. Once strategies are developed and implemented, the identified student's learning, behavior, or both are monitored. If positive changes do not occur, the educator rerefers the situation back to the team for reexamination. At this point, additional strategies may be recommended and other referrals outside the prereferral team may be suggested (i.e., testing to determine eligibility for special education, remedial education, school social worker/counselor, etc.).

In addition, a more extensive educational evaluation or psychosocial assessment of the student may be needed. Educators are again pivotal in this initial assessment and referral process because they are the most knowledgeable informants about students and their current situations. Through their daily interactions with students, they are able to monitor progress closely and respond quickly to noticeable changes and emergent needs. At this point, tools such as the Teacher/School Staff Referral Checklist (adapted and expanded on from Deniro Ashton, 2004) presented in Figure 15.1, become more useful. The checklist provides an extensive overview of the common "symptoms" that teachers may encounter among their students. It allows educators to better pinpoint the issues without having to formally diagnose conduct disorders, learning disabilities, and other problems among students. Their role is to identify current risk factors and needs evident among students and refer them to school-based mental health providers who can further assess and respond to the situation at hand. This checklist provides an assessment framework for educators and other school staff members to use in these scenarios. Once referrals are made, mental health personnel working in schools can respond further to identified needs.

THE EDUCATOR'S ROLE IN REFERRAL: BARRIERS TO THE SYSTEM

In essence, educators are key adults in the lives of children. Their job involves more than teaching students math and literacy skills. Educators are central figures who are constantly monitoring students' strengths, assets, and academic, social, and emotional learning needs. They do not have to be the only individuals providing supports and interventions, however.

Through strategic referrals to targeted school activities, community organizations, student assistance teams, and school-based supportive service personnel, educators can broaden the services and supports provided to students, thus further promoting healthy youth development and, ultimately, overall student success. In the end, educators' jobs will become easier. They will be able to better focus on teaching as the other factors that influence school success are addressed in partnership with others via their strategic referrals.

The literature, however, does provide some insights into the barriers existing in schools related to assessment, referral, and linkage within schools. Educators need to think through these issues and address them, if they are to truly incorporate the aforementioned strategies into their everyday work in schools. These barriers are discussed next.

PERCEPTIONS THAT EXPANDED MENTAL HEALTH IS OUTSIDE OF THE SCOPE OF SCHOOLS

With the advent of No Child Left Behind, schools have focused their reform efforts inwardly, concentrating on instructional strategies, curriculum alignment, and standards-based accountabilities. Education indeed is the mission of schools, and many educators problem solve by teaching "harder" and "longer," as opposed to reaching outwardly and differently by way of expanded mental health agendas. As educators often note, their jobs involve teaching and not providing mental health. Many teachers simply do not have the time in their day to be case managers for students' social and emotional well-being as well as seeing to their academic achievement (Stiffman et al., 1997).

The research identifies, however, many nonacademic barriers to learning that affect student success. Perceptions about the school's role in addressing these nonacademic barriers must change if the growing needs of youths today are to be met. The truth is that schools cannot do their jobs of educating unless students come to school ready, able, and motivated to learn. Educators will have to expand their roles to work in partnership with others to build strengths, reduce risk factors, and support whole-child development. Students will come to class with unmet barriers to learning that will impede educators' abilities to teach.

Most Educator Referrals Address Behavioral and Academic Needs

It is commonly believed that students' academic competence (e.g., Abidin & Robinson, 2002), is the primary reason motivating educator referrals (Gottlieb, Gottlieb, & Trongone, 1991). Research suggests, however, that student misbehavior is also a critical factor influencing educators' decisions about referral (Abidin & Robinson, 2002; Chalfant & Pysh, 1989; Giesbrecht & Routh, 1979; Hutton, 1985). In addition, most behavioral referrals focus on externalizing problems, and educators often underestimate the need to refer students with internalizing problems (Abidin & Robinson, 2002; Greene, Clopton, & Pope, 1996; Lloyd, Kauffman, Landrum, & Roe, 1991). Likewise, educators have low identification and referral rates for substance use issues and suicidality (Stiffman et al., 1997).

Together, these findings suggest that, typically, educator referrals are related to deficiencies and the outward display of problem behaviors (i.e., those that interfere with the educator's ability to teach in the classroom). In expanded mental health models, educators need to identify and refer students for supports that build competencies and address early risk factors

Figure 15.1 Teacher/School Staff Referral Checklist

TEACHER/SCHOOL STAFF REFERRAL CHECKLIST

Student Name: ____________________ Referent: ____________________ Date: __________

Primary Reason for Referral: ____

Please circle the level of concern for ALL ITEMS:	No Concern	Moderate Concern	Serious Concern
A. ACADEMIC			
1. Reading performance – grade level	0	1	2
2. Math performance – grade level	0	1	2
3. Written language – grade level	0	1	2
4. Attendance issues	0	1	2
5. Tardiness	0	1	2
6. Suspensions/expulsions	0	1	2
7. Lack of commitment to school/belonging	0	1	2
8. Problems following directions	0	1	2
9. Off-task behaviors	0	1	2
10. Potential or identified learning disability	0	1	2
11. Limited English proficiency	0	1	2
12. Speech and language	0	1	2
B. OTHER PROBLEM BEHAVIORS			
13. Substance use/abuse (specify):	0	1	2
14. Antisocial peer relationships	0	1	2
15. Gang involvement	0	1	2
16. Juvenile court involvement	0	1	2

Please circle the level of concern for ALL ITEMS:	No Concern	Moderate Concern	Serious Concern
D. BEHAVIORAL/MENTAL HEALTH			
33. Poor attention span	0	1	2
34. Hyperactivity, restlessness	0	1	2
35. Rebelliousness	0	1	2
36. Impulsivity	0	1	2
37. Attention-seeking behavior	0	1	2
38. Inability to control anger	0	1	2
39. Physically aggressive	0	1	2
40. Self-destructive behavior	0	1	2
41. Destructive behavior to property	0	1	2
42. Poor self-confidence/self-esteem	0	1	2
43. Poor social skills	0	1	2
44. Trouble getting along with others	0	1	2
45. Anxious, worried	0	1	2
46. Mood alterations	0	1	2
47. Sad, depressed, blue	0	1	2
48. Withdrawn, loss of interest in activities	0	1	2
49. Sleepy, lethargic	0	1	2
50. Thoughts of suicide	0	1	2

Please circle the level of concern for ALL ITEMS:	No Concern	Moderate Concern	Serious Concern
17. Suspected illegal activity (theft, drugs, etc.)	0	1	2
18. Sexual activity/teen pregnancy	0	1	2
19. Inappropriate sexual behavior	0	1	2
C. HOME/FAMILY			
20. Limited parental involvement in school	0	1	2
21. Limited parental education/literacy	0	1	2
22. Parental limited English proficiency	0	1	2
23. Concerns with basic needs (food, shelter, clothing)	0	1	2
24. Parental employment issues	0	1	2
25. Child care needs	0	1	2
26. Evidence of or suspected abuse and/or neglect	0	1	2
27. Foster care/out-of-home placement	0	1	2
28. Family conflict	0	1	2
29. Family management, discipline procedures	0	1	2
30. Death/illness of family member	0	1	2
31. Family history of problem behaviors	0	1	2
32. Family history of mental health problems	0	1	2

Please circle the level of concern for ALL ITEMS:	No Concern	Moderate Concern	Serious Concern
51. Grief and/or loss	0	1	2
52. Change in appetite (increase or decrease)	0	1	2
53. Eating problems/disorder	0	1	2
54. On medications (specify):	0	1	2
E. PHYSICAL HEALTH			
55. Vision	0	1	2
56. Hearing, earache, ear problems	0	1	2
57. Dental problems	0	1	2
58. Headaches	0	1	2
59. Stomach pains	0	1	2
60. Health, in general (specify):	0	1	2
61. Head lice	0	1	2
62. Fatigue	0	1	2
63. Hygiene, cleanliness	0	1	2
64. Weight concerns	0	1	2
65. Underdeveloped motor skills	0	1	2
66. Known or suspected chronic illness	0	1	2
67. Physical disability	0	1	2

SOURCE: Deniro Ashton (2004).

of problem behaviors. They must identify these needs early on within the process because these strategies will ward off problems and provide proactive approaches for supporting students and their families.

REFERRALS HAPPEN ONLY WHEN PROBLEMS ARE SEVERE

Research suggests that educators' perceptions of student needs are strong predictors of educator referrals (Stiffman et al., 2000). Often educators wait to refer students for services until problems are escalated and extreme. They work independently within the classroom to address the issues, often in isolation. Research tells us, however, that the probability of a successful intervention is related to the original severity of the problem (Chalfant & Pysh, 1989). In other words, the earlier the identification of need and the earlier the delivery of support, the easier it is for educators and their partners to deter future problems. Research presented earlier on strengths and assets, as well as risk factors, further points to these needs. As such, educators need to provide early assessment and referral, thus wrapping their arms around student needs before they become so severe they are too difficult to address. In addition, strategies to build competencies and assets will prevent the emergence and deter the escalation of problems in the future, such as some of the strategies initially tried by the following teacher.

During my second year as a special education teacher, I taught seventh-grade students with specific learning disabilities (SLD). The middle school was located in a poor, predominately African American, urban area. On the first day of school, I immediately noticed 12-year-old Leon Porter. He was nearly 6 feet tall and weighed over 250 pounds. I taught math first period, and Leon was one of eight students, all African American males. Leon was immediately noticeable not only for his stature but also for his behavior. He seemed eager to please, but he asked far more questions than the other students. After a few days, the other students began to settle into the new school routine. Leon, however, began to have difficulty. He disrupted class by talking out of turn and attempted to monopolize my attention. When reprimanded, he would cry, an action his peers considered completely unacceptable. By the second week of school, Leon was crying much of the day. The other teachers and I agreed that Leon was having difficulty with the transition from elementary to middle school. In addition to talking with Leon's mother, Mrs. Porter, about his behavior, I referred Leon to the school counselor. The school counselor was able to establish good rapport with Leon, but his behavior in classroom settings continued to regress. Although Leon's disability area was mathematics, the only subject for which he received special services, he did poorly in all subjects. In spite of being very bright and articulate, Leon turned in no assignments in any of his general education classes. He was receiving a grade of zero in most subjects by the end of the first 3-week grading period.

During the second month of school, Leon made suicidal statements when he became frustrated with his math assignment. I notified the school counselor immediately, and she notified Leon's mother. Mrs. Porter agreed to seek professional help for him. She took Leon to the family's physician that same day. The family physician diagnosed Leon with clinical depression, but said he felt he was not in any immediate danger of committing suicide and referred him to a psychiatrist. Mrs. Porter later took Leon to a family counselor but did not take him to the psychiatrist. As I continued to report problems, the school counselor and the school nurse both encouraged Mrs. Porter to seek help for her son, but Mrs. Porter was reluctant to get outside help. Leon cried less as the school year progressed, but he began talking, at times, in his own nonsense language. At other times, he would talk in a babyish voice similar to a small child or toddler. His classmates found his behavior amusing, but generally they dismissed Leon as "crazy" and ignored even his most disruptive behaviors. Months after the initial referral, Leon was seen by a different family practice physician. This physician asked all of Leon's teachers to fill out behavior rating scales. Noting problems with attention and completing assignments, the physician placed Leon on medication for Attention Deficit Hyperactivity Disorder (ADHD). Leon's behavior did not improve. In addition to classroom disruptions, he began threatening other students. He also hit and pushed students, even though he did not appear to be angry with them. When I asked Leon about this behavior, he said there was a little man in his brain telling him to do those things.

Although Leon was frequently disruptive in my classroom, he appeared completely unable to cope with larger regular education classroom settings. His regular education teachers sent him to the resource room or office daily because of volatile, out-of-control behavior such as hitting, yelling, or turning over occupied desks. At the beginning of the year, a complete reevaluation for Leon had been initiated to determine if Leon was still eligible to receive services in the SLD category. With the evaluation completed, an Individual Education Plan (IEP) meeting was held for Leon. The principal was unable to attend this meeting, but a consultant from central office sat in. At the meeting, the school psychologist reported that Leon was displaying symptoms of schizophrenia and noted that Leon's biological father was diagnosed with schizophrenia. Mrs. Porter and the local education agency (LEA) representative, who did not know Leon personally, disagreed with the psychologist's conclusions. They felt that Leon was having difficulty because he was an only child. I stated that Leon appeared to be having difficulties that weren't typical for children with learning disabilities or children with no siblings. The school psychologist and I proposed changing Leon's disability category from SLD to Emotional Behavior Disorder (EBD) so that he could receive services to address his needs. The parent and central office representative outvoted the school psychologist and me, so the IEP meeting ended with no changes to the existing IEP. Leon's behavior continued to worsen, and he spent much of the time in the principal's office. I continued to document my observations and communicate my concerns to the counselor, nurse, school psychologist, and principal. During the seventh month of the school year, under pressure from the principal, additional evaluations of Leon were done by the school system. Finally, during the last weeks of school, the IEP committee met again. During this meeting, the principal, the special education director, two diagnosticians, the school psychologist, three program consultants, all five of Leon's teachers, the school social worker, the school counselor, and Mrs. Porter were present. With some debate, Leon's disability category was changed from SLD to EBD. Leon would receive all academic subjects in the EBD classroom with assistance from the SLD teacher for math instruction. Mrs. Porter reluctantly agreed to the change of services.

Leon began going to the EBD classroom the last 2 weeks of school. With a more appropriate placement, Leon's behavior did improve somewhat. He began completing assignments in the EBD classroom and began forming friendships with some of the students in that class. Unfortunately, Mrs. Porter could not accept the possibility that her son might have schizophrenia, so she did not seek any psychiatric care for his illness.

It took the entire school year to get Leon's educational needs met. By continuing to push for services for my student, I gained the respect of some and the disdain of others. Although there is no real triumph in Leon's case, I am satisfied that I did all that I could.

EDUCATORS ARE FEARFUL OF IDENTIFICATION AND REFERRAL

Educators are sometimes fearful of the outcomes associated with identification and referral. Fantuzzo et al. (1999) found that fears about student stigmatization deter early childhood educators from referring students. Other research suggests that educators may not refer students because parents and the community often deny problems exist (Stiffman et al., 1997). It also has been proposed that some educators may also perceive that asking for help through a referral indicates they are not doing their job well. For instance, research found that educators experienced anxiety related to student support team processes primarily because they believed there was a covert evaluation process by administrators working simultaneously (Logan, Hansen, Nieminen, & Wright, 2001). As such, fears related to student labeling, as well as those related to self-evaluation, need to be addressed if educators are to buy into an expanded mental health model. Referrals related to student support need to be perceived as helpful and not hindering. This will involve altering other stakeholders' perceptions about referral and support seeking.

THERE IS NO ONE PERSON OR PLACE TO REFER, LITERALLY OR FIGURATIVELY

Another issue related to referrals involves broader systems issues within schools and communities. On a macro level, mental health services and other supports may be nonexistent, sparse, or inadequate (Fantuzzo et al., 1999). And often, educators and others do not identify and refer students because they perceive there are few supports available (Stiffman et al., 1997). The reality is this: The most effective screening and assessment procedures will be useless without available services that respond to needs (Fantuzzo et al., 1999).

When services are available, often, systems are not in place within schools to link educators and their students to these outside supports once student needs are identified (Adelman &

Taylor, 1999; Lawson & Briar-Lawson, 1997). Some educators may be unaware of the services (Stiffman et al., 1997), or they may not see these auxiliary or support systems as essential within the school and community structure (Adelman & Taylor, 1997). School-community partnerships through school-based and -linked services and interagency collaboration need to be in place to better link schools, students, and families to necessary supports within communities (Anderson-Butcher & Ashton, 2004; Adelman & Taylor; 1999; Lawson & Briar-Lawson, 1997). Schools also need to develop internal structures for student support, implementing strategies such as strategic referral systems, single points of contact, and even interagency student support teams so that educators know "who to call" once student needs are identified (Anderson-Butcher & Ashton, 2004). These strategic supports must be put in place to support educators within their classrooms.

RELATIONSHIPS BETWEEN EDUCATORS AND SCHOOL SUPPORT STAFF AND OTHER MENTAL HEALTH PROVIDERS ARE LIMITED

Similarly, sometimes referrals do not happen because educators and supportive service personnel are not working together or work in tandem. There are multiple barriers to collaboration among these professionals. For instance, there is little consultation time between mental health providers and educators (Catron & Weiss, 1994), school-based mental health is perceived as separate from education and schooling (Lynn et al., 2003), and supportive services are typically conducted "behind closed doors" and focus on individual needs, not on how educators and others can support intervention plans (Paternite, 2004). We do know, however, that consultation with educators is related to increased teacher competence, which in turn may enhance student success and achievement (Goldman, Botkin, Tokunaga, & Kuklinski, 1997). We also have seen that the emergence of school-based and -linked mental health initiatives has helped to build bridges between schools and others (Adelman & Taylor, 2003; Anderson-Butcher et al., 2004). Relationships and linkages between educators and school support personnel and other mental health providers need to be developed to further support the likelihood of educator referrals, as well as the likelihood of a targeted response to the referrals.

CURRENT REFERRAL SYSTEMS OFTEN ARE NOT USEFUL TO EDUCATORS

Referral systems commonly used in schools often do not work effectively (Adelman & Taylor, 2003). For instance, educators are often asked for student referrals through memos to educators or postings on bulletin boards (Ritchie & Huss, 2000). It is proposed, however, that a more interaction-focused process between teachers and school support personnel is a better way to facilitate student access to services and supports (Sullivan, 2002). Likewise, there is often the belief among educators that nothing will happen in response to a referral. For instance, referrals are associated with the degree to which educators believe there will be a benefit for referred students (Rosenfield, 1987).

Referrals also are affected by the educators' perceptions of the competence of the individuals receiving the referrals as (Christenson, Ysseldyke, & Algozzine, 1982). Similarly, many educators do not perceive referrals as useful to them and their immediate needs in the classroom (Fantuzzo et al., 1999). In other words, educators need classroom-based supports and interventions that help them work better with students in classrooms, not services that are provided tangentially to their work. Systems in schools that support educators in classrooms need to be enhanced, and mental health supports need to be better integrated with educators and students in the classroom. This is particularly important as the probability of modifying students' behaviors in classrooms is often related to the quality of the educators' implementation of the intervention plan (Chalfant & Pysh, 1989).

THERE ARE MANY UNKNOWN FACTORS RELATED TO EDUCATOR REFERRALS

Referral processes, in general, have not been studied at great length in the past (Cooper & Speece, 1988; Early et al., 2004; Skiba, McLeskey, Waldron, & Grizzle, 1993). When factors predicting referrals are identified, there are discrepancies within the findings. Abidin and Robinson (2002) found no demographic variables predictive of the likelihood of referrals to school counselors. Research in special education, however, suggests that males refer more often than females (Lloyd et al., 1991). Educators may refer minorities more to special education (Andrews, Wisniewski, & Mulick, 1997). Others have not found these differences (Harvey, 1991; Tobias, Cole, Zibrin, & Bodlakova, 1982). Some research suggests that students' socioeconomic status predicts referrals to special education (Low & Clement, 1982); however, others have found no differences (Harvey, 1991). Similarly, Drabman, Tarnowski, and Kelly (1987) found that younger children in classrooms were more likely to be referred, but Andrews et al. (1997) found no age effect.

In essence, there is a great need for a better understanding of the factors that influence educators' decisions to refer. Educators themselves may want to examine their own perceptions and assumptions to better understand their own biases related to providing expanded mental health supports in schools. This personal exploration may indeed help educators identify problems earlier, provide more strategic targeted referrals, and foster better support systems for students in schools. In turn, it is highly likely that educators' jobs will become easier and students' success in school will be further promoted.

SUMMARY

This chapter provides an examination of the role of the educator within an expanded school mental health model. It begins with prevention and early intervention strategies in classrooms and ends with important school linkages to intervention systems in communities. The role of the educator within this supportive service continuum is essential. Educators promote health and positive youth development as they build strengths and assets within their classrooms and provide referrals to other supports in communities. Educators are also central to identifying early risk factors and symptoms, proactively deterring the escalation of student needs and problems. Their response to this early assessment involves referring students to support service personnel in schools and communities. The professionals who are better trained to handle these issues address the various unmet needs, leaving educators to focus on teaching and learning within their classrooms. In the end, students and their academic, social, and emotional needs will be better met, ultimately promoting students' healthy development, academic achievement, and overall school success.

DISCUSSION QUESTIONS

1. As you reflect on the material in this chapter, can you think of responsibilities that teachers may have to foster mental health among students?
2. Is it overwhelming to consider your potential role in strengthening students' protective factors, or is it something that you have always thought of as part of your job?
3. What strategies do you use or do you plan to use to minimize the impact of risk factors associated with adverse mental health outcomes for your students?
4. Do you think that your school system and community actively engage in nurturing the mental health of children and adolescents, or do they primarily intervene with identified "mental illnesses" and diagnosed conditions?

FOR ADDITIONAL HELP

	Organization	*Web Address*	*Description*
The Role of the Educator in Early Identification, Referral, and Linkage	National Mental Health Association – Children's Mental Health Matters	http://www.nmha.org/children/children_mh_matters/index.cfm	The National Mental Health Association is the country's largest and oldest nonprofit organization devoted to mental health issues. Children's Mental Health Matters (CMHM) is a grassroots campaign designed specifically for teachers, other children's caregivers, and families. CMHM has several identified goals, including increasing awareness of childhood mental health needs and issues, improving identification and treatment of childhood mental health issues, and reducing the stigma of mental illness.
	President's New Freedom Commission on Mental Health	http://www.mentalhealthcommission.gov/index.html	Established by an executive order of President George W. Bush, the President's New Freedom Commission on Mental Health is charged with maximizing service access and utilization of mental health services for adults with serious mental illnesses. Several subcommittees have been developed to address other identified need areas, however, and one subcommittee that has been established is Children and Families.

NOTE

Please note that the specific role of the educator in supporting intensive interventions for targeted students with diagnoses, particularly in relation to monitoring students' progress, is discussed in other chapters of this text. Attention here is focused primarily on prevention, early identification, referral, and linkage.

REFERENCES

Abidin, R. R., & Robinson, L. L. (2002). Stress, biases, or professionalism: What drives teachers' referral judgments of students with challenging behaviors? *Journal of Emotional and Behavioral Disorders, 10*(4), 204–212.

Adelman, H., & Taylor, S. (1997). Toward a scale-up model for replicating new approaches to schooling. *Journal of Educational and Psychological Consultation, 8,* 197–230.

Adelman, H. S., & Taylor, L. (1998). Mental health in schools: Moving forward. *School Psychology Review, 27,* 175–190.

Adelman, H. S., & Taylor, L. (1999). Mental health in schools and system restructuring. *Clinical Psychology Review, 19*(2), 137–163.

Adelman, H. S., & Taylor, L. (2000a). Promoting mental health in schools in the midst of school reform. *Journal of School Health, 70,* 171–178.

Adelman, H. S., & Taylor, L. (2000b). Shaping the future of mental health in schools. *Psychology in the Schools, 37,* 49–60.

Adelman, H. S., & Taylor, L. (2003). *Developing resource-oriented mechanisms to enhance learning supports.* Los Angeles: UCLA, Department of Psychology, Center for Mental Health in Schools.

Anderson-Butcher, D., & Ashton, D. (2004). Innovative models of collaboration to serve children, youths, families, and communities. *Children & Schools, 26*(1), 39–53.

Anderson-Butcher, D., Lawson, H. A., Bean, J., Boone, B., Kwiatkowski, A., McGuire, R., et al. (2004). *Implementation guide: The Ohio Community Collaboration Model for school improvement.* Columbus: Ohio Department of Education.

Andrews, T. J., Wisniewski, J. J., & Mulick, J. A. (1997). Variables influencing teachers' decisions to refer children for school psychological assessment services. *Psychology in the Schools, 34*(3), 239– 244.

Benson, P. L. (1997). *All kids are our kids: What communities must do to raise caring and responsible children and adolescents.* Minneapolis, MN: Search Institute.

Browne, G., Gafni, A., Roberts, J., Byrne, C., & Majumdar, B. (2003). Effective/efficient mental health programs for school-age children: A synthesis of review. *Social Science & Medicine, 58,* 1367–1384.

Carter, J., & Sugai, G. (1989). Survey on prereferral practices: Responses from state departments of education. *Exceptional Children, 55,* 298–302.

Catron, T., & Weiss, B. (1994). The Vanderbilt school-based counseling program: An interagency, primary-care model of mental health services. *Journal of Emotional and Behavioral Disorders,* 2(4), 247–253.

Chalfant, J. C., & Pysh, M. V. (1989). Teacher assistance teams: Five descriptive studies on 96 teams. *Remedial and Special Education, 10*(6), 49–58.

Chalfant, J. C., Pysh, M. V., & Moultrie, R. (1979). Teacher assistance teams: A model for within building problem solving. *Learning Disability Quarterly, 2,* 85–95.

Christenson, S., Ysseldyke, J., & Algozzine, B. (1982). Institutional constraints and external pressures influencing referral decisions. *Psychology in the Schools, 19,* 341–345.

Cooper, H. M., & Speece, D. L. (1988). A novel methodology for the study of children at risk for school failure. *Journal of Special Education, 22*(2), 186–189.

Costello, E. J. (1989). Developments in child psychiatric epidemiology. *Journal of the American Academy of Child and Adolescent Psychiatry, 28,* 142–147.

Costello, E. J., Burns, B. J., Angold, A., & Leaf, P. J. (1993). How can epidemiology improve mental health services for children and adolescents? *Journal of the American Academy of Child and Adolescent Psychiatry, 32,* 1106–1113.

Deniro Ashton, D. (2004). *Community support team/families, agencies, and communities together (FACT) support services referral checklist.* Murray, UT: Murray School District.

Drabman, R. S., Tarnowski, K. J., & Kelly, P. A. (1987). Are younger classroom children disproportionately referred for childhood academic and behavior problems? *Journal of Consulting and Clinical Psychology, 55*(6), 907–909.

Dryfoss, J. (1990). *Adolescents at risk: Prevalence and prevention.* New York: Oxford University Press.

Early, T. J., Anderson-Butcher, D., & Burke, A. C. (2004). Referral of adolescents to substance abuse treatment: Process and expectations of potential referral sources. Manuscript submitted for publication.

Ellickson, P. L., McGuigan, K. A., Adams, V., & Bell, R. M. (1996). Teenagers and alcohol misuse in the United States: By any definition, it's a big problem. *Addiction, 9,* 1489–1503.

Fantuzzo, J., Stoltzfus, J., Lutz, M. N., Hamlet, H., Balraj, V., & Turner, C. (1999). An evaluation of the special needs referral process for low-income preschool children with emotional and behavioral problems. *Early Childhood Research Quarterly, 14*(4), 465–482.

Farmer, E. M. Z., Burns, B. J., Phillips, S. D., Angold, A., & Costello, E. J. (2003). Pathways into and through mental health services for children and adolescents. *Psychiatric Services, 54*(1), 60–67.

Giesbrecht, M. L., & Routh, D. K. (1979). The influences of categories of cumulative folder information on teacher referrals of low-achieving children for special educational services. *American Educational Research Journal, 16*(2), 181–187.

Goldman, R. K., Botkin, M. J., Tokunaga, H., & Kuklinski, M. (1997). Teacher consultation: Impact on teachers' effectiveness and students' cognitive competence and achievement. *American Journal of Orthopsychiatry, 67,* 374–384.

Gottlieb, J., Gottlieb, B. W., & Trongone, S. (1991). Parent and teacher referrals for psychoeducational evaluation. *Journal of Special Education, 25*(2), 155–167.

Greenberg, M. T., Weissberg, R. P., O'Brien, M. U., Zins, J. E., Fredericks, L., Resnik, H., et al. (2003). Enhancing school-based prevention and youth development through coordinated social, emotional, and academic learning. *American Psychologist, 58,* 466–474.

Greene, M. T., Clopton, J. R., & Pope, A. W. (1996). Understanding gender differences in referral of children to mental health services. *Journal of Emotional and Behavioral Disorders, 4*(3), 182–190.

Harvey, V. S. (1991). Characteristics of children referred to school psychologists: A discriminant analysis. *Psychology in the Schools, 28,* 209–218.

Hawkins, J. D., Catalano, R. F., & Miller, J. Y. (1992). Risk and protective factors for alcohol and other drug problems in adolescence and early adulthood: Implications for substance abuse prevention. *Psychological Bulletin, 112,* 64–105.

Hawkins, J. D., & Lam, T. (1987). *Teacher practices, social development, and delinquency.* Newbury Park, CA: Sage.

Hutton, J. B. (1985). What reasons are given by teachers who refer problem behavior students? *Psychology in the Schools, 22,* 79–82.

Jessor, R., Van Den Bos, J., Vanderryn, J., Costa, F. M., & Turbin, M. S. (1997). Protective factors in adolescent problem behavior: Moderator effects and developmental change. *Developmental Psychology, 31*(6), 923–933.

Kashani, J. H., Beck, N. C., Hoeper, E. W., Fallahi, C., Corcoran, J. M., McAllister, J. A., et al. (1987). Psychiatric disorders in a community sample of adolescents. *American Journal of Psychiatry, 144*(5), 584–589.

Lawson, H. A., & Anderson-Butcher, D. (2001). In the best interests of the child: Youth development as a child welfare support and resource. In A. L. Sallee, H. A. Lawson, & K. Briar-Lawson (Eds.), *Innovative practice with vulnerable children and families* (pp. 245–265). Des Moines, IA: Eddie Bowers.

Lawson, H. A., Anderson-Butcher, D., & Barkdull, C. (2002). *Cross-cutting findings from ten schools and recommendations for improvement: A Phase 3 evaluation report.* Salt Lake City, UT: Salt Lake City School District.

Lawson, H., & Briar-Lawson, K. (1997). *Connecting the dots: Progress toward the integration of school reform, school-linked services, parent involvement and community schools.* Oxford, OH: Miami University, Danforth Foundation and the Institute for Educational Renewal.

Lloyd, J. W., Kauffman, J. M., Landrum, T. J., & Roe, D. L. (1991). Why do teachers refer pupils for special education? An analysis of referral records. *Exceptionality, 2,* 115–126.

Logan, K. R., Hansen, C. D., Nieminen, P. K., & Wright, E. H. (2001). Student support teams: Helping students succeed in general education classrooms or working to place students in special education? *Education and Training in Mental Retardation and Developmental Disabilities, 36*(3), 280–292.

Low, B. P., & Clement, P. W. (1982). Relationships of race and socioeconomic status to classroom behavior, academic achievement, and referral for special education. *Journal of School Psychology, 20*(2), 103–112.

Lynn, C. J., McKay, M. M., & Atkins, M. S. (2003). School social work: Meeting the mental health needs of students throughout collaboration with teachers. *Children & Schools, 25*(4), 197–209.

Neisler, O. J., McInnis-Dittrich, K., & Mooney, J. F. (1999). Interprofessional collaboration in the process of assessment. In R. W. C. Tourse & J. F. Mooney (Eds.), *Collaborative practice: School and human service partnerships* (pp. 79–104). Westport, CT: Praeger.

Paternite, C. E. (2004). Involving educators in school-based mental health programs. In K. Robinson (Ed.), *Advances in school-based mental health: Best practices and program models* (pp. 6–21). Kingston, NJ: Civic Research Institute.

Payton, J. W., Wardlaw, D. M., Gracyzk, P. A., Bloodworth, M. R., Tompsett, C. J., & Weissberg, R. (2000). Social and emotional learning: A framework for promoting mental health and reducing risk behaviors in children and youth. *Journal of School Health, 70*(5), 179–185.

Pugach, M. C., & Johnson, L. J. (1995). Unlocking expertise among classroom teachers through structured dialogue: Extending research on peer collaboration. *Exceptional Children, 62*(2), 101–110.

Ritchie, M. H., & Huss, S. N. (2000). Recruitment and screening of minors for group counseling. *Journal for Specialists in Group Work, 25,* 146–156.

Rones, M., & Hoagwood, K. (2000). School-based mental health services: A research review. *Clinical Child and Family Psychology Review, 3,* 223–241.

Rosenfield, S. A. (1987). *Instructional consultation.* Hillsdale, NJ: Erlbaum.

Ruffolo, M. C. (1998). Mental health services for children and adolescents. In J. B. Williams & K. Ell (Eds.), *Advances in mental health research: Implications for practice* (pp. 399–419). Washington, DC: National Association of Social Workers Press.

Sindelar, P. T., Griffin, C. C., Smith, S. W., & Watanabe, A. K. (1992). Prereferral intervention: Encouraging notes on preliminary findings. *Elementary School Journal, 92*(3), 245–259.

Skiba, R. J., McLeskey, J., Waldron, N. L., & Grizzle, K. (1993). The context of failure in the primary grades: Risk factors in low and high referral rate classrooms. *School Psychology Quarterly, 8*(2), 81–98.

Stephens, T., Dulberg, C., & Joubert, N. (1999). Mental health of the Canadian population: A comprehensive analysis. *Chronic Diseases in Canada, 20*(3), 118–126.

Stiffman, A., Chen, Y., Elze, D., Dore, P., & Cheng, L. (1997). Adolescents and providers' perspectives on the need and use of mental health services. *Journal of Adolescent Health, 21,* 335–342.

Stiffman, A. R., Hadley-Ives, E., Dore, P., Polgar, P., Horvath, V. E., Striley, C., et al. (2000). Youths' access to mental health services: The role of providers' training, resource connectivity, and assessment of need. *Mental Health Services Research, 2,* 141–154.

Sullivan, J. R. (2002). The collaborative group counseling referral process: Description and teacher evaluation. *Professional School Counseling, 5*(5), 366–368.

Tobias, S., Cole, C., Zibrin, M., & Bodlakova, V. (1982). Teacher-student ethnicity and recommendations for special education referrals. *Journal of Education Psychology, 74*(1), 72–76.

U.S. Surgeon General. (2001). *U.S. Public Health Service report of the Surgeon General's Conference on Children's Mental Status: A national agenda.* Washington, DC: Department of Health and Human Services.

Chapter 16

Communication Between Parents and Professionals

Thomas A. Wood

S. Thomas Kordinak

PREREADING QUESTIONS

As you read this chapter, reflect on the following questions and issues:

1. What factors are involved in the development of communication skills?
2. How does the structure of the family unit affect the process of communication between parents and professionals?
3. How does a child's disability affect parent-professional communication?
4. How can parent-teacher communication be enhanced?
5. Why is it important to maintain confidentiality between parents and professionals?

Communication between parents and professionals is an important process in the education of children and youth. More often than not, a breakdown in communication results in the creation of a difficult situation or will make an already difficult situation worse. This chapter deals with issues surrounding the process of communication in general and suggests approaches to developing and improving communication between parents and professionals. In addition, issues related to communications with parents of children and youth with disabilities are discussed.

Owens (2001) described **communication** as the process of exchanging ideas, information, needs, and desires. Communication involves a sender and a receiver. It is highly valued in school and society as a way to give and receive information, develop relationships, express our feelings, control situations, and persuade others. Guerin (2003) has suggested four purposes for using language: to get people to do things, to get people to say things, to keep people's attention, and to maintain social relationships. We communicate every day in a variety of situations and take the process much for granted. Even within ourselves we use a sophisticated communication system. We try to control and monitor our own behavior through "self-talk" (Weiten & Lloyd, 2003). Although spoken language is the most common form of communication, we also communicate in nonverbal ways. **Nonlinguistic communication** refers to a message delivered from the sender to the receiver with symbols other than words. This type of communicating often occurs concurrently with verbal communication. Examples include gestures, facial expressions, body posture, and eye contact. There are unspoken rules and nuances in the communication process that vary from culture to culture. Unless one is aware of these variances, they can become major hindrances to effective communication.

As receivers of the message, we also may react in certain ways depending on how these variations of sent messages are perceived. Communication takes place in other than face-to-face situations. The recent development of the cellular telephone provides the opportunity to communicate at almost any time or any place. Electronic mail (e-mail) is still another recent form of communication that has made communicating both faster and easier for many people. Although telephone and e-mail are effective methods of transmitting information, they lack the gestures, body language, and voice inflection (in the case of e-mail) that are often key in accurately interpreting the full meaning of the information received. Nonetheless, these forms of communication are being used more and more between parents and teachers.

Culture is another factor that plays an important role in both verbal and nonverbal communication. People from various cultures or geographical regions may have different dialects or use different gestures or body language. Also, many students come from families where English is a second language. Communication between parents and professionals who do not share a common language presents unique problems.

In this chapter, you will discover the skills a teacher needs to communicate effectively in a variety of situations with the parents of his or her students. These skills will help to ensure that the needs of each student are identified and provided for.

DEVELOPMENT OF COMMUNICATION SKILLS

As previously mentioned, communication can be defined as a process. When we talk to ourselves, we are experiencing intrapersonal communication. Interpersonal communication involves at least two people—a sender and a receiver. This simple, straightforward process can be complicated by the content and context of the message. For example, when a teacher is talking with a parent about his or her child who has exhibited negative behavior, different interpersonal dynamics will be elicited than in a situation where the conversation is about the student's outstanding achievement. The context of the message also affects the dynamics of communication. For example, a parent talking to a teacher in the classroom versus talking to the teacher in the parking lot of the local grocery store provides an example of a situation when the setting can affect the content of communication. The dynamics of communication are also complicated by interference due to other environmental or situational factors or the psychological set of the sender or receiver or both. A good communicator attends to the factors of content, context, possible interferers, and psychological sets of the receiver when formulating the message.

As seen with the discussion of the context and content, communication is not limited to exchanging words. Information is also exchanged through nonverbal channels. Many individuals are unaware that they may be communicating one message by the words they are using but another message in the tone, pitch, and amplitude with which they communicate the verbal message. Many times in our lives, we heard a verbal message and by the person's voice quality or body position, we knew their words were not true. Weiten and Lloyd (2003) describe the dimension of nonverbal communication as having a number of aspects. First, it is multichanneled; the voice quality, body position, and body movements all play into the message. It is ambiguous; the receiver is interpreting unclear signals that make it hard to identify the true message. It portrays emotions; our voice, tone pitch, and amplitude convey the full range of human emotions, anger, anxiety, or joy. It is also culturally bound. Consider the example of interpersonal space. **Interpersonal space** is the amount of space an individual allows between himself or herself and another person for a friendly or intimate conversation and may be based on cultural and ethnic differences. Nonverbal messages can be sent through several channels at the same time but may mean different things to different people. Caution should be exercised when making inferences between nonverbal communication and emotions (Krauss, Morrel-Samuels, & Colasante, 1991). Nonverbal messages are the most reliable when sent along with confirmatory verbal messages. When verbal and nonverbal communication contradict each other, it may be better to acknowledge the nonverbal signs (DePaulo, LeMay, & Epstein, 1991) or to probe into the possible meaning of nonverbal communication.

As noted, a major element in nonverbal communication is interpersonal space, or the distance between two or more people during the communication process. The most comfortable distance for individuals is related to one's cultural background, social status, personality, age, type of relationship, and gender (Weiten & Lloyd, 2003). For example, in mainstream U.S. culture, a boyfriend and his girlfriend are usually physically very close to each other in their interactions, less than a foot apart, whereas the young man or woman would be farther away (3–4 feet) when they are interacting with their teacher. According to Hall (1966), the social distance zone is between 4 and 12 feet, with the personal distance zone less than 4 feet and the public distance zone greater than 12 feet. Women and people of similar social status seem to communicate at a closer distance. Individuals will usually adjust the social distance during interaction. If someone invades an individual's intimate social space when the relationship is not intimate, the individual will usually step backward to increase the social space to a more appropriate and comfortable distance. It is important not to invade an individual's personal space during communication. When this is done, the nonverbal communications will be dominant and the verbal communications may be lost due to a violation of social boundaries. Because the social distance varies in different cultures, the teacher needs to be sensitive to these differences. This awareness of one's own cultural bias is important to ensure that communication is received without threat or rejection due to physical distance.

Other elements of nonverbal communication important to the communication process include facial expressions, eye contact, body language, and touch. Facial expressions can convey emotions through the six basic types: anger, disgust, fear, happiness, sadness, and surprise (Eckman, 1994). In cross-cultural studies, it has been found that these facial expressions are universal. They seem to be a basic human response regardless of culture. Although these expressions appear to be universal, they are used differently in certain situations and are related to culture. People may be feeling one emotion while communicating another through their facial expressions. The individual with a classic "poker face" may not reflect his or her true emotional state. The cultural norms that govern the display of emotions are called *display rules* (Weiten & Lloyd, 2003).

Establishing and maintaining eye contact is another important element of nonverbal communication. Duration is considered the most critical aspect of eye contact as prolonged eye contact or lack of eye contact can make the other person feel uncomfortable (Kleinke, 1986). Because eye contact also varies according to sex, race, and social status, it is important to be sensitive to normative eye contact behavior and not to misinterpret it as being negative in the communication process. For example, an individual may maintain eye contact while speaking but not while listening or vice versa.

Body position and touch are two additional elements of nonverbal communication. Posture, in particular, may provide an indication of one's level of tension or relaxation and attitude. When we use the expression of someone's being "uptight," we are probably responding to the way they are holding themselves. Many people use hand gestures when they speak to emphasize a point; however, the meaning of hand gestures is not universal. A gesture that is acceptable in one culture can be obscene in a different culture. For example, the peace sign in the U.S. is a vulgar sign in some foreign countries (Weiten & Lloyd, 2003). Touch conveys a number of messages depending on the relationship and varies according to sex and age. Women tend to touch other women more than men touch other men, although younger men touch women more than older men (Weiten & Lloyd, 2003). Touching in the United States has become an area of concern. With allegations of sexual harassment, sexual abuse, and inappropriate touching, the professional should be cautious about touching because it is so easily misinterpreted.

Nonverbal communication plays an important role in the communication process. Teachers need be aware of the context and content of their own communication. You must be aware that your own cultural conditioning, reflected in your verbal and nonverbal characteristics, may interfere with other individuals who have different patterns of nonverbal communication. Often, nonverbal behaviors are so engrained that one is not aware of them. A red flag that those nonverbal factors have not been properly attended to is when communications fail; the communicator (sender) has attended to the verbal dimension of the message, but it does not seem to be reaching the receiver. The teacher needs to look at how his or her nonverbal communication is affecting the words being said. It is also important to remember that these mistakes can occur between people from a similar cultural background, as well.

COMMUNICATION WITH PARENTS

Family Structure

The first factor that must be taken into consideration in regard to teacher-parent communication is the family structure. The family is the child's primary social group. Today's

Table 16.1 Family Types and Factors That May Affect School Communications

Type of Family	*Legal & Financial Responsibility of Both Parents*	*Emotional Support*	*Target Communication*
1. Traditional intact	Yes	Very likely from both parents	Both parents
2a. Single parent (SP)—traditional, family rupture due to divorce	Yes	First 2 years after the divorce, family is usually distressed. Supports depend on the age and sex of the child and the parents' postdivorce relationship.	Custodial parent, possibly noncustodial parent
2b. Single parent (SP)—traditional, family rupture due to death	Yes	Only one parent, who is emotionally wounded after the death	Surviving parent
2c. Single parent (SP)—cohabitation, relationship that has ruptured	Maybe, depending on paternity proof	Probably not a lot of involvement from nonresidential parent	Custodial parent
2d. Single parent (SP)—short term, relationship father unknown	No, unless father is found and paternity is proven	Probably none unless the paternity is shown; then it may be questionable	Custodial parent
2e. Single parent (SP)—Single female, artificial insemination, no male involved	No	Only one parent's involvement	Custodial parent
2f. Single parent (SP)—Adoption by single individual	No	Only one parent's involvement	Custodial parent
3. Stepfamilies (blended families)	Yes	Stepfamilies have difficulties if the parental roles are not clearly defined; the stepfamily is a high-risk family.	Depends; biological custodial parent

families reflect a wide range of caregiver arrangements, from the traditional intact two-married-parents family to the single-parent family. In fact, the word *family* may have a broader definition than in previous times because it now often refers to a diverse group of caregiver circumstances. Table 16.1 outlines some factors that may affect teacher-parent communication, including legal and financial responsibility, emotional support, and target parent in school communications. This table reflects general trends and may vary by different family situations.

Today, a student has a much greater chance of spending some time of his or her childhood in a single-family household. Over 24% of all children less than 18 years old are in single-parent homes, with higher percentages for black (59.5%) and Hispanic (29.1%) children (U.S. Department of Education, 2001). The percentage is even higher for students with disabilities. Students from single-parent families and stepfamilies are at greater risk for school suspension and experience less academic success than do students from two-parent intact households (U.S. Department of Education, 1996). One possible explanation for the increase in school problems is less available support than usually exists in the traditional intact family. In the traditional intact family, both biological parents are typically involved and the child customarily experiences more parental support. In addition to the support the child is given, coparenting provides support for the parents themselves. Even though one parent, typically the mother, may be the only participant in the child's school program, it still helps to have the other biological parent available as a source of support. A single-parent household, on the other hand, may not have the support of the other biological parent to share the responsibility of child rearing and decision making. Financially, the single-parent household income is often lower than for an intact two-parent family. Almost 40% of households with a single mother as a parent of a child with a disability are at the poverty level (Fujiura & Yamaki, 1997). With more financial problems, the single-parent family's housing, transportation, and other areas of basic need are affected.

In addition to single-parent families, there are families with stepparents—the blended families where parents bring children from previous relationships. Approximately 40% of remarriages involve stepchildren. In these cases, which involve more than two parents, shared custody may become an issue. The stepfamily may be at greater risk for family stress and is also at greater risk for divorce (Weiten & Lloyd, 2003). More recent family configurations include a single parent who has a live-in partner or a child who has parents who are gay or lesbian. There are also a growing number of people who adopt children. In some families, grandparents are serving as guardians. These examples of diverse family structures suggest that there is no set formula for the makeup of a family. The great diversity in family structures can make communication more complex.

Other family structure issues can result in challenges to communication, including the size of the family, number of children involved, sex of the child, sex of the custodial parent, cultural background, family socioeconomic status, and geographic location. The family structure has much to do with how the demands of everyday life affect the mood, temperament, and receptiveness of the parent. Of principal concern is the nature of the relationship of the child and the caregiver, regardless of legal link to the caregiver. When we consider the stresses of modern-day life and the diversity of family units, the communication process becomes much more challenging for the educator. Thus, to communicate more effectively, the professional needs to be aware of the child's family structure.

Defense Mechanisms

The teacher-parent interaction can be an additional burden on what may already be an overburdened parent, especially if the child is having academic or behavioral difficulty. To adequately communicate, teachers must be sensitive to the verbal and nonverbal cues of interactions. They must attend to content and context of communication. Along with family structure, teachers should be aware of the defenses that parents and teachers bring into an interaction. Ego defense mechanisms are unconscious processes that protect an individual's self-concept. Parents who have a child with school difficulties or a disability may become defensive because of the threat to their self-image. For example, they may feel that they are incompetent as a parent, that their child is not as good as their friends' children, or that they are at fault for their child's difficulties or disability. These defenses are manifested in a number of different ways. Parents may deny that their child has a problem ("there is nothing wrong with my child"). They may project the blame for the problem onto the teacher rather than the child ("my child can learn, but the teacher does not like him" or "the teacher cannot teach"). They may rationalize ("I am a single parent, and I do not have the time to check his or her homework"). Teachers must also be aware of their own use of these defenses in communicating with parents. Sometimes when a student has problems, the teacher will be a focus of blame. This message may be threatening to the teacher and cause him or her to respond with a defensive message to the parent. It is important that teachers be prepared to respond to the defenses used by parents in a way that shows respect and genuine concern while calmly presenting evidence to support why they are concerned about the child. If conflict or disagreement persists, it is useful to remember that it *is* the child's caregiver with whom you are speaking, and this person clearly has a right to offer legitimate feedback about his or her child; it is wise to acknowledge that, indeed, the behavioral concerns observed in the school setting may not be problematic at home. Acknowledging this may lead to a common ground in which you can work with caregivers to develop useful interventions.

Children With Disabilities

A number of studies have proposed that families go through a grief cycle related to the presence of a child with a disability (e.g., Kubler-Ross, 1969; Leff & Walizer, 1992). The stages proposed were similar to the reaction to death and dying, such as shock, denial, guilt, anger, shame, depression, and then finally, acceptance. Parents may experience these feelings when a child is born with a disability or when the child is later diagnosed with a disability. For example, mild mental retardation, specific learning disability, or Attention Deficit Hyperactivity Disorder may not be diagnosed until the child enters school. Certain developmental disorders, such as muscular dystrophy, may manifest symptoms in the early childhood years. Other researchers (e.g., Blacher, 1984) suggest that parents experience grief especially when they first learn of their child's disability, but they do not necessarily go through a set of sequential stages. Nonetheless, it is important to realize that parents may experience some type of grief reaction in response to their child's having a disability. Also, these grief reactions may reoccur during particular transitions. For example, parents might feel secure with a self-contained elementary school setting, but when the child moves to middle school, they may have to adapt to a departmentalized program. Suddenly, instead of one teacher, parents may have to deal with five or more different teachers who have specialized interests and more limited knowledge about their child. It is important to recognize that parents have different feelings related to the stage or transition they are experiencing at the time.

PARENT-TEACHER MEETINGS

Meetings between parents and the teachers foster mutual understanding of the child, identify behavioral assets and deficits, and generate potential solutions to problems. With the exception of caregivers, the teacher spends more time with the child than any other person.

Sometimes the teacher spends more time with the child than the caregiver does, especially if the parents have full-time jobs. The child's behavior may be similar or different in home and school settings. Therefore, the teacher may corroborate the parent's reports or shed light on behavior at school that does not occur at home. Helpful information can be obtained from parents about social interactions between their child and other children in the neighborhood, the number of friends in the child's social circle, and the parent-child interaction style. It is also useful to know the type of discipline the parents use. Teachers can provide parents with information about specific problems the child manifests at school in academic performance and behavior. The following case is provided to outline communication recommendations that we made to a teacher who was preparing for a parent-teacher meeting that was likely to result in an evaluation for placement in special education services.

Juan Perez is a 13-year-old Hispanic male who has just entered middle school in a small East Texas community. Juan emigrated from Mexico with his family when he was 9. He has two sisters and one brother, all younger, who attend an elementary school in their neighborhood. Juan's parents have very limited use of English. Juan's father earns minimum wage working in the warehouse of a large discount store. One of Mr. Perez's primary duties is unloading trucks as they arrive at the store daily. He also cleans up the warehouse each evening. Mrs. Perez is a stay-at-home mom but supplements her family's income by selling homemade tamales in her neighborhood and at the elementary school. Neither of Juan's parents has applied for U.S. citizenship, which creates a lot of anxiety for the family. The family lives in a subsidized housing project and attends the local Catholic Church.

The major educational issue for Juan is that English is his second language. When Juan and his family immigrated, he was placed in a bilingual classroom in elementary school. Subject matter was primarily taught in Spanish. Juan has learned a great deal of English since he started school but has had problems reading in both languages. He has not passed the state standardized test, and his problem in reading has affected his achievement in science and social studies. Juan's performance in mathematical computation is above average. Due to his problems in achievement, Juan has exhibited some behavior problems, and he recently started hanging out with a "bad crowd." Juan's parents are afraid that he is going to join a gang.

Because Juan has experienced several difficult years in elementary school, his teachers have decided to refer him for a special education evaluation. It is hoped that the testing will determine if Juan has a disability or if his problems are more related to second-language acquisition.

Because of Juan's circumstances, a number of things need to happen. First, his parents have to be notified that Juan is experiencing difficulty and needs to be evaluated. Neither of Juan's parents are English speakers, so the written notice required by law should be in the parents' native language (Spanish). Second, when the evaluation is conducted, the diagnostician or school psychologist should be bilingual. It may be necessary to test Juan in both English and Spanish to determine if he has a true discrepancy between his aptitude and achievement. When the Individualized Education Plan (IEP) committee meets to discuss the results of the evaluation, every effort should be made to make sure that at least one, but preferably both, of Juan's parents are present. It would be helpful to Juan's parents if an advocate who is bilingual is present. It is also a good idea for Juan to attend the meeting. If the committee members are not fluent in Spanish, a translator should be designated. It is not appropriate to use Juan or any other family member or friend of the family as a translator. Juan's parents should be provided with an adequate opportunity to provide input about Juan's behavior and study habits at home. The booklet describing their legal rights should be provided to them in Spanish and explained to them.

The committee will discuss the results of the evaluation and determine if Juan has a disability and needs special education services to improve his achievement. Of particular interest will be his problem in reading. Two other areas also need to be addressed. First, if his behavior is determined to be a significant problem, then it may be necessary to develop a behavior intervention plan (BIP). The BIP will be based on a functional analysis of behavior and describe how Juan's teachers will respond to his behavior. Second, because Juan is rapidly approaching his 14th birthday, the committee should begin to think about transition planning for when he graduates from high school, such as planning for a vocation. Will Juan pursue college or a vocational school? Will he leave high school to pursue a job in the community? His educational program and special services should be geared toward the future.

When the IEP committee meets to discuss Juan, the committee members should be aware of the cultural and language differences that may be a factor. Because Juan's parents are recent immigrants, they may not be comfortable in the school environment and feel "outnumbered" by the number of professionals on the committee. The committee members should make them feel comfortable by involving them in small talk before the meeting begins. If a translator is present, committee members should speak directly to Juan's parents, not the translator, and in sentences short enough to manage. The translator should not try to explain things or enter the discussion. He or she should simply translate. Committee members should not be offended if the Perezes do not make prolonged eye contact. They may also get closer to the professional than the professional is accustomed to.

Following the meeting and the development of the IEP, the committee must meet at least once a year to discuss Juan's progress. The committee may meet more often if necessary. Juan's teachers should stay in touch with his parents. In this case, it will have to be done by sending notes home with Juan or through the mail because the Perezes have no telephone or e-mail access. The teachers may need to get help writing the notes in Spanish.

There are a number of ways to communicate with parents and to obtain and convey information concerning a child, including interviews, developmental schedules, behavioral checklists and scales, parent conferences, written communications, and other forms of communications.

Interviews

The use of interviews involves close interaction between the teacher and parents. It is preferable to invite all caregivers to attend the interview session, but more often than not, the mother will attend by herself. It is important to begin by immediately establishing rapport with the parent. The teacher needs to pay attention to eye contact and body posture as mentioned earlier. The teacher should not be threatening or confrontational. During the interview, the teacher should avoid using technical language or language beyond the parent's capacity to understand. It is also important not to talk down to the parents. The purpose of the interview is to get as much information about the child as possible. Gathering demographic information is usually a nonthreatening way to begin the interview. The teacher may occasionally share some personal information when appropriate. This may help the parent to feel more comfortable and perceive the teacher as a fellow human being. The use of humor may also release tension and strengthen rapport. Throughout the interview, the teacher should demonstrate an empathetic attitude toward the parents.

A critical component of interviewing parents is the use of "open-ended" questions. This type of question yields much information and allows for follow-up questions. Questions should provide conversational openers with caregivers and not be questions that could be interpreted as threatening or overly intrusive. This type of questioning should be thought of as "relationship building," and it is logical to realize that, if an occasion arises that requires you to discus behavioral difficulties with a caregiver, that discussion will be facilitated by your already having a positive relationship with the parent. For example, the teacher might ask, "What does your child do after school?" "What are some activities that your child really likes?" "What are some things your child really dislikes?" There are no hard-and-fast rules to this except one: Keep your questions open-ended. Closed-ended questions do not foster communication, and a long series of closed-ended questions may begin to be interpreted as forced or intrusive.

If you do find a need to discuss behavioral concerns with a caregiver, an important component is getting parents to describe their child's behavior in specific, observable terms. Teachers should ask parents how often, how long, to what degree, and under what conditions targeted behavior occurs. This information will provide the basis for a behavioral intervention plan. Other questions that can yield valuable information include what alternative behavior the parents would like to see in their child and what reinforcers or punishers seem to be effective with their child.

Developmental Schedules

An interview that is very structured, usually for young children, involves a developmental schedule. During this interview, the teacher asks questions about the mother's pregnancy and delivery and the child's developmental milestones. For example, when the child sat up, walked, talked, was toilet trained, and so on would be included. The teacher would also ask about accidents and illnesses as well as social development. Although informal in nature, this approach does provide a structure that assists in obtaining information. Some school systems will not expect teachers to complete developmental schedules, but they are certainly something that teachers can do if given training.

Behavioral Rating Scales

Behavioral rating scales or checklists are designed to be completed by school psychologists, teachers, parents, or the students themselves. The advantage of these instruments is that information provided by both parents and teachers can be compared across home and school settings. These rating scales involve pencil-and-paper tasks that normally take between 10 and 45 minutes to complete. The items are specific behavioral statements such as "acts silly" and are rated on a Likert-type scale such as *always, sometimes,* or *never.* Many of these scales are standardized so that scores can be computed and a particular child's behavior can be compared to the "norm." In addition, factor analyses provide subscale scores that indicate specific problem areas such as hyperactivity or depression. Information obtained from these scales can be considered along with information gained from unstructured interviewed and interviews with developmental schedules. The Child Behavior Checklist (CBCL; Achenbach, 2001) is a behavioral rating scale that includes a form specifically designed to be completed by teachers.

Parent Conferences

Conferences with parents sometimes involve groups of professionals meeting with one or both parents. A disadvantage for the parents is that they are outnumbered by the professionals. An example is the IEP meeting, which might include an administrator, an assessment person, and several others in addition to the child's teachers. The parents may feel overwhelmed, and if a disagreement occurs, it can easily be perceived as the professionals against the parents. When a parent conference is scheduled, the facilitator should give the parents sufficient advanced notice of the date, time, and place of the meeting. The date and time may need to be negotiated based on the needs of both parents and educators. Everyone involved should be notified and an agenda prepared. Educators should thoroughly review the child's case folder in advance of the meeting. As with individual meetings, it is important to establish rapport. This may involve initially exchanging information that seems irrelevant. Everyone should be introduced, and the parents should be thanked for coming to the meeting. It is important to clarify the specific reasons for having the meeting, then proceed and stay on task. Cultural differences may require a variation in communication style as discussed in the previous case study and elaborated on later in this chapter.

Written Communication

Communicating with parents in writing is a useful way to exchange information. Two methods of written communication are the traditional method of sending home information on paper and electronic media. Using the traditional method may be as simple as a handwritten note to inform the parents about progress in an academic or behavioral area. This method of communicating could also be in the form of a school handbook or handouts providing information about upcoming events or specific school policies. Newsletters are often produced by schools, grade levels, or even individual classrooms. These can contain a range of information about school events, student accomplishments, and the like. A procedure used by many teachers is the daily or weekly folder. Teachers and parents can effectively communicate back and forth about day-to-day accomplishments and concerns. The folders are of particular value for communicating homework assignments. Some students have significant difficulty in remembering their assignments when they arrive home. Davern (2004) states that daily folders provide the student's caregiver(s) with an awareness of what happened during the child's school day, provide assurance that the child was actively participating, share information about instruction, and inform about homework assignments. The folders also function as a method of receiving information from the caregiver(s), thereby eliciting caregiver participation in the student's school activities. She cautions, however, that if a problem with the student needs to be communicated, written communication should not be the method chosen. Meeting face-to-face may be required.

Electronic media has brought a newer mode of written communication. As more and more families are being connected to the World Wide Web, e-mail has become a viable form of communication for many families. It can be of great convenience to both teachers and parents and will probably become the communication mode of choice. Schools or classrooms may develop a Web site and periodically post messages. Parents can connect to the Web to find out about class activities, events, and so on.

A drawback to written communication (traditional or electronic) is that it lacks the voice inflection of the telephone and the nonverbal signals of face-to-face communication. For this reason, most written communication should provide positive messages. As mentioned by Davern (2004), significant problems in behavior or academic achievement should be discussed during a parent-teacher meeting. For families with English as their second language, every effort should be made to translate the written material into their native language.

Telephone Communication

The telephone can also offer an efficient means for parent-teacher communication. Conversations should be short and to the point. Appropriate telephone etiquette should be observed. Again, significant problems should be addressed in person whenever possible. Teachers should find out if parents are comfortable being called at their place of employment. If not, then early evening may be more appropriate. Teachers should return calls from school as soon as possible. Teachers may be willing to provide their home phone numbers to parents but may want to designate a time frame for receiving calls. Another efficient use of the telephone is to use an answering machine with a recorded message that includes assignments, spelling words, and so on. One caution about telephone and electronic communication is that some families do not have access to them and can easily, if unintentionally, be excluded if their needs are not accommodated.

RECORDS AND CONFIDENTIALLY

Teachers should take notes during meetings and conferences that become part of the child's record. Some meetings (i.e., IEP meetings) require a written record of the meeting. This information may be needed later and should be kept in files with limited access. Normally, parents have the expectation that information divulged in a conference or meeting is done so in confidence. Information should be shared only with other professionals on a "need-to-know" basis. The **Family Rights and Privacy Act (FERPA)** of 1974 (Public Law 93-380) states that information cannot be released to other persons or agencies without the parent's written consent. This law, commonly referred to as the Buckley Amendment, also allows parents full access to any information collected on their child and the right to challenge that information. Although records are usually considered privileged information, they can be subpoenaed by the court.

CULTURAL CONCERNS

One of the greatest barriers to communication is cultural differences. If the student's family comes from a different culture or speaks a different language than does the teacher, communicating effectively will, most likely, be a challenge. The most efficient approach is to have a professional with the same language and cultural background as the family. That situation is often rare; some school districts have students from over 100 culture or language backgrounds. The second most effective approach is to bring in a translater who is an educational professional. It is not advisable to use a family member or friend to do the translating during a parent-teacher conference. When using a translator, the teacher should follow essentially the same format of communication during a conference but should make brief statements and pause so the translator can communicate the information to the parent.

There are a number of things that professionals can do to increase their own cultural awareness and cross-cultural competence. First of all, it is important that the professional understand himself or herself. The teacher needs to know how his or her background, values, and beliefs will affect relationships with families from other cultures (Kroth & Edge, 1997). In general, people tend to view their own perceptions as accurate and those of others as wrong. To form viable relationships with others, the teacher must be able to understand that his or her own cultural interpretation is only one of many.

A second way to develop cultural awareness is to learn all that one can about the other person's culture. This can be done in a number of ways. The teacher can ask the family about its background, traditions, and the like in a nonjudgmental way. The professional can also ask other professionals of the same culture or those who have knowledge or experience with that culture. The students and parents can be invited to share a "tradition" about their culture with the class. Parents can be invited to read a book from their culture to the class. The teacher can visit the family's home and participate in community activities of that particular culture. As the teacher gains knowledge of the culture(s), he or she can share this information with other professionals and teachers to extend awareness and appreciation of various cultures across the school. Students can celebrate different cultures through the use of classroom experiences with costumes and food. To be effective in communicating with students and parents from other cultures, it is important to gain as much information as possible. Be aware that highlighting a child as being "different" might contribute to isolating that student from the primary culture. This can be avoided by proactively implementing a multicultural curriculum consistently throughout the school year. This may help to minimize the "shock" value of the introduction of students from diverse backgrounds.

Although it is important to learn all we can about different cultures, Turnbull and Turnbull (2001) caution about stereotyping. They point out that "Hispanics" represent over 20 separate nationalities and Asian Americans originate from three major geographic areas that include 15 different countries. In addition to knowledge about the cultural differences, it is important to know the degree of **acculturation** the family has experienced. Depending on how long the family has been in this country, the family may embrace some of the beliefs and values associated with the culture of this country. Some may continue to hold on to the traditions of their native land, whereas others may become bicultural. Again, the best way to gain an understanding of cultures represented in the classroom is to ask the parents.

The most important feature in communicating effectively with parents of different cultures is respect. The teacher must be able to move beyond language and dress as well as values and beliefs and develop an alliance with the caregivers and family. In the United States, we tend to believe that our culture is the right one and the only one. In communicating with people of different cultures, we have to move beyond this notion. Professionals need to focus on family strengths and facilitate the development of goals and strategies that serve the best interests of the student.

ENHANCING COMMUNICATION

Nonverbal Communication

Nonverbal communication between parents and professionals can be enhanced by using a number of techniques and by becoming aware of how different cultures use these techniques. Eye contact is very important but must be culturally appropriate. In some cultures, an individual makes more eye contact when listening than speaking, whereas in other cultures it may be the reverse. Physical closeness is another thing to be aware of; the teacher should be aware of how it is important that he or she not misinterpret physical closeness on the part of the parent from another culture. Positive and varied facial expressions should be used, but it is important for the teacher to recognize that parents from other cultures may not use facial expressions that express their real mood (Sileo & Prater, 1998). Gestures are important but do not have the same meaning across all cultures. Listening is of utmost importance in the process of communication and involves concerted effort. It is necessary for the professional to engage in "active listening," whereby the listener focuses on the speaker and indicates throughout the conversation that the speaker is being heard and understood. This is accomplished as easily as repeating back to the parent what the parent has just said before responding. The professional may nod his or her head, say "mn-hm," ask questions, make comments, or in other ways indicate that the speaker is being heard and understood.

Verbal Communication

Turnbull and Turnbull (2001) mention five verbal responses important to facilitating communication. These are furthering responses, paraphrasing, response to affect, questioning, and summarizing. Furthering responses are similar to active listening described above. Paraphrasing involves repeating what the speaker has said with slightly different wording to check for accurate understanding. In response to affect, the listener tries to verbalize the speaker's feelings and attitudes. Questioning, as discussed previously, can be done effectively by soliciting open-ended rather than closed-ended information. Last, summarizing reviews the important points in the conversation and makes sure both parties have effectively communicated their main points.

Dealing With Anger

One of the most difficult situations that a professional can encounter is an angry parent. The first thing to consider is that the parent is usually not angry with the teacher but, rather, with the system or situation. The teacher should listen to the parent without becoming defensive. The teacher should speak in a soft, calm voice and ask the parent for his or her opinion on how to solve the problem(s). After the parent has settled down, the teacher and parent are more likely to be able to have a more productive conversation.

PARENT SUPPORT AND EDUCATION

For many parents who have a child with a disability or a mental health issue, groups that provide information and support can be very helpful. Parents have a great need for information about their child's disability. Support groups, often specific to a particular disability or mental health need, focus on the exchange of information by parents with similar circumstances. Parents share their own experiences as well as information about resources in an informal setting such as a member's home, a church, or a community center. These groups may be sponsored by a parent organization such as the Learning Disabilty Association or the Association for Retarded Citizens. It is often helpful for parents to talk to others who have experienced the same or similar circumstances. More experienced parents can act as advocates for parents who are having difficulty accessing the appropriate educational programs for their child.

Parent education groups are more structured than support groups in that they use a trained leader who provides a specific type of education or training. Sometimes the training provided is focused on parenting skills such as effective behavior management. Parents of a child with a disability are often presented with behavior that they are not prepared to manage. Although there are a number of packaged commercial programs available, training is more successful if tailored to the parents in the group. The groups generally are made up of 4 to 12 parents, and training is more effective if both parents attend all of the sessions together. Programs typically range from 6 to 12 sessions.

SUMMARY

This chapter has discussed the importance of communication between professional and parents. Within interpersonal communication, both verbal and nonverbal components are important. Nonverbal components in particular can vary according to gender, cultural background, and social status. Professionals must consider family structure and cultural factors as integral parts of the communication process with parents. In particular, family structure can affect how the family relates to the professional, and cultural differences can influence how parents relate to the professional. In terms of families with children with disabilities or mental health issues, the way the family responds to the disability may also affect the communication process. Information about families can be collected in various ways, such as through structured and unstructured interviews, behavior checklists, and parent-professional conferences. There are also effective ways to communicate with parents through written and electronic formats. It is the teacher's responsibility to ensure that spoken and written communication is kept confidential according to ethical and legal procedures. Parent education and support groups can be helpful in providing necessary information and coping skills to parents. The more skillful the professional is in communicating with the parent, the more successful the educational program will be for the child.

DISCUSSION QUESTIONS

1. As a classroom teacher, explain the steps you would take to ensure that effective communication was taking place with the caregiver of a child in your class who was having academic difficulties or behavioral problems.
2. Discuss some of the communication strategies that might be needed in working with a family that has a different cultural background than do the professionals.
3. As a member of an IEP committee, discuss the information you would need to help make recommendations and how you would handle the confidentiality.
4. Discuss the importance of nonverbal communication in the overall communication process.
5. Discuss at least three factors that might influence how a family would participate in the parent-professional communication process.

FOR ADDITIONAL HELP

	Organization	*Web Address*	*Description*
Communication Between Parents and Professionals	KidSource OnLine®	www.kidsource.com	KidSource OnLine® is a group of parents who want to make a positive and lasting difference in the lives of parents and children.
	OnlineSchool Reports.Com	http://onlineschool reports.com	This is a free online grading and record-keeping system that allows students and parents to access their grades and other important classroom information via the Internet.

REFERENCES

Achenbach, M. (2001). *Child behavior checklist for ages 6–18 (CBCL/16–18).* Burlington, VT: ASEBA.

Blacher, J. (1984). Sequential stages of adjustment to the birth of a child with handicaps: Fact or artifact? *Mental Retardation, 22,* 55–68.

Davern, L. (2004). School-to-home notebooks, what parents have to say. *Teaching Exceptional Children, 36*(5), 22–27.

DePaulo, B. M., LeMay, C. S., & Epstein, J. A. (1991). Effects of importance of success and expectations for success on effectiveness of deceiving. *Personality and Social Psychology Bulletin, 17,* 14–24.

Eckman, P. (1994). Strong evidence for universals in facial expression: A reply to Russell's mistaken critique. *Psychological Bulletin, 115,* 268–287.

Family Educational Rights and Privacy Act (FERPA). Implementing regulations, 34 C.F.R. Sec. 99.3 (1976).

Fujiura, G. T., & Yamaki, K. (1997). Analysis of ethnic variation in developmental disability prevalence and household economic status. *Mental Retardation, 35*(4), 286–294.

Guerin, B. (2003). Language use as a social strategy: A review and an analytic framework for social success. *Review of General Psychology, 7*(3), 251–298.

Hall, E. T. (1966). *The hidden dimension.* Garden City, NY: Doubleday.

Kleinke, C. L. (1986). Gaze and eye contact: A research review. *Psychological Bulletin, 100*(1), 78-100.

Krauss, R. M., Morrel-Samuels, P., & Colasante, C. (1991). Do conversational hand gestures communicate? *Journal of Personality and Social Psychology, 61*(5), 743–754.

Kroth, R. L., & Edge, D. (1997). *Strategies for communication with parents of exceptional children: Improving parent-teacher relationships* (2nd ed.). Denver, CO: Love.

Kubler-Ross, E. (1969). *On death and dying.* New York: Macmillan.

Leff, P. T., & Walizer, E. H. (1992). *Building and healing partnerships: Parents, professionals and children with chronic illness and disabilities.* Cambridge, MA: Brookline Books.

Owens, R. (2001). *Language development: An introduction* (5th ed.). Boston: Allyn & Bacon.

Sileo, T. W., & Prater, M. A. (1998, November/December). Creating classroom environments that address the linguistic and cultural backgrounds of students with disabilities: An Asian Pacific American perspective. *Remedial and Special Education, 19*(6), pp. 323–337.

Turnbull, A. P., & Turnbull, H. R. (2001). *Families, professionals, and exceptionality: Collaborating for empowerment.* Upper Saddle River, NJ: Merrill.

U.S. Department of Education. (1996). *National Center for Education Statistics. Parent and Family Involvement Survey of 1996* (PFI-NHES). Washington, DC: National Household Education Surveys Program.

U.S. Department of Education. (2001). *Fathers' and mothers' involvement in their children's school by family type and resident status* (NCES 2001-032). Washington, DC: National Center for Education Statistics.

Weiten, W., & Lloyd, M. (2003). *Psychology applied to modern life* (7th ed.). Belmont, CA: Wadsworth Thompson Learning.

Chapter 17

Mental Health Needs and Problems as Opportunities for Expanding the Boundaries of School Improvement

Hal A. Lawson

Kevin P. Quinn

Eric Hardiman

Robert L. Miller, Jr.

PREREADING QUESTIONS

As you read this chapter, reflect on the following questions and issues:

1. What do you see as the needs of children with emotional and behavioral disorders?
2. Can you think of gaps that exist in the school's response to children with mental disorders?
3. Are there components of the school environment that could be changed to be more supportive of students with mental health needs?

A free, democratic society requires educated citizens who enjoy health (including mental health) and well-being. Public schooling influences all three characteristics—education, health, and well-being. When children and youth enjoy all three, they have the best chance of becoming competent citizens. When any of these three is compromised, the others are difficult to obtain and maintain. In brief, today's slogan is perfectly apt: No child can be left behind. Democracy depends on it.

What will it take to ensure that no child is left behind? This question transcends our schools because other social institutions, especially the family, also influence children's education, health, and well-being. That said, every initiative designed to help children and youths must involve schools because schooling is the only universal entitlement for the nation's children and youths.

Consequently, this chapter focuses on school improvement, albeit in an unconventional way. Mental health needs and problems are presented as opportunities for expanding the boundaries of school improvement. More specifically, expanded models for school improvement are needed, especially coherent models that incorporate and integrate school-based and school-linked mental health services and systems (e.g., Adelman & Taylor, 2000a, 2000b; Lawson & Briar-Lawson, 1997). These emergent models offer benefits to children, educators, parents, and entire families.

Two needs and problems serve as examples: (a) The needs of children with emotional and behavioral disorders and (b) the organizational climate needs of entire schools. Each receives a two-sided analysis. One is critical; it is aimed at identifying gaps and unmet needs. The other side is constructive and action oriented.

The underlying logic is straightforward, and it builds on the above-referenced relationships between education, health, and well-being. Every unmet mental health need or problem represents a barrier to children's learning, academic achievement, and success in school, thereby increasing the probability that some children will be left behind. And when children and youth are left behind, problems multiply. For example, when children's mental health needs and problems are not met, their families are challenged. Furthermore, every need and problem adds to the formidable challenges that teachers, principals, and other school professionals confront, including challenges to their own mental health on the job, and perhaps influencing whether they'll remain in the education profession.

Clearly, expanded models of school improvement, designed to ameliorate mental health needs and problems, should be a top priority. Planning and implementation activities begin with a critical analysis of conventional models and assumptions for school improvement.

FRAMING THE CHALLENGES AND THE OPPORTUNITIES

The American social experiment with universal public schooling is a never-ending one, and it is fraught with endemic conflicts and contradictions. Basic questions of purpose and responsibilities invite conflicting opinions and structural arrangements. What are the purposes of schooling? Is the provision of mental health services a primary purpose of schooling? Should teachers be involved in mental health services? What should schools not do? What population(s) should schools serve—and not serve? How much responsibility should classroom teachers assume for children's mental health? What are the accountabilities for parents and entire families? These questions drive democratic debates locally, regionally, and nationally. They suggest that initiatives aimed at expanding the boundaries of school improvement will invite controversy.

The Traditional Model of School Improvement

Standardized testing in core subject areas—operating under the guise of choice, accountability, or both—indicates how some politicians view the fundamental purposes of schooling. Similarly, the long-standing national goal to the effect that "all children should enter school ready and able to learn" suggests that the purpose of schooling is, first and foremost, learning and academic achievement.

Several main assumptions drive this line of thinking. For example, mental health needs and problems are caused by outside influences (e.g., Deschenes, Cuban, & Tyack, 2001). They are not the school's responsibility; they belong to families and community agencies. More important, schools don't cause mental health problems, and teachers are not implicated in their development and maintenance. Likewise, school climates and cultures have nothing to do with the development of mental health problems.

These assumptions make up a distinctive historical tradition. They are legacies of industrial-age thinking and institutional designs. Mirroring factories and their assembly lines, specialized schools, social service agencies, mental health agencies, health agencies, and other public systems have historical trajectories as specialized, single-issue, and categorical systems. In this framework, mental health needs and problems are assigned to mental health providers, delinquency-related needs are assigned to juvenile justice specialists, educators are assigned learning and academic achievement needs, and so on.

Little wonder that the dominant model of school improvement is essentially a building centered, or walled-in, model, led by educators and site-based teams. For example, learning and academic achievement are walled in; other needs and problems, especially mental health priorities, often are walled out.

This walled-in model for school improvement is flawed, especially in public schools serving vulnerable children and youths challenged by poverty and its correlates. For example, children and youths spend only 9% to 15% of their nonsleeping hours in schools (e.g., Gardner, 1999), and even with "academic press" initiatives aimed at maximizing academic learning time, approximately 25% of time in school is not devoted to academic learning. As research grows on the influence of family, peer, and neighborhood characteristics on children's learning, academic achievement, success in school, mental health, and overall well-being (e.g., Honig, Kahne, & McLaughlin, 2001), the limitations of the conventional school improvement model become even more apparent.

THE MENTAL HEALTH SYSTEM

Mental health care is distributed across many settings and systems today, including primary care, juvenile justice systems, foster care, and child welfare systems in addition to schools (U.S. Public Health Service, 2000). Mental health services in all sectors tend to be underused. One reason is the stigma associated with seeking and receiving services. Another is the lack of coordinated, coherent systems that ensure access, quality, improved outcomes, and, where needed, integration with other systems. Yet another is the quality of treatment needy people receive from service providers. A fourth is the absence of coherent, integrated systems designed in relation to population needs.

Problems with traditional models of mental health care delivery spill over into schools. These models, which emphasize identification, diagnosis, and treatment of disorders, may further stigmatize and set apart students with mental health needs. Preventive approaches are needed, ones that emphasize the importance of designing holistic, future-oriented, supportive environments for children and youths. Here, mental health *promotion* rather than *treatment* becomes the primary emphasis.

Classifying Mental Health Needs to Catalyze New Models for School Improvement

Thanks to recent research, it's possible to classify mental health needs and problems. Risking oversimplification, a three-part categorization is useful, and it paves the way for comprehensive service system planning.

The first kind of need or problem is associated with, or caused by, forces and factors outside the school. Schools are merely one of the places, and a convenient one at that, where the problems and needs are expressed. Gang violence, and the mental health issues it implicates (e.g., fear, anxiety, insecurity), represents an obvious example. Substance abuse and co-occurring depression are another.

School-induced mental health needs and problems compose the second category. Many of these needs and problems stem from the social organization of schools, including the school's climate, culture, and practices. Examples include tracking students, disproportionate suspensions and expulsions for students of color (e.g., Ferguson, 2000), and poor and minority students' lack of access to classes for the gifted and talented. Examples of mental health challenges stemming from these practices include depression; a lack of efficacy, resulting in learned hopelessness; aggressive and violent personalities; despair; and a lack of attachment to peers and little sense of connection to school, even alienation from schools and other mainstream institutions (e.g., Wyn & Dwyer, 2000).

Mental health needs and challenges that stem from the interactions among schools, peer groups, families, neighborhoods, and neighborhood community agencies make up the third category. So-called "cross-over kids" and "multisystem families" are an obvious example (e.g., Lawson & Sailor, 2000; Wandersman & Florin, 2003). These kids and families have co-occurring and interlocking needs (e.g., substance abuse, delinquency, mental health, child abuse and neglect, violent behavior, and problems at school) that require simultaneous, coordinated interventions aimed at multiple correlates and causes.

SCHOOL-BASED AND SCHOOL-LINKED SERVICE PLANNING

Services and service system planning may proceed in relation to this simple categorization. This planning requires an inventory of school-owned and operated and community-owned and operated mental health services and resources (e.g., Adelman & Taylor, 2000a, 2000b), ensuring maximization of resources and preventing duplication and fragmentation. It also involves a continuum of services spanning prevention, early intervention, and crisis-response models (e.g., Biglan, Mrazek, Carnine, & Flay, 2003).

School-based mental health planning also needs to be integrated with individual school improvement plans. For example, the National Association of School Psychologists (2004) suggests that children's mental health should be supported through interventions on three distinct levels. The *environmental level* emphasizes the creation of a healthy, supportive school climate, such as was done with Adam in Chapter 4. The *programmatic level* involves curricular and educational programming addressing specific mental health issues, such as the Good Behavior Game discussed in Chapter 10. The *individual level* focuses on the provision of mental health interventions to students with identified needs, as occurred with Melissa in Chapter 5.

Where the multiple, co-occurring needs of children and their families are evident, and several systems are involved, walled-in school mental health systems tend to be insufficient and ineffective. School-family-community connections and service systems are needed. They bring opportunities to expand the boundaries of school improvement at the same time that they pave the way for comprehensive, community-based systems of care in which no person, adult or child, is left behind (Lawson, 2001; Wandersman & Florin, 2003). These comprehensive systems typically involve intermediary organizations that act as bridging mechanisms between schools and communities. They relieve educators and schools of the burdens of administering complex systems, and they help prevent fragmented, duplicated services involving schools and community agencies.

Children With Emotional and Behavioral Disorders

Children with emotional and behavioral disorders (EBDs) illustrate the need for integrated school-based and school-linked systems. They also illustrate the need for classroom-focused interventions in which the boundary between pedagogy and mental health services is at least blurred, if not erased (Mooney, Kline, & Davoren, 1999). For example, children's mental health challenges often provide ripe opportunities for engaging pedagogy, and their needs for socioemotional learning and development can be integrated with academic instruction (e.g., Greenberg et al., 2003).

Status of Children and Youth With Emotional and Behavioral Disorders

EBDs can manifest as externalized problems (e.g., opposition, defiance, aggression) or internalized problems (e.g., depression, anxiety, withdrawal) (e.g., Kauffman, 2001). Approximately 5% of all school-age children and youths have the kind of EBD that constitutes an extreme functional impairment. Eleven percent, or about 1 in 10, have an EBD that manifests as a significant functional impairment (U.S. Department of Health and Human Services, 1999). In communities with high rates of poverty, the percentage of young children at risk for EBD swells to 25% (e.g., Kaiser, Hancock, Cai, Foster, & Hester, 2000).

Of all young children with externalizing disorders, 75% predictably progress from lesser kinds of unacceptable behavior (e.g., disobedience, temper tantrums) to more severe kinds such as fighting, and stealing (e.g., Reid, 1993). Left without effective interventions, these children and youths eventually exhibit highly troubling, law-violating, antisocial behavior (Patterson, Reid, & Dishion, 1992). When these externalizing behavior problems co-occur with language, cognitive, and achievement problems, as they often do, the likelihood of troubling outcomes increases (e.g., Dodge et al., 2003).

Early identification and intervention are vital. In the words of Walker, Colvin, and Ramsey (1995), "If antisocial behavior is not changed by third grade, it should be treated as a chronic condition like diabetes. That is, it cannot be cured, but managed with the appropriate supports and continuing intervention" (p. 6). In other words, like internalizing behaviors such as depression, anxiety, and withdrawal, these externalizing behaviors tend to be stable once they are established (e.g., Kauffman, 2001).

Influence on Learning, Academic Achievement, and School Improvement

Children and youths with EBDs often have co-occurring needs such as cognitive impairments, social incompetence and rejection, and language deficits. When their academic achievement is assessed, they tend to be a year or more below grade level in math, reading, and most other content areas. Almost half have grade point averages below 1.75 (4.0 being the top), and they tend to fail one or more courses each year (Kauffman, 2001). More than half drop out of school, nearly double the dropout rate found in the general student population (U.S. Department of Education, 2001). Nearly half fail to engage in further education, vocational training, or employment after exiting school. Those who do work typically do so part-time for minimum wage. More than half of all students with EBDs are arrested within 3 to 5 years of leaving school; among youths with an EBD who drop out of school, the figure exceeds 70% (Wagner, Blackorby, Cameto, Hebbler, & Newman, 1993). Students with EBDs, it seems, are getting left behind.

In brief, without expanded models for school improvement that incorporate interventions and services for them, children and youths with EBD will likely encounter educational, social, vocational, and intrapersonal problems throughout adolescence. Because these problems will continue into adulthood (Kazdin, 1995), kids with EBDs will not enjoy the benefits of a solid education, positive physical and mental health, and overall well-being.

A CRITIQUE OF EXISTING SYSTEMS AND MODELS

The disconcerting status of students with EBDs is at least partially attributable to educators' and other professionals' widespread failure to consistently apply evidence-based best practices (Chesapeake Institute, 1994). Classroom practices and overall school improvement models also are implicated.

For example, Knitzer, Steinberg, and Fleisch (1990) criticized "the curriculum of control" (p. 148). Two main features of this control curriculum are (a) the suppression of student behavior through an exclusive reliance on aversive consequences and (b) the complete absence of a motivating academic curriculum and sound instructional practices.

Other researchers have documented problematic classroom practices. For example, interactions between teachers and students with EBDs are rarely positive; they consist mostly of teacher reprimands for inappropriate behavior. Teachers rarely praise or reinforce appropriate behavior. Perhaps only 30% of all teacher-student interactions occur in the context of academic instruction!

Apparently, the more significant the student's behavioral problem, the less likely it is that the teacher will offer academic instruction to the student. In fact, teachers inadvertently may actually strengthen and stabilize the very student behaviors they find so troubling (Van Acker, Grant, & Henry, 1996). *This finding suggests that changing the behavior of teachers, parents, and other adults in the lives of EBD children should be as much of a priority as changing the children's behavior.* Here, then, is one target for expanded models for school improvement. It involves school-family-community partnerships that expand the boundaries of school improvement so that no child may be left behind.

Other gaps and needs are easily documented. For example, most schools serving students with EBDs count some combination of counseling, therapy, life skills, occupational therapy, and individualized tutoring among the services they provide. However, nearly half of all students with EBDs receive none of these services (Marder, 1992). Of all students with EBDs, 66% receive no specific counseling or therapy services. Even fewer EBD students receive tutoring (15%) and life skills (20%) services. And only 17% of these students received multiple types of services from their schools.

Gaps in the Community and the Need for Linkages With Schools

Students with EBDs and their families often present needs that bring them into contact with a variety of service providers in the community (Quinn & Epstein, 1996). But just as best practices are often not evident in schools, service availability and quality has also been found lacking within mental health (Friesen & Poertner, 1995), child welfare (Trupin, Tarico, Low, Jemelka, & McClellan, 1993), and juvenile justice (MacIntyre, 1993) systems.

Furthermore, when families simultaneously use multiple sources of care, the helping professionals providing that care often fail to collaborate and involve families effectively (Stroul & Friedman, 1996). For example, in one study, only 25% of schools serving students with EBDs averaged at least monthly contact with other community-based agencies, and the vast majority of schools reported only a couple of contacts per year or less (Marder, 1992).

UNDERUSE OF TESTED MODELS AND STRATEGIES

The status of services for students with EBDs is especially troubling because compelling evidence exists to support the efficacy of numerous approaches to intervention for these children and youths and their families. In other words, the lifetime of pervasive, complex, and chronic difficulties associated with EBDs might be considerably ameliorated if only professionals would use the available, evidence-based models and strategies.

Evidence-based interventions for students with EBDs are grounded in a number of perspectives, including behavioral, cognitive-behavioral, social learning, and social ecology theories. Detailed explication of various interventions associated with each theoretical perspective is beyond the scope of this chapter. Instead, a broad overview of some empirically based approaches is provided.

Walker and colleagues (1996) articulated a state-of-the-art behavior management model composed of three tiers: (a) universal interventions for all students, (b) individualized interventions for students distinctly at risk for emotional and behavioral problems, and (c) comprehensive interventions for students with severe and chronic emotional and behavioral problems. Each tier is briefly described below.

Tier 1: Universal Interventions

Universal interventions are prevention oriented, and they draw on the principles of applied behavior analysis. Interventions in this category include strategies all teachers should use with all students. These interventions are designed to ensure that students' disruptive behaviors are not occasioned or maintained by teacher practices and organizational structures (Lewis & Sugai, 1999).

These interventions are implemented in a well-defined sequence, as listed here:

1. Schoolwide normative and behavioral expectations are defined explicitly by staff and, in some cases, students.
2. Then, these expectations are taught to students through direct instruction.
3. Subsequently, teachers model and students practice. Both positive and negative examples of rule-following behavior are provided to ensure that students' understanding is explicit.
4. Then, as students meet behavioral expectations, they are systematically reinforced. When they do not, they are systematically corrected while any reinforcement available for the inappropriate behavior is minimized.
5. Data are collected to document the intervention's effectiveness and make prescriptive changes where needed. (Horner, Sugai, Todd, & Lewis-Palmer, 2000)

Tier 2: Individualized Interventions

Individualized interventions are for those students who do not respond sufficiently when provided with universal interventions (Walker et al., 1996). Here, there is empirical support for a plethora of individualized interventions, including contingency contracts, differential reinforcement procedures, shaping and fading procedures, time-out, and response-cost (Dunlap & Childs, 1996). These individualized interventions depend on theoretically sound hypotheses regarding the inappropriate behavior's causes (Sugai, Lewis-Palmer, & Hagen-Burke, 2000). These causes are determined through two formal, related procedures—functional behavioral assessment and the ensuing provision of positive behavioral supports (Sugai & Horner, 2000).

O'Neill, Horner, Albin, Storey, and Sprague (1990) identified the following salient outcomes of functional behavioral assessment (FBA):

- An operational definition of the problem behavior(s)
- Identification of environmental variables that predict occurrence and nonoccurrence of targeted behavior(s)
- Identification of environmental consequences that maintain the behavior

- Development of hypotheses regarding the behavior's function
- Development of summary statements that describe specific behaviors' relationship to environmental variables that occasion and maintain occurrence
- Articulation of a competing pathway model for teaching new, prosocial, replacement behaviors

Horner et al. (2000) identified the following key aspects of well-constructed positive behavior support (PBS) plans:

- Understand the particular ways in which the target child views the world—that is, his or her idiosyncratic perceptions and interpretations of surrounding events that may be related to an existing disability.
- Carefully attend to the environmental conditions the FBA identified as predictors of targeted behavior (in order to prevent it).
- Systematically teach positive replacement behaviors for those behaviors targeted for suppression, using both direct and embedded instruction.
- Systematically reinforce the replacement behavior while carefully withholding reinforcement for targeted undesirable behavior.
- Stay well prepared for particularly intense episodes of acting-out behavior. (Future occurrences of problem behavior, equal in intensity to the most severe previous occurrences, should be anticipated and systematic responses planned.)

To implement these twin strategies, teachers need a "mental flowchart" consisting of their preferred cognitive and behavioral strategies. In other words, teachers develop a contingency format consisting of "if the child does this, here's what I'll do to secure the outcome we need." Of course, this means that teachers and other adults in the child's life need to understand both FBA and PBS, and they need to be fluent with the dialogue and skillful with the behaviors that make up each decision point in the flowchart.

Recently, researchers have focused anew on both the cognitive and affective functioning of students with EBDs. For example, Fraser, Day, Galinsky, Hodges, and Smokowski (2004) have incorporated into their Making Choices intervention an understanding of the idiosyncratic ways in which troubled students process information, regulate emotion, and allocate behavior. In addition to sound application of behavioral theory, the inclusion of cognitive- and affective-behavioral components helps students perceive and interpret social cues more objectively, gain conscious awareness of their emotional states, use self-talk to control impulsive behavior, and choose solutions that make things better rather than worse. The results are promising. Children who participate in the program display greater social competence, more social interaction, greater cognitive concentration, and less oppositional behavior.

Tier 3: Comprehensive Interventions

Comprehensive interventions are designed for so-called deep-end and multisystem children and youths. These are the kids with the most severe, complex, and challenging behavioral problems. These problems place the student at risk for restrictive placement outside the school, home, and community (Quinn & Epstein, 1996).

Wraparound services is the term frequently used to capture the type of support these students and families require. A service team consisting of school and community agency professionals and, ideally, family members develops the wraparound service plan. The plan entails bringing intensive, integrated services to the child or youth (rather than sending the child or youth to the separate service providers in a one-at-a-time sequence). The two aims are to remove the threats posed by the child's extremely troubling behavior and to do so without removing the child from the school and the home (i.e., institutionalizing the child). Wraparound takes into account the child and family ecology and is aimed at developing consistency and coherence across the boundaries of schools, families, community agencies, and neighborhoods. Ideally, it is family centered; parents and other family members are partners in service planning, delivery, and evaluation (e.g., Briar-Lawson & Drews, 1998).

These wraparound services are integral to school improvement when teachers are involved in the service planning and when the service planning is integrated with instruction in the classroom (e.g., Lawson & Briar-Lawson, 1997). When teachers are not involved, serious gaps result. In fact, it's not unusual to have teachers contradict what the other adults on the service team have worked so hard to establish. Teachers are not to blame here. The problem stems from the view that EBD-related needs are the province of service providers, that teachers are not responsible for them, and that school improvement need not focus on wraparound strategies for EBD students.

TOWARD MENTAL HEALTH-ENHANCING SCHOOL CLIMATES

Schools have a responsibility to provide safe, mental health-enhancing environments. Innovative concepts such as positive psychology (e.g., Seligman, 2002) are now being applied to educational settings, and they are associated with an emergent shift in the paradigm for working with children (and their families) in schools.

This shift is also grounded in the notion that schools need to adopt elements of a public health approach. This public health approach is proactive; it focuses on prevention and protective factors in lieu of merely focusing on risks and responding to crises (e.g., McLoughlin & Kubick, 2004; Terjesen, Jacofsky, Froh, & DiGiuseppe, 2004). And it emphasizes organizational and neighborhood environments in addition to the long-standing emphasis on the behaviors, attitudes, and norms of individuals and groups.

CONCEPTUALIZING THE SCHOOL CLIMATE

When their schooling finally ends, children will have spent years of their lives in classrooms and in schools. Like the messages kids receive from their family systems, all children receive powerful, loud messages about themselves, others, and the world around them from their classroom and school environments. These environments, the tone they set, and the messages and metamessages they convey implicate the school's climate. A health-enhancing, supportive school climate is vital to their education, health, and well-being, and it is a major determinant of whether children and youth develop a sense of connection to school. A sense of connection to school is vital to educational outcomes, healthy development, and overall well-being (McNeely, Nonnemaker, & Blum, 2002).

School climate, broadly defined, includes social and behavioral norms, patterns of communication, role expectations, and approaches to discipline (Reinke & Herman, 2002). Although climate is related to school culture, it is also analytically distinct. Climate is a sociopsychological construct. It affects how people feel, perceive, and behave.

The Importance of School Climate

When the school's climate is a problem, academic performance declines (e.g., Rutter et al., 1997), school violence (including bullying) may occur (e.g., Hunt et al., 2002), antisocial behavior may be cultivated (e.g., McEvoy & Welker, 2000), children's sense of connection to school declines (e.g., McNeely et al., 2002), and school dropouts may result (e.g., Persaud & Madak, 1992). School climate thus is a priority for expanded models for school improvement.

Surprisingly, direct links between school climate, mental health, and wellness promotion have received scant attention in the research literature. Traditional approaches to mental health in the schools have predominantly focused on classroom behavior management, problem identification, assessment, and intervention.

One reason for this neglect is that a medical model has long held sway in schools; the focus has been on individuals and programs, usually at the expense of school climate and surrounding social environments. This medical model has been reinforced by the advent of pharmacological interventions in the area of children's mental health. Arguably, it's easier to medicate a child than it is to create health-enhancing environments, especially when mental health gets short shrift in the overall health system and in school systems.

Toward a Preventive, Organizationwide Approach

Viewed from a preventive framework instead of the more deterministic and disease-based medical model, schools represent an exciting opportunity for the creation of positive spaces and environments that can have long-lasting protective impacts on the development of children's worldviews about physical health, wellness, and mental health. Under such a model, the complete school environment becomes the primary source of mental health support and promotion. If such a proactive approach is taken, mental health in school settings can truly become about mental *health* rather than the "Band-Aid" approach of addressing problems only as they arise and become unmanageable in the classroom. Teachers, principals, and other staff members trained in mental health promotion could construct school climates characterized by normative views of mental health, reduction of stigma, and the positive promotion of positive characteristics such as self-awareness, hope, optimism, and efficacy, both individual and collective. Everyone in the school, not just the children, would benefit, and so would families and other neighborhood residents.

Targeting Peer Relations as One Aspect of Climate

Peer-based interventions include mentoring, mediation, support groups, counseling, and befriending. These and other creative interventions have been tried in varied school settings that emphasize the promotion of positive mental health among students. One such program, the *Peer Navigator* Model in Española Valley, New Mexico, uses social work systems theory to train peer volunteers—high school students able to serve as role models, mentors, and advocates for other students (New Mexico School Mental Health Initiative, 2004). Program elements include conflict mediation, mental health awareness education, suicide prevention, substance use services, advocacy, and programming on interpersonal violence.

Such programs use theoretical concepts of peer support, which have been linked to positive impacts for youth (e.g., Cowe, Naylor, Chauhan, & Smith, 2002). Drawing directly from established models of peer support and mutual aid in adult mental health, the preliminary documentation of success of these approaches suggests that supportive and reciprocal peer relationships play a paramount role in buffering students from the effects of school-related distress. Peer-based initiatives and interventions should thus be considered in the creation of positive social learning environments within schools.

From Health and Wellness Programs to Strong Normative Settings

Schools seeking to establish positive environments promoting mental health have tremendous room for creativity and innovation. Other organizational interventions include school-based wellness centers and healthy school environment initiatives. Some of these are dovetailed with state and national initiatives from comprehensive health education and promotion, especially those fostered by the Centers for Disease Control and Prevention. Yet these special programs are only a small part of a larger climate change.

Special programs must be accompanied by concurrent shifts in all levels of the school. Simply stated, the school's norms, principles, values, and desired behaviors—involving not just students but also all the adults—are determined by consensus, and everyone accepts shared responsibility for demonstrating and reinforcing them. Typically, the principal serves as the facilitative leader for this consensus-oriented work, and it can be dovetailed with the special efforts to serve EBD students, as identified earlier. In this way, the school, through its climate, becomes what some researchers call "a strong normative setting" (Coleman, 1990). Normative settings emphasizing positive mental health, while also normalizing the seeking of support, can radically change how students and their families view mental health problems.

It's not an exaggeration to claim that as the climate changes, the entire school changes. Specifying characteristics of "positive" school climates (i.e., strong normative settings) is crucial. The following list includes some of the definitive features. Ideally, these features are modeled and stewarded routinely by all the adults and students in the school. When they are, they tend to be contagious. And when newcomers join the school, they are "inoculated" with the same norms, attitudes, and behaviors. A positive school climate does the following:

- Fosters membership and feelings of belonging, which promote self-worth and dignity and inspire efforts for self-improvement
- Develops, promotes, and reinforces strength-based, nonstigmatizing language
- Disavows and sanctions antidemocratic policies and practices, especially repression and discrimination
- Promotes understanding and maximizes opportunities for the full realization of each member's potential
- Builds individual and collective efficacy among students, educators, parents, and social and health service providers
- Encourages diversity and emphasizes its strengths, assets, and opportunities

- Rejects and prevents the isolation and marginalization of individuals and groups
- Provides regular occasions for positive interactions among diverse individuals and groups
- Communicates routinely high expectations for everyone in the school community
- Promotes strengths-based, solution-focused cooperative inquiry; mutual responsibility; social competency; and democratic participation in decision making
- Promotes open discussions and strategic planning focused on mental health needs of students, staff members, and parents, ensuring ready access, quality, and improved outcomes from mental health services
- Promotes norms of caring and concern for the dignity and worth of every person in a safe, secure school environment
- Provides conflict resolution leaders and mechanisms aimed at preventing violence
- Empowers everyone to be a steward of health, mental health, and educational development
- Ensures that rules and regulations are purposeful, vital, and flexible
- Emphasizes that mistakes are opportunities for learning, development, and improvement
- Promotes self-determination, social responsibility, and empowerment among all members
- Emphasizes solid alliances with the multiple stakeholders in the community, including wraparound services and strategic school-community-university partnerships

Even more ideally, these same norms and behaviors are adopted by families and community organizations that serve a school's children and families. In brief, normative settings that promote positive mental health, wellness, and positive social functioning can provide the supportive environments necessary for improved child, family, school, and community level outcomes. These settings, a key feature of positive school climates, are one of the linchpins for connecting mental health services and school improvement.

SUMMARY

When the results of national assessments were published in 2004, it was expected that nearly half the nation's public schools would be categorized as "underperforming" (Popham, 2004). Such findings do not bode well for anyone associated with schools. No doubt there will be another round of finger-pointing and blaming dynamics aimed primarily at teachers, principals, and parents. Blaming people, especially teachers, under the guise of accountability, fundamentally misses the point.

Arguably, when so many schools fail to meet performance expectations, systems issues are implicated, including the kinds of systems issues identified in this chapter (e.g., schools as stand-alone organizations). Arguably, industrial-age schools with egg-crate classrooms in which teachers work alone, indeed in isolation from mental health services and providers, simply cannot yield the results everyone expects, wants, and needs. Expanded models of school improvement are needed, especially models that integrate mental health systems and services with school improvement. These expanded, integrated improvement models require new assumptions and strategies.

The good news is that there is solid evidence to support them. Moreover, progress is under way in the United States in developing effective models.

Although this chapter did not and could not provide all the salient details, ideally, it has achieved its aim—to stimulate action-oriented planning dialogue in relation to urgent needs and exciting possibilities. Clearly, the work of expanding the boundaries of school improvement promises to benefit everyone—children, teachers, parents, service providers, and community members. Not just another special project destined to become "this year's new thing," this work promises to reform and integrate school and mental health systems. As this work is done, schools and mental health systems, individually and in combination, will be ready to meet the emergent needs of 21st-century America, especially its rapidly changing demographic, economic, social, political, and global realities.

DISCUSSION QUESTIONS

1. Do the ideas presented in this chapter fit in with your ideas on the purpose of school, or do you think that the ideas expressed here go beyond what should be expected from the educational system?
2. Do you think that the school can induce mental health needs? What are some things that educators can do to avoid this?
3. What responsibilities do the schools have to meet the needs of students with EBDs and mental health needs?
4. Reflect on the material that you read in the previous chapters. Do you think that schools are taking a leadership role in confronting the needs of students with mental health challenges? What agency, if not the schools, should be leading the charge to meet the challenge of students with mental health and emotional needs?

FOR ADDITIONAL HELP

	Organization	*Web Address*	*Description*
Mental Health Needs and Problems as Opportunities for Expanding the Boundaries of School Improvement	North Central Regional Educational Laboratory/Pathways to School Improvement	www.ncrel.org/sdrs	Pathways to School Improvement synthesizes research and best practices for educators involved in school improvement.
	Tools for School-Improvement Planning/Annenberg Institute for School Reform	www.annenberginstitute.org/tools	The Tools for School-Improvement Planning Web site contains observation protocols, focus group samples and questions, surveys, questionnaires, and other techniques to help you examine your specific school improvement concerns.

REFERENCES

Adelman, H., & Taylor, L. (2000a). Looking at school health and school reform policy through the lens of addressing barriers to learning. *Children's Services: Social Policy, Research, & Practice, 3*(2), 117–132.

Adelman, H., & Taylor, L. (2000b). Moving prevention from the fringes into the fabric of school improvement. *Journal of Educational and Psychological Consultation, 11*(1), 7–36.

Biglan, A., Mrazek, P., Carnine, D., & Flay, B. (2003). The integration of research and practice in the prevention of problem youth behaviors. *American Psychologist, 58*, 433–440.

Briar-Lawson, K., & Drews, J. (1998). School-based service integration: Lessons learned and future challenges. In D. van Veen, C. Day, & G. Walraven (Eds.), *Multi-service schools: Integrated services for children and youth at risk* (pp. 49–64). Leuven/Appeldorn, The Netherlands: Garant.

Chesapeake Institute. (1994). *National agenda for achieving better results for children and youth with serious emotional disturbance*. Washington, DC: U.S. Department of Education.

Coleman, J. (1990). *Foundations of social theory*. Cambridge, MA: Harvard University Press.

Cowe, H., Naylor, P., Chauhan, L. T. P., & Smith, P. K. (2002). Knowledge, use of and attitudes towards peer support: A 2-year follow-up to the Prince's Trust survey. *Journal of Adolescence, 25*, 453–467.

Deschenes, S., Cuban, L., & Tyack, D. (2001). Mismatch: Historical perspectives on schools and students who don't fit them. *Teachers College Record, 4*, 525–547.

Dodge, K. A., Lansford, J. E., Burks, V. S., Bates, J. E., Pettit, G. S., Fontaine, R., et al. (2003). Peer rejection and social information processing factors in the development of aggressive behavior in children. *Child Development, 74,* 373–393.

Dunlap, G., & Childs, K. E. (1996). Intervention research in emotional and behavioral disorders: An analysis of studies from 1980–1993. *Behavioral Disorders, 21,* 125–136.

Ferguson, A. (2000). *Bad boys: Public schools in the making of black masculinity*. Ann Arbor: University of Michigan Press.

Fraser, M. W., Day, S. H., Galinsky, M. J., Hodges, V. G., & Smokowski, P. R. (2004). Conduct problems and peer rejection in childhood: A randomized trial of the Making Choices and Strong Families programs. *Research on Social Work Practice, 14,* 313–324.

Friesen, B. J., & Poertner, J. (1995). *From case management to service coordination for children with emotional, behavioral, or mental disorders: Building on family strengths*. Baltimore, MD: Brookes.

Gardner, S. (1999). *Beyond collaboration to results: Hard choices in the future of services to children and families.* Fullerton: California State University, Center for Collaboration for Children.

Greenberg, M., Weissberg, R., O'Brien, M., Zins, J., Fredericks, L., Resnik, H., et al. (2003). Enhancing school-based prevention and youth development through coordinated social, emotional, and academic learning. *American Psychologist, 58*, 466–474.

Honig, M., Kahne, J., & McLaughlin, M. (2001). School-community connections: Strengthening opportunity to learn and opportunity to teach. In V. Richardson (Ed.), *Fourth handbook of research on teaching* (pp. 998–1028). New York: Macmillan.

Horner, R. H., Sugai, G., Todd, A. W., & Lewis-Palmer, T. (2000). Elements of behavior support plans: A technical brief. *Exceptionality, 8*, 205–216.

Hunt, M. H., Meyers, J., Davies, G., Meyers, M., Rogers Grogg, K., & Neel, J. (2002). A comprehensive needs assessment to facilitate prevention of school dropout and violence. *Psychology in the Schools, 39*(4), 399–416.

Kaiser, A. P., Hancock, T. B., Cai, X., Foster, E. M., & Hester, P. P. (2000). Parent reported behavioral problems and language delays in boys and girls enrolled in Head Start classrooms. *Behavioral Disorders, 26,* 26–41.

Kauffman, J. M. (2001). *Characteristics of behavior disorders of children and youth* (7th ed.). Columbus, OH: Merrill.

Kazdin, A. E. (1995). *Conduct disorders in childhood and adolescence* (2nd ed.). Thousand Oaks, CA: Sage.

Knitzer, J., Steinberg, Z., & Fleisch, B. (1990). *At the schoolhouse door: An examination of programs and policies for children with behavioral and emotional problems*. New York: Bank Street College of Education.

Lawson, H. (2001). Back to the future: New century professionalism and collaborative leadership for comprehensive, community-based systems of care. In A. Sallee, H. Lawson, & K. Briar-Lawson (Eds.), *Innovative practices with vulnerable children and families* (pp. 393–419). Dubuque, IA: Eddie Bowers.

Lawson, H., & Briar-Lawson, K. (1997). *Connecting the dots: Progress toward the integration of school reform, school-linked services, parent involvement, and community schools*. Oxford, OH: Danforth Foundation and the Institute for Educational Renewal at Miami University.

Lawson, H., & Sailor, W. (2000). Integrating services, collaborating, and developing connections with schools. *Focus on Exceptional Children*, *33*(2), 1–22.

Lewis, T. J., & Sugai, G. (1999). Effective behavior support: A systems approach to proactive school-wide management. *Focus on Exceptional Children, 31*(6), 1–24.

MacIntyre, T. (1993). Behaviorally disordered youth in correctional settings: Prevalence, programming, and teacher training. *Behavioral Disorders, 18*(3), 167–176.

Marder, C. (1992). *Secondary school students classified as serious emotionally disturbed: How are they being served?* Menlo Park, CA: SRI International.

McEvoy, A., & Welker, R. (2000). Antisocial behavior, academic failure, and school climate: A critical review. *Journal of Emotional and Behavioral Disorders, 8*, 130–140.

McLoughlin, C. S., & Kubick, R. J. (2004). Wellness promotion as a life-long endeavor: Promoting and developing life competencies from childhood. *Psychology in the Schools, 41*(1), 131–141.

McNeely, C., Nonnemaker, J., & Blum, R. (2002). Promoting school connectedness: Evidence from the national longitudinal study of adolescent health. *Journal of School Health*, *72*(4), 138–146.

Mooney, J., Kline, P., & Davoren, J. (1999). Collaborative interventions: Promoting psychosocial competence and academic achievement. In R. Tourse & J. Mooney (Eds.), *Collaborative practice: School and human service partnerships* (pp. 105–135). Westport, CT: Praeger.

National Association of School Psychologists. (2004). *Position statement on mental health services in the schools*. Retrieved May 14, 2004, www.nasponline.org/information/pospaper_mhs.html

New Mexico School Mental Health Initiative. (2004). *Peer navigators: A youth-focused systems model*. Retrieved May 14, 2004, www.nmsmhi.org/programs_pn.html

O'Neill, R. E., Horner, R. H., Albin, R. A., Storey, J., & Sprague, J. (1990). *Functional analysis of problem behavior: A practical assessment guide.* Sycamore, IL: Sycamore.

Patterson, G. R., Reid, J. B., & Dishion, T. J. (1992). *Antisocial Boys*. Eugene, OR: Castalia.

Persaud, D., & Madak, P. R. (1992). Graduates and dropouts: Comparing perceptions of self, family, and school supports. *Alberta Journal of Educational Research, 38*, 235–250.

Popham, W. J. (2004). Shaping up the "no child" act: Is edge-softening really enough? *Education Week*, *23*(38), 26.

Quinn, K. P., & Epstein, M. H. (1996). Characteristics of children, youth, and families served by local interagency systems of care. In M. H. Epstein, K. Kutash, & A. Duchnowski (Eds.), *Community-based programming for children with serious emotional disturbance and their families: Research and evaluations* (pp. 81–114). Austin, TX: PRO-ED.

Reid, J. B. (1993). Prevention of conduct disorder before and after school entry: Relating interventions to developmental findings. *Development and Psychopathology, 5,* 311–319.

Reinke, W. M., & Herman, K. C. (2002). Creating school environments that deter antisocial behaviors in youth. *Psychology in the Schools, 39*(5), 549–559.

Rutter, M., Maughan, B., Meyer, J., Pickles, A., Silberg, J., Simonoff, E., et al. (1997). Heterogeneity of antisocial behavior: Causes, continuities, and consequences. In D. W. Osgood (Ed.), *Motivation and delinquency* (pp. 45–118). Lincoln: University of Nebraska Press.

Seligman, M. P. (2002). *Authentic happiness: Using the new positive psychology to realize your potential for lasting fulfillment.* New York: Free Press.

Stroul, B. A., & Friedman, R. M. (1996). The system of care philosophy. In B. A. Stroul (Ed.), *Children's mental health: Creating systems of care in a changing society* (pp. 3–22). Baltimore, MD: Paul H. Brookes.

Sugai, G., & Horner, R. H. (2000). Including the functional behavioral assessment technology in schools. *Exceptionality, 8*, 145–148.

Sugai, G., Lewis-Palmer, T., & Hagan-Burke, S. (2000). Overview of functional behavioral assessment. *Exceptionality, 8*, 149–160.

Terjesen, M. D., Jacofsky, M., Froh, J., & DiGiuseppe, R. (2004). Integrating positive psychology into schools: Implications for practice. *Psychology in the Schools, 41*(1), 163–172.

Trupin, E. W., Tarico, V. S., Low, B. P., Jemelka, R., & McClellan, J. (1993). Children on child protective service caseloads: Prevalence and nature of serious emotional disturbance. *Child Abuse & Neglect, 17*, 345–355.

U.S. Department of Education. (2001). *Twenty-third annual report to Congress on the implementation of Public Law 94-142*. Washington, DC: Government Printing Office.

U.S. Department of Health and Human Services. (1999). *Mental health: A report of the Surgeon General.* Retrieved April 21, 2004, from www.mentalhealth.org/features/surgeongeneralreport/chapter3/sec1.asp

U.S. Public Health Service. (2000). *Report of the Surgeon General's Conference on Children's Mental Health: A national action agenda.* Washington, DC: Department of Health and Human Services.

Van Acker, R., Grant, S. H., & Henry, D. (1996). Teacher and student behavior as a function of risk for aggression. *Education and Treatment of Children, 19,* 316–334.

Wagner, M., Blackorby, J., Cameto, R., Hebbler, K., & Newman, L. (1993). *Influences in postschool outcomes of youth with disabilities: The third comprehensive report from the National Longitudinal Transition Study of Special Education Students*. Menlo Park, CA: SRI International.

Walker, H. M., Colvin, G., & Ramsey, E. (1995). *Antisocial behavior in school: Strategies and best practices*. Pacific Grove, CA: Brooks/Cole.

Walker, H. M., Horner, R. H., Sugai, G., Bullis, M., Sprague, J. R., Bricker, D., et al. (1996). Integrated approaches to preventing antisocial behavior patterns among school-age children and youth. *Journal of Emotional and Behavioral Disorders, 4,* 194–209.

Wandersman, A., & Florin, P. (2003). Community intervention and effective prevention. *American Psychologist, 58*, 441–448.

Wyn, J., & Dwyer, P. (2000). New patterns of youth in transition. *International Social Science Journal, 164*, 147–160.

Glossary

acculturation: the process of people adopting behaviors and customs of another culture.

Anorexia Nervosa: an eating disorder that involves the refusal to maintain body weight at or above a minimally normal weight for age and height, the intense fear of gaining weight or becoming fat even though underweight, a disturbance in the way one perceives one's body weight or shape, and the interruption of menstrual cycles.

antecedent events: events that precede certain actions. Presenting an antecedent stimulus previously correlated with reinforcement will evoke behavior; presenting an antecedent stimulus previously correlated with punishment will suppress behavior.

applied behavior analysis: the engineering aspect of behaviorology; behavior-change technology derived from well-established experimental analyses of socially significant behavior.

aversive stimuli: stimuli that are perceived as noxious or unpleasant.

behavior intervention plan (BIP): a written plan that describes a behavioral intervention designed to correct a problem behavior. The aim of a BIP is to replace problem behavior with equally effective appropriate behavior.

behavior rating scales: instruments designed to measure behavior. Professionals and parents respond to items that describe specific behaviors of the subject. Some scales have subscales that indicate specific behavioral problem categories (e.g., hyperactivity).

behaviorology: the natural science of contingent relations between behavior and other events. It excludes accounts of behavior based on notions of a personal inner agency such as ego, self, or similar trait-type psychological concepts.

best practice: in education, the most current, practical, and evidence-based methods for working with students. Practices are not classified as "best practices" without substantial research support, although the amount of research necessary to be considered "substantial" is a matter of ongoing debate.

Bipolar Disorder: a mood disorder often characterized by recurrent, alternating episodes of depression and mania. Sometimes referred to as manic depression.

body mass index: a statistic used to ascertain if someone's weight is appropriate for his or her height. It is usually calculated by taking one's height in inches, dividing it by weight in pounds squared, and multiplying it by 703.

Bulimia Nervosa: an eating disorder that involves recurrent episodes of binge eating; recurrent inappropriate compensatory behavior to prevent weight gain, such as self-induced vomiting; misuse of laxatives, diuretics, enemas, and other medications; fasting; excessive exercise; and self-evaluation that is unduly influenced by body shape and weight.

child maltreatment: an umbrella term that some professionals in the field prefer that includes any form of mistreatment of a child that results in nonaccidental harm. This term could be used interchangeably with the term *child abuse.*

child protective services (CPS): the common term applied to state organizations substantiating reports of child maltreatment in adherence to individual state laws and policies.

coercive exchanges: interactions in which one person attempts to dominate another by force, such as through threatening, yelling, or aggression. Coercive exchanges between children and their parents maintain and exacerbate the development of disruptive and antisocial behaviors.

communication: the process of exchanging ideas, information, needs, and desires. The exchange requires a sender(s) and a receiver(s).

comorbid: specifically, occurring simultaneously. For example, conduct disorders are commonly comorbid with Attention Deficit Hyperactivity Disorder.

comorbidity: the existence of two or more illnesses in an individual at the same time.

consequences: *postcedent events* produced by one's own actions.

construct: a complex concept that represents an abstract idea that we accept as a real phenomenon. An example is "intelligence."

contingencies: functional relations between actions and other events. Some events are *antecedents* that set the occasion for certain actions. Other events are *postcedents,* events that immediately follow certain actions. When the actions produce those postcedent events, they are called consequences; those that affect subsequent behavior are either *reinforcing consequences* or *punishing consequences.*

cooperative learning: teaching strategy designed to promote learning among students by emphasizing structured groups and cooperation.

developmental disabilities: any severe, chronic disability that has an onset prior to adulthood.

discriminative stimulus: a stimlus that sets the occasion for a response to be reinforced.

double depression: a mood condition in which an individual is diagnosed with both major depressive disorder and dysthymic disorder.

Dysthymic Disorder (dysthymia): a mood disorder characterized by a chronically depressed mood. Other symptoms include feelings of guilt, hopelessness, and inadequacy; low self-esteem; fatigue; indecisiveness; and an inability to enjoy pleasurable activities.

efficacy: practices that have demonstrated efficacy are those that have been supported by research findings. Contrast with effectiveness, which describes practices supported by compelling, replicated research findings that have a great deal of support within a profession. Researchers are generally very measured in their pronouncement that a practice is effective.

emotional abuse: in simplest terms, the regular denigration of a child in a manner that can disrupt normal development.

emotional disorders: a disability group recognized by federal law that indicates the presence of specific emotional problems in children that interfere with academic performance.

empirical: based on practical research findings rather than theory.

explanatory fictions: accounts that appear to explain the behavior of concern but in reality explain nothing. For example, "Jack continues to hit other children because he is aggressive" (see *folk psychology*).

externalizing disorder: psychosocial problems in which behaviors are directed outward, often toward other people, frequently to a degree that impairs social relationships with other people.

Family Educational Rights and Privacy Act (FERPA): commonly referred to as the Buckley Amendment, this law was designed to protect the confidentiality of information regarding families and their children.

folk psychology: a "commonsense" approach expressed in ordinary talk about putatively causal psychological phenomena. Folk psychology looks at the form but not the function of the behavior (see *explanatory fictions*).

functional behavior assessment (FBA): assessment procedures that use interviews, paper-and-pencil measures, and direct observation to identify the function of a target behavior.

gateway providers: service providers who are often the first legitimate contact for those in need. Our supposition is that educators often serve as the first professionals to confront mental health needs in children.

gender dysphoria: a persistent discomfort with one's gender identity or a sense of inappropriateness in the gender role of that sex.

gender identity: the psychological sense of being male or female.

Gender Identity Disorder: a mental disorder, outlined by the *Diagnostic and Statistical Manual of Mental Disorders* (*DSM-IV-TR*), characterized by both a strong and persistent desire to be or insistence that one is the other sex and a persistent discomfort about one's assigned sex or a sense of inappropriateness in the gender role of that sex.

gender role: the public image of being male or female that a person presents to others, including the ways males and females are expected to behave within their society.

grooming: the behavioral progression by a sexual perpetrator from less intrusive to more intrusive behaviors. Through a methodical progression, the perpetrator tests the victim's readiness and trust of him or her.

hyperfocus: completely focus on some activity, sometimes prompted by a crisis or approaching deadline.

hypersomnia: a change in sleep patterns characterized by prolonged sleep or excessive daytime drowsiness.

incidence: rate of new cases of a given disorder occurring during a specific time period (usually 1 year).

inclusion: to allow people into a group; in a school setting, inclusion involves educating all children in general classrooms to the maximum extent possible.

insidious onset: occurs when symptoms of an illness manifest themselves so gradually that it is difficult to pinpoint the exact beginning of the illness.

internalizing disorder: psychosocial problems that occur "within the self." Examples of internalizing disorders would include depression and anxiety. Historically, internalizing disorders have been referred to by other names, such as "neuroses."

interpersonal space: the amount of space an individual allows between himself or herself and another person for a friendly or intimate conversation. Cultural differences and relationships dictate how close people get to each other when communicating.

intersexuals: persons having both male and female characteristics, including in varying degrees reproductive organs, secondary sexual characteristics, and sexual behavior. Also included are persons who have ambiguous sex characteristics resulting from hormone abnormalities or atypical genital formation during fetal development.

juvenile delinquency: criminal behavior committed by a juvenile. It should be noted that some behaviors, called status offenses, are criminal acts for a juvenile but not for an adult. Examples of status offenses include being ungovernable (disobedient to caregivers) and truancy.

learning disability: any of a variety of disorders that result in a marked discrepancy between overall functioning and one or more specific cognitive domains, such as reading and math.

Major Depressive Disorder: a mood disorder characterized by depressed mood; feelings of guilt, hopelessness, and worthlessness; fatigue; loss of interest in pleasurable activities; changes in appetite or sleep patterns; and thoughts of death or suicide.

mania: a mood disturbance characterized by hyperactivity, agitation, rapid and confused thinking and speaking, excessive elation, and inflated self-esteem. Generally seen as a component of Bipolar Disorder.

mastery learning: teaching approaches based on the idea that all children can learn when provided with the appropriate learning conditions in the classroom.

mental health problem: loosely defined, any emotional problem severe enough to result in a reduction in school, social, or academic performance. In this book, the term may be used interchangeably with the terms *mental disorder, psychiatric disorder, psychopathology,* and *mental illness.*

mixed state: occurs when the criteria for both a manic episode and Major Depressive Disorder (except duration) are met nearly every day for at least 1 week.

mood disorder: a category of mood disorders that includes Major Depressive Disorder, Dysthymic Disorder, and Bipolar Disorder. Sometimes referred to as depressive disorders.

mores: customs or norms of a social group.

neglect: the most common form of child maltreatment, the failure to meet the basic needs of a child.

neurotransmitters: chemicals in the brain that transmit messages from one nerve cell to another.

nonlinguistic communication: the message is delivered between the sender and receiver with symbols other than words. It may be used concurrently with verbal communication.

obesity: usually defined in terms of the body mass index [BMI]. Some researchers define obesity as having a BMI at or above the 95th percentile. It is also sometimes defined as having a BMI score above 30. Another definition of obesity is weight that is 20% above the ideal based on growth charts.

operant: a class of actions selected by their common consequent effect. In contrast to reflex-like responses, operant behavior *operates* on the environment and is said to be emitted, not elicited (i.e., so-called voluntary behavior).

Oppositional Defiant Disorder: a persistent pattern of negativistic, defiant, disobedient, and antagonistic behavior toward people in authority.

overweight: usually defined in terms of the body mass index (BMI). Some researchers define overweight as having a BMI at or above the 85th percentile based on an appropriate reference population. Others have defined overweight as having a BMI score between 25 and 30.

peer-mediated interventions: a system in which students teach other students or classmates; also referred to as *peer tutoring.*

physical abuse: the most visible form of child maltreatment, involving deliberate physical injury inflicted on a child.

postcedent events: events that follow certain actions—including *reinforcing consequences, punishing consequences,* and events that follow particular actions but are not produced by those actions (i.e., adventitious events, some of which may nonetheless affect subsequent actions).

prevalence: measure of the proportion of people in a population affected with a particular disorder during a specific time period.

protective factors: factors that make it less likely that an individual will develop a disorder by enhancing psychological resilience and increasing resistance to risk.

psychoanalytic theory: theory of the development and treatment of mental health problems that focuses on unconscious and unacceptable fantasies of a sexual or aggressive nature; developed by Sigmund Freud.

psychological resilience: ability to cope successfully in the face of significant adversity or risk.

psychomotor agitation: excessive physical activity associated with feelings of inner tension.

psychomotor retardation: visible slowing of physical and emotional reactions.

psychopathology: the manifestation of a diagnosable mental health problem.

psychosocial: the acknowledgment of the important interplay between psychological factors and social issues in the determination of overall mental health.

punishing consequences: consequences that decrease the actions they follow. If the out-of-seat behavior decreases following teacher's reprimands, then the reprimands are punishing consequences (at least temporarily).

recidivism: recommission or rearrest for subsequent crimes.

reinforcing consequences: consequences that increase actions they follow. If the out-of-seat behavior increases following teacher's reprimands, then the reprimands are reinforcing consequences.

risk factors: factors associated with increasing the odds of developing a disorder.

self-management: engaging in activities that monitor and manage symptoms and signs of a disorder.

setting events: situational or contextual factors that affect how a student will respond to antecedent and consequent events. "Setting events may be divided into three categories: physiological/biological, physical/environmental, and social/situational" (see Chandler & Dahlquist, 2002, p. 55).

sexual abuse: any sexual contact between an adult and a child.

sexual identity: one aspect of an individual's personal identity. Sexual identity refers to the development of an individual's understanding of how to develop close relationships; his or her own sexual orientation; his or her sexual impulses, desires, and needs; and ultimately, his or her sexual role in life.

sexual orientation: the direction of one's sexual interest toward members of the same, opposite, or both sexes.

social maladjustment: a term regularly used in educational settings that refers to the behaviors associated with Conduct Disorder. However, federal law has not provided a definition for social maladjustment, so no standard definition exists.

somatic: related to the body, specifically manifesting physical symptoms as a result of a mental health problem.

treatment validity: the extent to which a functional behavioral assessment contributes to an effective behavioral intervention program. Did the use of the assessment information result in a plan for behavior intervention that actually produced the desired change in the target behavior?

INDEX

About the Editor

Raymond J. Waller is the Coordinator of the Graduate Program in Emotional and Behavior Disorders at Piedmont College and is on the faculty of the School of Social Work at the University of Georgia. He has been an advocate for children and the promotion of children's mental health for years and has worked in support of this cause in a number of settings. He has been a teacher of special education and taught students with a variety of disabilities and mental health needs. He has been an administrator in a psychoeducational facility serving students with severe behavioral problems and has worked with children with mental health needs in the public mental health system, the juvenile justice system, Head Start, foster care, and the school system.

About the Contributors

Dawn Anderson-Butcher, MSW, PhD, is Associate Professor in the College of Social Work at Ohio State University (OSU). Her primary research interests include school-family-community partnerships, youth development, after-school programming, and interprofessional collaboration. She is the lead principal investigator for the Ohio Department of Education's Ohio Community Collaboration Model for School Improvement project, an expanded school improvement model focused on addressing nonacademic barriers to learning through school-family-community partnerships. She oversees the College of Social Work's school social work licensure program and is actively involved in the OSU P–12 Project. Her work is published in key journals such as *Social Work, Children & Schools, Social Work in Education,* and *Journal of Community Psychology.* She also is a member of the Society for Social Work Research, the National Association of Social Workers, and the American Alliance for Health, Physical Education, Recreation and Dance. She received her BA, BS, and MS degrees from Miami University and her MSW and PhD from the University of Utah.

Diane J. Bresson is a second-grade teacher at J. H. House Elementary School in Conyers, Georgia. She is currently obtaining her graduate degree in elementary education from Piedmont College and will graduate in May of 2006.

Jeffrey P. Douglass has 32 years experience in mental retardation/developmental disabilities services with the state of Georgia. He has been a CARF (Commission on Accreditation of Rehabilitation Facilities) surveyor since 1998, evaluating mental health and mental retardation facilities for compliance with accreditation standards. In addition, he has served as an emergency services team clinician doing crisis mental health assessment and disposition for more than 10 years. He received a BS in sociology from Georgia College in 1973 and an MSA from Georgia College in 1981.

Daniel J. Fischer, MSW, is Clinical Assistant Professor and Associate Director of the Pediatric Anxiety and Tic Disorders Program at the University of Michigan, Department of Psychiatry, Child/Adolescent Section. An active clinician, teacher, and researcher in the area of anxiety disorders and cognitive-behavioral therapies, he is also the Chief of Social Work in Psychiatry and Director of Graduate Education at the University of Michigan Health Systems Department of Social Work and an Adjunct Lecturer at the University of Michigan School of Social Work. He completed his MSW at the University of Michigan in 1984.

Denise M. Green, LCSW, PhD, teaches and conducts research at the School of Social Work at the University of Georgia. For the past 20 years, she has maintained a focus on the effects of mental illness on individuals, their families, and the systems that serve them. She is particularly interested in the outcomes of programs that serve disabled individuals. She obtained her master's in social work at UNC Chapel Hill and her doctorate at the University of Georgia, Athens.

Sarah Hamel is currently a graduate student in the School of Education at the University of North Carolina at Chapel Hill. She is pursuing an MEd in school psychology. She is also a research assistant at the Frank Porter Graham Child Development Institute. Her professional interests include prereferral intervention teams, crisis intervention, and curriculum-based assessment. After graduating, she hopes to work as a school psychologist in a public school district. She received her BA in psychology and educational studies from Denison University.

Eric Hardiman is Assistant Professor of Social Welfare at the State University of New York, Albany. He conducts research with a focus on mental health service delivery and use for adults facing psychiatric disabilities. His primary areas of scholarly focus are peer support and mutual aid, consumer and peer-provided services, homelessness and housing, and psychiatric recovery. He has also conducted research in the delivery of peer-provided mental health services following large-scale mass disasters such as the September 11, 2001, World Trade Center attack and the December 2004 tsunami in Indonesia. His current research continues to focus on peer support, the consumer-delivered mental health services, psychiatric recovery, supportive housing models for homeless individuals, and collaboration between consumer-run and traditional provider-based organizations. He teaches courses in social work practice methods, the evaluation of clinical practice, and advanced social work practice in mental health settings.

Joseph A. Himle, PhD, is Assistant Professor at the University of Michigan School of Social Work and Department of Psychiatry. An active clinician, teacher, and researcher in the area of anxiety disorders, he is also Associate Director of the Anxiety Disorders Program at the University of Michigan Department of Psychiatry. He completed his doctorate in social work and psychology at the University of Michigan in August of 1995.

Miriam Johnson is currently completing her master of arts in teaching from Piedmont College in special education. She is employed in the Department of Special Education at Piedmont College and gives private lessons in piano. She received a BA in psychology and German from Guilford College in 2001.

Michael Kelly is a doctoral student in social work at the University of Illinois–Chicago. He also teaches in the Family & School Partnerships Program at the University of Chicago's Center for Family Health and is a school social worker in Oak Park's District 97, where he has instituted numerous counseling and community-building projects, including a service project for New York Disaster Relief that was featured in *Time* magazine. He received his BA in social science at the University of Michigan and his MSW at the Jane Addams College of Social Work at the University of Illinois at Chicago.

Steve Knotek is Assistant Professor in the Human Development and Professional Studies Department in the School of Education at the University of North Carolina at Chapel Hill. He has been a practicing school psychologist and therapist specializing in crisis intervention and therapy for students with mood and anxiety disorders. His research focus is on the use of consultation to enhance the ability of teachers and administrators to respond to students' mental health needs in school settings.

S. Thomas Kordinak, PhD, is Professor of Psychology at Sam Houston State University, in Huntsville, Texas. He is a licensed psychologist and health service provider by the Texas State Board of Examiners of Psychologists, and is licensed by the Texas Board of Examiners of Marriage and Family Therapists. He is also certified by the Council of the National Register of Health Service Providers in psychology and as a family life educator by the National Council on Family Relations. He has a teaching and research interest in families, family dynamics, divorce and divorce adjustment, as well as behavioral therapy. His practice has focused on these areas.

Hal A. Lawson is Professor of Social Welfare and Professor of Educational Administration and Policy Studies at the University at Albany, State University of New York. He served previously on the faculties of the University of Washington, the University of British Columbia, Miami University, and the University of Utah. School-family-community-higher education partnerships make up his primary specialty. Over the past 35 years, he has focused on the most vulnerable schools, families, and neighborhood communities. He is a noted international expert in various forms of collaboration and in interprofessional education and training aimed at preparing people to collaborate. His extensive experience includes work in several nations and has resulted in books, monographs, and journal articles; consultations with schools, universities, community organizations, and state agencies; and grants from governments and charitable foundations. Beginning in 1992, his work encompassed public child welfare agencies, their relationships with other service systems, and workforce recruitment, retention, and optimization for public child welfare systems. He has degrees from Oberlin College and the University of Michigan.

Michelle Van Etten Lee is Training Director for the Cognitive Behavioral Therapy Program at the University of Michigan Psychological Clinic and Adjunct Assistant Professor of Psychology and Psychiatry at the University of Michigan. An active clinician, teacher, and researcher in the area of anxiety disorders, she completed her doctorate in clinical psychology at the University of Vermont in 1996, and completed postdoctoral fellowships at Johns Hopkins University and the University of Michigan Anxiety Disorders Program.

Robert L. Miller, Jr., LMSW, MPhil, PhD, is a social work researcher and Professor at the State University of New York, Albany. He explores the intersection of spirituality, social welfare, and public health. He has examined spirituality in the lives of African Americans affected by AIDS, decision-making processes of African American clergy in HIV prevention efforts within their congregations, coping strategies for African American women over 50 living with AIDS, and community health collaborations between federally qualified health centers and urban churches.

Jordana R. Muroff, MSW, PhD, is a postdoctoral fellow at the VA Ann Arbor Healthcare System Center for Practice Management and Outcomes Research and the University of Michigan Center for Behavioral and Decision Sciences in Medicine. Her practice experience, teaching, and research are in the areas of mental health assessment and cognitive behavioral interventions with a particular focus on anxiety disorders, and the influence of culture on clinical decision making. She completed her doctorate in social work and psychology at the University of Michigan, Fall 2004.

Laura L. Myers, PhD, MSW, is Assistant Professor for the Division of Social Work at Thomas University in Thomasville, Georgia. Her main research interests include human diversity and social discrimination, eating disorders and healthy eating habits, and child foster care and adoption. She has written several articles and chapters on eating disorders and is currently concerned with discrimination issues involving obesity and the increase in obesity and eating disorders among children and young adolescents. She lives in Tallahassee, Florida, with her husband, Dr. Bruce Thyer, and their four children.

W. Sean Newsome, PhD, is Assistant Professor at Miami (Ohio) University and teaches social welfare and its impact on diverse groups and social work practice. His current research interests include the use of solution focused brief therapy (SFBT) with at-risk K–12 populations, risk and protective factors associated with school truancy, bullying behavior and school violence, and the impact of grandparents raising grandchildren in K–12 settings. Before pursuing his doctorate in social work, he practiced as a treatment coordinator for Boysville of Michigan and as a school social worker in Birmingham, Michigan. He received his doctorate in social work from Ohio State University.

Ramona M. Noland, PhD, is a licensed psychologist and licensed specialist in school psychology, with 9 years of experience working as a psychologist and consultant for both school personnel and parents. She is also Assistant Professor in the Department of Psychology and Philosophy at Sam Houston State University, where she teaches courses in Human Sexuality, Psychological Assessment, and School Consultation. Her current research interests include various topics related to sexuality and behavior, assessment of autism spectrum disorders, and the provision of psychological services in the school setting.

Julie Sarno Owens, PhD, is Assistant Professor of Psychology in the Department of Psychology at Ohio University. She works collaboratively with community agencies and elementary schools in the design and implementation of school-based mental health programming for elementary school children and is the director of the Youth Experiencing Success in School (Y.E.S.S.) Program (www.yessprogram.com). Her applied research examines the effectiveness of school-based mental health programming that incorporates evidence-based services and the extent to which such services can be disseminated through university-community partnerships. Her laboratory-based research examines self-perceptions and attributions in children with ADHD. Her work can be found in journals such as *Journal of Consulting and Clinical Psychology, Journal of Attention Disorders,* and *Journal of Clinical Child Psychology.* She obtained a PhD in clinical psychology from Purdue University in 2001.

Julie Roberts Palmour, PhD, is Associate Professor of Education at Piedmont College in Demorest, Georgia, teaching in the graduate education program offering the EdS degree in Curriculum and Instruction. Her background includes work in the field of marriage and family therapy and drug and alcohol rehabilitation. Early teaching responsibilities included work with mild and moderate special needs children in Grades K–12 and regular classroom teaching at the pre-K and elementary levels. Her administrative responsibilities have included supervision of district special needs early childhood programs and administration of a K–5 private school. She has received specialized training and is well versed in the reporting and prevention of child abuse. In addition to her current faculty responsibilities, she is a course author for an established e-learning service company, writing courses for a variety of educational topics. She received a BS from Georgia State University, an MS from Butler University, and a PhD from Bowling Green State University.

Kevin P. Quinn, EdD, is Associate Professor of Special Education in the School of Education at the State University of New York (SUNY), Albany. He has extensive experience working with children and youths with emotional and behavioral disorders (EBDs) including teaching at and administering Rose School, an award-winning interagency, alternative school for children and youths with EBDs living in Washington, D.C. Also, as a project manager and research associate at a nationally recognized research institute, he implemented several federally funded projects to develop and examine various interventions for children and youths with EBDs and their families. He continues to collaborate with several schools and communities in developing and evaluating interventions for children and youths with EBDs and has had his research in this area published in major professional journals.

Lauren Richerson is a doctoral student in the Department of Psychology at Ohio University. She has worked as a clinician in the Youth Experiencing Success in Schools (Y.E.S.S.) Program, a school-based mental health program for children with disruptive behavior problems, for over 2 years. She also has worked with a number of children referred for mental health treatment at the university's psychological clinic. Her research interests include the study of factors associated with children's outcomes in the context of school-based interventions as well as factors that contribute to the development and maintenance of children's conduct problems. She obtained an MS in clinical psychology from Ohio University in 2004.

Rachel Schoolman, a school psychology student in the School of Education at the University of North Carolina at Chapel Hill, is currently doing her school psychology internship with Stafford County Schools in Virginia. Her interests lie in the areas of early intervention and prevention in school systems. In addition, her research focuses on the application and utility of positive behavior support. She earned her BA in psychology from the State University of New York College at Geneseo.

Michelle Madden Schramm is currently obtaining a master's degree in emotional and behavior disorders from Piedmont College in Athens, Georgia. After graduating from Auburn University with a BA in 1990, she pursued a career path working with children of all ages and is currently working with high school students with emotional disabilities. In addition to working with children, she and her husband, Mark, enjoy spending time with their three young boys.

Natalie Siegel is currently a doctoral student in the school psychology program at the University of North Carolina at Chapel Hill. Her research interests are in student victimization and bullying, peer relationships, PTSD, and anxiety. After graduation, Natalie hopes to practice as a school psychologist in a school or clinical setting and conduct research. Originally from Philadelphia, she graduated from Temple University with a BA in psychology and a minor in anthropology.

Amy C. Traylor, MSW, is working toward a doctorate in social work at the University of Georgia. Her clinical experience includes work with severely emotionally disturbed children in Southeast Wyoming Mental Health Center's treatment foster care program in Cheyenne, Wyoming, and at Southwest Education Center in Phoenix, Arizona. She received her master's in social work from the University of Alabama.

Jerome D. Ulman is Professor of Special Education at Ball State University, where he has taught courses in the areas of applied behavior analysis and behavior disorders since 1974. He received bachelor's and master's degrees in psychology from the University of South Florida in 1965 and 1968 and a doctoral degree in educational psychology from Southern Illinois University in 1972. Before joining the Ball State faculty, he was employed as a school psychologist in Florida, a research scientist at Choate Mental Health and Development Center in Illinois, and a behavioral consultant in Indianapolis, Indiana. His research interests include behavioral research methodology, behaviorological technology in special education, the operant analysis of verbal behavior, and the sociocultural implications of behaviorology. He serves on the editorial board of *Behavior and Social Issues* and is the current secretary-treasurer of the International Society for Behaviorology.

Susan Mortweet VanScoyoc, PhD, ABPP, is Associate Professor of Pediatrics at the University of Missouri at Kansas City School of Medicine. She is also a staff psychologist at the Children's Mercy Hospitals and Clinics in Kansas City. In her role as staff psychologist, she serves children with behavioral and emotional disorders. She also is the primary psychologist for children with diabetes and other endocrine disorders. Her publications have been in the areas of parenting and empirically supported treatments for children. She received her PhD in developmental and child psychology from the University of Kansas and is also board certified in behavioral psychology.

M. Elizabeth Vonk is Associate Professor and the Director of the Doctoral Program at the School of Social Work, University of Georgia, Athens, Georgia. She teaches advanced-practice classes in the MSW program. Her research interests include social work practice evaluation, treatment of depression and trauma, and parent education for transracial adoptive parents. She has published numerous articles and book chapters in these areas. Prior to receiving her doctoral degree, she practiced clinical social work with children, adolescents, and young adults in a variety of settings. She completed her MSW degree in 1980 from Florida State University and her doctoral degree in social work in 1996 from the University of Georgia.

Katherine S. Waller, MEd, is an instructor of Education at Piedmont College and a veteran schoolteacher. She began her work in general education, but her focus changed to special education early in her career. She has taught children across many disability areas and with many mental health needs. She regularly volunteers her time to community agencies and activities that foster the positive mental health needs of children.

Thomas A. Wood, BS, MEd, EdD, is Professor of Psychology and Education at Sam Houston State University (SHSU) in Huntsville, Texas. He also served as Dean of the College of Education and Applied Science at SHSU. Prior to his current position, he served as Department Chair and Associate Dean at the University of Texas at El Paso. He also has held faculty positions at Auburn University and Murray State University. He has been interested in families of children with disabilities or chronic illness for much of his career and has worked in clinical settings and conducted research. He has held leadership positions in organizations at the local, state, and national levels and is the author or coauthor of numerous grants and referreed articles. He received his doctor of education degree from George Peabody College of Vanderbilt University in special education and school psychology and completed a postdoctoral fellowship in pediatric psychology at the University of Texas Medical Branch in Galveston, Texas.

Nina Yssel, PhD, is Associate Professor in the Department of Special Education at Ball State University, Muncie, Indiana, where she teaches undergraduate and graduate classes in high-incidence disabilities. She also serves on the editorial board of *Behavior and Social Issues* and is the current secretary-treasurer of the International Society for Behaviorology. Her research interests have included students with disabilities in higher education, paraprofessionals in special education, and professional development schools. Currently, she focuses on exceptional children and serves as director of a residential summer camp for learning disabled and gifted middle school students. Born and raised in South Africa, she values international collaboration in research and teaching. She received her bachelor's and master's degrees in psychology from the University of South Florida in 1965 and 1968 and her doctorate in educational psychology from Southern Illinois University in 1972.